ACES, WARRIORS
&
WINGMEN

Typhoons

Aces, Warriors & Wingmen

Firsthand Accounts of Canada's Fighter Pilots in the Second World War

Wayne Ralph

WILEY

John Wiley & Sons Canada, Ltd.

National Library of Canada Cataloguing in Publication Data

Ralph, Wayne, 1946-Aces, warriors and wingman : the firsthand accounts of Canada's fighter pilots in the Second World War / Wayne Ralph.

Includes index.
ISBN-13 978-0-470-83590-6
ISBN-10 0-470-83590-7

1. Canada. Royal Canadian Air Force—Biography. 2. World War, 1939-1945—Aerial operations, Canadian. 3. World War, 1939-1945—Personal narratives, Canadian. 4. Air pilots, Military—Canada—Biography. I. Title.

D792.C2R34 2005   940.54'4971'0922   C2005-900324-3

Production Credits:
Cover design: Mike Chan
Interior text design: Mike Chan
Front cover photo:
Upper left - Spitfires of 417 Squadron RCAF in Italy (Courtesy of the Airforce Magazine Collection)
Upper middle - F/L Harry Hardy, DFC, Typhoon pilot with 440 Squadron RCAF, in Holland (Courtesy of the Harry Hardy Collection)
Upper right - Tropical model Hurricane in Africa (Courtesy of the Al and Lennie McFadden Collection)
Lower left - F/O Robert Middlemiss, DFC (left), with F/L George Beurling, DSO, DFC, DFM and Bar, with 403 Squadron RCAF in England (Courtesy of the Robert Middlemiss Collection)
Lower middle - Typhoon being refuelled at 143 Wing RCAF gunnery camp in England (Courtesy of the Roy Burden Collection)
Lower right - S/L James Edwards, DFC and Bar, DFM, in Italy (Courtesy of the James Edwards Collection)
Back cover photo:
Hurricane with rocket rails in Scotland, 1944 (Courtesy of the Roy Burden Collection)

Printer: Friesen

John Wiley & Sons Canada Ltd
6045 Freemont Blvd.
Mississauga, Ontario
L5R 4J3

Printed in Canada

10 9 8 7 6 5 4 3 2 1

To my wife, Patrice Shore, for her loving, patient support in all things. A woman with a crystal spirit and a fighter pilot's heart.

Seafire

CONTENTS

Acknowledgments.. xi
Prologue... xiii
Introduction... 1

PART ONE: KITTYHAWK ACE OF THE WESTERN DESERT CAMPAIGN..... 3
James Francis "Stocky" Edwards, Wing Commander[1].. 3

PART TWO: CANADIANS IN THE SIEGE OF MALTA..................................... 9
Roderick Illingsworth Alpine Smith, Squadron Leader... 9
   The Seige of Malta... 9
Robert George "Bob" Middlemiss, Flight Lieutenant... 18
Ian Roy Maclennan, Flight Lieutenant.. 21
   Memories of George Frederick Beurling in Malta.. 25
   Rod Smith's October Bailout... 27
Robert Carl "Moose" Fumerton, Wing Commander.. 29
Leslie Patrick Sandford "Pat" Bing, Flight Lieutenant (Fumerton's navigator)....................... 29
Gordon Henry Taylor Farquharson, Flight Lieutenant.. 31
   Memories of the Loss of Liberator AL511 at Gibraltar... 31

PART THREE: THE WESTERN DESERT, 1942–43, AND ITALY, 1943–44.......... 35
   Death of a Luftwaffe Ace in the Western Desert... 35
John Terrance "Terry" Field, Flight Lieutenant... 38
Rex Howard Probert, Flight Lieutenant... 39
Milton Eardley Jowsey, Flight Lieutenant.. 43
Stanley John Kernaghan, Flight Lieutenant.. 45
Irving Farmer "Hap" Kennedy, Squadron Leader.. 49
   Edwards at Anzio Beachhead — Six Downed in One Op... 53
David Goldberg, Squadron Leader... 54

PART FOUR: THE WORLD OF THE UNARMED PHOTOGRAPHIC RECONNAISSANCE PILOT.................. 59
John William "Brick" Bradford, Flying Officer.. 59
William Keir "Bill" Carr, Flight Lieutenant.. 60

PART FIVE: CANADIANS IN THE RAF AND FLEET AIR ARM, 1939–40........... 67
William Lidstone "Willie" McKnight, Flying Officer... 67
   (letters home to Canada from Willie McKnight)... 68
Arthur Henry "Art" Deacon, Flight Lieutenant.. 70
Richard Edward Bartlett, Lieutenant... 72

PART SIX: THE DEADLY YEARS: RHUBARBS AND CIRCUSES AND MANY, MANY WULFIES............. 79
William Barry Needham, Flight Lieutenant.. 81
George Dennis Aitken, Flight Lieutenant... 82
Lloyd Vernon Chadburn, Wing Commander 84

[1] Ranks shown are the highest attained by war's end.

Robert Dulmage "Dagwood" Phillip, Flight Lieutenant.. 85

Arthur John "Jack" Moul, Squadron Leader.. 86

Michell Johnston, Squadron Leader... 87

Norris Edmund Hunt, Flight Lieutenant.. 90

Roman Roy Wozniak, Flight Lieutenant... 91

    Fighter Sweep, led by Alan Deere, RNZAF, June 2, 1942.. 91

Douglas Warren, Flight Lieutenant.. 93

Bruce Warren, Flight Lieutenant.. 93

    The Dieppe Raid, August 19, 1942... 96

Allan Robert McFadden, Flight Lieutenant... 96

    Interned by the Vichy French in Africa... 98

Richard Drummond Forbes-Roberts, Flight Lieutenant... 100

Arthur Hazelton Sager, Flight Lieutenant... 100

Richard Douglas Booth, Flight Lieutenant.. 101

    Booth's Bailout over the English Channel.. 107

    Ramrod 290: November 3, 1943.. *108*

William Francis Joseph Mason, Flight Lieutenant... 108

PART SEVEN: THE WORLD OF THE BEAUFIGHTER AND MOSQUITO IN BRITAIN............... **113**

Robert Ross "Bob" Ferguson, Squadron Leader... 115

    Competition at West Malling.. 118

Rayne Dennis Schultz, Squadron Leader... 119

Ian Anderson March, Flight Lieutenant.. 122

William Horace Vincent, Flight Lieutenant... 123

Harold Douglas McNabb, Flight Lieutenant.. 126

George "Red" Sutherland, Squadron Leader.. 129

David John "Blackie" Williams, Wing Commander.. 129

    The Personalities of Pilots and Navigators in Night-Fighter Operations...................... 133

Clarence Joseph Kirkpatrick, Flight Lieutenant (navigator with Williams, Bannock)..... 135

James Davidson Wright, Flight Lieutenant (navigator with Squadron Leader McFadyen)..... 136

Ross Hunter Finlayson, Flight Lieutenant.. 136

William Lloyd Marr, Flight Lieutenant.. 138

John Harold "Jack" Phillips, Flight Lieutenant.. 142

Russell William "Russ" Bannock, Wing Commander.. 147

Sydney Simon Shulemson, Flight Lieutenant... 152

    The story of Canada's Coastal Command fighters off Norway and France.................... 153

PART EIGHT: TWO AMERICANS IN THE RCAF.. **161**

Philip Gordon (Bockman) Vickers, Flying Officer.. 161

Howard Lynn Phillips, Flight Lieutenant.. 164

PART NINE: RCAF SPITFIRE OPERATIONS, FROM BRITAIN AND EUROPE........................ **169**

Kenneth Charles Lett, Flight Lieutenant... 169

    Memories of Richard Joseph "Dick" Audet.. 172

James Douglas Lindsay, Flight Lieutenant.. 173

    Memories of Beurling at 403... 174

Donald Currie Laubman, Squadron Leader... 173

Robert Bruce Barker, Flight Lieutenant.. 176
    Memories of Donald Mathew Pieri... 176

PART TEN: CANADA'S TYPHOON PILOTS... **181**
Harry James Hardy, Flight Lieutenant... 181
William Ivan Mouat, Flight Lieutenant.. 184
John Wallace Porter, Flight Lieutenant... 185
Donald Edward George Martyn, Flight Lieutenant...................................... 186
Herbert Roy Burden, Flight Lieutenant... 189
Robert Edward Spooner, Squadron Leader... 193
Martin John "Pat" Peterson, Leading Aircraftman (fitter)............................ 197

PART ELEVEN: THE FIGHTER PILOTS' WAR IN INDIA AND BURMA......... **203**
Atholl Sutherland Brown, Flight Lieutenant... 204
Harold Taylor Hope, Flight Lieutenant.. 207
Bert Dennis Madill, Flight Lieutenant... 211
Frederick Howard Sproule, Flight Lieutenant.. 213

PART TWELVE: THREE PILOTS OF THE FLEET AIR ARM IN THE PACIFIC THEATRE.......... **219**
Robert Hampton Gray, Lieutenant... 219
Donald John Sheppard, Lieutenant.. 221
William Henry Isaac Atkinson, Lieutenant.. 226

PART THIRTEEN: REHABILITATION, READJUSTMENT AND RE-ENTRY...... **233**
Stories of Ivan Mouat, Jack Moul, Roy Burden, Stocky Edwards, Geoff Northcott,
Doug Booth, George "Pat" Patterson, Al McFadden, Derrick England, Frank Hubbard,
Bill Roddie, John "Red" Francis, Rod Smith, Burdette Gillis, and Don Walz.................. 233

APPENDICES.. **243**
"Overheard at the Bar": Recollections by Various Anonymous Fighter Pilots about
Friendly Fire and General Stupidity, Fleeting Affairs and Tragic Outcomes................ 243
Profile of the Men Interviewed for the Book... 244
The Interviewees.. 246
Glossary of Most Common British Empire Awards to Fighter Pilots............ 249
Air Force Ranks — RCAF and RAF—Second World War............................ 250
Primer on RCAF and RAF fighter structures... 251

References... 252
Index.. 260

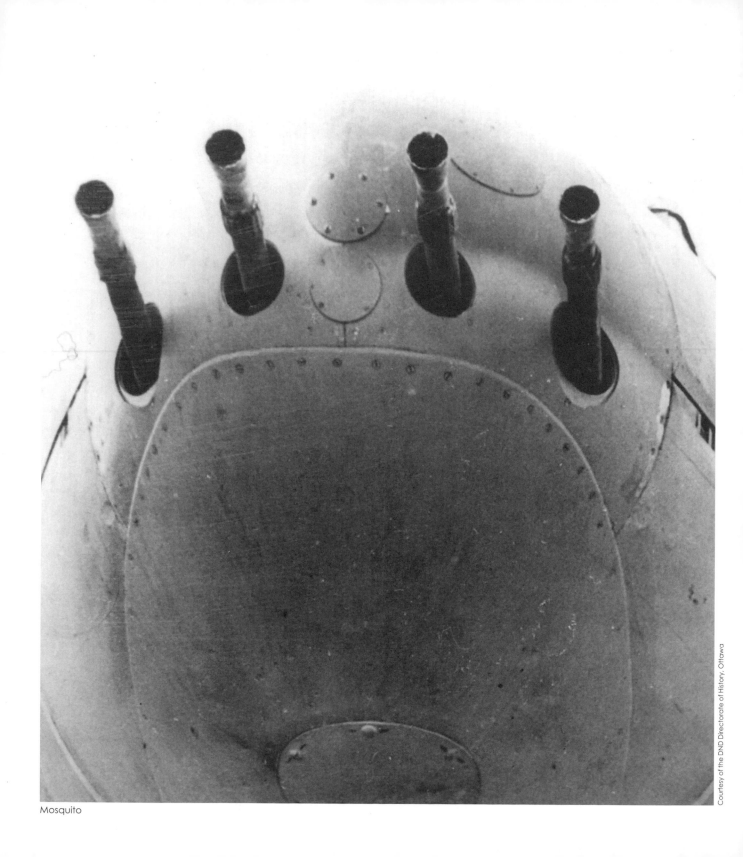

Mosquito

ACKNOWLEDGMENTS

My work has been sustained and fostered through the help and guidance of many generous people. I am most deeply indebted to the more than one hundred men and women who agreed to be interviewed (they are listed in the Appendices), as well as others who were too modest or too ill to speak to me personally but provided guidance. Many veterans pushed forward the names of their colleagues, insisting I interview them because they were far more talented; I frequently was to hear the exhortation, "You've got to interview him, he's a great fighter pilot." It was impossible to include the stories of everyone I met, but those stories not told here informed the rest. Sixteen per cent of the people I interviewed died during the research and writing of the book. With so many fighter pilots "gone west," I was spurred on to write their stories as soon as possible.

At the start of my journey I received invaluable assistance from the late Wing Commander Rod Smith, DFC and Bar, and, after his death, from his sister Wendy Noble. Wing Commander Douglas "Duke" Warren, DFC, provided many insights and gave this project a big impetus by arranging a lunch in 2001 with fighter pilots in and near Comox, BC. Wing Commander James "Stocky" Edwards, DFC and Bar, DFM, MiD, OC, and his wife Toni provided a home and hospitality at Comox, as did Squadron Leader Bob Ferguson, MiD, OC, and his wife Norma at Ft Qu'Appelle, Saskatchewan, and the late Flight Lieutenant Don Walz, CdeG, at his farm south of Moose Jaw, Saskatchewan.

Flight Lieutenant Zella Gibson, widow of Flight Lieutenant John M. "Gibby" Gibson, provided books, enthusiasm and encouragement from Exeter, Ontario. In Ottawa I owe thanks to Squadron Leaders Bill McLaughlin and Joe Scoles, RCAF and Transport Canada retired, for their homes and hospitality during my research, and to military archivist Tim Dubé, author Hugh Halliday, and *Airforce Magazine* editor Vic Johnson, for ongoing guidance and help with that research. My thanks to the staff at the Directorate of History and Heritage, Department of National Defence, for being generous with their Second World War squadron and biographical files. Don Pearsons and Captain Brendan Bond, 1 Canadian Air Division, Heritage and History, Winnipeg, have been supportive and found answers for a variety of obscure questions, as have the Comox Air Force Museum, BC and the Commonwealth Air Training Museum, MB. The western branch of the Canadian Fighter Pilots Association gave me a membership list, and kindly invited this outsider to attend their reunions, where I met many veterans and heard many stories. Flight Lieutenant Harry Hardy, DFC, leader of the western Typhoon Pilots Group, has been a great source of information on lots of topics, and has always included me in the group's social activities, for which I am most grateful. I also salute Leading Aircraftman Fred Berg, RCAF armourer, and the late Leading Aircraftman Martin J. "Pat" Peterson, RCAF fitter, a man with great wisdom and much beloved in our family.

My good friends and fellow history buffs Bob Ough, CD, in Peterborough, Stephen Heinemann, in St Catharines, Squadron Leader Jerry Vernon, CD, in Burnaby, and Stéphane Guevremont in Calgary have been welcome participants in the research process, and provided stimulating conversations. Gary Ross, author, publisher, and now editor of *Saturday Night*, offered encouragement and many trenchant insights over several years.

In the greater Vancouver region, including Surrey and White Rock, many Second World War fighter pilots have become friends, providing me with a wealth of information and insight. They include Group Captain R.B. "Bill" Barker, DFC; Commander Bill Atkinson, and his wife Val; Wing Commander John "Jack" Phillips, DFC, and his wife Sunny; Squadron Leader Harold G. "Curly" Edwards; Flying Officer John "Brick" Bradford, DFC; and Flight Lieutenants H. Roy Burden, MiD; R.D. "Doug" Booth; Al McFadden, and his wife Lennie; Ian Maclennan, DFM; Bill Marr, AFC; Ivan Smith; Bill Doyle. The many published and unpublished memoirs of the men I interviewed helped me immensely; they are listed in the bibliography.

I want to thank the Canada Council for the Arts, Ottawa, for providing financial support in 2002 through its emerging authors' program. The money allowed me to visit and interview many additional fighter pilots across Canada and as far south as Arizona. Sadly, quite a few have since died and will not see their stories in print, but I had the privilege of meeting and getting to know them, albeit all too briefly, because of the Canada Council. My thanks also to Bard's Ink Writer's Group and Surrey International Writers' Conference.

Don Loney, my editor at John Wiley & Sons Canada, has supported this project for several years, and been a great source of enthusiasm and encouragement. I want to thank my copy editor, Cheryl Cohen, for her vigilance and sensitivity.

My love and thanks to my wife, Patrice Shore, and the Shore family; to my sister and brother, Elaine and Dan Ralph, and their spouses, Charles Taylor and Lise Hawkins, and their children. Without the encouragement of family and loved ones, the process of writing this or any other book would be lonely work indeed.

Wings and ribbons of James Edwards.

Courtesy of the DND Directorate of History, Ottawa

PROLOGUE
CHASING STORIES IN A FOREIGN COUNTRY

"The past is a foreign country; they do things differently there."
L.P. Hartley, *The Go-Between.*

This book is not an operational history of the Second World War and, intentionally, is not narrated chronologically from 1939 to 1945. Other authors have done that difficult historical work before me, and are better at it. The book I chose to write is more about people than campaigns, about humanity rather than fighter aircraft, about sociology rather than technology.

For fifteen years I have hunted after men to hear their war stories. At the start of my journey through that foreign country where they did things differently, a ninety-year-old said to me, "All old men, we like to talk about the past ... we don't give a damn about the future." He knew he didn't have a future, at least not one he wanted to talk about.

The men I am in search of die on me. Some only weeks after our first and final meeting. The death of virtual strangers should not distress me so, yet I take it personally. Their deaths often surprise me, despite the oxygen bottles and cancerous tumours I see. A man of eighty or ninety is certainly entitled to check out. But his passing never fails to upset me. I have lost the chance to ask one more war veteran: "What was it like?"

I seem to have chosen an avocation that causes me anxiety. My ignorance is at the root of that anxiety. I never know enough. As well prepared as I try to be, with extra pens, plenty of tapes, loaded camera, I lose my way in the interview. I forget to ask the right questions. I don't know what the right questions are. The men I interview have a habit of remembering the wrong things and forgetting the right things. They want to talk about what is compelling for them rather than what is useful to me.

Quite a few are losing command of their memories—what is left is like a cigar box filled with punched train tickets, curled-up photographs, old mess bills and dry-cleaning receipts. In these interviews time slows down. The ticking of the mantel clock becomes clearly audible, the hourly and

quarter-hourly chimes louder. To salvage something out of the interview, I will read to these pilots from history books of the war, or their personal logbooks, the latter being the most important summary of their wartime flying. This sometimes helps the memories flow, but sometimes not. As one pilot apologized, "I guess that must have happened on that trip, if I wrote it down." Still others know they flew on a particular op yet have no record of it in their logbooks.

They tell me that the dramatic events of the war seem to have happened to someone else, a feeling that intensifies with age. Many have the documents to prove that all of it really did take place. For others the evidence was sold at a garage sale, or simply went missing in action. I met one decorated flyer featured in the history books who could not even find his medals and logbook. He spoke one of the saddest lines of the many sad lines recorded, "I think I got the Croix de Guerre. But I don't remember."

I have learned by interviewing dozens of pilots that facts, opinions and legends are knotted together. Untying the knots is my job. To prove beyond reasonable doubt what is a fact, what is a legend. Often there are only fragments of stories, about people whose last names have gone missing, their trail gone cold. Legendary exploits, the "right stuff" that makes it into the history books, are invariably full of contradictions. Signed combat reports confuse as much as clarify. Who shot whom down, who was a witness to the flaming wreckage, which wingmen were even present at the making of history is not so easily determined. Apparently innocuous questions about such exploits can lead to rebuke: "Don't use that word 'mission.' We didn't fly missions, we were on a 'do' or we flew an 'op.' Perhaps on a 'trip,' but never on a mission! The Americans used that word, but we didn't."

Some flyers remember old grudges, dismissing the official accounts as bullshit. The wrong characters in the drama have been credited, these flyers complain, while men of sterling character have been overlooked. I, the investigator, have arrived just in the nick of time to rewrite the past. Here is the real story, they will say, get it down. Or more often and discouragingly, here is the real story, but you can't put this in your book. Turn that damn tape recorder off and I will tell you what really happened.

Frequently, the past has never been revealed to anyone and, for the first time, I hear a story that is resonant, sad and truthful. An old man stops talking, fumbling with his glasses, starts to weep, quickly gathers himself, moves forward. Why am I so cruel, I wonder, poking at old scars? Still, he wants to talk about it, and sometimes the question is the vehicle, the permission, to relive the memory. A man may save his most moving story until the end, as you are shaking hands at the front door, your tape recorder packed away. Memory taps him, and he grabs you by the arm and starts talking.

Interviewing these veterans has taught me that the mythology of that knight of the twentieth century called the fighter pilot is so strong that more dramatic truths are obscured. To get at any deeper insight, at the underlying truth, one must get past that mythology. One must be brazen enough to ask the rude questions, and listen carefully to the responses and what they imply. The answers are often as rude as the questions, but also surprisingly candid.

For example, I have learned that a man can volunteer to be a fighter pilot, perform competently, and yet hate the work. He sees nothing glamorous in it, being merely a warrior for the working day. One fighter pilot who excelled at aerial combat told me that he was paid during the war to be a serial killer. Another who had strafed many kinds of ground targets said that a fighter pilot strafing people is simply "a one-man execution squad." This same man wiped tears from his eyes as he remembered the bravery of the crews of torpedo bombers he escorted that fell in flames, exploding in the English Channel, one after another after another.

I have even met two or three men who volunteered for the job so they could be certain that nobody innocent died at their hands, that like killed only like, combatant only combatant. Even in the callowness of youth, the moral ambiguities faced by the bomber pilot were not for them. This dark, cynical view of the daily duties of the fighter pilot is by no means universal. Most believed then and now that their war was about patriotism, the love of country and a hatred of evil. It was a war

that had to be fought and won, a fact so obvious to that generation that one's decision to join was confident and effortless.

> existentialism... n. 1. A movement in philosophy with roots in 19th-century German romanticism, especially in the thought of Kierkegaard and Nietzsche, whose chief exponents have been Heidegger and Jaspers in Germany and Sartre in France. It stresses the active role of the will rather than reason in confronting problems posed by a hostile universe. The nature of man is regarded as consisting in decisive actions rather than in inner or latent dispositions. 2. A cult of nihilism and pessimism popularized after World War II, supposedly based on the doctrines of Sartre and other existentialist writers.
> *Funk & Wagnalls Standard College Dictionary.*

A fighter pilot who has survived a tour of operations understands existentialism without ever reading Heidegger or Sartre. As the specialist in war with arguably the greatest control over his destiny, he knows that his life can be saved only by himself or, if he is lucky, another specialist like himself. His death will often go unwitnessed. He knows that ultimately his war is solitary and, because he is alone, his decision-making absolute. If he has the paramount talent of all great fighter pilots, to see what others cannot, he will live and someone else will probably die.

It is this unwitnessed quality of a fighter pilot's war, and the wish to execute without being seen, that creates such a compelling moral tableau. The gift of exceptional sight, inherited by very few, offers frequent opportunities for moral decision-making. He who sees first has already won half the battle, can escape or choose to fight, disengage or engage at will.

Most of the men I have interviewed see no morality in aerial combat, only an opportunity to do or be done. One high-scoring ace admitted candidly that he did not like his enemy to survive. If there was any chance to kill the opponent in his aircraft or even on the ground as he climbed out of the burning wreckage, this ace took it. After all, that pilot might be back to kill a friend the next day. Why give him that opportunity? While drinking in the bar, one of the famous and accomplished Mosquito pilots was criticized by others like himself for killing German crew members who had been sitting on the wing of their downed bomber. He made no apology, admitted he had done so and said he would do it again.

Not all fighter pilots conform to this ruthless stereotype, one created in the early days of air warfare by legendary aces, especially Richthofen, Fonck and Mannock. Another high-scoring Canadian ace declared that he had never strafed an opponent whose aircraft had been downed. Moreover, he said, on any squadron he commanded he would not have tolerated a pilot who deliberately killed an enemy who was hanging in a parachute. He had two reasons. First, he said, it was unfair, and second, it was unprofessional to make subsequent attacks. What about the enemy watching you from a high-sun position, rolling into a dive to clobber you?

The quality of mercy in aerial warfare, however, depends on time and place and, most importantly, the background and character of the individual. A Polish fighter pilot, his country occupied by Nazi Germany, viewed such fair play as misguided sportsmanship. A Typhoon fighter-bomber pilot, witnessing the death of a good friend in a ball of flames, pointed his machine straight down at the offending German anti-aircraft battery, fiercely determined to wreak personal vengeance against its gunners. I have spoken to a Spitfire ace who killed others like himself without a moment's compunction, but stopped firing at soldiers as they tumbled blood-streaked from a truck and started running in terror across a field.

I have learned also that a gesture of mercy, a withholding of fire, can pale when compared to an impetuous or deliberate act of malice recollected in old age. I asked an ace if he had ever killed an unarmed pilot in his parachute. He said he didn't think he could do that, but he would not blame any pilot who did. Fortuitously, however, my question reminded him of how ruthlessly he had fought to shoot others down. He spoke about how relentlessly obedient that younger man had been to the goal of ending the war as quickly as possible. In memory he could still feel his Spitfire vibrating from his burst of cannon and machine-gun fire aimed directly into the open doors of a French factory, workers scattering and falling.

Another pilot, a carrier-based Navy ace, recalled Japanese soldiers raising a flag at sunrise in a jungle clearing while lined up in parade-square formation, completing their daily sacred ritual. He, merely passing by to a better target, squeezed the trigger on his control column; his six .50-calibre guns vibrated, and soldiers fell. The act is over in a second but lives on, the soldiers falling again and again in memory and sometimes in dreams.

Who of us, non-combatants of this luckier age, would not have been corrupted by such God-like destructive power in our youth? Would we not lose our way on the path, or even risk the loss of our soul? What happens to those who, pro patria, sign up to be warriors in that most challenging of warrior occupations? What did their experiences in the Second World War do to them, and how did their lives turn out? It was in search of answers to these questions that this book came to be written. If, in the process, mistakes have crept in, they are my responsibility, and readers are invited to contact me at my email address listed below to let me know about them, or anything else that comes to mind.

Wayne Ralph,
White Rock, British Columbia, Canada
<wayneralph@telus.net>
January 10, 2005

We master archers say: one shot — one life! What this means, you cannot yet understand. But perhaps another image will help you, which expresses the same experience. We master archers say: with the upper end of the bow the archer pierces the sky; on the lower end, as though attached by a thread, hangs the earth. If the shot is loosed with a jerk there is a danger of the thread snapping. For purposeful and violent people the rift becomes final, and they are left in the awful center between heaven and earth.
Zen Master Kenzo Awa in conversation with student and author Eugen Herrigel, *Zen in the Art of Archery*.

Flight Sergeant F. Lindy Cliff of Kingston, Ontario, in the Western Desert with 94 Squadron, cleans his canopy before a flight.

INTRODUCTION
A BRIEF PRIMER ON THE FIGHTER ACE

A fighter pilot who is called an ace has achieved at least five victories in aerial combat. The coveted accolade, born out of the aerial battles of the First World War, was first coined by the French in 1915. There are no governing international bodies controlling the label or screening entry into the club. The enemy you fight does not have to die for you to be credited with a victory. Therefore the expression "kills" used when discussing aces is misleading. It is confirmed victories, not deaths in air combat that produce aces.

Unfortunately, books about aces create mythologies of good, better and best, portraying air-to-air combat as a kind of international sporting event where bronze, silver and gold medals are awarded based on scores. Any conclusions drawn from such simplistic ranking are meaningless. Comparing aces, within or between nations, based solely on their victory scores is an absurd exercise, and does a great disservice to all fighter pilots.

Why is this so? Well, to begin with, the standard of due diligence in crediting victories to individual pilots varies according to the country, the war being fought, how well or badly the war is going, the doctrine of the opposing air forces, and the leaders in command of individual fighter squadrons and flights.

Many other variables affect these alleged rankings. The process of crediting victories is not immune to subjective concerns such as ambition, both individual and institutional, and exaggeration, either deliberate or inadvertent. Aerial combat is almost always confusing. The oft-used term "fog of war" applies equally to air war.

Victories credited in aerial combat are prone to error, frequently because several pilots report shooting at the same enemy aircraft. In the First World War, the Second World War and also the Korean War, overclaiming was common; it varied by theatre, nation and individual, but it was inevitable.

While many fighter pilots in the Second World War aspired to be aces, only a small minority achieved that status. Hundreds of fighter pilots could have

been aces had opportunity come their way. Many skilled fighter pilots, through no fault of their own, have no confirmed victories. One fighter ace I interviewed, Wing Commander Rod Smith, observed that some of the finest fighter pilots he knew and served with never shot anyone down. Moreover, the occupation of fighter pilot encompasses a great deal beyond the destruction of aerial targets.

The most important ingredient to a successful outcome is a target-rich environment. Opportunity has to combine with skill and luck to create success; without opportunity, no talent, however brilliant, can be brought to bear. Those who have plentiful opportunities — a target-rich environment — and the requisite skills — become aces.

Of the thousands of young men who served operational tours as fighter pilots in the Second World War with the Royal Canadian Air Force (RCAF), Royal Air Force (RAF) or Royal Navy Fleet Air Arm, about 150 had five or more victories.[1] That is an estimate as there is no official list.

The RCAF had no formal system for recording or ranking the scores of its own aces in RCAF squadrons. The four highest-scoring aces born in Canada achieved either all or the majority of their victories with RAF squadrons.

The last surviving Canadian ace from the First World War, Gerald A. Birks, MC and Bar, died in 1991. Many of our Second World War aces had productive lives and successful careers and have, as First World War flyers used to say, "Gone west."

The three Canadians credited with twenty or more victories are no longer with us. George Beurling was killed in Rome in 1948 in a flying accident caused by sabotage; Wally McLeod was killed in combat in 1944; Vernon Woodward died in 2000 in Victoria at the age of eighty-three.

This book tells their stories but, intentionally, does not stop there. It is about every kind of fighter pilot who served, and includes the stories of those who flew mainly at night, in close air support and in anti-shipping roles, and in the solitary world of photographic reconnaissance.

[1] Halliday, *The Tumbling Sky*.

First solo for James Edwards, 1941.

KITTYHAWK ACE OF
THE WESTERN DESERT
CAMPAIGN

Profile – JAMES FRANCIS EDWARDS

Born – June 5, 1921, Nokomis, SK, raised in Battleford, SK

Father – Wilfrid Edwards, farmer

Mother – Alice Scott

Decorations & Medals – DFC and Bar, DFM, MiD, CD and Two Clasps

Degrees & Awards – Order of Canada, 2004

Post-war occupation – Air force officer, Wing Commander, RCAF/CAF

Marital status – Wife Alice "Toni" Antonio; daughters Dorothy, Jean and Angel; son James

Hobbies – Oil painting, fly fishing, golf, gardening

Fighter pilots come in all sizes, shapes and personalities. There is no standard profile, despite Hollywood's attempts to stereotype them. Once in a while, however, you meet an individual who fits the stereotype and Wing Commander James Francis "Stocky" Edwards is one of those. He is Canada's highest-scoring fighter ace of the Western Desert campaign, and one of only three living Canadian aces with fifteen or more victories.

The Western Desert, for those who fought there, encompassed a coastal strip of land westward along the Mediterranean Sea from Alexandria, Egypt, past Benghazi on the Gulf of Sirte to Tripoli, Libya, a distance about equal to that between Moscow and Berlin. The southern boundary went inland as far as Siwa in Egypt and Jagjbub in Libya. This beautiful and daunting landscape was a war zone from the evening of June 10, 1940, when Italy's Benito Mussolini declared war on Britain and France, through to May 13, 1943, when all Axis forces surrendered in that theatre.

On meeting Edwards, I sensed immediately that I was in the presence of a natural leader, unflappable, with preternatural calm. He was just born wise

and old. Yet he looks deceptively boyish. During his wartime career he did not shave with any regularity because, physically, he did not need to. He neither smoked nor drank, believing that clarity of thought contributed to his self-discipline and helped him be a better fighter pilot.

Edwards believes that his own personal guardian angel provided by God kept him safe in battle. If the thought occasionally crossed his mind that he might be killed, he simply moved on to a more cheerful thought. He is still a practising Roman Catholic, after a long war and a thirty-year military career. He joined the air force because his country was at war and needed him. It was not a complicated decision.

Once in the air force, Edwards rose quickly. At twenty, he was a sergeant pilot; at twenty-three, a wing commander (flying). He was decorated four times for gallantry. A natural, he led his squadron in combat in the Western Desert while still a sergeant pilot. When his wing commander found that a sergeant was leading a squadron, he arranged for Edwards to be commissioned in the field and simultaneously promoted to flight lieutenant and commander of one of the two flights in the squadron. He logged 373 operational trips between 1942 and 1945, one of the highest totals for any Canadian fighter pilot in the war. He has co-authored his own memoir, *Kittyhawk Pilot*, and two histories of the Western Desert campaign, *Kittyhawks over the Sands* and *Hurricanes over the Sands*.

Like all Canadian fighter aces, his achievements are far better known outside Canada than within the country. Edwards sees little evidence that young Canadians know anything about their own history or why his generation fought and died so long ago. Sixty years after the war ended, he is still receiving letters from enthusiasts in other countries who want his autographed photo for their "aces" collection. He is famous to them, if not in Canada.

Like many fighter pilots a simple pragmatist, he acknowledges the absurdity of war and the absurdity of young men doing their best to shoot each other down. He says, "The thought occurred to me at the time: I'm saying a prayer in my cockpit, and that other pilot is saying the same prayer to the same God. What a ridiculous thing that we should be at war with each other. He was probably just as good a type of fellow as I was."

Edwards has had ample opportunity to study young men under stress and wonder about the nature of courage and cowardice. One of war's lessons about human nature was that "you could never tell how a guy would turn out. You never know if he will last. The meek fellow in the corner may be the deadliest in the air, while a big strapping fellow might break down."

Growing up in Battleford, Saskatchewan, Edwards was known simply as Jimmie to his family and friends—Stocky was his post-war nickname. He had never been up in an aircraft and had no driver's licence when he volunteered for pilot training with the RCAF in the summer of 1940. The fall of France to German invaders had been playing in the newsreels at the movie house that spring, and Britain might soon be invaded. Two of Jimmie's buddies, Gerry and Bill, had already enlisted and learned to fly. They had even brought their aircraft back to Battleford for a visit, landing alongside the Canadian National Railways tracks.

Jimmie practised reading the post office clock in the town centre from a distance of a mile or more as he walked home from hunting expeditions. He closed each eye in turn, making sure that when his time came to enlist, he would have no trouble passing the test. He knew that he had a scar on the retina of one eye, and it worried him. He had also suffered throughout his childhood from migraine headaches. He didn't go to the movies very often because the flickering image on the screen could set off an attack.

Jimmie was a natural athlete. He was a star with the St Thomas College Flyers hockey team of the Intercollegiate League—in seventy-two games over three years, the team tied only once and never lost at all. He graduated in 1940 from St Thomas. Father Simon, a priest who had once been a semi-pro hockey player, knew somebody with the Chicago Black Hawks. He told Jimmie that a tryout with the Hawks might just be a possibility. Gonzaga University down in Spokane, Washington, had invited Jimmie the year before to join its hockey team while also getting a university education.

But Edwards had decided that he wanted to be a fighter pilot. The nearest RCAF recruiting centre was more than ninety miles away. With his birth certificate and report card in his pocket, he walked from Battleford towards Saskatoon along the gravel road that was Highway 5. Many cars and trucks whistled past the small figure as he trudged along, the dust coating his clothes and best shoes, a pair of Sisman Scampers. Nobody stopped to pick him up.

The recruiting officer was happy to see Edwards. Here was a healthy, athletic nineteen-year-old, complete with senior matriculation. He had a shock of unruly dark hair, an infectious giggle and an easy, happy-go-lucky smile. There was a new movie star in Hollywood who was getting a lot of attention. His name was John Garfield and he played tough-guy roles. Jimmie looked a bit like John Garfield.

A First World War pilot who had downed sixteen Germans in aerial battle walked into the recruiting centre to visit. The medical doctor examining Jimmie pointed this man out, saying, "If you can achieve what he did in the last war, young fellow, you will have made quite a contribution."

The paperwork and medical tests, including eye examination, took most of the day. One of the tests required every recruit to hold his breath—Edwards set a record of more than three minutes. He was ready to start training immediately, but the RCAF was still training instructors and building aerodromes. The war was in its early stages, and Canada's armed forces were struggling to expand fast enough for the battlefield. The recruiting officer told him to go back home and wait for a letter. This was an unexpected turn of events, but it never entered Jimmie's mind to tell the recruiting officer about his dilemma.

The problem was that he had only enough money for one more night's stay at the hotel in Saskatoon. He hadn't planned on returning home so soon because he was joining the air force that day, or so he thought. He had bought his mother a gift at the five- and ten-cent store: salt and pepper shakers in the shape of ducks. He had no money for bus fare and the RCAF was not responsible for getting him back to Battleford. Jimmie left the hotel early the following morning; by 5 p.m. he had walked forty miles northwest to the town of Borden. His feet were very sore, and his Scampers were starting to fall apart. The proprietor of the roadside restaurant in Borden took pity on the kid. He loaned him $3.75 for bus fare, and fed him a meal while he waited.

Jimmie spent the summer working on a friend's farm. His call-up letter finally arrived in October, on a day when he was getting a team of black Percherons to pull a hay rack for the wheat harvest. The RCAF had sent him a rail warrant and meal tickets to the RCAF Manning Depot[1] at Brandon, Manitoba. This time he would not have to walk. The career of Edwards as one of Canada's most brilliant fighter leaders was underway.

The Western Desert south and west of the Libyan port of Tobruk looked nothing like the rolling terrain of northern Saskatchewan. As Edwards said, "Even though I was born on the Prairies where I could see for miles, the desert is completely different really, with the sun blazing all the time, and endless fields of sand ... nothing is recognizable."

Posted to 94 Squadron, RAF, in January 1942, Sergeant Edwards arrived at an inauspicious time for both the unit and the British Army in Africa. The Afrika Korps and the Luftwaffe dominated the battlefields and skies of the Western Desert, being better equipped, better trained and better led than their British opponents. Only two days before Edwards's arrival, the commanding officer, a flight commander and six other pilots of 94 had been shot down by two German fighter pilots. The Hawker Hurricanes had assumed an ineffectual defensive circle to protect themselves, and the Messerschmitt Me109s picked them off in attack after attack, one by one.

Edwards and nine other Canadian pilots were sobered to learn that their new squadron had been practically wiped out. There were only three Hurricanes left to fly, and it soon got worse. Two days later, General Oberst Erwin Rommel's Afrika Corps pushed General Neil Ritchies British Eigth Army eastward. To avoid being captured, the pilots piled aboard trucks travelling the coast road parallel to the Mediterranean. The Eighth Army managed to dig in thirty miles west of Tobruk, forming a new front line at Gazala.

By March 21, 94 Squadron was back to full strength, stationed at an airfield at Gasr el Arid, southeast of Tobruk. The unit had traded its Hurricanes for a US-designed fighter, the Curtiss P40 Kittyhawk. The early P40 models had been immortalized in stories in *Life Magazine* in 1942, battling against the Japanese fighters and bombers in the skies of Burma and China. General Claire Chennault's pilots serving in the American Volunteer Group of the Chinese Air Force in 1941 had seen photographs of the shark's mouth paint scheme on 112 Squadron's P40 Tomahawks fighting in the Western Desert. They copied the RAF squadron's paint scheme, and the legendary Flying Tigers were born—John Wayne played the lead in the 1941 Hollywood movie of the same name.

SAND AND THE DESERT...

Sand is the foundation of the visible world ...When a mug of tea is finished there is a sediment of sand at the bottom. There is sand in the food, no matter how recently it has been taken from a sealed tin. The hairs of the body are individually outlined by a coating of fine powdered sand. Everywhere the body is invaded by the desert ...This clinging pervasiveness is a quality of the desert sand, like the wetness of water. The atmosphere of the desert resembles that of the sea. There is the same sweep of space. There is a vastness and an overwhelming sense of personal minuteness, of the living flesh submerged by the immense, dead, physical world ... The desert is; it is undeniable, it is immemorial. It is the immemorial world of which we are a trifling and temporal part.

-Neil McCallum, Journey with a Pistol.

[1] In the RCAF, induction centres for recruits were called Manning Depots and were located at Edmonton, Brandon and Toronto.

Even though 94 Squadron had no dramatic symbol such as the tiger shark on its machines, the squadron's Kittyhawks were an improved model of the original P40 Tomahawk, and better than the obsolescent Hurricane, with larger-calibre .50-inch guns and bomb racks. One-on-one its performance still did not match the Messerschmitt Me109F, but a Kittyhawk pilot using tactics to suit the aircraft's strengths could hold his own. A gifted Kittyhawk pilot could inflict a lot of damage.

On March 23, Edwards flew his first operational trip—providing fighter escort to twelve Boston medium bombers in an attack against the German airfield at Martuba. In a remarkable foreshadowing of his future success, Edwards accomplished something few novice fighter pilots do—he shot down an enemy aircraft on his first operational trip, likely saving his flight leader's life.

RCAF and RAF fighter pilots had little or no training in aerial gunnery in 1941–42, and Jimmie had to fall back on years of hunting experience:

I had grown up on the Prairies, where a shotgun was something you carried with you at all times in the fall. We shot birds. So I knew all about deflection shooting, and how to lead a flying target. But most of the guys did not know ... One of the Me109s wheeled in behind my No. 1, who was about 75 yards in front of me. Jeez, I just pulled the trigger. I don't know what made me do it. I could see the black crosses on the German aircraft, and he was going to shoot him down, so I pulled the trigger, and he just went all to pieces—exploded.

Edwards almost became a victim himself that day because another 109F was already in position to kill. The German fighter, with an MG151 cannon firing through the propeller shaft and prop spinner, seemed to fill the sky when Edwards looked over his shoulder:

I'm lookin' right at a big white spinner, like this *big*, with a hole in it, this *big*. I am looking right at it, and I saw him just dip his nose—God, I pushed the stick right forward because I could see he was going to hit me. He was

dropping the nose of his aircraft to get the proper deflection ... his bullets went just over the top of my cockpit as I dove straight down to the ground. All the stuff, dust on the floor of the cockpit floated to the top of the cockpit ... I went straight down. Straight down to the ground. There was nobody behind me, which was lucky. I often thought about that after. All the German pilot had to do was follow me down, and I would have been dead.

Alone, flying a few hundred feet above the sand dunes, Edwards now had to navigate in a vast landscape that might have been the face of the moon. He knew he had to follow the Mediterranean coast to find his way home, but it all looked so unfamiliar. He finally recognized a bomber base that was some miles past his own airfield. Retracing his path to Gasr el Arid, Edwards landed without incident and walked to the operations tent.

His distracted squadron commander was worried about the missing pilots who had not yet landed. He had no time for a novice on his first op. Edwards was bursting to shout out that he had been successful in his first aerial battle, but when Squadron Leader MacDougall finally turned his attention to the kid from Canada, all Edwards could manage was a mouse-like squeak: "I shot down a 109." With the return of the leader of the mission, Flight Sergeant Phillips, "Eddie" Edwards's story was confirmed (Eddie was his squadron nickname during the war).

Wing Commander Beresford, leader of 233 Wing, was pleased with the results of the attack, labelling the new chap the Hawk of Martuba. Edwards was now singled out within 233 Wing as a pilot who could shoot. It was the perfect nickname for Canadian journalists seeking out Canadian heroes for the folks back home. In 1942 there were not many good news stories coming out of the Western Desert, and few Canadians knew they had sons fighting over there. Within a few months, Edwards became the outstanding Canadian fighter pilot and leader in that theatre of war. Newspapers back in Canada heralded Jimmie Edwards of Battleford, Saskatchewan, as the "Beurling of Western Desert Fighting," reporting his many victories, his rapid promotion and his gallantry awards, the Distinguished Flying Medal (DFM) and Distinguished Flying Cross (DFC) for valour.

About five hundred Canadian pilots served in the Western Desert, alongside other young pilots from South Africa, Rhodesia, New Zealand, Australia, Britain and the United States. From all parts of the British Empire and very different family backgrounds, they got along in the Western Desert as though they had grown up together. Rank and military formalities meant little to these young men living in tents, shaking scorpions and sand from their boots each morning and subsisting on a diet of tinned corn beef.

About 120 Canadian pilots served on Kittyhawks, and 50 were either killed or shot down and taken prisoner. The deaths were in part the result of unsophisticated fighter tactics training, non-existent gunnery training, obsolescent flying machines and inadequate leadership. After a few weeks of operational flying, Sergeant Edwards knew that the haphazard way in which the RAF conducted its operations, with its absence of coordinated teamwork and frequent changes of flight leaders, was never going to win this war. Edwards may have been just twenty years old, but he had an extraordinary blend of self-discipline, self-confidence and creative thinking. He soon realized that the high turnover in squadron and flight commanders and the severe casualties being suffered by the RAF in the Western Desert could lead only to defeat.

But good planning and discipline in the air saved lives, and Edwards quickly showed that he was a natural leader. Mirroring his three undefeated years with the St Thomas College Flyers hockey team, he applied the unbeatable combination of teamwork and discipline to the challenges he faced. As Edwards said: "You could fool around on the ground. But in the air, in combat, there are do's and don'ts, and you never do the don'ts. That way, you get to live to fly another day."

In that fateful summer of 1942, while Edwards was learning to become a leader in the life-or-death skies of the Western Desert, two other young men from Saskatchewan, Roderick Illingsworth Alpine Smith, of Regina, and Ian Roy Maclennan, of Gull Lake, were growing up fast in an intense air war only a few hundred miles to the northwest on the besieged island of Malta.

EDWARDS RECOLLECTS PRINCIPLES AND PROBLEMS OF AIR COMBAT LEADERSHIP

We had quite a few of those types, pilots who just wanted to survive. They took a lot of looking after on a squadron in the air. You had to include them in your flight patterns, your attack patterns. In other words, you had to look after them like a mother hen. Some of the leaders didn't give a damn—they would say, 'You're on your own.' But I felt that if I led four or eight pilots, we were a team and I had to help them out. If you have the chance, you direct them: 'Go there, stay here, stay up.'

I recall a young flying officer who had done about twenty trips, and the flight commander asked him to become a section leader. This fellow was upset because he had to take notes during the briefing; the heading out, the heading back. Well, you see, for him everything was changed. He had to look after somebody besides himself. He had to start thinking differently.

But you have to have a background and knowledge to cope with all this. Flying instructors coming over with the rank of flight lieutenant were sometimes made flight commanders, but they could not cope. They didn't know anything about ops or teamwork.

It is nice to go out with someone [in whom] you have confidence. Then you think to yourself, well, I don't have to worry about his leadership of that section.

You always look for potential leaders, not just someone to be the head of the arrow, but lead the people behind him, and also look after them on the ground.

Rod Smith, of Regina, 1944.

CANADIANS IN THE SIEGE OF MALTA

Profile – RODERICK ILLINGSWORTH ALPINE SMITH

Born – March 21, 1922, Regina

Died – April 16, 2002, Vancouver

Father – Donald Alpine Smith, civil engineer, land surveyor

Mother – Blanche Robertshaw

Decorations & Medals – DFC and Bar

Degrees & Awards – BSc, LLB

Post-war occupation – Lawyer and partner at Campney, Owen & Murphy, Vancouver; Wing Commander, RCAF Auxiliary

Marital status – Bachelor (he preferred the phrase "never married")

Hobbies – Military historian

Rod Smith and Ian Maclennan arrived on the strategically pivotal Mediterranean island of Malta on July 15, 1942, after launching their fighter planes from the Royal Navy aircraft carrier *Eagle* as it steamed at twenty-five knots directly into the wind north of the Algerian coast. This was no mean accomplishment because they had never flown from the deck of an aircraft carrier. The Royal Navy had provided the Spitfire pilots with one lecture on how to take off and no information on how to land. The pilots en route to Malta were forbidden to attempt a landing back on the *Eagle* if their engine faltered. Instead, the navy told them to ditch in the sea, where someone might come by and pick them up. Unfortunately, the Spitfire had poor buoyancy and ditching was not recommended by the manufacturer.

Smith and Maclennan did not know each other at this point; they served on different squadrons in both Britain and Malta, and became friends long after the war.

Smith climbed his Spitfire up to ten thousand feet and joined a formation of seven other aircraft. They were led by an experienced pilot from Malta who was navigator for the formation. They flew seven hundred miles east to the tiny island, across the middle of an inhospitable sea, avoiding German, Italian and Vichy French aircraft. It was particularly important to steer clear of the African coastline, where pilots loyal to Marshal Pétain—whose regime based in Vichy, France, was never recognized by the Allies—had orders to shoot down British aircraft.

It was Rod Smith's longest flight in the Spitfire, a short-range fighter with eighty-five Imperial gallons of internal fuel, good for about an hour and a half operational flying. An extra ninety-gallon "slipper" tank under the belly extended the Spitfire's range. No ammunition was loaded in the machine, so the pilot could not fire back if attacked by enemy fighters.

Smith landed at a hot, dusty, bomb-cratered airfield named Luqa after a three-hour flight. He was directed to park in an aircraft pen on the far side of the airfield. His limbs stiff from the flight, he unfolded himself from the small cockpit. He opened the Spitfire's empty ammunition chambers in the wings and removed his cache of ten pounds of personal belongings, a few shirts, underwear and socks. Sweat trickled down his back as he squinted at the yellow chalky soil of the island. The walls of the aircraft revetment were made of sand-filled gasoline cans, something Smith had never seen.

A tan-coloured Ford, flying a large Royal Air Force flag, pulled up by Smith's Spitfire. Out of the vehicle stepped a tall, thin man with, as Smith recalls, "a face like an eagle." He was the highest-ranking RAF officer on Malta, Air Vice-Marshal Keith Park, who had been one of the senior commanders in the Battle of Britain of 1940. He had arrived just the day before to take command of the RAF on the island from Air Vice-Marshal Hugh Lloyd. The New Zealand-born commander offered the young Canadian

US Navy photo coutesy of the Wendy Noble Collection

US Navy sailors tie down Jerry Smith's Spitfire on the USS *Wasp*. The carrier's F4F Wildcats provide cover.

S P I T F I R E L A N D S
O N D E C K O F U S S *W A S P*

Jerry Smith had flown off USS *Wasp* on May 17, 1942. In contravention of orders, he landed back on the flight deck of the *Wasp* because his drop tank failed to feed the fuel to his engine. His landing was safely accomplished without arrester gear, though it was a close-run thing. The feat was deemed so impressive that the US Navy liaison officer for President Roosevelt, Douglas Fairbanks Jr. (the movie star) offered Jerry a whisky from an illicit cabinet on the *Wasp*. US Navy ships, being "dry," carried no drinkable alcohol, unlike Royal Navy ships with daily rum tots. Jerry was also presented with US Navy aviator wings. He hitched a ride out of Gibraltar to Malta on a B24 the following day, and immediately was thrown into air combat.

a ride across the airfield. Smith was flattered. Unaccustomed to such kindness from senior officers, he sat quietly.

He noticed another pilot—a bit bedraggled, just back from an air battle—trudging along with his parachute and Mae West over his shoulder. Something about his appearance seemed familiar, and Rod, with a start, recognized his brother, Jerrold. Rod shouted, "Stop the car!" The air vice-marshal obliged, and Rod turned to Park and said, "This is my brother, sir, Pilot Officer Smith." To Rod's embarrassment, in the shock of the moment, he could not remember his brother's first name.

"Jerry," not quite a year older than Rod, had made his takeoff from the USS *Wasp* in May and was already flying on operations with 126 Squadron, which Rod was joining. Due to the customary secrecy of wartime operations, Rod had no idea where Jerry was serving. By accident Jerry and Rod had made it to the same squadron during one of the most intense air battles of the Second World War. Nobody expressed any concerns about two brothers flying not only in the same squadron, but also in the same flight. The two were thrilled to be on operations—Jerry leading, Rod as No. 2.

Rod Smith was the first Second World War fighter pilot I interviewed for this book, and the tallest, at six feet three inches. Yet the plane he flew operationally throughout the war was the Vickers Supermarine Spitfire—the Allied fighter with the smallest cockpit. Even at the end of his life he preferred compact quarters at high altitude. His home was a one-bedroom apartment on the fourteenth floor of a high-rise co-op building on Pendrell Street tucked up close to the famed Stanley Park in Vancouver's West End. He enjoyed the panoramic view of English Bay, where large tankers and small sailboats anchor at sunset. Float planes and helicopters flew by Rod's living-room window every day, and he could gauge with an experienced eye the deflection that might be necessary to shoot them down.

He lived by himself with Boofuls, an old Siamese cat who was deaf and blind. Rod adored the cat, even when he clawed his sweater. But if the sweater in question was the cashmere one that his sister Wendy had given him, he would take it off and put on his oldest sweater so the cat could keep

clawing. The first paragraph of Rod's last will and testament told the executor about the cat's welfare and future owner. Further down in the document were instructions for payments to six significant women in Rod's life. Rod had never married and liked to say that he gave up proposing after the first woman who turned him down said that she loved him too much, and the second woman chastised him for not loving her enough. Boofuls, who came to Rod late in life, was "a neutered male, just like me!" The cat pointedly ignored any visitors, and liked to sleep under a goose-neck lamp on Rod's desk, his nose against the wall, his rump pointed towards the intruder.

Britain's highest-scoring fighter pilot of the Second World War, Air Vice-Marshal J.E. "Johnnie" Johnson, was a good friend of Wing Commander Smith. When Johnnie came to Canada to visit the beloved Canadian fighter pilots that he had led in combat, he liked to sleep on Rod's long couch and go boating on his yacht. Johnnie liked to talk of the war and lost friends, and was proud of his connection to Canada. He autographed a few of Rod's history books, inscribing an admonition, "Rod, keep the memory green."

Retired from the daily grind of corporate law, Rod Smith had become a military historian, writing his memoirs at the dining-room table, but broadening his personal story with thorough research on strategy, tactics, aircraft and weapons. He had a natural flair for teaching, and enjoyed holding forth at length from his armchair. If we went to the Sylvia Hotel just around the corner for lunch, Rod asked the young waitress to microwave his beer; he did not like cold beer. As we spoke about the ambitions of fighter aces, he reached across and took french fries off my plate, raising his eyebrows to ask permission.

At one point in a long conversation, Smith lowered Boofuls gently to the floor, got up from his armchair, disappeared into the bedroom and came back holding gun cartridges. He laid them out on the table before me—a .303, a .50 inch, a 20mm and a 30mm. A succinct lecture was provided about calibre, weight and hitting power. He then effortlessly shifted from ballistics to Sir Winston Churchill's memoirs of the war. Smith said that during the Battle of Britain, because of the Enigma code-breaking machine, the prime minister knew day to day how few German fighters had really been shot down versus how many the RAF had claimed.

There was a big difference, Smith noted, between the overheated claims of battle and the reality. He was a man who wanted to know the truth, however unpalatable. Sustaining legends was, in his opinion, no virtue ("The Brits, you know, they don't want to give up their legends"). At some point I used the polite phrase, "He passed away, didn't he?" Rod barked at me, "You can pass water, but you can't pass away. You die." He could not abide euphemisms or comforting illusions, particularly when they pertained to the defining period of his life—the war and especially Malta in 1942.

When the war broke out, Rod Smith was determined to be a fighter pilot and the sooner the better. He recalled the warning he received on his first visit in 1940 to the RCAF recruiting centre in Regina: "Should you fail to get your pilot's wings, you are too tall to be trained as an air gunner or navigator. The air force will assign you to general duties, pushing a pen or a broom." "Well, sir," said Rod, "I've never failed anything in my life, and I don't intend to fail this."

His cockiness and maturity impressed the recruiting officer, himself a First World War pilot. Rod was granted a "distinguished pass" at No. 2 Service Flying Training School (SFTS), Uplands, Ontario, placing eighth out of forty-four, and was granted a commission.

Three days after having his wings pinned on, Rod celebrated his nineteenth birthday. To make it, in his own words, "a clean sweep," he was assigned to fly fighters overseas. He travelled to Britain on the armed merchant cruiser HMS *California*, making friends on the voyage with a twenty-one-year-old pilot from North Battleford, Saskatchewan, named Robert Wendell "Buck" McNair. The two young men competed with each other at No. 58

NCO OR COMMISSIONED OFFICER ON GRADUATION?

Pilots graduating from an SFTS of the British Commonwealth Air Training Plan were promoted to one of two ranks based on their marks on flying and written examinations, their education and maturity. Along with your pilot's wings, you instantly were elevated from leading aircraftman to non-commissioned officer (NCO), a sergeant pilot, or the commissioned officer's rank of pilot officer (P/O). The latter rank conferred a King's scroll, a considerably better rate of pay and nicer uniforms and, in some circles, the label of "gentleman," as in "an officer and a gentleman."

If your best friend in training was commissioned and you were not, your futures might parallel each other but across the divide. It was a huge divide separating a flying NCO, disapproved of by "real" NCOs who had served decades in the ranks, and a youthful pilot officer who nonetheless was usually regarded (in British circles) as of the right social class to receive a commission in His Majesty's forces.

On board ship going overseas, NCO pilots were provided with a hammock for sleeping; commissioned officers had cabins, albeit crowded with three or more together in one tiny space. In Britain the norm was that aircrew NCOs ate in a separate mess from aircrew officers. The problems this created for men flying and fighting as a flight, crew or squadron were so great that on many stations and in many wings and groups, aircrew of all ranks ate and lived together.

It was common for buddies separated by rank to falsely wear officers' epaulets or spare tunics so they could socialize together on leave in bars and restaurants from London to Cairo to Calcutta. NCO pilots could date NCO women, for example their mechanic, but commissioned officers could not fraternize with or date them (at least not officially).

During the war, Canadian NCO pilots were commissioned after a period of service, sometimes jumping from NCO directly to flight lieutenant. Canadians serving with RAF squadrons frequently did not know that they had been promoted within the RCAF, and were sometimes "lost" administratively for long periods of the war.

Operational Training Unit (OTU), Grangemouth, Scotland, graduating as the top two on the Spitfire course in total hours flown. Every chance they got to fly, they flew.

Wing Commander Mark Henry "Hilly" Brown, who was an ace and a veteran of the 1940 Battle of France and Battle of Britain, took Smith and McNair up for their first formation trip in the Spitfire. Brown was interested in the two because he also was a Canadian from the Prairies, born in Portage la Prairie, Manitoba, in 1911. He had been in the RAF since 1936. Smith chuckled as he recalled the experience:

We were trying to come in so close on him in formation, showing off, trying to look good. God, we were in close ... he must have been nervous. Anyway, we landed and he said, "You did very well, boys. Smitty, you were a little too close for your experience." That means, "You frighten me, and I want you to stay a little farther out!" Of course, he was right.

For their first tour of operations, Buck McNair and Rod Smith were sent to RCAF squadrons, 411 and 412 respectively. Riding in a private compartment on the train up to Digby, Lincolnshire, Rod was horrified to watch Buck open his sealed dossier and look over his assessment. Written assessments were not for the graduate pilot to read but rather for his new squadron commander to use as a helpful tool in assessing capabilities and shortcomings. Buck's jaw dropped. He swore about his OTU flight commander and handed the report to Rod. "It had been signed by Tony Lovell," Rod recounted, "and one sentence said: 'Pilot Officer McNair is a good pilot, but wants everyone to know it.' That may be true, but Buck was one of the finest ever ... he got very morose and, of course, I really wanted to burst out laughing, but I didn't."

In 1942 both men arrived on Malta, McNair in March, a few months before Smith. In the Malta battles, McNair was credited with destroying five enemy aircraft, Smith with six, and both received the

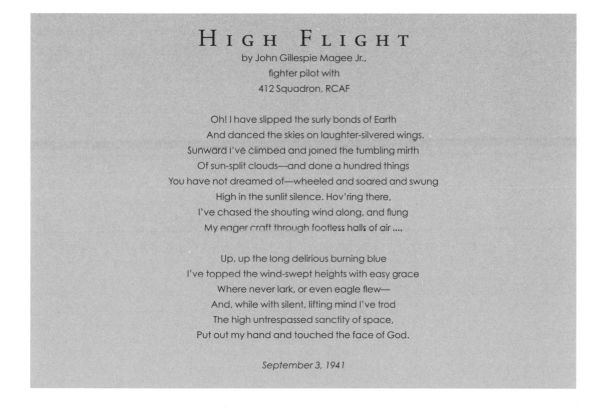

HIGH FLIGHT
by John Gillespie Magee Jr.,
fighter pilot with
412 Squadron, RCAF

Oh! I have slipped the surly bonds of Earth
And danced the skies on laughter-silvered wings.
Sunward I've climbed and joined the tumbling mirth
Of sun-split clouds—and done a hundred things
You have not dreamed of—wheeled and soared and swung
High in the sunlit silence. Hov'ring there,
I've chased the shouting wind along, and flung
My eager craft through footless halls of air ....

Up, up the long delirious burning blue
I've topped the wind-swept heights with easy grace
Where never lark, or even eagle flew—
And, while with silent, lifting mind I've trod
The high untrespassed sanctity of space,
Put out my hand and touched the face of God.

September 3, 1941

DFC. Wing Commander McNair survived the war as one of Canada's most decorated fighter aces, with four British and two French gallantry medals and 16 victories. In addition to Malta, Squadron Leader Smith completed a tour of operations in Europe, commanded 401 Squadron, received a Bar to his DFC and was credited with 13 and 1/5 victories, his last being a shared victory over an Me262 jet.

In the fall of 1941, while his squadron was stationed at Wellingore, Lincolnshire, Smith had become friends with another teenager, Pilot Officer John Gillespie Magee Jr., who had graduated from No. 2 SFTS at Uplands three months after Smith had received his wings there. Less than a month before Magee's death in a mid-air collision on December 11, 1941, a poem he had composed on the back of a letter to his family in Washington, DC, was published in the *Pittsburgh Post-Gazette*.

The poem, "High Flight," struck a chord in the United States and was put on display with other war poems at the Library of Congress.[1] It has become a kind of anthem of flight—not just for fighter pilots, but for all those who fly in war or peace. It is the best evocation of what it feels like to fly a high-performance fighter, especially one so beautifully crafted as the Spitfire. It is often read at the funeral of flyers, symbolizing as it does the exaltation of flight and its sometimes spiritual epiphany. It has also been read at the funerals of astronauts, who have taken the tradition of high flight to new dimensions.

In the war, however, the poem symbolized something more: international sacrifice in defence of freedom. "High Flight" had been composed by a nineteen-year-old product of the British public-school system—a graduate of Rugby—who happened to have been born in China of an American father and British mother, both Christian missionaries. Magee trained as a pilot in Canada and died serving with a Royal Canadian Air Force Spitfire squadron in defence of Britain.

T H E   S I E G E   O F   M A L T A

The Siege of Malta is one of the most dramatic stories of the Second World War. An ally of Britain since the Napoleonic Wars of the early nineteenth century, the island was an essential linchpin in the land battles of the Western Desert. The country that controlled it could dominate the supply routes from Gibraltar and Italy.

The tiny island, just seventeen miles long and only nine miles wide at its widest point (about one hundred square miles of rugged terrain) had a quarter of a million citizens in 1940. For more than two years, from June '40 to December '42, the goal of the Axis powers was to blockade the island and so deplete its stocks of food, fuel and ammunition, starving the Maltese people and destroying their will to fight.

At the peak of the Malta Blitz in 1942, the bombing by Italian and German aircraft surpassed in intensity anything that had taken place to that point in the Second World War. In the spring of '42, there were 150 days of continual day and night bombing, and more than 6,500 tons of bombs landed on towns, villages, harbours and airfields. In April and May, twice as many bombs were dropped as during the entire twelve months of the London Blitz.

How could Malta be defended in the air against bombers? How could convoys be protected as they neared the island? The answer was in air power, including day fighters and radar-equipped night fighters. Due to the strategic emphasis on northern Europe, Malta had to defend itself with less capable aircraft, in 1940–41 with Gloster Gladiator biplane fighters borrowed from the Royal Navy, then with Hawker Hurricanes—both Mk Is and IIs. They were not adequate opponents to the German Me109s and Italian Macchi fighters flying from the island of Sicily only sixty miles to the north. One answer was the Spitfire Mk V, but the Spitfires were needed, or so the RAF leaders in Britain believed, for British defence and fighter sweeps over occupied France. After much lobbying, a plan was developed to supply Malta with the tropical model of the Mk V by launching the fighters from aircraft carriers sailing out of Gibraltar.

The first Canadians to serve in Malta were those who had joined the RAF before the war. Wing Commander Hilly Brown arrived on the island in October 1941. He had been the first Canadian to shoot down an enemy aircraft, in November '39. Allen Angus, from McCreary, Manitoba, and Brown, from Portage la Prairie, were respectively Canada's first and

[1] Linda Granfield, *High Flight*.

THE MALTA RUN

Malta could be resupplied only by sea. It was essential that convoys of ships carrying food, fuel, ammunition and spare parts make it to the Grand Harbour at Valletta, the island's capital. These convoys, which sailors nicknamed The Malta Run, had to navigate through a gauntlet of enemy submarines, surface ships, high-altitude bombers and dive bombers, as well as low-flying torpedo bombers. Once inside Grand Harbour, the ships still had to be unloaded while under attack. Many were sunk at their anchorages or at pier side.

Convoys were uneventful in 1940, encountering little opposition from the Italian air force and navy. But a January 1941 convoy, Operation Excess, departing from Alexandria, Egypt, and Gibraltar, almost lost its escorting aircraft carrier, the Royal Navy's HMS *Illustrious*.

Around midday on January 10, waves of Italian air force Ju87 Stukas attacked the ship, and six or seven thousand-pound bombs hit their target, set fire to aviation fuel below decks and destroyed the carrier's steering system. The attack took only ten minutes.

By heroic efforts the *Illustrious* stayed afloat and limped into Valletta after dark. The Axis air forces continued bombing her at the docks for another twenty-four hours. The convoy's cargo ships and tankers made it to Valletta as well. However, the success of future convoys had been put into question by these aerial attacks. Aircraft could sink ships that were not adequately protected by air cover.

American air-power prophet Brigadier General William "Billy" Mitchell had forecast what aircraft could do to ships back in 1921. In peacetime bombing exercises off the North Carolina coast, he had shown the vulnerability of large ships to aerial attack. The success of his attacks with Martin bombers against the battleship *Ostfriesland* were generally discounted by naval experts as unrealistic.

But the lesson was there to be learned in 1921 and 1941—ships without local air superiority cannot guarantee their survival against aerial attack. Some convoys made it to Malta unscathed under the cover of bad weather, and others by secrecy and the decoding of German secret messages. But air superiority was essential in clear weather, especially as the convoys approached Malta.

The Royal Navy's Mediterranean commander, Admiral Andrew Browne Cunningham, recognized that without aircraft carriers, and without land-based air cover against attack, convoys could not arrive intact. He lobbied to have more fighter aircraft transferred to the Mediterranean and to Malta.

German airborne troops successfully occupied the island of Crete in June 1941, and many of the Royal Navy's major warships were damaged or sunk defending the Greek island, including the aircraft carrier *Formidable*. The German general staff had been countermanded by Hitler—they wanted to invade Malta, not Crete, a more difficult objective but more crucial to the outcome of the Western Desert fighting. Field Marshal Erwin Rommel had forecast that if Germany did not possess Malta, his Deutsches Afrika Korps could not take Egypt and the Suez Canal.

What targets that aircraft had failed to sink, submarines took care of. In November '41, U-Boat 331 sank the battleship *Barham*, and in December U81 sank the carrier *Ark Royal*.

That same month the Japanese navy's carrier-based aircraft attacked the United States naval and military installations at Pearl Harbor in the Hawaiian Islands.

The coordinated efforts of Japanese navy high-altitude bombers and low-flying torpedo bombers sank the Royal Navy battleship *Prince of Wales* and the battle cruiser *Repulse* in the Gulf of Siam, near Singapore, on December 10.

Nine days later, Italian navy two-man submarines penetrated the harbour at Alexandria and severely damaged two battleships, *Queen Elizabeth* and *Valiant*.

The Royal Navy was losing the resources needed to wage war and protect convoys in the Battle of the Atlantic and the Mediterranean. Where were the ships and men to come from to save Malta? Without carriers or air cover from land, could convoys even make it through to Valletta in 1942?

second aces. Angus was killed in May 1940 during the battles over France. Brown was killed during the Siege of Malta while on operations over Sicily in November '41, and was buried there by his enemies. In an act of gallantry reminiscent of the Great War, the Italians dropped a note over Malta telling the RAF that he had died fighting, and been accorded full military honours.

One of the first arrivals in 1942 was a twenty-eight-year-old naturalized Canadian in the RAF who had flown with the legendary amputee RAF ace Douglas Bader. His name was Percival Stanley Turner, born in Devon of British parents but raised in Toronto from childhood. He was a veteran of the Battle of Britain, having shot down at least ten German aircraft before arriving in Malta to take command of 249 Squadron, and he would serve as a group captain in the last months of the war. Turner was brutally frank towards inexperienced or stupid pilots serving under him. He could, when provoked, be equally insolent to senior officers. At his first meeting with Squadron Leader Douglas Bader, during Bader's inaugural speech as the new commander of 242 Squadron in 1940, Turner's only response to his public-school-style pep talk was one word, spoken in a loud voice from the back of the room: "Horseshit!" After a long silence during which Bader became red in the face, Turner added a second word, "Sir."

Turner despised unprofessional flying and just the sound of his voice on a frequency—"This is Dogsbody …" —brought an abrupt end to any RT chatter. Pilots did not contradict him; they became accustomed to his blistering rebukes, spiced for emphasis with adjectives and adverbs starting with the letters *f* and *c*.

The RAF squadrons on Malta, as in the Western Desert, were a multinational conglomerate of young men from all over the world. More than 100 Canadians and Americans served there in 1942 during the peak of the siege, and a memorial has been erected on Malta in their honour. The names of 44 RCAF personnel are engraved on the memorial. Some 120 fighter pilots were killed in action or died, including 56 Britons, 11 New Zealanders, 9 Australians and 4 Rhodesians. Twenty-four fighter pilots of the RCAF were killed in action from January to November '42. Six Americans in the RCAF, plus 5 others serving in the RAF, also died. In ad-

SERGEANT GEORGE FREDERICK BEURLING ARRIVES IN MALTA

Beurling was the highest-scoring ace in the Siege of Malta, becoming a legend in a few months and the most identifiable war hero of the aerial campaign. The twenty-year-old kid from Verdun, Quebec, landed on Malta on June 9 as a sergeant pilot. He seemed more troubled and reclusive than most twenty-year-olds, and was a difficult subordinate to understand, manage or care about.

It was the unfortunate habit of some squadron commanders in Britain to transfer their hard cases out to Malta—pilots who were disobedient or accident-prone. Sometimes inexperienced rookies were also sent, and some of these almost immediately became cannon fodder in the high-intensity war over the island. Others were sent back home for their own protection.

Beurling's reputation for being both difficult and "weirdly antisocial" was already known when he arrived at 249 Squadron. His squadron buddies quickly nicknamed him Screwball, partly because Beurling himself used the word to describe many aspects of the world he saw around him.

There were other Canadians already on the island with excellent reputations as leaders and wingmen, so Beurling was viewed as an eccentric anomaly, not at all characteristic of the Canadians as a whole. However, his eyesight and deflection gunnery were unequalled by any pilot of any nation in the battle for Malta, and he was credited with about twenty-five victories in four months. He was given four gallantry awards for this achievement and—unwisely, and clearly against his wishes—an officer's commission.

Courtesy of the Bob Middlemiss Collection

Bob Middlemiss and George Beurling in England in 1943.

dition, of the 10 pilots lost on Spitfire ferry flights to Malta from the aircraft carriers in 1942, 5 were serving with the RCAF.

Very few of the Canadians defending Malta became household names. They were young men from all across Canada, from farms, small towns and the cities. The following is a representative sampling of some of the Canadians and other nationalities in the RCAF who served: James Ballantyne; G.D. "Jerry" Billing; Mickey Butler; William K. "Bill" Carr; Bud Connell; Gerry de Nancrede; Wilbert Dodd; Gordon Farquharson; Robert "Moose" Fumerton and his navigator, L.P.S. "Pat" Bing; Frank Jones; Irving "Hap" Kennedy; Carl "Ozzie" Linton; Chuck MacLean; Ian Maclennan; John McElroy; Henry Wallace "Wally" McLeod; Robert "Buck" McNair; Andrew McNaughton; Bob Middlemiss; Geoffrey

Wilson Northcott, Chuck Ramsay, Donald Reid, John Sherlock; Rod and Jerrold Smith; and John "Willie the Kid" Williams.

Many Canadians became aces over Malta, and quite a few were promoted to flight commanders in the RAF squadrons on the island. Quite a few of these flight leaders went on to serve with distinction in northwest Europe in 1944–45 as squadron and wing commanders. Many were killed in subsequent air combat or died in flying accidents. The most famous of the Canadians and the one whose name is forever linked with the defence of Malta was George Frederick Beurling, of Verdun, Quebec. He will feature in this narrative only as a supporting player, seen mostly through the eyes and memories of men who admired him, liked him or, in some cases, despised or pitied him.

Profile – ROBERT GEORGE MIDDLEMISS

Born – July 30, 1920, Montreal

Father – Edwin James Middlemiss, CPR policeman

Mother – Mary Bennett

Decorations & Medals – DFC, CD and Clasp

Post-war occupation – Air force officer, Wing Commander, RCAF/CAF, Honorary Colonel of 427 Squadron

Marital status – Wife Crystal Scott, sons Dan and Rob, daughter Dale

Hobbies – Golf, 427 Squadron, air force history

Robert George "Bob" Middlemiss arrived on Malta in May 1942, a month ahead of Beurling, launching from HMS *Eagle* as one of thirty-one pilots flying their fighters together across the Mediterranean. On approaching Malta they were intercepted by Me109s from Sicily and had to fight their way in. Low on fuel, they kept turning in defensive circles and edging their way to the island. Four Spitfires were shot down, including one in Middlemiss's section. It was a harrowing introduction to the high-intensity battles that took place daily over Malta. The miracle was that so many survived and managed to park their Spits in revetments, even with the enemy circling overhead.

A twenty-three-year-old from Montreal with operational experience that included one victory and one damaged enemy aircraft over France, Middlemiss had a short, intense tour on Malta with 249 Squadron. He flew both as a wingman to his flight commander, Edward Daddo-Langlois—who was referred to in the squadron as Daddy Long Legs—and occasionally as a section leader. On June 27, he destroyed a Regia Aeronautica (Italian air force) Macchi 202 and damaged another; Middlemiss destroyed a Luftwaffe Me109 on July 2, following up two days later with a Regia Aeronautica Cant Z1007, a three-engine bomber.

On July 7, flying as No. 2 to Daddo, he covered his six o'clock while his leader shot down a German Ju88. The Me109 that was behind Daddo was, in turn, shot down by Middlemiss. Looking over his own shoulder (there were no other Spits to cover Middlemiss's tail), he had a mere fraction of a second to absorb the fact that he was under attack by another Me109. Abruptly his hand flew away from the control column and his Spitfire began to spin towards

the blue waters below. Bullet fragments had struck his arm and tracked along the right side of his back. He was unable to bail out because of the centrifugal force caused by the aircraft spinning. He managed to recover the crippled fighter and roll it upside down, falling out of the cockpit at low altitude. The carbon-dioxide cartridge was empty, but despite his serious wounds he was able to pump up his dinghy manually and crawl into it. As he recalled:

> I wondered if there were any sharks. Now the squadron was looking for me on the wrong side of the island. I could see the island, five or so miles off … Luckily two of our chaps, Brennan and de l'Ara, were covering the mine-sweepers … they called back for the air-sea rescue boat. The crew hauled me aboard, gave me a big shot of Navy rum. My eyes just about popped out. "It was a good job," the doctor said to me in the hospital, "you were turning and looking over your shoulder. Had you been sitting back in your seat you would have been a goner."

Bob Middlemiss and Gerry de Nancrede had been shot down on the same day. Their hospital beds were end to end on the balcony of the hospital, from where they could watch German bombers attack the harbour and the airfields. No one on Malta was a non-combatant and the hospital had been struck by bombs several times. As bombs started falling closer to the hospital, they moved inside, and finally they were sheltering in a cave. The underground caves on Malta seemed the only place that provided comfort against a relentless enemy.

His operational tour on Malta cut short, Bob was patched up and shipped out. He finished his convalescence in England, but did not want a rest flying at an OTU for six months. He wanted to be back on operations and one day went looking for a job in 41 Squadron—stationed at Merston, England—which was a unit of the Tangmere Wing. On the way he stopped in at The Unicorn, one of the squadron's favourite pubs in Chichester, to have tea. His hands started to shake as he picked up his cup. They shook so badly that he had to lay the cup down. Nothing had fazed him about his experiences

Courtesy of the Wendy Noble Collection

Blanche Smith, the mother of Jerry and Rod Smith.

Courtesy of the Wendy Noble Collection

Jerry (left) and Rod Smith as children in Regina.

on the island, his dramatic bailout or the subsequent bombings while he was a wounded flyer in a Maltese hospital. After all, Bob was a self-described fatalist—what point was there in worrying? However, back in Britain the intensity of it all caught up to him in a British pub, his hand shaking so badly that he could not even hold a teacup. Nevertheless, he was hoping to talk his way back on operations.

* * *

Within three days of Rod Smith's arrival on the island, he and Jerry had shared a probable victory against a Ju88 bomber. It was last seen limping just above the Mediterranean, steering for Sicily. On July

24, 1942, each brother shot down a Ju88, Jerry's third confirmed victory, Rod's first.

A fighter pilot's first victory is all-important. Like all victories it is an intensely felt experience. Fighter pilots—some of them, at least—have said that victories are akin to sexual orgasm, but in some ineffable sense more intense, more memorable. The feelings evoked by victory are frequently a mixture of relief, sadness and glee. As soon as Rod's bullets hit the left engine of the bomber, white glycol smoke and brilliant white flames streamed aft. Rod recalled that "when the Ju88 caught fire, and the flames moved to the fuselage, I thought, God, there are men in there! I had a feeling of absolute exultation—that is the only way to describe it. You see, you are frightened so many times, and when you score like that, it is a huge feeling of victory." One of the four crew members of the Ju88 bailed out; the others died in the crash.

There was little time to savour a victory on Malta. The German and Italian bombers and fighters far outnumbered the British, by as many as ten to one. Rod learned quickly that war plays no favourites. Within a couple of days, Jerry's Spitfire was damaged by gunfire, and his engine seized. Malta was a far cry from the Canadian Prairies—it was an awful place to attempt a forced landing. The low stone fences that ringed the rocky fields on Malta could easily destroy any Spitfire. It was better to bail out than hit one of those. But pilots hated to bail out if they could save the aircraft; Spitfires were so scarce and valuable. Rod escorted his brother down, weaving back and forth above Jerry, anxiously scanning the sky for enemies:

I could see Jerry's shadow on the ground, getting closer and closer to the aircraft itself. Boy, I thought, I hope that shadow doesn't join him before he makes it over that last fence ... Well, he just got over the fence, in a forced landing with the wheels and flaps down ... He stopped in the middle of Takali and got out and waved, and I went back to my aerodrome, to Luqa ...

When I got back, our C/O's airplane was there and he [the C/O, Squadron Leader Phil Winfield] had gone to hospital ... A bullet had gone into his stomach, just one bullet hole through the side of the Spit. There was blood and yellow bits of fat scattered around the cockpit. It smelled like hell in the hot sun on a hot day. That was rather a gruesome sight... Anyway, the ground crew came along and put a fabric patch over the bullet hole on right starboard side—I don't know whether they washed out the cockpit or not, but they put it back on the line. I didn't have to fly it, thank God!

On August 10, Rod and Jerry were waiting at the airfield on the flight line, ready to scramble at a moment's notice. Rod was Jerry's No. 2, as he had been during the previous trips, and where his brother went, he went. Nothing much was happening and 126 Squadron was put on a thirty-minute readiness status. Jerry, now expecting at least half an hour of

notice before flight, said to Rod, "Why don't you go get us some new silk liners for our gloves?" A dispatch rider gave Rod a lift on his motorcycle over to supply section, located inside one of the island caves.

While Rod was away—just a few minutes—Jerry and another pilot were scrambled to provide air cover for two minesweepers being threatened by incoming bombers. Exactly what happened is not known, but Jerry did not return to Luqa. Rod recounted the story: "Jerry left the minesweepers he was escorting. He shouldn't have done that. He went haring north towards Sicily ... He obviously found one, because [a Ju88] was shot down and nobody ever claimed it. The guy with Jerry said, 'I couldn't keep up.' And he never even got as far as the bombers."

When no word had arrived by late afternoon, Rod asked his squadron commander if he could take a Spitfire and search off the coast after the sun went down. Rod knew that Jerry had rigged up a flashlight on his Mae West, and he hoped to see the bright beam in the darkness. Rod went about two-thirds of the distance to Sicily, forty miles along the track that German aircraft routinely flew. There was no moon that evening, and looking down onto the black surface of the Mediterranean, he saw no life raft, no Mae West, no flashlight gleam.

He felt that it was an imposition to his squadron for him to be out looking for Jerry in the dark. The officers' mess was nine miles from Luqa airfield, and the bus driver was waiting patiently to take him home to bed. He did not want to keep the bus driver waiting just for him. Turning back to Malta, Rod looked at his instruments, glowing red in the small cockpit. Jerry's body was never recovered; he was simply one of the missing in the Siege of Malta.

Profile – IAN ROY MACLENNAN

Born – April 9, 1919, Gull Lake, SK

Father – Joseph Maclennan, Superintendent of Schools

Mother – Constance Wood

Decorations & Medals – DFM

Degrees & Awards – BArch, FRAIC, member of RCA

Post-war occupation – Architect, New York, Venezuela; vice-president, Canada Mortgage and Housing Corporation, retired 1977

Marital status – Wife Nina Olive Barry, son Bruce, daughter Joss

Hobbies – Bridge (Life Master); owner of a barge in France

Courtesy of the Ian Maclennan Collection

Ian Maclennan, DFM, on Malta in 1942.

Ian Maclennan has spent his life since the war as an architect, designing buildings in the United States, Venezuela and Canada. He is a Fellow of the Royal Architectural Institute of Canada and a member of the Royal Canadian Academy of Arts. After being appointed by Order in Council as a vice-president to Canada Mortgage and Housing Corporation (CMHC), he shepherded architect Moshe Safdie's Expo '67 Habitat housing exhibition through the bureaucracy. He has been involved in some of the most important community projects in Canada, most notably with federal cabinet minister Ron Basford on the redevelopment of Granville Island, on Vancouver's waterfront. Maclennan has served in retirement on planning boards and architectural committees. In summary, his life since the war has been about building community.

Maclennan had many reasons to want to forget the war in 1945. He had seen death and mass destruction in the air and on the ground, and was a prisoner in Stalag Luft III, southeast of Berlin, from June '44 till near the end of the war. Stricken with asthma, he was in the prison camp hospital when "The Long March" eastward in late January '45 began. Asthma may have saved his life—instead of having to trudge through the winter snow, he was shipped in a railway boxcar with other sick men to Nuremberg and onward from Munich to the Austrian redoubt. He escaped and evaded by walking and hitchhiking his way back to Paris. When he arrived in London on May 8, he went in search of his twenty-year-old brother. He learned at RCAF headquarters that Bruce, a wireless air gunner with 419 Squadron RCAF, had been killed south of Hamburg during a daylight raid by No. 6 Bomber Group on March 31.

Air Marshal Arthur "Bomber" Harris had decided to operate round the clock in 1945. However, RCAF bomber squadrons had had no training in tight formation providing protective crossfire with .50 calibre machine guns—the kind of formation that Americans had pioneered in their daylight campaign against Germany. The Lancaster and Halifax bombers were equipped with smaller-calibre .303 machine guns, and they were no match against Me262s equipped with 30mm cannons. It was one of these jet fighters that destroyed Bruce Maclennan's aircraft.

The news of Bruce's death came as a stunning blow to Ian after he had survived the war himself, and it made him deeply angry and despairing. He remembered a sweet, nice kid who was unable to tell even a simple joke without cracking up before the punchline. Ian pushed aside his grief and did not talk to his parents about the war or how needlessly his brother had died. More than twenty years passed before he attended a reunion of wartime pilots. In a 1997 interview with a young newspaper columnist on Remembrance Day, Ian Maclennan offered the following explanation:

You know, when I was 15 or 16, I was aware of the Canadian Legion and the World War One veterans, but there was never really any comprehension on my part of what they went through. And I could see how someone your age might find it terribly difficult to connect with that. I don't know how you could connect, because I never connected. And, well, here I am.

Even myself, after the war ended, I just put it out of my mind. I never thought about it. I mean, all your friends were dying and you had formed very passionate friendships. But once a year, on Nov. 11, I allow myself to remember.[2]

Ian Maclennan started his Tiger Moth training in February 1941 at No. 6 Elementary Flying Training School (EFTS), Prince Albert, Saskatchewan, with a well-known bush pilot named Floyd Glass, "a wonderfully kind and intelligent guy, the kind of guy who instilled confidence." He graduated from the first course at No. 10 SFTS Dauphin, Manitoba, on July 1. Ian and his best friend at SFTS, an American named "Tex" Lynton, used to practise mock dogfights in Harvards. One day they went low flying, and according to Ian "we took off the top of an outdoor toilet near a rural school house." The low flying was reported and probably as a result the two were not commissioned when they received their wings.

As a green fighter pilot newly graduated from No. 52 OTU at Aston Down in England, Sergeant Ian Maclennan had a degree of confidence that exceeded his experience. In his own opinion: "I was very young, and did some incredibly stupid things!" He did not lack for audacity, and it got him into trouble early in his flying career. It also made him an ace. His citation for the Distinguished Flying Medal stated: "Flight Sergeant Maclennan has displayed great courage and tenacity. He has destroyed four and damaged several more enemy aircraft." Ultimately, he was credited with seven victories in the battle for Malta, plus several damaged. But he might never have made it to the island had he not gotten into several scrapes with authority.

Not long after joining 610 Squadron in Yorkshire in February 1942, Maclennan performed some

Courtesy of DND Directorate of History, Ottawa

Donald James Matthew Blakeslee, of Fairport Harbour, Ohio, Colonel (ret.), USAF, joined the RCAF at Windsor and trained at No. 1 SFTS, Camp Borden, Ontario, was commissioned and served with No. 411 and 401 Squadrons. He then transferred to No. 133 RAF Eagle Squadron, and later commanded the Fourth Fighter Group of the Eighth Air Force. He is credited with fifteen victories, but his fellow American pilots believe his score is much higher.

[2] Pete McMartin. "Dawn Patrol Gather to Remember Comrades Who Didn't Make It Back." *The Vancouver Sun*.

impromptu aerobatics on arrival at a bomber airfield at Pocklington. He was on an unauthorized visit to see Fletcher Taylor, his future brother-in-law. On takeoff he damaged his propeller and was grounded while it was repaired. Ian brazenly pretended that he had gotten lost and landed at Pocklington quite incidentally. For this escapade, his flight commander at 610, Denis Crowley-Milling (later Air Marshal Sir Denis Crowley-Milling KCB, CBE, DSO, DFC, AE), tore a strip off him.

After Maclennan transferred in April to 401 Squadron RCAF, one of the most colourful and successful fighter pilots of the war took him flying for his formation evaluation. It was the usual initiation test for all rookies and newcomers, to determine if their skills were up to the standard needed to start operational flying. American Don Blakeslee not only fitted the stereotype of a fighter pilot, but looked like the movie star cast to play one. Just like Rod Smith and Buck McNair when meeting Hilly Brown, and just like all other keen newcomers to squadron life, Maclennan was not going to have anyone say he couldn't hang in there, no matter what:

> We went low flying, and I kept very close, tucked right under his wing, and I didn't look at anything but his wing ... no matter what he did, I stayed there. We came back and Blakeslee said, "You'll do."... I wasn't scared; [in my mind I thought] if he killed me, he killed me.

While flying with 401, Ian had two incidents where his airmanship was called into question. On one occasion he had damaged two Spitfires in a collision on the aerodrome. After this episode his flight commander, Eugene "Jeep" Neal, called him in and said they were looking for pilots to *volunteer* for Malta. Ian recalled: "Neal liked me, but he was rather angry at me ... I was one of his up-and-coming pilots, and I had let him down. I was pleased to go to Malta; I knew there was lots of action there. But it was put in such a way that I couldn't really refuse."

Ian's last flight with 401 was on June 26, 1941; on July 15 he landed on Malta. In the customary way of the RAF, Maclennan was interviewed by the com-

manding officer of his third squadron in less than a year. Maclennan remembers a handsome man with a lean face like that of an austere saint:

> Wonderful guy, Tony Lovell, a patrician. Anglo-Irish. I tell him I am Roman Catholic. "Good, you can come to Mass with me in the mornings." So everybody else got up at 4 a.m.; he and I were up at 3:30 a.m. for Mass. When I arrived, 1435 Squadron was forming. Wally McLeod was flight commander of "A" Flight, and later I took over that flight. Wally McLeod's father was a school inspector in Regina, so my father, who was superintendent of schools, knew him well ... Because of this, Wally kind of adopted me. He witnessed and confirmed my first victory in Malta, so that put me in good standing with him ... Tony Lovell said to us, "I can't get enough Canadians." He liked Canadian pilots.

McLeod's family was also known to the Smiths in Regina. Rod and Jerry's mother, Blanche, knew Wally's mother when they were growing up. Born in December 1915, Wally was six years ahead of Rod and Jerry in school. When McLeod, the RCAF's highest-scoring ace, was killed in September 1944, it was Blanche Smith and daughter Wendy who went to visit the McLeod family to offer condolences. The relationship between Wally and Ian continued after Malta. In 1944 Ian asked Wally to rescue him from a posting at Bagotville, Quebec; he was transferred back overseas to fly in 443 Squadron where Squadron Leader McLeod, DSO, DFC and Bar, was the commanding officer.

Malta was the ideal theatre of war for tenacious pilots who could shoot well. Maclennan excelled at shooting. This was all the more remarkable because he had been given no formal gunnery training. His first shots in a Spitfire were in anger. Amazingly, many RAF pilots went to war in 1941–42 after logging less than an hour of airborne gunnery practice. By autumn, Maclennan had been promoted directly from flight sergeant to flight lieutenant and taken command of "A" Flight.

Maclennan believes it was the contributions of the many rather than the few that won the Siege

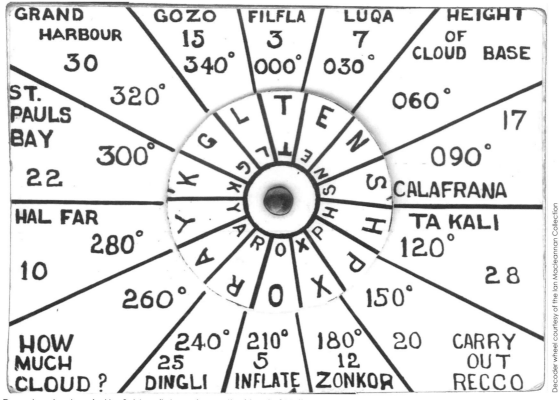

Decoder wheel carried by fighter pilots serving on the island of Malta.

of Malta. He says the most credit must go to the experienced fighter controllers in the operations room of RAF headquarters near Valletta harbour, and the laminated decoding wheel carried by every pilot (see photo): "Without the ground controllers and the code wheel we had and, in addition, the line abreast formation, we could never have won the battle of Malta."

Food on Malta was strictly rationed. Fighting men received only a little more than the rations for the average civilian, and less than half the amount necessary to maintain good health. The two staple food items were locally made bread (nine ounces each per day) and corned beef. And most of the beef, say those who had to eat it, had been packaged during the First World War. Maclennan recalled:

The corned beef was tinned by Fray Bentos in 1918 in Argentina or Brazil. Because of that smell of fried corned beef, I couldn't eat it for ten years after the war. At teatime they would come around to the flight line with a piece of bread, thin, with a thin scrim of margarine and thin scrim of jam. They handed it to the pilots, but the ground crew got nothing. I cannot tell you how terrible that is, because you are sitting under the wing, away from the heat, and you are trying to give it to them, and they won't take it. They get tea only, you get bread for energy because you are flying, but the ground crew won't touch your bread.

If the enemy didn't get you quickly in Malta, illness and malnutrition took you down slowly and inexorably. The intensity of the war and the lack of food meant that, as the weeks went by, fighter pilots became weaker and thinner. Virtually all who served a tour succumbed to illness and battle fatigue. Three

Sculpture of Flight Lieutenant George Frederick Beurling, DSO, DFC, DFM and Bar, Canada's highest-scoring ace, by sculptor Alexandra E. Whitney. A gift to the Canada Aviation Museum, Ottawa, by Countess Vivian Crespi, 1998.

Sculpture of Squadron Leader Henry Wallace McLeod, DSO, DFC and Bar, the RCAF's highest scoring ace, by sculptor and former Spitfire pilot the late Philip Gordon (Bockman) Vickers. On display at the RCAF Officers' Mess, Ottawa.

months of fighting on the island was a very long time. Pilots typically lost twenty to thirty pounds in those three months. Dysentery (the "Malta Dog") was common, along with sandfly fever or jaundice, or some sequence of all three.

Rest and relaxation was limited on an island being bombed day and night—perhaps a swim in the ocean on your day off. Alcohol was difficult though not impossible to obtain, and feminine companionship (don't even mention sex) was an unlikely treat in a culture with a strong religious tradition stretching back two millennia.

MEMORIES OF GEORGE BEURLING IN MALTA

Canada's most successful fighter ace of the war was a complicated young man, and everyone who met him, even briefly, came away with a vivid memory. The stories they tell about him are often contradictory, making his true personality virtually impossible to decipher. As a Canadian hero of the war years it somewhat impaired his prospects that he was the son of working-class immigrants raised devoutly according to the tenets of, by Quebec standards, an obscure religious sect. With this background one suspects that his impetuosity and disobedience seemed more bizarre than colourful. Had Beurling been of United Empire Loyalist stock and a graduate of Upper Canada

College, would his treatment have been different, and his eccentricities overlooked by the RCAF?

Those Canadians who seemed to find him most objectionable came from comfortable, middle-class, educated circles whose members were accustomed to long-established traditions. Ironically, it was the RAF, not the RCAF, that smiled tolerantly on brilliant non-conformers, finding a niche for them and allowing such leaders to excel or self-destruct in battle for the greater good of the service.

As a generalization, the author has learned that the closer you were in social class to Beurling, the more certain it was that you would like him. Many of those interviewed for this book with similar upbringings to the young ace expressed the opinion that he was mistreated and misunderstood. They felt he deserved a better fate—perhaps to live or die as a lone wolf in a P51 Mustang rather than be cast aside in the manner he was.

Without exception, men (but also the women who dated him) speak about his eyes—piercing, vivid blue, unsettling in their coldness. Those who flew on operations with George Beurling witnessed a quality of distance vision that was, well, there is no other word for it, supernatural. It was so superior to the vision of ordinary men that if you flew ops with him you had confidence that the enemy could not bounce you. George always saw them first. That was a comfort. However, his unpredictability once the enemy was sighted could be unsettling. Flight and squadron leaders who had bad operational experiences flying with him were on guard when they flew with George. A few leaders disliked him intensely, in particular Frank Jones on Malta.

On a night flight in August '42, Frank Jones and Beurling disagreed loudly on an open-radio frequency about Jones's navigation. Jones said that Beurling had not only been insubordinate in the air but also hysterical in his criticisms, on a frequency where all could listen in. A section leader at the time with 249 Squadron, Jones admired Beurling's flying and gunnery skills but, despite Beurling's apology the following morning, he refused to fly again with him. He asked the squadron commander to move him to "B" Flight.

Beurling was a gifted teacher and, particularly rare in a fighter ace, he could explain with clarity how to shoot aircraft down. He was happy to provide speed and deflection charts to any pilot who wanted to learn more, and he had great patience in imparting his knowledge. Gunnery schools and squadrons often issued printed deflection charts based on Beurling's math. There are quite a few RCAF pilots happy to credit Beurling with a significant part of their shooting success in combat. Air gunnery is a frustrating discipline for most men, but if pilots were willing to apply Beurling's technique, and practise it assiduously, their victory scores improved.

Ian Maclennan never flew on operations with Beurling, but paints a subtle portrait of him that contrasts with the more colourful accounts:

I met George in Malta in 1942, while out walking, and we became friends. We were both flight sergeant pilots, he with 249 Squadron at Takali ... I was with 1435 Squadron at Luqa. He had arrived in Malta before me on June 9th. He was already becoming well known. I didn't know him very well or for very long. He was younger (twenty), impatient and non-conformist, whereas I was older (twenty-three) and more conventional. I thought he was intelligent and tough, and he had to be. He was stubborn but I never thought he was intransigent. In the conversations I had with him, he was often frustrated and often uncertain but I felt he was essentially modest, and I liked him very much.

George had a surprisingly kind and thoughtful side to him. I had bought a Maltese lace tablecloth for my mother and when I knew he was leaving I asked him to deliver it to a small place in the middle of nowhere (or so he thought) and he promised. He left, with the tablecloth in his duffel bag, on October 31st, '42, on a Liberator. The aircraft crashed into the shallow sea off the end of the runway at Gibraltar, killing fourteen passengers, including three Canadian fighter pilots [see pages 31–33]. George had a wounded foot cast in plaster, but survived, with the duffel bag.

On the war-bond drive across Canada, he arrived in Moose Jaw and the RCAF invited my mother and father to come from Gull Lake where my father was superintendent of schools

... George gave my mother the tablecloth and a photograph. The tablecloth is gone now, but I have the photo here, addressed to my parents with best wishes, and signed by Flying Officer George Beurling.

In the space of three months, Ian Maclennan accomplished a great deal on the island. In August, he shot down an Me109 and an Italian Reggiane Re2001. On a single day, October 11, he destroyed two Ju88s and damaged three Me109s. As a result, he was awarded a Distinguished Flying Medal. The following day he damaged another 109 and destroyed a third Ju88. On October 16, he damaged a Ju88; ten days later he destroyed an Me109. In November, as commander of "A" Flight, he destroyed a seventh enemy aircraft, an Italian Savoia Marchetti SM82.

ROD SMITH'S
OCTOBER BAILOUT

After the loss of his brother Jerry, Rod Smith occasionally flew as No. 2 with Wing Commander Peter Prosser Hanks, an ace in the Battle of France. On an op on October 15, 1942, Hanks gave the lead to Smith, who had keener eyesight and had spotted two enemy aircraft down low. The wing commander was unaccustomed to the job of being No. 2, protecting his leader's tail, which he had to do as Rod Smith attempted to shoot down the fleeing enemy fighters:

I suddenly saw two Me109s on the water, right on the surface, going north for Sicily. We rarely got above the 109s, and so I pointed them out to Prosser, who was pretty blind. So Prosser says, "Lead on, Red Three." So the two of us dove down, and I thought we had them cold. But they were so fast that ... we wound up seven hundred yards behind them, out of range ... so I thought I had a brilliant idea that I would aim over and ahead of him ... my shells will splash in the water ahead of him. If he turns, I will cut the corner, and get inside him. I'll get him, I hope.

I fired a one-second burst, ten rounds. They splashed in the water. Then another one-second,

ten rounds, splashed in the water. His No. 2 then broke off to the right. I thought, "Lucky Prosser, he's going to reap the benefit of my bright idea." ... Anyway, I just assumed that Prosser went after the one who had broken off to the right ...

I looked down and I saw a bullet hole in my left wing about six feet away from me, a machine-gun bullet. Oh, I did not notice that earlier, I thought to myself, I must have got that dogfighting over Valletta. Anyway, I fired a second burst over the 109. Then I looked back down and there was a bullet hole a foot away from the one I had just seen! ...

Somehow, I became aware that Prosser Hanks was level on my right, and I broke violently off to my left, and as I broke left, I was hit on the left side of the engine. I couldn't actually see the strikes, but, boy, I could see the flashes, *smell* the smoke, I could *smell* the exploding 20-mm shells ... I had run into the stream of his machine guns and his 20-mm cannon going directly over my port wing—I broke right into them ... As I am breaking, I looked at my engine instruments—the oil pressure dropped in seconds, and the temperature rose.

As I pulled around I could see this fellow's aircraft had a yellow nose—I think he must have been the No. 2 that broke off and came around behind me—he came *so close* to me, his wing came *so close* to mine [it's a miracle we didn't collide].

Rod had to gain altitude and head back to land if he was going to survive. He did not know how long the engine could maintain full power. He eventually made it up to four thousand feet, calling "Mayday, mayday, mayday" on the air-sea rescue frequency, and they got a radio fix on his position. But the engine gave out just as he approached Valletta, so he turned out over the sea and bailed out of his machine:

I felt the tail hit me on the hip as I went past it ... not very hard. Then I was on my back looking up at the sky, my pants rippling in the breeze (that is my clearest memory). I looked down for the D-ring, the rip cord, and I pulled it, I saw this white ball going out between my legs. Then, suddenly, a terrific shock, and I went out briefly, because when I came to, I could see I was hanging directly below the parachute, and I could see coloured lights going by me. I thought, "Are they shooting at me?"... It was coloured lights inside my head, not someone shooting at me.

Rod's problems were not over. Being so tall, he had removed the flotation kapok from his Mae West to give him more room to look over his shoulder in the confined cockpit of the Spitfire. First, his Mae West was failing to keep his head above the water, and then his rubber dinghy deflated and sank. His wet flying gear weighed him down as he tried to tread water:

I was so weak because I had been in Malta for months ... so I thought, at one point: "I am so tired. Why not just let go." Then I thought: "Well, you know, my mother and father will be very disappointed." ...

I kicked and I kicked, and made it to the surface, and, for some lucky reason, was able to blow all the water out of my mouth and take a full breath of air. Then I went down like a stone again, but I was blowing into the [Mae West manual inflation] air tube with every last ounce of my last breath. I thought, "If this does not work, nothing will." This brought my nose above the surface; I got another breath, and topped the Mae West up and squeezed the valve closed ...

I saw a man fishing in a boat ... his boat was so small I knew I couldn't get into it. He was standing up, using one oar as a paddle, backing the transom of the boat up to me. The Maltese used to club people who came down—they didn't like the Germans. So I said to this guy, "I'm British." I didn't say I was Canadian. I thought they would know British more in Malta than Canadian! ...

Then the air-sea rescue boat came along right off the stern, and went into reverse beside me ... so they pulled me aboard. It was good to be inside the cockpit of that boat, I can tell you.

Rod was driven back to his living quarters to take a hot bath and recuperate before his next operational trip.

The woman who was the house mother to us ... gave me a kettle of water ... I had taken over my brother Jerry's small room after he had gone missing in action. I was changing my clothes, and got into the tub ...

I noticed a bottle of Black and White Scotch with a candle stuck into the top ... I was at the end of the table changing, I could see a surface inside the bottle ... took the candle out, and lo and behold, here was two-thirds of a bottle of Scotch. My brother had been holding out on me, I guess. We had to go to Valletta to get Scotch, it was hard to get. So there I was—I partook of this Scotch, more than a bit, I guess.

I was sitting in the living room of the house that was our mess, and Prosser Hanks came in. And he said to me, "Christ, I'm glad to see you! I felt guilty." Because he should have been looking after me, but I guess he was so used to being No. 1.

Since Rod had been bruised when he hit the tail of his Spitfire on the bailout, they gave him the next day off. Over the next week, his squadron commander was killed and Rick Jones, his flight commander, was killed, as well as several other pilots. Rod took command of "A" Flight. The October Blitz, the final push by the Axis for that fall, was finally coming to an end. Rod shot down his sixth enemy aircraft, a Ju88 on October 25—he had now been on operations since mid-July and it was showing. He flew into November, losing weight and energy:

I woke up on November 8th feeling rotten. I got to the aerodrome; they said the Americans and British had landed in the Western Desert. The doctor came by on his bicycle, and I said, "I'm not feeling very well." He lifted up my eyelid and said: "You've got jaundice—you're finished."

It was a great relief, the Blitz was over, and in the Western Desert we had the feeling that it was the beginning of the end ... So I was driven to the hospital. I was there about a month ... I remember feeling terribly depressed. I weighed 134 pounds when they let me out, and I was terribly weak. I went for a walk. I got about one block, and I had to sit down, my feet in the gutter ...

Courtesy of the Pat Bing Collection

Moose Fumerton and Pat Bing hold a piece of enemy aircraft, first victory for 406 Squadron RCAF.

In mid-December I flew back to Gibraltar, in a Lockheed Hudson, my first trip in a twin-engined aircraft ... We had three approaches in Gib, and I started to feel sick. [One of the passengers] a lady with her baby walked by me as I vomited by the tail wheel of the aircraft—me with my new DFC on my chest!

Profile – ROBERT CARL FUMERTON
Born – March 20, 1913; Fort Coulange, QC
Father – George Fumerton
Mother – Katherine Parr
Decorations & Medals – DFC and Bar, AFC
Post-war occupation – Real-estate executive, Toronto
Marital status – Wife Madeleine Reay; daughters Gail, Maureen, Debbie and Pattie; son Richard
Hobbies – "Don't have any of those"

Profile – LESLIE PATRICK SANDFORD BING
Born – July 28, 1920, Regina
Father – Gerrard Bing, accountant with the provincial government
Mother – Gladys Pearce
Decorations & Medals – DFC and Bar, CD and Clasp
Post-war occupation – Air force officer, Squadron Leader, RCAF/CAF
Marital status – Wife Anna Hughes died in 2001; son Gerry; daughter Leslie
Hobbies – Golf, woodworking, gardening

Not all the Canadians serving on Malta were Spitfire pilots. There were also Canadians serving on bomber and night-fighter aircraft. A childhood friend of Rod Smith, Leslie Patrick Sandford "Pat" Bing, was serving as a radar operator with a pilot from Fort Coulonge,

Quebec, Robert Carl "Moose" Fumerton. Their aircraft was the twin-engine Bristol Beaufighter and their job was to shoot down enemy aircraft attacking Malta after dark. The team of Fumerton and Bing arrived at Luqa, Malta, on detached duty from 89 Squadron at Abu Sueir, Egypt, in June 1942. As one of four night-fighter crews of "C" Flight detachment and the squadron's only Canadians, Fumerton and Bing shot down nine enemy aircraft in three months. They became the outstanding all-Canadian night-fighter team in the Second World War in aerial victories, shooting down a total of thirteen enemy aircraft.

Moose Fumerton had an unpredictable streak and an independence of thought that rivalled Stan Turner. Like Turner, he could be impetuous. He had no patience with wrong-headed superior officers and gave no thought to his career aspirations before speaking. Revered by the men who served with him for his aggressive competence, he was somewhat older than the average, twenty-six, when he enlisted in the RCAF. He had been making a living in a rough world since he was eighteen, first as a timber cruiser and then as a mining prospector. He already had a private pilot's licence when he volunteered and was among the first to graduate from wartime training. The famed ace of an earlier war, Air Marshal William "Billy" Bishop, presented Fumerton with his wings on May 23, 1940.

Looking back on the war, Fumerton, like many flyers, felt that he "would not have missed it for the world." He believes that, as a fighter pilot, "the beauty about the war was that no one was chasing the dollar." He met his airborne-interception (A/I) radar operator, Pat Bing, in June 1941 at 406 Squadron, stationed in Northumberland at Acklington north of Newcastle-upon-Tyne. He thought that Bing looked "pretty smart." Recalling his early impression of the young navigator, Fumerton says: "He got to the point. He wasn't jabbering all the time." Bing remembers Fumerton affectionately, and always admired his calmness and optimism. He says that Moose liked to tell stories while he flew and frequently sang songs at the top of his lungs; one of his favourite ditties was "They are removing father's grave to dig a sewer."

The Beaufighter's radar was not functioning normally on the night of September 1, 1941, when

Bing picked up his first enemy target over Acklington. Fumerton saw the Ju88 silhouetted against the moon and after two attacks, the twin-engine bomber exploded. It was the first victory for the Fumerton/Bing team, the first-ever victory at night by an RCAF fighter pilot and the first successful attack by the newly formed 406 Squadron of the RCAF.

Posted out to Egypt with 89 Squadron of the RAF in December 1941, Fumerton and Bing scored three more victories in the night skies over Egypt before being sent to Malta. On the evening of August 10, the day Jerry Smith went missing, Fumerton and Bing were returning from a hunting expedition over Sicily. Without warning, both engines stopped. When Fumerton reached for the throttles to attempt a restart, he could not move the levers. It was as though they were in poured cement.

Bing still believes today that they had been struck by gunfire, though Fumerton is non-committal about the cause. There were German night fighters hunting for the British night fighters, and perhaps it was one of those that did the damage. In any case, the two men were some thirty miles off the Sicilian coast, the throttles were jammed, and Fumerton—despite repeated attempts—could not get either engine restarted. He now had to ditch in the Med without power on a dark night with no moonlight. As the plane neared the water's surface, Moose could see that the waves were high. He landed crossways to the waves with a surprisingly smooth touchdown, and the two men scrambled out of the sinking aircraft.

Bing's dinghy did not inflate, so the two large men had to clamber into Fumerton's dinghy. They immediately set course for Malta and by dawn had managed to paddle within five miles of the island, at which point an air-sea rescue launch picked them up. Shaking from the cold, Fumerton and Bing were offered a brandy by the captain of the launch. The wrong bottle of brown liquid was poured into glasses. Instead of brandy, the captain had selected a bottle of iodine. Fumerton later noted, after spitting the foul-tasting liquid out: "It helped clean my teeth, I suppose."

Wing Commander Fumerton later became the commanding officer of 406 Squadron, ending the war as the RCAF's highest-scoring night-fighter pilot in aerial victories. While commanding officer of 406, he fell in love with a fighter controller who had vectored him back to the home aerodrome of Anglesey in northwest Wales after a night flight. According to Moose, the sound of her voice intrigued him. He looked her up and asked for a date. Flying Officer Madeleine Reay, eight years younger than Moose, accepted his proposal of marriage, immigrated to Canada and made a life with this rough-edged Canadian. Together they raised five children.

MEMORIES OF THE LOSS OF LIBERATOR AL511 AT GIBRALTAR

Profile – GORDON HENRY TAYLOR FARQUHARSON
Born – May 10, 1921, raised in Toronto, London, and Corbyville, ON
Died – June 13, 2004, Peterborough, ON
Father – Robert Farquharson, stationary engineer, Corby Distilleries Limited.
Mother – Jean Goudie
Decorations & Medals – DFC
Degrees & Awards – BA, LLB. LSM
Post-war occupation – Lawyer, QC, at Peterborough. ON
Marital status – Wife Elizabeth Ashbury; daughters Jean and Ann; son Robert

Rod Smith was not the only Canadian to be shot down on Thursday, October 15, 1942. Warrant Officer Gordon Farquharson's luck ran out that same morning when a German fighter pilot put several rounds through his cockpit, shattering the instrument panel. With his right knee bleeding from bullet fragments and his plane only five hundred feet above the ocean's surface, Farquharson was well below the minimum safe altitude for a bailout. Nevertheless, he rolled inverted, pushed forward hard on the stick and fell free of his crippled Spitfire. Pulling the D-ring on his parachute immediately, he had just enough time to see the splash of his aircraft before he himself hit the Mediterranean directly behind it. It was as though the Spit had carved a hole in the blue water for his chute to land in, creating just enough of a hollow to cushion the hard impact.

Farquharson, who had flown off the USS *Wasp* the day before his twenty-first birthday, was now at least thirty pounds lighter in weight, weakened physically due to inadequate food and diarrhea. He had not transmitted a distress call, but a rescue launch looking for another downed pilot came across him and pulled him aboard. He was then shipped to hospital, and his right leg was stitched up and bandaged. As he recuperated from his wounds, the good news arrived that his tour in Malta was over. He had achieved several victories, some probables and damage, and now he was going to get a rest.

At about 2:30 a.m. on Sunday, November 1, Gordon Farquharson boarded a B24 Liberator bomber along with many other wounded and tour-expired fighter pilots, including the top Allied ace of Malta, George Beurling, whose left foot was in a cast. Beurling's pal and fellow ace John Williams, of Kamloops and Chilliwack, BC, aged twenty, was also aboard. "Willie the Kid" Williams had received his wings with Farquharson in July 1941 at No. 32 Service Flying Training School (SFTS), Moose Jaw. The passenger manifest comprised a total of six Royal Australian Air Force (RAAF), five RCAF and thirteen RAF pilots. There were also ten civilians, including two husbands with wives as well as four other wives and two young children. The senior RAF officer aboard was the famous Wing Commander Arthur H. Donaldson, whose left hand had been mangled by Me109 gunfire on October 14. The Liberator was headed for Gibraltar and then onward to the green fields of England.

This particular Liberator, number AL516, belonging to 511 Squadron, RAF, out of Alexandria, Egypt, was just a standard four-engine bomber without passenger seats, flying with a crew of six. Most of the passengers were gathered in the bomb bay, sitting or lying on baggage and parachutes. Some shouted above the noise of the engines, others tried to nap in the darkness. The pilots were glad to be going home, to abundant food and drink and clean sheets. Well, almost all the pilots were glad. Beurling, to his disgust, was leaving behind what some experts have called the fighter pilot's heaven. His squadron commander, Laddie Lucas, has written: "Something told me that he was made for this rarefied form of island warfare … he proved to be, in this environment, a genius. Malta was made for him."

Beurling was ordered to return to Canada for public relations events and to assist the government of Prime Minister William Lyon Mackenzie King in a war-bond tour. In fact, George Beurling belonged to the RAF not the RCAF, which had turned him down for pilot training in 1939 because he did not have the required education. The hypocrisy of the Canadian government in forcing him home did not sit well, and he was dreadfully unhappy about this, or any other, non-operational duty.

He had the most victories of any Canadian fighter pilot in the war, four decorations awarded in only four months, and an officer's commission. It was this latter fate that especially aggravated him—what most young men in his position might have coveted at the time, a step up in social class and military hierarchy, made him only uneasy and inadequate.

He was malnourished, his gunshot wounds hurt like hell, but that was not what upset him most. Above all he wanted to fight on in Malta, not give pep talks to naive Canadians. Beurling had a finely tuned sixth sense, and he knew that the death-or-glory intensity of Malta was never going to be repeated. The future could never offer what he had experienced in that one intense summer. According to biographer Brian Nolan he talked of going to China after this war ended; he figured there was always a war of some sort raging in China.

The Liberator was on approach to Gibraltar, but the ceilings were low and the winds off "the Rock" were fierce, making the big aircraft difficult to control. The two pilots, Walton and Saunders, had their hands full keeping the sixty-thousand-pound machine on the glide slope as they approached the runway threshold from north to south. The B24 was one of the most important Allied bombers in the Second World War, but it had weaknesses. B24s burned like torches when damaged by gunfire. When they crashed, their backs broke easily, just behind the wing, and they sank like stones when ditched in deep water. Halfway down the runway at Gibraltar, still not on the ground, the fighter pilots in the back realized this approach and landing was not routine. The engines roared to life as Flight Lieutenant Walton attempted an overshoot, but his airspeed was too low and the Liberator stalled only one hundred yards from the end of the runway.

Almost all the passengers were hurled forward and found themselves immediately underwater. The fuselage broke in half just behind the wings, but since the landing gear had not been raised for the overshoot, the aircraft ground to a halt with its wheels on the floor of the ocean. This was fortunate because it meant that the top of the long narrow wing was awash just at the surface. Soldiers on shore witnessing the accident dived into the water to rescue whomever they could find; some soldiers rowed out in boats.

Beurling and fellow pilot Art Roscoe had left the bomb bay at sunrise and moved aft to talk to the two so-called waist gunners in the rear fuselage. Beurling told journalist Leslie Roberts that he actually dived out of the Liberator's side hatch as it crashed. Swimming to shore with his foot in a cast almost did him in, and he was taken to hospital on a stretcher.

Sitting in his law office in 2002, still practising law at the age of eighty-one ("I can only spare a few minutes of my time for you. I have an appointment with a judge at 11:30 …"), Gordon Farquharson is certain that he was the last person to make it out of the submerged Liberator. As the traffic flowed along Hunter Street in downtown Peterborough, the Queen's Counsel vividly recalled the aftermath of the impact:

> I swallowed gallons of water, so much so I didn't think I was going to get out … I remember thinking "Maybe I can" and I saw this doorway and got through it, and saw light on the ceiling of the aircraft. That was open air, and I got up to there … I had an Irvin coat on, and I popped out of the water. I was absolutely spent. There were two men on the wing of the aircraft: one was "Ping" Powell, a Canadian pilot (who subsequently joined 416 Squadron and was killed); the other was an Aussie.

Flight Sergeant Mahar, RAAF, standing up on the wing, hollered at Farquharson: "Grab my leg and hold on. Be careful because I think it is broken." Without this quick thinking by the Australian pilot, Gordon believes he would have drowned:

> We were not too far out. The army knew we had crashed, and they picked us up in rubber boats … I had the greatest difficulty telling

them my name—my teeth were chattering … I was in the hospital for a week in Gibraltar, and flew out in a Lockheed Hudson with Wing Commander Donaldson.

As the Hudson flew in darkness northward to England, Farquharson looked down to see an unusual image—a city, jewel-like and peaceful:

[It was such] a thrill seeing the bright lights of Lisbon … my head was shaved due to wounds. I didn't have a hat and was dressed in summer clothing. I arrived by train in London on a Saturday. I didn't have any money so I stayed at the Union Jack Club. I slept there on the pool table. Then Sunday morning I went to Lincoln's Inn Fields to RCAF headquarters, where the duty officer gave me some money. I had been commissioned in Malta, so I was entitled to back pay, and a clothing allowance. I went to Austin Reed on Regent Street on Monday and got a uniform.

We had seen this large invasion fleet prior to my flight out of Malta … it was the invasion fleet going to North Africa [Operation Torch]. When I got up on the Tuesday, I could hear the church bells of London. I knew why they were ringing. I said to the Irish maid cleaning my room: "We have invaded North Africa."

Farquharson, in his new officer's uniform, wandered over to Denman Street, not far from the favourite hotel of flyers, the Regent Palace. If you had a little more money, the Strand Palace was tonier; if you had a lot more money or were a senior officer you stayed at the Park Lane. On Denman were many clubs, two favourites of the Canadians being the Crackers Club and the Chez Moi. They were places to drink and smoke, exchange stories and look for familiar faces. Because the clubs were below street level and not well ventilated, the cigarette and pipe smoke hung thickly in the air, making it difficult to see.

At the Chez Moi was a statuesque blond hostess, a Maltese woman named Marie (other names have been resurrected from memory, but there is more agreement on Marie). She liked to drink, and she adored Canadians and especially Malta veterans. Once you were known to her as one of them, her greeting at the foot of the club (the stairs to the club led down from the sidewalk on Denman Street) was enthusiastic. Farquharson always remembers her shouting in a full voice, "Hello, Malta!" and planting a kiss on his cheek.

A month after Farquharson, Rod Smith arrived in London, emaciated and cut adrift from all he had experienced in Malta. He checked into the Regent Palace and had a bath in the bathroom down the hall. Ignoring the rationing signs, he changed the water three times to get the dirt off his skin from his overseas sojourn. He put on his one clean uniform and went down to the hotel bar. He longed to see a familiar face. But no one knew him, so he ordered a drink and sat down in the corner, where "a terrible wave of loneliness came over me. I knew no one, and for days walking the streets of London I looked eagerly for men wearing Canada flashes, anyone I might have trained with or knew from Saskatchewan, any familiar face."

BEURLING REMEMBERS …

I lay abed that night and looked out the window on the lights of Gibraltar. So this was how it had to end. You fly and you fight and live for the minute, and you team up with guys who know nothing about you and about whom you know nothing. All you know is the other guy is full of guts and does the job.

Then the break comes and you all fly away together, each to go his own way at the journey's end, but each with something to share with the others that none of you will ever forget. Then this …

George Beurling with Leslie Roberts, *Malta Spitfire*.

DAY		NIGHT		DAY			NIGHT			PASS-ENGER	FLYING (incl. in cols. (1) to (10))	
DUAL	PILOT	DUAL	PILOT	DUAL	1ST PILOT	2ND PILOT	DUAL	1ST PILOT	2ND PILOT		DUAL	PILOT
(1)	(2)	(3)	(4)	(5)	(6)	(7)	(8)	(9)	(10)	(11)	(12)	(13)
69·30	460·25	2·00	28·15							1·25	27·15	17·15
	·50											
	1·15											
	·55											
	·45											
	1·10											
	·20		·20									
	2·25											
	1·30											
	2·10											
	1·00											
	1·10											
	1·15											
	1·05											
	·10											
	·30											
	·30											
	1·06											
	·45											
	·40											
	1·25											
	19·50		·20									
69·30	480·15	2·00	28·35							1·25	27·15	17·15
(1)	(2)	(3)	(4)	(5)	(6)	(7)	(8)	(9)	(10)	(11)	(12)	(13)

Search for Jerry 10 miles North of St. Pauls Bay.

Late Search for Torch. No Luck.

Ammo ship Blew up.

1 S.M. 79 DESTROYED
Confirmed

Gave 4 sec. Burst. Stbd engine caught fire. Crashed in sea. It was OVER convoy AT 800'. MASS OF FLAMES.

S.M. 79

Nothing Seen.

J. B. ___ s/c.
O.C. 126 Sqdn.

A clipping from the log book of Rod Smith detailing his search for lost brother Jerry, August 1942.

THE WESTERN DESERT, 1942–43, AND ITALY, 1943–44

After a promising start at 94 Squadron, James Edwards and four other pilots, including William E. "Bill" Stewart, were transferred to 260 Squadron, also in the Western Desert, in May 1942. Stewart had enlisted at Montreal in 1940, because his hometown was Sherbrooke, Quebec; he was, however, an American citizen. Edwards greatly admired Stewart who was exceedingly modest, "the most self-effacing fighter pilot I ever knew." He frequently neglected to fill out an aerial combat report. Edwards remembers Bill fondly as a great fighter pilot who always looked mystified when you asked him to put in a claim: "Why would I want to do that?" he would say. Flight Sergeant Stewart later was awarded the DFM for his leadership and ground attack work, his citation stating: "He is a fearsome fighter whose fine example has proved inspiring."

Edwards and Stewart had a great opportunity to show their squadron leader at 260, O.V. "Pedro" Hanbury, what they were capable of because from the last week of May through June 1942 combat was ferocious for Allied flyers in the Western Desert. Morale was high among the flyers, but the British Eighth Army was retreating before the superior leadership of Germany's Afrika Korps. Air warfare while retreating presents additional terrors. Combine limited sleep with a steady diet of hardtack biscuits and canned bully beef and you get exhaustion. At times during the June retreat, pilots wrapped themselves in blankets to sleep under the wings of aircraft. The fatigue of multiple operations, with limited food and rest, led to mistakes in the air, mistakes that cost dearly.

DEATH OF A LUFTWAFFE ACE IN THE WESTERN DESERT

Flight Lieutenant Wally Conrad, formerly of Melrose, Ontario, was huddled near the engine of his crashed Hurricane. He was being strafed, and was attempting to make himself as small a target as possible. He didn't know it at the time, but he had been shot down by Oberleutnant Otto Schulz, a German ace. Schulz wasn't happy to see the enemy fighter simply lying there on the desert sands; he wanted the Hurricane on fire and its pilot dead. He came down low for his strafing passes. It was a practice he had gotten into during his meteoric career in the Western Desert. His victory score was now fifty, second only to the Luftwaffe's premier *grosse Kanone*, Hans-Joachim Marseille.

Conrad's radio had failed during his op and despite his repeated calls, he could not warn his section about the four Me109s that only he had seen. In self-defence Conrad, a member of 274 Squadron, simply did what any fighter pilot under attack must do: turn towards his attackers. But he was alone, one against four. In a Hurricane the outcome was inevitable. Cannon shell fragments had passed through the cockpit, wounding the twenty-two-year-old pilot. As Conrad jumped over the side of the cockpit, he saw the white-nosed Me109s coming towards him, fast and low. There was no point in running away. Where could he hide in the desert?

Flight Sergeant James Edwards, like Conrad, had gotten separated from his section during an air battle while defending a formation of Boston bombers. In the melee he had damaged an Me109. He was headed back home, cruising his Kittyhawk at more than three hundred miles an hour less than one hundred feet above the desert. Edwards was no longer a novice, and the early label "Hawk of Martuba" had been vindicated—he had flown thirty-three operational trips and had three victories and a probable victory to his credit, as well as a couple of damaged enemy aircraft.

However, he wasn't looking for a fight. He was alone, without a wingman to protect him. Edwards was prudent and wanted only to get back to the safety of his airfield. By chance, his route took him within half a mile of Conrad's downed machine, just as Schulz's section had finished its strafing attack. Edwards saw Me109s ahead, but not what they were shooting at. Schulz levelled off only three hundred yards away from Edwards, above him to the right, but on a descending flight path that took him across and in front of the nose of the Kittyhawk.

Calculating in an instant the necessary lead to fire a burst into this target of opportunity, Edwards banked his aircraft just slightly to the left and squeezed the trigger. The .50-calibre bullets found their mark along the left side of Schulz's fuselage. The thirty-one-year-old native of Treptow, Germany, veteran of four hundred operational trips in the battles of France, Britain, Russia and the Western Desert,

crashed to his death. Schulz had committed two mistakes—assuming his six o'clock was clear and hanging around after downing his target. Edwards did not even circle the flaming wreckage, simply glancing over his shoulder as he left the scene. Wally Conrad stood up, but failed in his attempt to read the squadron markings of the Kittyhawk fighter that had saved his life.

For Conrad the name of the pilot who had saved his life would remain a mystery for more than thirty years.

Pedro Hanbury was strict about victory claims—no witnesses, no credit. Edwards decided to file a combat report, claiming only a probable, Schulz's machine. He did not mention the 109 he had damaged earlier because he did not want to appear boastful. After all, putting forward two destroyed claims without witnesses might seem like grandstanding to the close-knit multinational group of pilots at 260. Nevertheless, back in the privacy of his tent he penned two swastikas in his pilot's logbook for the trip on June 17, confident in his own mind that the enemy aircraft had gone down.

He was not wrong, and post-war research confirmed this. In addition to Schulz, Leutnant Wolf Schaller's Me109, which Edwards had damaged in the engine, crash-landed in the desert near Tobruk, Libya. Schaller was taken prisoner by the British Army that morning but liberated only two days later when Rommel's Afrika Korps overran Tobruk.

Conrad and Edwards never met during the war. Thirty-five years later the story of how Edwards saved

NEW ZEALAND ACE COLIN GRAY LECTURES CANADIAN BILL OLMSTED ON HIS SHORTCOMINGS

Billie, you're young, eager and impetuous. You must learn to cool down, to look everywhere, but most of all, behind you. You've been here ten days and that was your fifth op [operational] trip. Under the circumstances you did well, but you won't live long enough to do better if you don't use your eyes. Learn to look around. Get into that habit. A chap who sees all and is a poor pilot has a one hundred percent better chance of living than a good pilot who sees little.

Bill Olmsted, *Blue Skies.*

Conrad's life was finally published, and also provided confirmation for Edwards's fifth victory.

It takes a special amalgam of character and ability to excel in the unforgiving world of air combat. Edwards was recognized soon after his arrival in the Western Desert as special. A young Australian, Ron Cundy, was already serving at 260 Squadron when Edwards arrived. "Eddie," as his 260 Squadron mates called him in the war, had presence on the ground and was utterly unflappable in the air. This is how Cundy remembered Eddie in his memoir:

Quiet, undemonstrative, and if anything introspective, he was a man of great courage. Perhaps it was his background as a country boy from [a] small town … in the Canadian prairies but his calmness in action was extraordinary. I flew with him many times and could only admire his coolness under fire. He had remarkably keen eyesight and seemed to be able to take in the whole panorama of an engagement with enemy fighters and position himself to maximum advantage. I recall one occasion when we were heavily engaged with the 109s. He was flying a few hundred feet above me on my starboard side when a 109 slid in some hundreds of yard behind him. I called a warning but I believe he had seen it. It all happened in seconds but as I watched the 109 close in, Eddie applied a lot of right rudder and skidded out of the way. The 109 was coming in too fast to make the necessary adjustment and as he overshot, Eddie swung back to the left, opened fire and shot him down. It was the coolest piece of aerial combat I had ever witnessed.[1]

Edwards's shooting abilities were enhanced by his understanding (self-taught) of ballistics. He knew that for bullets to strike their target accurately, his aircraft had to be in stable flight, with no slipping, no skidding. Any slip or skid, in level flight or a turn results in the bullets going to a location different from that in which they are aimed. It is no simple thing in the heat of battle to remember this essential truth because the aircraft must be flown aggressively and yet smoothly when firing the guns. There is an instrument, typically called the slip and skid, or the turn and bank, consisting of a needle plus a ball suspended in liquid inside a glass tube. It is useful for flying stable turns and all instrument flying, hence the time-honoured phrase "needle, ball and airspeed." In flight the needle provides the aircraft's angle of bank; the ball, the amount of slip or skid.

In the P40, the turn and bank indicator is in the middle of the instrument panel, not the best place to be looking during aerial battle, when eyes and brain must focus only on the outside world. Today's fighter aircraft have a head-up display (HUD) controlled by computers, reflecting the aircraft's flight status onto the front windscreen. In 1942 only the reflector gunsight was above the instrument panel, in line with the pilot's vision.

Edwards asked his mechanics to install a second turn and bank instrument on the cowling above the instrument panel, directly in his line of sight, next to the gunsight. He could then see the slip indicator, the little white ball suspended in the glass tube. It is by use of the rudder pedals that a pilot keeps the ball in the centre of the tube. With the ball centred, the P40 is neither slipping to the inside of the turn nor skidding to the outside of the turn.

Edwards demonstrated such outstanding gunnery ability in action that he was appointed in June 1943 to teach at the Middle East Central Gunnery School at El Ballah, Egypt. To show his students how simple it could be, he had his armourer load a mere nine 20mm cannon shells in the left-hand 20mm cannon of his Spitfire. He would fire these nine rounds, sometimes while flying inverted, and shred the tow plane's cloth target drogue. Sometimes his rounds would sever the cable and the cloth target would flutter to earth. Only George Beurling showed an equal flair—it was his habit as well to fly inverted for many of his gunnery passes at drogues, since it was too boring to hit them flying upright.

On June 28, 1942, Jimmie Edwards and Ron Cundy were among the tired pilots of 260 Squadron flying from early morning until dusk, dropping five-hundred-pound bombs from their P40s and strafing German vehicles with their six .50-calibre machine guns. At dusk, Australian Cundy was sitting in his P40 waiting for orders for the next retreat, watching a personnel carrier with towed anti-tank gun drive up to his machine. A British Army captain asked:

"What are you fellows doing here?"

"Waiting for orders to move."

"Well, you had better not wait too long. The enemy tanks are less than two miles away."

The squadron took off after dark, lucky to have a full moon to light the way. The pilots could see Rommel's tanks approaching the western edge of landing ground (LG) 109; the ground crew had to escape by truck, and were quite fortunate to evade the Germans. The region around Gazala, Libya, was lost, says Cundy, due to the British Army's "inept tactical leadership":

> Our flight east to LG 106 near El Daba took only twenty minutes, but we had to land by moonlight with the aid of some drums filled with petrol-soaked sand set alight by our thoughtful ground crews. A very dicey landing but everyone made it without mishap.

Profile – JOHN TERRANCE FIELD
Born – September 24, 1921, Vancouver
Father – Patrick Willoughby Robert Field, sales manager, roofing and paper business
Mother – Gladys Connell
Post-war occupation – Businessman, military flying instructor, airport manager
Marital status – Wife Pat Stewart; sons Michael, Shane, Patrick and Brady; daughter Cindy
Hobbies – Tennis

A much less experienced Western Desert pilot than Cundy was also caught up in the debacle at Gazala, having arrived only two days before. John Terrance "Terry" Field of Vancouver had been flying P39 Aircobras with 601 Squadron in Britain in 1941, but he did not accompany that unit to Malta; instead, he was sent with a draft of twelve Hurricane pilots to the Western Desert. His journey by sea via South Africa took more than seventy days. Field had the misfortune to be in the Gazala sector just as Rommel's Afrika Korps pushed east. The squadron he was joining, 213, had already flown towards Alexandria and he was hoping to hitch a ride by truck in that direction. The previous night, five Spitfires had been ferried out of Malta to Gazala. Some of the

Canadian Gordon Wilson in Hurricane, 213 Squadron, Western Desert.

Courtesy of the Terry Field Collection

ferry pilots were known to Field, and he was chatting to them as the sun went down.

When the news broke that the Germans were on the move, the flight lieutenant in charge received a telephone call. His face paled, and then he turned to Field and asked him if he could fly a Spitfire. He pointed towards a machine with "VC—P" on the side. Field was not trained to fly a Spitfire, having had only one fifteen-minute familiarization flight in Britain. He allowed as how he could manage a take-off, if the flight lieutenant could refresh his memory on starting the Rolls-Royce Merlin engine:

"Well, I am going to start the engine for you. Then you take this aircraft and get out of here."

"Well, where am I going and why am I going?" Terry asked.

"The line is broken at Sidi Bahrain," he responded, handing Field the binoculars. Terry could see only clouds of dust on the horizon. It meant little to him, being a newcomer to desert war. The sun was now setting and the ground crews on the defensive airfield guns had started shooting—at what, Terry could not see. Following orders, he climbed in the aircraft and took off: "I got the Spitfire up to five hundred feet … I had not flown for several months. I had not flown at night, except for my ten hours on Harvards. It was no longer dusk, it was dark. By the time I got to ten thousand feet, it was jet bloody black … I knew if I turned right I was headed for Cairo."

He flew along in darkness, uncertain of the fuel remaining, without a clue as to his destination. Just when it seemed likely that he must bail out rather than risk a forced landing or a ditching in the Mediterranean, Terry saw a bright flash of light on the ground and the unique shape of a Spitfire wing. He lowered his landing gear, descended, pulled up over an anti-aircraft gun at the last moment before round out and touched down without even bouncing, almost as though he knew what he was doing. As he observed later: "When I looked down I could just see the gun post I had just leaped over … I made a landing of sorts, and was extremely relieved."

It certainly fooled the ground crews who witnessed his arrival. They started jumping up and down with excitement, shouting "What a landing!" They told Field that seventeen other aircraft had tried to land in darkness at the aerodrome, located near

Fuka, and all had been damaged to one degree or another. The following morning the ground crew raised Field's Spitfire where it had sunk in the sand and found there was no undercarriage damage at all. Field had made his second successful flight on a Spitfire at night to an unknown destination, with pilot and machine delivered intact.

Profile – REX HOWARD PROBERT
Born – March 19, 1921, Moose Jaw, SK
Father – William Probert, merchant
Mother – Elsie May Tomilson
Decorations & Medals – DFC
Post-war occupation – Manufacturers' representative for clothing lines
Marital status – Wife Dorothy Hellings, daughters Heather and Colleen
Hobbies – Musician (trombone), skiing, sailing, motor boating, golf

By late July the front lines in the Western Desert had stabilized near El Alamein, Egypt, and some squadrons were re-equipping with newer aircraft, and fresh flying personnel were arriving. On July 29, Lance Wade, a twenty-six-year-old American born in Texas and raised in Arizona, greeted Rex Howard Probert at 33 Squadron, RAF. Rex took an immediate liking to Lance, a short man with a wide grin and a full moustache.

Sergeant Probert had been a charter member of 416 Squadron, RCAF, when it was forming at Peterhead, Scotland, in the autumn of 1941. He arrived in December, and his early operational experiences were uneventful. He provided aerial escort to shipping and chased bombers, when the weather of northern Scotland permitted. By watching 416 evolve, Probert also learned that leadership is critical to success. The first squadron commander, in his opinion, lacked the experience to help the squadron improve, and by the time Lloyd Chadburn, the second squadron commander, had fully transformed 416, Probert was gone. He and seven other 416 pilots were taken from the unit and shipped to Takoradi, Gold Coast (today the country of Ghana) in May 1942, aboard the newest and fastest Royal Navy light cruiser, HMS *Manxman*.

Looking back at those who served at Peterhead in late '41 and early '42, Rex Probert says the most

LIFE IN THE DESERT, BY BERT HOULE

Pilots slept four in a ridge tent with their folding beds arranged to give the most leg-room. All clothing was kept in a parachute bag which made it fairly dust proof. The bed had a blanket wrapped completely around it. This collected inches of dust during a dust storm and was shaken out at night before retiring. There were no batmen on an operational squadron, no deadwood of any kind. Everyone did his laundry in a canvas basin which fitted on a folding stand. The ration of two quarts of water per man per day had to do for laundry, washing, shaving and sponge baths. None of it was wasted and, sometimes, after being used a few times, the water was strained through sand and used again. It was a toss up whether to shave with the extra tea water or make tea from the shaving water.

Our dressers were five-gallon gasoline drums set on top of each other just outside the tent door. The airmen slept beside the aircraft. Many of them were stung by tarantulas and scorpions, which found their way into their blankets. The main messes were formed by two or three large EPIP tents fastened together. A bar was usually constructed at one end, a kitchen at the back, and we ate from rough folding tables which were always carried as part of the furniture. We always dug a small slit trench near each tent and a larger one near the mess.

Albert U. Houle with J.P.A. Michel Levigne (co-author), G/C A.U. "Bert" Houle, DFC & Bar.

LIFE IN THE DESERT, BY NEVILLE DUKE

It was winter once more and in the keen air of the desert we developed enormous appetites; food became more than usually important, particularly as supplies were not always adequate as they might have been. A habit developed of a "yaffle" box being kept in every tent. In it was stored any food that we could lay hands on: gazelle meat, which tasted like venison, collected during shoots in the desert and butchered expertly by the Aussies, Ted Sly and Glendinning being particularly useful with their knives; sausages, cocoa, tinned food, flour, raisins, sugar, and biltong or salted antelope from East Africa. The Aussies and Canadians in the squadron usually had well-filled yaffle boxes, replenished regularly by food parcels from their friends and relatives.

On cold nights, when the wind had a bitter touch and sand seemed to be flying everywhere, it was one of the more pleasant things in life to gather four or five in a tent, and with the help of a petrol fire in a cut-down tin filled with sand, to contrive a hot meal. I can still see the inside of a tent, a few rather ragged looking types grouped round the petrol fire, the solemn and anxious looks on their faces picked out by the soft lighting, intent on producing yaffle. And then, when the cooking was completed, the sharing of the food, which warmed and cheered us and thawed us into general conversation until a move was made to turn in for the night. We talked of many things, usually closely associated with our lives—the trouble we were inclined to get with sand jamming our guns, battle formations and enemy tactics.

Neville Duke, Test Pilot.

memorable for him was Flight Sergeant Robert Andrew "Bob" Buckham: "He was a born leader, the most outstanding pilot on the unit, a damn good fighter pilot." Buckham, an elderly twenty-eight-year-old in December 1941 who had been a driver for a dairy company in Vancouver before the war, rose to wing commander, shot down at least six enemy aircraft and received the DFC and Bar and American DFC.

A fighter pilot's early indoctrination is critical to his self-confidence, and having a mentor makes all the difference. At the time 33 Squadron was commanded by a Rhodesian Air Force pilot who seldom flew on operations. Most of the squadron leadership in combat was provided by the flight and section leaders. Lance Wade was a good teacher to his pilots, with a brilliant grasp of aerial tactics—which was important for survival in the inadequate Hurricane II. In his southwest Calgary apartment in 2001, Rex recalled his operational limitations:

I never fired my guns until I went on my first operation in the desert. Our gunnery training was non-existent. For the first fifteen trips or so I couldn't see anything of the enemy—I didn't know what to look for or where to look. It was strictly defensive on the Hurricane. By comparison with us, the American P40 pilots of the US Army Air Corps arriving in the Western Desert had 250 hours on type and full gunnery training. They were great pilots ... Wade was a super leader; just call for help, and he was there if it was possible to be. "Sandy" Kallio, another American, worshipped Wade. Wade kept a lot of us alive and we would have been long dead without him.

Oliver Charles "Sandy" Kallio was from Ironwood, Michigan, and had enlisted at Ft William, Ontario, receiving his RCAF wings and commission in the summer of 1941. He served through the war with the RAF and RCAF, receiving the DFC and the DSO, the latter for his outstanding work as a commander with the RAF's 145 Squadron and with the RCAF's 417 Squadron, the only RCAF fighter squadron based in the Middle East.

The Royal Air Force in the Middle East had a few faults, but also had a knack for recognizing

VERNON CROMPTON WOODWARD
Outstanding Ace, Outstanding Leader

One of the aces of 33 Squadron in the darkest period of 1940–41 had been a Canadian named Vernon Crompton Woodward, born in 1916 in Victoria, BC. He is not a household name today, but in the summer of '42, "Woody" was the highest-scoring Canadian fighter pilot of the war. George Beurling surpassed Woodward in victories, but Woodward had demonstrated more talent as a leader.

Like Beurling he was one of the hundreds of Canadians with a Grade 11 education who had been awarded a short-service commission in the RAF. He had first tackled the Italians and Germans in 1940 while flying a lovely-handling biplane, the Gloster Gladiator. He became an ace alongside the highest-scoring South African Air Force ace, Marmaduke "Pat" Pattle, who was killed in April 1941 with a victory score that may have surpassed forty. Woodward had about twenty victories, though the exact total is unknown and nearly impossible to corroborate.

He was awarded a DFC and Bar, and he stayed with the RAF after the war, retiring as a wing commander. He worked for twelve years for the Corps of Commissionaires at a West Coast naval facility, retiring at age seventy-four; he needed the job due to his failed financial investments and abiding love of exotic cars such as Lamborghinis, Jaguars and Jensons. Born into a well-to-do Victoria family from whom he was somewhat estranged, he died in 2000, little known by Canadians. According to the obituary written by Jack E.G. Dixon of the *National Post*, Woody was a fixture at Herman's Jazz Club in Victoria on Sunday nights, and Herman's burned to the ground the day Woody was cremated. Woody's wife, Nora, had died in 1974, leaving two daughters, Gail and Piaf.

SERGEANT ALAN JAMES HARRIS, RDF TECHNICIAN, RCAF, WITH 243 AND 450 SQUADRONS

All photos courtesy of the Alan Harris Collection

While serving at 96 Squadron, RAF Wrexham in Wales, Leading Aircraftman Alan Harris, of Ottawa, was sent on a short but demanding commando course and issued a khaki uniform and STEN gun. He was assigned to 243 Squadron—based in Turnhouse, Scotland, and equipped with Mk V Spitfires—and travelled to the Middle East in secrecy along with other ground crew aboard SS *Sobieski*, there to join the invasion forces for Operation Torch. The first landfall was Philippeville, Algeria, in November 1942, and the first airfield was in the same country, at Constantine. The speed of the invasion and the rate of advance from airfield to airfield meant few creature comforts. The hard rains and winter weather made tent living miserable. The first task at any new airfield was to dig a slit trench for protection against German bombing. Owning a STEN gun meant that Harris served on firing parties at the funerals of pilots who had been killed in action or in flying accidents.

Food is a critical component of morale in any military unit, and the food in North Africa and the Western Desert left a lot to be desired. In Algeria, oranges were plentiful, and the ground crew lived on them. The corned beef, some of it tinned many years earlier, was always fried, and the bread, when it finally arrived, usually tasted of vinegar. As Harris noted to the author: "When you are young, you take all that adversity in stride—you give it no thought ... everybody is the same. The fact is, as I think back on my war career, all I remember is four years of bad food."

youthful talent and for accommodating eccentric leaders who did not fit the traditional model. In time of war the RAF often promoted talented men no matter where they had been born and educated. Wade and Kallio were typical of the hundreds of foreign-born men who rose to command squadrons and even wings in the RAF.

The RAF in the Western Desert and Italy, somewhat like the American forces in the Southwest Pacific, received too few weapons, many of them second-rate, and the barest minimum of other comforts. The Middle East was not a glamorous posting and in the hierarchy of important theatres was regarded

as second or third tier by the Allies. The theatre was the last to get improved aircraft.

For example, Alan Harris, an RCAF radio-detection-finding (RDF) technician who served with RAF and RAAF squadrons there, recalls a singsong refrain of mechanics working in the desert in 1942: "Polish and shine and you'll get Spit 9s," a jibe at the obsolete machines with which the Western Desert and North African units were equipped.

The destiny of Allied pilots in the Middle East was controlled by RAF Middle East HQ, not RAF UK HQ as was the case on the island of Malta. A posting to the Middle East in times of peace had traditionally been four years for officers and six years for airmen. This pre-war tradition did not bode well for flyers from the other dominions. The RCAF had a very modest presence in Cairo, despite the hundreds of Canadian combatants, and had limited insight into or control over its personnel.

It sometimes wasn't much better for the British pilots. Even the highest-scoring ace in the Western Desert, Neville Duke, who had about thirty victories and six hundred operational hours behind him, was refused a transfer back to his home in Britain after his second tour of operations. He twice had to crash-land in the desert after coming under attack by German fighters. The young ace, born in 1922 at Tonbridge, southeast of London, served in the Italian campaign as a squadron commander and ended the war with a total of more than seven hundred operational hours and nearly five hundred sorties. When Rex Probert and Milt Jowsey served under Duke at 92 Squadron, the expression often heard in the squadron, says Probert, was: "92 and Neville Duke are up!"

Profile – MILTON EARDLEY JOWSEY

Born – May 21, 1922, Ottawa

Died – August 14, 2004, Copper Cliff, ON

Father – Harry Jowsey, various jobs including selling insurance, dairy faming

Mother – Florence Moir

Decorations & Medals – DFC

Degrees & Awards – BSc, PEng

Post-war occupation – Mining engineer, vice-president of Inco in Ontario

Marital Status – Wife Mary Honeyman; daughters Carol, Christine, Kim and Ellen; son Peter

Hobbies – "Nothing that you could call a hobby"

A week after Probert arrived at 33 Squadron, Milton "Milt" Jowsey (pronounced *Joe-see*) joined him and was assigned to Kallio's flight. Milt had graduated near the top of his Service Flying Training School (SFTS) class and was dismayed to learn that he was being posted to Trenton, Ontario, to take a course for new instructors. He wanted to go overseas and become a fighter pilot. There were married fellows who did not mind instructing, but Milt was only nineteen years old.

He was discouraged about the instructional assignment and crafted an escape plan. In those days Ottawa was more like a village than a city and it was not that difficult to get appointments with senior civil servants or military officers. Milt had been the paper boy for many military officers before the war, including Air Vice-Marshal Lloyd Breadner, a Royal Naval Air Service ace in the Great War.

Jowsey visited Breadner's office at RCAF Headquarters, Ottawa, without an appointment and asked his receptionist to fit him in. Breadner congratulated his former paper boy for receiving his pilot's wings and sergeant's stripes. Milt then showed the rotund, round-cheeked Breadner his orders to Trenton, complaining, "I don't want to instruct, I want to be a fighter pilot." Breadner was delighted that here was a young man as keen to get overseas as he had been twenty-five years earlier. He replied, "Leave it with me, Sergeant Jowsey." The next day, fresh orders arrived posting Milt to "Y" Depot in Halifax for embarkation on an armed merchant cruiser (SS *Leopoldville*) to Britain via Iceland. At the same time a telegram arrived informing Jowsey that he was being commissioned and had permission to outfit himself with a pilot officer's uniform. Perhaps his meeting with Breadner speeded up his advancement in rank.

When he left Canada, Jowsey didn't know the odds that awaited him in the Western Desert. But he commented in conversation in 2004 that even in 1942 he and his squadron mates knew the Hurricane was hopelessly outclassed. Milt says the rule of thumb at 33 Squadron was that about thirty Hurricanes had to be shot down before the squadron scored one victory against a German fighter. Since many aircraft were salvaged to fly again, Jowsey calculates that a few Hurricanes were shot down two or three times.

When Jowsey and Probert moved on to Spitfires at 92 Squadron, renowned as the high-scoring squadron of the RAF, they fought in the Sicilian campaign and both received DFCs for a lopsided aerial battle over Sicily. The citations for their gallantry awards summarize what they achieved in just a few short minutes:

One day in July 1943 this officer, in company with a pilot in another aircraft, engaged a

Hurricane of 260 Squadron RAF in the Western Desert undergoing maintenance.

formation of more than twelve enemy fighters over Catania airfield. In the engagement two of the enemy aircraft were destroyed and another was seriously damaged. Pilot Officer Probert personally destroyed one and damaged another. The enemy force, greatly superior in number, was so completely outflown that this pilot and his companion were able to return to base with both aircraft unscathed. Pilot Officer Probert has always set a high standard in flying and his courage and determination have been of the highest order.

Recently with another pilot Flying Officer Jowsey attacked a large force of enemy aircraft over Catania airfield. During the ensuing engagement he personally destroyed one of them bringing his victories to at least four enemy aircraft destroyed. A cool and capable leader, his courage and determination to engage the enemy have set a fine example to his fellow pilots and have contributed in no small measure to the successes achieved by his squadron.

Probert, Jowsey and two others, Doc Savage and Brendan Baker, had been asked by the RAF to stay on for an additional 50 ops after Africa to keep the experience level up on the squadron. When Savage was killed and Baker taken prisoner, Probert and Jowsey were hauled out of combat, but not before each of them had reached 185 operational trips.

After serving as an instructor on an operational training unit (OTU) in Canada, Probert in 1944 asked to go back overseas for a second tour. His request was turned down, probably because of previous deaths in the family: his older brother, William, an air gunner on Stirlings with 15 Squadron, RAF, had been killed in September 1942, and a cousin, Kenneth, a navigator on Marauders, had been killed on takeoff in British Guyana in April 1944. However, after a rest, Jowsey left Canada for his second tour, and from September through December 1944 served with 442 Squadron, RCAF, in northwest Europe, where he was promoted to squadron leader and took command of the unit. He was shot down in February '45 and evaded capture until April, when he made it back to Allied lines. At war's end he had flown 390 hours in 290 operational sorties.

Michell Johnston, who led 442 Squadron after Jowsey was shot down, felt that of all the squadron commanders he had served with from 1941 onwards, Jowsey was the best. Johnston, who was well liked and respected, commanded 442 when it converted to long-range Mustang IIIs; when it flew the last op of the war on May 9, 1945, over the Channel Islands; and when it disbanded in August 1945. However, Squadron Leader Johnston received no official recognition for his 1941–45 service, not even a Mention in Despatches.

* * *

Profile – STANLEY JOHN KERNAGHAN
Born – May 30, 1921, Cartwright, MB
Died – April 16, 2001, Vancouver
Father – Robert Kernaghan, farmer
Mother – Ruby Beach
Decorations & Awards – AFC, DFM
Post-war occupation – Entrepreneur; founder of insurance, security and travel businesses
Marital status – Wife Agnes Terese Borody; daughters Josie, Karen, Patti and Jennifer; son Darcy
Hobbies – Hospital volunteer, aircraft owner

While Jowsey and Probert were starting their operational education at 33 Squadron, a Canadian from Cartwright, Manitoba, arrived at 252 Squadron in Egypt, on the evening of July 31, '42. The unit was equipped with twin engine Beaufighters armed with four 20-mm cannon and eight machine guns. Unlike the Hurricanes that struggled to survive against German fighters, the Beaufighter was the match of its twin-engine counterparts in the Luftwaffe. With a top speed over three hundred miles an hour, it was the most heavily armed British fighter-bomber and an excellent ground-attack and anti-shipping fighter. Stanley John "Stan" Kernaghan had trained on the Beaufighter at No. 2(C) OTU at Catfoss in Yorkshire.

He and his navigator, Sergeant Bernard Andrews, were sent to West Africa by ship, from where they would ferry an aircraft to Cairo. They took off in a night-fighter model of the Beaufighter (serial number 7753) from the airport at Takoradi, Gold Coast, for Luxor, Egypt, with an overnight stop at El Fasha. After arrival at No. 108 Maintenance Unit near Cairo on July 12, many of Stan's buddies, including

A Bristol Beaufighter stationed in Italy.

his navigator, soon fell ill with malaria at the Almaza holding camp in Egypt. Stan alone remained healthy and was the only one of his group out of Britain to go directly to an operational squadron.

He arrived in Edku to report for duty at 252 on the evening of July 31, and early on the morning of August 1, Sergeant Kernaghan and his navigator, Sergeant Tom Armstrong, were sent out in a formation of eight to strafe four German barges bringing in supplies to the Afrika Korps. The barges were large, more than 160 feet long, weighing between 200 and 280 tons, capable of carrying up to 150 three-ton trucks, and drawing only six feet of water. They were dangerous to attack because they were well armed with several large-calibre anti-aircraft guns. The 252 fighters inflicted little damage, but one of the eight Beaufighter crews was shot down and killed. Kernaghan greatly impressed the more experienced Armstrong by demonstrating that he was an able rookie pilot, showing no sign of nerves or novice stupidity on what was his first op without any field training.

On September 3, during his seventh operational trip, Stan Kernaghan provided escort cover for Beaufort torpedo bombers. He destroyed his first of four enemy aircraft, a Heinkel 111, on this op, by which time he had been rejoined by his original navigator, Bernard Andrews, now recovered from malaria. The Beauforts did not complete a successful attack against an Italian convoy made up of three merchant vessels and four torpedo boats. But the Beaufighters attempted to shoot down the enemy's aerial escort of two Ju88s and a He111. Kernaghan was able to close with the 111, which was flying on one engine after an earlier attack, as it attempted to escape at low altitude, and his accurate shooting forced the 111 into the sea.

On September 13 and 14, 252 Squadron provided aerial cover for Operation Agreement, a Royal Marine commando raid against Tobruk supported by a large flotilla of Royal Navy ships and boats. The raid was one of those irregular operations beloved by Churchill and parodied by British author Evelyn Waugh, who had been in the Royal Marines at the time. It was an unmitigated disaster. Kernaghan remembered it late in his life as one of the biggest snafus he witnessed during the war. He recalled that

there was much incompetence and cowardice, including flyers on top cover who headed home as soon as the shooting started.

On September 14, enemy Ju87 Stukas in large formations repeatedly bombed the cruiser HMS *Conventry*. Stan and Bernard attacked and damaged a Ju87 and were in turn set upon by three Ju88s. Stan's wingman on this op left for home immediately, leaving his leader to fight on alone. Stan and Bernard were able to damage one of the Ju88s and disable its rear gunner. Two other Ju88s then attacked him and he turned into their attacks, flying between the No. 1 and No. 2 aircraft, escaping unharmed.

The Royal Navy lost the *Coventry*, the destroyers *Sikh* and *Zulu* and several smaller vessels. Virtually none of the Royal Marines and other troops taking part in the Tobruk raid, five hundred in all, were recovered, either dying or being taken prisoner of war. Aboard the *Coventry* was Squadron Leader Stan Turner, recently of Malta, who had taken a reduction in rank from wing commander to squadron leader so he could serve as air resources coordinator for Operation Agreement. For his troubles he was obliged to dive off the sinking ship and hope for rescue by one of the other assault vessels. Turner survived his swim and later commanded 134 and then 417 Squadrons in the Mediterranean theatre.

After a two-week rest for the squadron, Kernaghan went back on operations with a new navigator, Sergeant Archie Powell of Middlebury, England. On October 12, he and Powell set fire to a Junkers (Ju) 52 transport, forcing it down in the desert and then destroying it with gunfire. On the way home they strafed a road convoy. Return fire from the convoy destroyed the elevator cables of the Beaufighter, but Kernaghan was able to fly the remaining 225 miles to his home aerodrome using the elevator trim wheel for pitch control. Kernaghan offered Powell a chance to bail out because he was uncertain whether he could land the machine on trim only, but Powell declined, and his pilot successfully put the damaged Beaufighter down on the runway at Edku.

Two weeks later Kernaghan and Powell participated in an escort operation with the Beauforts of 39 Squadron and engaged a formation of five He111s. In a head-on attack against one bomber, Stan said that the shooting of the German gunner was so accurate that he told British author Roy Nesbitt "it was like sitting in a car during a hailstorm." With more than forty bullet holes in his machine, Stan still managed to attack the left-hand He111 in the formation and drive it into the Mediterranean. In the ensuing explosion, parts of the 111 struck the starboard wing of the Beaufighter.

By the end of November, Sergeant Kernaghan had served four months and flown one hundred operational hours at 252. Rated an average pilot by the RCAF on graduation from Cessna Cranes at No. 12 SFTS, Brandon, Manitoba, and average on graduation from the Blenheim/Beaufighter OTU course at Catfoss, Stan already had three confirmed victories. In addition, by his own assessment, there was a probable against a Ju88, as well as a damaged Ju87 and many ground vehicles and barges damaged or destroyed. He achieved his fourth victory on December 8 during another convoy escort, destroying a Ju88. His squadron commander recommended Stan for the Distinguished Flying Medal, and the citation said that he was "a first class pilot with a

fine operational record … this airman has displayed courage and determination of a high order."

After 267 hours of operational flying, Stan was sent to Britain for a rest and for assignment as an OTU instructor on the Beaufighter at Catfoss, then back to Canada to Greenwood, Nova Scotia, where he taught on de Havilland Mosquitoes. His operational experience, instructional expertise and quick wits at the controls of a Mosquito at Greenwood's No. 8 OTU earned him an Air Force Cross, his citation commenting that he was "an inspiration to the many pupils who have passed through his capable hands."

I first met Stan in 1996 as we were both members of the Air Force Officers Association (AFOA), Vancouver. Stan had followed me as president of the AFOA and in writing about him in a news release I mistakenly listed him as Stanley Kernaghan, DFM, AFC. He chastised me. I thought that decorations should be listed in the order they had been awarded, but Stan pointed out that in the RAF a decoration to an officer was always listed ahead of a medal to

Kernaghan (on right) and Powell.

a non-commissioned officer. As a sergeant he had received the DFM; as a flight lieutenant he had received the AFC. Though both gallantry awards were equal in the hierarchy of awards, in the British tradition an officer's gallantry awards precede those won as a ranker, with the sole exception of the Victoria Cross. It was because of this lesson in the nuances of British military awards that I often listened closely to Stan when he spoke about the past.

He liked to talk to me about the war, but his equanimity about it had been hard won. Stan said that when the war ended he felt cut adrift from life, depressed and uncertain about who he was or what he wanted. He did not want to stay in the RCAF and he did not want to go to university. He once said, more as an observation than a regret: "I could have become an ace on my second tour … I knew the ropes. But I think I made a greater contribution to the war in teaching others."

When Stan was home on leave in Manitoba in 1943, he went looking for a girl he used to know before the war. He searched for her at The Denver Cafe on Portage Avenue, Winnipeg, not far from the Bay and Eaton's department stores but on the north side of Portage. Agnes, whose father John Borody operated and owned The Denver Cafe, saw this tall, handsome pilot enter the restaurant; he looked just like the movie star Errol Flynn. Agnes talked with Stan and learned he was leaving for Nova Scotia. Stan sent her roses from Montreal but provided no address. By writing that she was his friend, but not mentioning her gender, she obtained Stan's address from his mother, Ruby, who was living in Cartwright. Agnes wrote to Stan during his tour at Greenwood, her first letter coming as a surprise to Kernaghan since he did not remember who she was.

After leaving the RCAF, Stan went home to Cartwright to assist his father in selling off his farm. After the auction, Stan returned to Winnipeg and brought his parents to live there. Jobs in Winnipeg in 1946 were few and far between and no one in the city gave Flight Lieutenant Kernaghan much credit for his distinguished combat record. It was at this time that Stan and Agnes Borody got to know each other better. They married in 1947, going on to raise a family of five children—four daughters and a son.

Once Stan finally found his way in civilian life, he never looked back. He bought and flew his own light aircraft to help his business prosper. He became a

wealthy entrepreneur and the owner of several companies. He was the founder of the largest privately owned insurance adjusting company in Canada, SJ Kernaghan Adjusters, with twenty-three offices from Halifax to Victoria; a security company called Securiguard; and the owner of a printing company called Calabar Printers, as well as Travelex and RSVP Travel.

Stan and I were invited to the Billy Bishop VC Legion branch in Vancouver in 1998 for a ceremony to unveil a Robert Hyndman painting of George Beurling. Among the invited guests was a former Luftwaffe pilot and fighter ace with more than twenty victories, a well-known émigré within the British Columbia aviation community. Stan did not know this Luftwaffe veteran and he did not wish to. Before the unveiling ceremonies, as I drank my beer and Stan his soda, Stan said to me: "I don't feel so good that he is here. I lost a lot of my friends in the Western Desert to pilots like him. I don't think it is wrong for him to be here, but I don't feel comfortable about it. I don't want to shake his hand."

Profile – IRVING FARMER KENNEDY
Born – February 4, 1922, Cumberland, ON
Father – Robert James Kennedy, accountant and treasurer of Cumberland Township
Mother – Eva Farmer
Decorations & Medals – DFC and Bar; awarded French Legion of Honour, 2004
Degrees & Awards – MD
Post-war occupation – Doctor and family physician
Marital status – Wife Fern Dale; daughters Ann, Carol, Nancy and Martha
Hobbies – Gardening, carpentry; an evolutionary naturalist

A surprising number of fighter pilots became medical doctors and surgeons, including well-known heroes such as Wing Commander Hugh Godefroy, DSO, DFC and Bar, Croix de Guerre. One of the highest-scoring RCAF aces, Squadron Leader Irving Farmer Kennedy, DFC and Bar, practised family medicine for thirty-five years in the county in which he was born. His nickname growing up in Cumberland County on the Ottawa River was "Buster" and in the war he was called "Happy" or "Hap" for short.

Tall, blond and blue-eyed, he had felt a deep-seated patriotism; he believed that service in war was his duty. He reflected at age eighty about the values that served as his moral foundation as a youngster: "The gravity with which I accepted the war cannot be over-emphasized. We were imbued with the gravity of the situation and my father who had served in WWI and was badly injured in 1917 at Vimy Ridge actually took me into the recruiting centre."

Like that other high-scoring ace, "Stocky" Edwards, Hap was a clean-living, principled young man who did not drink or chase women (see box on next page). He devoted himself to mastering his aircraft, so that he would know it intimately in any position and at any speed without looking inside the cockpit very often.

Now retired from family medical practice but still living within a short distance of his birthplace, Dr Kennedy remembers the young pilot who was so intent on service to his country:

> I considered it my duty to be as competent as I could. That is what I aimed towards, and eventually when I encountered enemy aircraft in the Middle East I felt competent and, strangely enough, I was not afraid … that may sound boastful. I became competent in Malta to the degree that I welcomed the enemy and waded into them with anticipation … We took the war very seriously, it was full throttle and get the bastard.

In reflecting upon his happy childhood, he recalls his father as a warden in the local Church of England, his mother playing the organ. Every Sunday was devoted to church. The discipline instilled through childhood resulted in a motivated young pilot:

> I never drank during the war. Those who did were often unprepared for combat … one I knew got shot down because he was hungover … I went through the war without getting tangled up with women at all—the odd dance, a very innocent affair … I didn't learn to dance until I arrived in England.

Trained on Harvards at No. 10 SFTS in Dauphin, Manitoba, in 1941, Kennedy, like Edwards, graduated as a sergeant pilot and was immediately sent overseas on a convoy that stopped over in Iceland. Although he

had trained on single-engine planes, Kennedy was assigned by the RAF to a twin-engine fighter squadron, an Army Cooperation unit, 263, flying a little-known, heavily armed fighter called the Westland Whirlwind. As he explained to me, the Whirlwind could have done far more good in the Western Desert and North Africa supporting the Eighth Army, but it was committed to Channel duties and an occasional sweep into France. After about nine months at 263, Kennedy transferred to an RCAF Spitfire squadron in June 1942, No. 421. With about 125 operational hours in Britain, Kennedy shipped out to Gibraltar and the Middle East. He arrived in Malta on December 15 and joined 249 Squadron.

> We were young lads who went overseas in 1941. We matured in Churchill's England. In the Mediterranean we were well informed by the BBC of German successes in the North Atlantic, Russia and Africa. In 1942-43 we did not know the horrors of Auschwitz, but we

Dr. Kennedy as a fighter pilot in the Second World War.

Courtesy of the Hap Kennedy Collection

read intelligence reports of [the] freight train exodus of people from occupied Europe ... I knew Hitler's beliefs about the Germans as a master race. [When I shot down a Focke-Wulf on a beach in Italy] and it hit the ground in a great ball of flame, my first emotion was satisfaction at having overcome a Luftwaffe aircraft and pilot—they went together. Whether the pilot baled out, or was killed, was immaterial; I felt no remorse. Air combat was an impersonal duel. I felt that if there had to be a war, surely this is the way it should be fought, this clean, unrestrained, impersonal duel ... Had there ever been a war in which the issues were so clearly defined? I recall saying to Church, my No. 2, "So much for the damned master race, Jack."

And yet, when I once encountered three Junkers 52 transport aircraft, fair game but sitting ducks unable to fight back, I set the port engine of each one on fire without injury to the crew, allowing the pilot to set the aircraft down on the water, presumably to survive. And I was never in a squadron in three and one half years where shooting a man in a parachute would be condoned. That was simply not done.

Kennedy was a natural fighter pilot with the three essential gifts: sharp eyesight, accurate gunnery, and aggression. Despite his sunny exterior on the ground, he had a killer instinct in the air and was not one to make a single pass and hurry home. If a German pilot wanted to scrap, Kennedy fought until he was victorious. If he could not achieve vic-

tory, he stayed in the battle until there was no hope of a successful outcome. He chased large formations while alone and attacked without hesitation once the situation turned to his advantage. By the summer of 1943 he was already an ace and well on his way to ten victories. He achieved one victory in October 1943 by following a German squadren of 12 Me109s all the way to its home airfield near Monte Cassino, Italy. Hap waited for the exact moment to destroy the rearmost fighter as the formation leader did a flypast for his pals on the ground.

The "tail-end Charlie" escaped by parachute and landed safely on the airfield. Kennedy reported the successful outcome of his patience and tenacity back at Capodichino airfield adjacent to Naples. The wing intelligence officer or the air officer commanding, Air-Vice Marshal Harry Broadhurst, disallowed the victory claim as it was unwitnessed and unsupported by any cine-camera pictures. (Spitfires in Italy did not have camera-guns.) It seemed clearly to be just an unlikely "line shoot." Hap was not discouraged or even fazed when his claim was not endorsed. After all, he knew what he had done and he knew what his eyes had seen.

Four decades after the war, British author Christopher Shores was able to determine from German records that Kennedy's shooting had resulted in Han-Werner Maximow, pilot of Me109 "Yellow 13," bailing out of his machine. Belatedly, Kennedy increased his victory score; officially he is shown in various publications as having eleven or twelve, but in his own estimation his score is actually fourteen when Maximow's Me109 is included along with one other Ju52. Kennedy received the Distinguished

---

BILL OLMSTED RECALLS SQUADRON LEADER HAP KENNEDY, DFC AND BAR

Tall and blond, with a perpetual grin that stretched from ear to ear, he was a very spontaneous and fun-loving person. Although a teetotaller at parties, he could give the impression that he had imbibed as much as any of us ... Hap's main and consuming interest, despite his carefree attitude, was to fight and kill the enemy ... [today] he is still the modest, almost shy person he was in the air force.

Bill Olmsted, *Blue Skies.*

Flying Cross for his work in Malta and Italy, and a Bar to that gallantry award near the end of his subsequent tour of operations in France in 1944.

Like many families, the Kennedys of Cumberland County had several children serving in uniform. In addition to Hap there was his older brother, Bob, who was a radio technician in 6 Bomber Group, and a younger brother, Carleton, who trained as a bomb aimer. It was worrying to any family to have three sons overseas, but to have two flying on operations ratcheted up the anxiety immeasurably. A telegram arrived for the Kennedys in August '44 advising that Hap, now squadron leader and commanding officer of 401 Squadron, RCAF, had bailed out and his whereabouts were uncertain.

He had successfully parachuted out of his flak-damaged burning Spitfire a few miles northwest of Paris on July 26. Kennedy escaped and evaded the enemy for a month. He ran and crawled through grain fields with German soldiers in pursuit, hid in haystacks and barn lofts and, with the help of the French underground, reconnected with his unit in late August. He learned that his successor as commanding officer, Charlie Trainor (Squadron Leader Hugh Charles Trainor, DSO, DFC and Bar, from Charlottetown, PEI, b. 1916, d. 2004), had also been shot down, and there was a vacancy for the slot he himself had held in July. He was immediately sent on leave in London, where he made efforts to talk his way back on operations, meeting with Air Marshal Breadner at RCAF HQ. Breadner said he would look into the possibilities, but a two-week leave after the tribulations of France was mandatory.

Kennedy decided to look up his younger brother, now stationed at Croft, south of Darlington, with 434 Squadron on Halifax III bombers. Hap was looking forward to seeing Carleton. He wanted to give him some practical advice. As an experienced combat leader and survivor of more than four hundred hours on operations, he wanted to tell Carleton not to take any foolish chances. He wanted to advise his brother to "take nothing for granted" and, above all, to exercise due care and self-discipline when flying. He arrived in the officers' mess late on the evening of September 2, and asked the strangers at the bar if they knew Flying Officer Kennedy. One asked if his brother belonged to Pilot Officer Todhunter's crew. When Hap said he

thought so, the response was: "I'm sorry, old chap, but we buried the whole crew today"

Returning from their first operational trip to Germany on August 30, Todhunter's Halifax plunged into a farmer's field from fifteen hundred feet while circling the airport to land. No precise cause of the crash was determined, but all seven aboard died instantly and were buried at Stonefall Cemetery, Harrogate. After a conversation with the station padre, Hap went for a walk in the rain and tried to grapple with the incomprehensible. As he recalled in his memoir *Black Crosses off My Wingtip*:

> For the first time in the war I was really hurt. I was overwhelmed by the sudden finality of it all. I was glad that it was raining softly because the rain would hide a grown man's tears.
>
> Getting shot down myself had not been a problem. I had treated the whole thing as an adventure. I played a game with the German soldiers. But this was completely different. This was not fair. These young lads didn't have a chance; they were killed before they learned a thing about survival …
>
> I thought of my mother. My parents would know by now. Dad, an old soldier badly wounded on the Somme in the First World War, would not say much. Long before, in Flanders Fields, he had seen the row of crosses. Mother would derive a great deal of comfort from her faith. It was appropriate that she would. Walking in the rain I was grateful for that. I was quite conscious of the fact that I had not such faith myself from which to seek solace. I thought that a spiritual existence in another life was a beautiful concept. It was hope when there was no hope. I wished that it were true for Tot's sake. But in the rain that night in Yorkshire, it was an ancient myth that I could not resolve. I only knew that my brother's life was over, abruptly terminated at twenty-one years. And I was angry that fate should have been so unkind.

When Air Marshal Breadner learned that Squadron Leader Kennedy's younger brother had died on operations, and that Hap had two tours of operations behind him, he told him that he was sending him home because he had done enough. So Hap did not get to command 401 and replace fighter ace Charlie Trainor, himself a second-tour pilot now held prisoner at Stalag Luft I in Germany. Instead, Rod Smith, Malta ace, was promoted and given command of the squadron.

EDWARDS AT ANZIO BEACHHEAD — SIX DOWNED IN ONE OP

After his stint as instructor at the Middle East gunnery school, James Edwards finally got to fly Spitfires in combat: the Mk Vb, Mk VIII and Mk IX. He later wrote that everyone should have to fly a P40 on a tour of operations before the Spitfire to "really understand and appreciate the grace and beauty of a Spitfire." The Mk IX was his favourite of all models of the famous fighter, but he also loved the Hawker Tempest for its sheer speed. He joined 417 Squadron at Canne, Termoli, Italy, did about ten ops, then was transferred to 92 Squadron RAF located north of Naples at Marcionize, where the squadron was assigned to provide air cover for the Allied landings at Anzio.

As a flight commander in 92 he flew several patrols over the beachhead in February 1944. The Germans made a determined effort to repel the amphibious forces, inflicting terrible losses on the American troops trapped on the beach. For this battle the Luftwaffe flew many sorties, and quite a few dogfights took place in the skies above.

On February 19, Edwards has probably the most dramatic aerial combat of his career, while leading a section of four Spitfires at fourteen thousand feet near Anzio. They are orbiting for a rendezvous with American B26 Marauders. The air controller reports that there are many bandits at fifteen thousand feet. The aerial battle that ensues because of this call is typical of most—fast, complex, confusing. This is how James Edwards remembers it today:

We were on patrol flying east-west at right angles to the coast. When we turned west, the Luftwaffe

are flying south parallel to the coast, so when we see this formation of Me109s and FW190s, they are at about two o'clock and above us. If they had seen us, we would have been in big trouble because there were four of us and at least twelve of them. But for whatever reason they did not, perhaps because they are flying an unusually tight formation with the 190s below, the 109s above, or their leader is inexperienced.

In any case I want to intercept them, and I turn my section towards the south and climb. I am actually a little in front of them but below, and they still do not spot us. I signal to my No. 3 and 4 to cross over to starboard. They don't move. So I make the request over the radio. I am quite concerned that they have not moved, because I want to set up the attack and I want them on my right side. To my dismay, No. 3 and 4 pull straight up into the enemy formation. It was simply finger trouble on their part; they clearly did not see any German aircraft.

I am now so close, looking up at a distance of only seventy-five yards, that I can see oil on the underbelly of the enemy fighters. Since No. 3 and 4 are now in front of me, I have to switch targets. I fire at one and it goes down, then another and it goes down, then about half of the formation do a wingover and dive. I roll with them, diving steeply, and I am pointed almost straight down at Anzio beachhead.

At this moment, the two 20mm cannons on Edwards's aircraft jam in the on position. Unable to do anything about this, he alternately applies left and right rudder to yaw his Spitfire. He can see strikes on several German fighters below him. Aware that at least one German fighter pilot did not descend, worried about where he was, Edwards pulls up in a high-G turn, with so much G force that he blacks out. When he comes to, he is at thirteen thousand feet, over Anzio beachhead, with his Spitfire pointed east, flying at a low airspeed. He now sees a 190 on his starboard side, several thousand feet below, apparently heading for home. Edwards dives and pursues this 190 at low altitude eastbound and manages to shoot it down with his machine guns.

On his 180-degree, low-altitude reversal at a mere one hundred feet above the ground, in a high-G turn with vortices streaming off his wingtips, Edwards looks down to see a Tiger tank firing its main gun, apparently at him. In the next moment, still in his steep turn, Edwards's cockpit fills with smoke. To his great surprise he hears the voice of his No. 2, a South African pilot named Johnny Gasson: "Boss, I can see right through your aircraft." This is the first time he has given thought to where No. 2 is, and is amazed that he is still hanging in there with him. The Tiger tank had hit the Spitfire right behind the cockpit, fortunately without destroying anything vital.

Back on the ground, the 92 Squadron intelligence officer (IO) has to make some sense out of all that has taken place. Unfortunately, No. 3 and 4 have landed and reported nil contact to the IO. Since No. 2 did not witness all the shooting that had taken place, he cannot corroborate what Edwards is claiming. To further complicate the decision, the US Army telephones to say that six German fighters have crashed in their sector. They ask: "Do you fellows know anything about that?"

The commanding officer of 92 Squadron adjudicates the combat and decides arbitrarily to assign three of the six enemy machines downed at Anzio to the squadron, without attribution to any pilot. Edwards is credited with two destroyed and one damaged, but is not pleased at all. Since he was the only shooter on this sortie, who else could have downed the six machines? Had he been credited it would have set a record for most aerial victories in a single sortie by one RCAF fighter pilot in the entire war.

After taking command of 274 Squadron in March 1944, Edwards flew with them briefly in Italy and then had a forced landing on a mountaintop due to a bad glycol leak. He has no memory of the forced landing, as he was catapulted out of the cockpit on touchdown and knocked unconscious. When he regained consciousness he was looking into the face of a woman surrounded by what seemed to be a cloak. For a moment, he imagined that God had decided it was time, and he was looking at the face of an angel. Edwards had crashed near a religious centre on the mountainside, and the face he woke to was that of a nun in a habit. He eventually walked his way back to 274, head bandaged, right eye swollen shut, and flew some further sorties with his head still bandaged up.

His squadron was repatriated back to Britain for D-Day, along with 229 and 80 Squadrons, to form a Spitfire Wing at Hornchurch. Edwards led on two ops on D-Day and stayed with 274 when it converted to the Tempest, at that point in the war being assigned to V1 buzz bomb work because it was so fast.

* * *

Profile – DAVID GOLDBERG
Born – March 20, 1917, Hamilton, ON
Father – Harry Goldberg, owner/manager King George Hotel, Hamilton
Mother – Sophia Gerstein
Decorations & Medals – DFC, CD
Degrees & Awards – BS in Business Administration, Boston, 1939, LLB, QC, LSM
Post-war occupation – Lawyer, Hamilton; Group Captain, RCAF Auxiliary
Marital Status – Wife Alice Dickey, daughter Mary
Hobbies – "None at all"

Group Captain David Goldberg, age eighty-eight, lives four blocks from his childhood home in Hamilton, Ontario, with his wife, Alice, and daughter, Mary. He has a self-deprecating sense of humour, referring to himself as "an old crock." He retired from the business of commercial law at eighty-two, sixty years after his graduation from Boston University with a bachelor of science in business administration. When the war broke out he immediately returned home from Boston and attempted to get into the army as an officer but they wouldn't take him. He was told that he had to go on a waiting list. So he went to the RCAF recruiting centre and was immediately sworn in. He has immense fondness for the military system that nurtured him as a young pilot, saying:

> The RCAF system of training was sensible, orderly, remarkably sound … I have come across nothing to equal it since in my life … I joined as an AC2 in the fall of 1940 and went to Manning Pool in Toronto, to the "bullpen" at the CNE Grounds … The RCAF knew from nothing in those days and was thinly spread. We had double-decker bunks, and no privacy. But to me this was all new; the best time in my life, I enjoyed it … and most of the men I met were a great bunch of guys.

Group Captain Goldberg paused for a moment, and then added with a smile, "You know, it is amazing to me how few bastards there were in the RCAF."

When David was growing up in Hamilton, there was no Jewish enclave or neighbourhood, and he had a mixture of friends of different religious backgrounds and from all walks of life. In his memory it was a happy childhood, full of variety. If on rare occasions anyone referred to him as "a dirty Jew," they immediately found out that David Goldberg was good with his fists; as he says "I learned how to fight!" His father, Harry, who had come over from Poland as a small boy and ended up working many years in the hotel trade, owned the King George Hotel on MacNab at Market. He married Sophia Gerstein when he was almost forty and they had three sons, David, Irwin and William, and one daughter, Ruth.

David's only childhood flying was a $5 ride in a seaplane at Lake Placid, New York, which he remembers as "utterly thrilling." When he graduated from SFTS at Saskatoon in February 1941, he had done well in his training and was immediately commissioned, being assigned serial number J4242. As he points out, he had little idea what commissioning entailed: "I didn't know, for example, that officers had to buy their own uniforms." He was selected to instruct and says:

I was disappointed, the most disappointed person in the whole world. But I later became a testing officer, and it was a great education. I hate to think what I would have been without all that. But I wanted to go overseas and I was asked to do some exhibition flying at Dunnville [Ontario]. Well, I did stunts and then some, and was called before the group captain. He banned me to the satellite substation at Welland. However, they relented and I went overseas on *Empress of Scotland*, no convoy, one ship, in December 1942, crossing alone to Greenock, Scotland.

Courtesy of the David Goldberg Collection

David Goldberg during the Second World War

Courtesy of the Wayne Ralph Collection

David Goldberg at his Hamilton home in 2002.

I checked out on the Miles Master at the AFU [Advanced Flying Unit] at Turnhill, then Eshott for OTU on Spitfires. When I did my gunnery training I was amazed at how few of my shots hit the drogue. I was awful, but it was a good education. I joined 416 Squadron in the summer of 1943, and was hardly ever in a scrap. In the early days I had to be told that the aircraft off in the distance was an enemy. I don't believe I fired my guns in my eighty ops …

On my eightieth I was shot down by ground flak at low altitude over an airfield in France near St André. It was March 8th, 1944. I picked a field, crash-landed, got out, not a scratch. I knew I didn't want to be captured, so I started running towards the trees, bumped into a chap. 'Where are the Germans?' I asked. I started to run where he told me to, and evaded for two days … I was hungry and tired … I walked all night, in daytime hid in any shelter. It was colder than hell; the electric suits [we wore in the Spitfire] were not worth a damn. I decided to walk northeast, though that made no sense, yet it worked! I approached an old farmer, he was wonderful, took me into his house, gave me a most wonderful meal, eggs, bread, wine, insisted that I stay in his bed.

David was taken to Paris by the French underground and waited there several weeks, meeting up with other evading flyers, including Gordon Crosby, a Typhoon pilot. They needed to get out of France through Spain to Gibraltar. A woman who was in the French underground took the flyers to a station in Paris. David recalls his amazement at being a fugitive on the run:

I see all the Germans walking around like we had seen in the movies; there were wanted posters on the walls. We (there was some thirty in all, but only five were flyers, others being agents and miscellaneous characters needing to leave France) travelled by train to Toulouse. We stayed for about ten days in the foothills of the Pyrenees. We started out across the Pyrenees but the trip was aggravated by bad weather and a guide who disappeared after going off for assistance. We crossed over through Andorra [a small country

between France and Spain]. Many of our party were in bad shape, having been ambushed on a previous attempt. Gordon Crosby, being a geologist, knew we were lost, he knew we were not at the border. We could see catastrophe ahead, we had no food, and bad weather had driven us into a cave. So seven of us decided we were going to take a crack at it on our own, with the boy who had been assisting the now-missing guide. Well, we got into Spain, and the boy got us to the British Consulate … after a week in Barcelona we were taken to the British Embassy in Madrid, from where we were taken to Gibraltar.

Two months after being shot down, David wanted to get word to his family that he was alive. He was strolling along a street in Gibraltar, much relieved to have made it, and spotted a British wireless office. His brother Irwin was an engineering officer at the RCAF's No. 6 Bomber Group, and he sent him a telegram, with no address, no details, just a short message: "Dave is on The Rock."

After being debriefed in England, Goldberg was sent home to Canada for thirty days' leave. He had worries that he might never fly again operationally; the RAF did not allow aircrew back on ops if they had used the French underground escape system. Their knowledge could compromise others should they be captured again by the Germans. The RCAF HQ in Ottawa, however, said he could fly in another theatre; where did he want to go? The invasion of Italy was underway, so the RCAF said he could join 417, the only RCAF squadron in the Desert Air Force, stationed at Fano, Italy.

When Goldberg arrived there, Sandy Kallio was 417's commanding officer. The main duty of the Mk VIII Spitfire they flew was ground attack and close air support to the army advancing north. It was rare to see a German fighter aircraft at this point in the war in Italy, and there were few opportunities to dogfight with the Mk VIII. Goldberg completed 155 ops with 417; within a few months he was promoted to squadron leader, taking command of the unit in November 1944. He recollects that the squadron was his life, and combat flying was the centre of his whole existence:

I never took holidays, so one day I went to Rome. It was a great disappointment, and

I didn't take leave again. There is some luck to the whole thing [of surviving combat]. I never had a malfunction of an engine, other than due to enemy action … it was always a challenge, even coming in for a landing was a challenge. You had to have all your wits about you, particularly if you were anxious to make a good landing.

We did not have a fixed number of trips at 417, but we took people off ops when we thought it was prudent to take them off, and we never told someone in advance. Most people were relieved when you told them it was over.

The ground crew were the unsung heroes, particularly as our guys had no hangars; they worked outside in all kinds of weather. It was amazing what they accomplished for us in those conditions.

Goldberg was at Padua, Italy, when the war ended. Some of the targets he had attacked were in Yugoslavia, and the airfield at Padua was just thirty minutes by Spitfire from Aviano. It was from the North Atlantic Treaty Organization (NATO) base at Aviano that, in the 1990s, Canadian Forces F18s flew missions into Kosovo—the former autonomous province within Yugoslavia that had come under Serbian control.

David Goldberg says that when peace was announced in 1945, "it was a quiet affair at 417. We did not party." He claims, with a chuckle, that he was the only Spitfire pilot of the RCAF who got a gong without shooting down a single aircraft. His citation for the DFC praises his leadership, stating in part:

During his 3½ months service with this Wing [No.244 Wing, Desert Air Force] he has shown outstanding courage and skill as a fighter-bomber leader. He took command of the squadron at a time when it was very deficient of experienced leaders, and by his magnificent example, enthusiasm, gallantry and cheerfulness has kept the squadron operational record on the top line. He has personally completed 78 fighter-bomber sorties since August, practically always in the face of considerable flak opposition, which, in spite of his previous bad experience, he coolly ignores in pressing home his attack.

When the war ended and David came back to Canada, it was a major adjustment for him, and he says:

I was lost, like a lot of people, I really was … everything was uneventful after all we had gone through. You had to start worrying about how to make a living … it was hard to realize it was over … I went to law school, to Osgoode Hall in Toronto … I never went with a big firm, I practised commercial law. I served with the Auxiliary Wing, RCAF, in Hamilton, and was officer in charge of flying. We flew Vampires, but I did less and less flying … age takes care of these things, you know.

Courtesy of the Airforce Magazine Collection

Spitfires of 417 Squadron in Italy.

Photo taken by Brick Bradford in his Spitfire at 10,000 feet above the Hoogley River in the city of Calcutta, India. Boats can be seen in the river, and at the top the large swimming pool of the Calcutta Swimming Club.

THE WORLD OF THE UNARMED PHOTOGRAPHIC RECONNAISSANCE PILOT

Of all the uses for fighter aircraft in the Second World War, one of the most successful and sophisticated was photographic reconnaissance. The fighters perhaps most famous for this work were the Spitfire, the Mosquito and the Mustang. Other types of aircraft saw service, including the Typhoon and the Lockheed P38 Lightning. Antoine de Saint-Exupéry, the renowned French author (*The Little Prince*; *Wind, Sand and Stars*) and pilot, disappeared on a photo reconnaissance op in a P38 on July 31, 1944. He was on a flight from Bastia near Algiers, North Africa, to Lyon, France. Recent evidence suggests his P38 lies at the bottom of the Mediterranean off Marseilles, possibly shot down by a Luftwaffe fighter pilot, but perhaps not. The day he went missing his reconnaissance squadron recorded a characteristic diary entry: "Pilot did not return and is presumed lost."

In a similar manner a brilliantly competent, flamboyantly independent thinker named Wing Commander Adrian Warburton, DSO and Bar, DFC and Bar, DFC (US), disappeared on a photo op out of Malta after years of successful photography and occasional scraps with enemy fighters. This was the most common kind of ending for recon pilots: no radio transmission, no wreckage, no search party, a death unconfirmed and without details, an unknown grave.

More than any other pilot, the specialist in photo reconnaissance worked alone. I have interviewed two Spitfire photo reconnaissance pilots and they tell similar stories of their independence from many of the aggravations of operational life.

When he went into the RCAF recruiting centre, John William "Brick" Bradford was deemed to be too short at five feet, four inches, until he showed them his pilot's licence. They promptly made him a flying instructor. After several years of instructing, Warrant Officer First Class Bradford was offered his choice of any kind of fighter aircraft upon his arrival in Britain. He had the great good fortune, in his mind, to drink with a photo reconnaissance pilot in the Crackers Club shortly after getting off his ship. This adviser, whose name is unrecorded, enthused to Brick about the best job in the air force. Why was it the best? Well, you worked alone, planned your own trips, and were the complete master of your own domain, accountable only for bringing back photographs.

Profile – JOHN WILLIAM "BRICK" BRADFORD

Born – May 6, 1920, Hamilton, ON

Father – William Ashford Bradford, jeweller

Mother – Alma Victoria Carpenter, United Empire Loyalist

Decorations & Medals – DFC

Post-war occupation – Airline pilot, KLM, ONA; Corporate pilot, McNamara Const, Sholl Investments; Cargo pilot, Morningstar Air Express; retired from commercial flying at age 77

Marital status – Wife Mary Kathleen Kirkpatrick, sons John Scott and David Andrew

Hobbies – Aviation, coin collecting

At the suggestion of this pilot in a London bar, Bradford asked for the best job in the air force and got it, but in Southeast Asia.

Unlike Bradford, William Keir "Bill" Carr was not offered any choice; he simply did what he was told and was happy to do so. In June 1943, with dreadful weather between RAF Portreath, England, and the Middle East, Carr was released by the dispatcher to fly alone, non-stop, to Gibraltar in his

At No. 2 SFTS, Uplands, July 1942, famous First World War ace Air Marshal Billy Bishop, VC, DSO and Bar, MC, DFC, pins pilot's wings on nineteen-year-old Bill Carr, of Grand Bank, Newfoundland.

brand new Spitfire PR Mk XI. All the other twin-engine aircraft were staying on the ground because the weather was deemed too challenging for them, but Carr, aged twenty, climbed from a foggy airfield up through twenty-nine thousand feet of cloud. He set course for Spain and three hours and fifteen minutes later landed at Gibraltar.

After arguing his way past the operations officer, who had no record of him, he rested and went onwards to Malta, there to be interviewed by the legendary Warburton. After a short conversation, he deemed Bill acceptable as a member of 683 Squadron RAF. Warburton had absolute authority to accept or reject pilots. What Carr saw outside the squadron tent—wicked heat, yellow soil and a brilliant yellow sun—was nothing like his birthplace in Grand Bank, Newfoundland.

Profile – WILLIAM KEIR CARR

Born – March 17, 1923, Grand Bank, NF

Father – Percy Lee Carr, manager with the Bank of Nova Scotia; CEO, Samuel Harris Export Company, later renamed Grand Banks Fisheries Limited; died in 1943

Mother – Eleanor Harris, BA (Hons), 1913, Mount Allison, RN in pediatrics (Massachusetts General Hospital, Boston)

Decorations & Medals – CMM, DFC, OStJ, CD with 4 Clasps, CMLJ, US Legion of Merit

Degrees & Awards – BA, BSc; member, Canada's Aviation Hall of Fame

Post-war occupation – Air force officer, Lieutenant General, RCAF/CAF; VP International Marketing, Canadair, Bombardier

Marital status – Wife Elaine Mulligan; daughter Virginia; sons David (deceased) and Peter

Hobbies – Woodworking, golf, fly fishing

Bill Carr's maternal grandfather, Samuel Harris, had a Grade 6 education and vowed that none of his children would be similarly deprived. He was the founder of the Samuel Harris Export Company, a shipping empire based in Grand Bank, Newfoundland, that at its peak had some thirty-two schooners, and his sons and daughters were educated abroad. Bill's mother, Eleanor Harris, received her honours BA from Mount Allison University in Sackville, New Brunswick, in 1913 and her RN in pediatrics from Massachusetts General Hospital in Boston; her brother became a medical doctor. She married Percy Carr, a bank manager born in Prince Edward Island and raised in New Brunswick, and had six children: a daughter, Eleanor, who grew up to become the first ordained female United Church of Canada minister and a missionary in Africa; and five sons, George, Bill, Bob, Hugh and Jim. They grew up on Newfoundland's south shore, the children of one of several well-to-do merchant families typical of that region of the island.

Carr graduated at age eighteen with his BA from Mount Allison; his brother George at nineteen already had an engineering degree from the University of New Brunswick. Bill joined the Canadian Officer Training Corps (COTC) at the university, in part for the money. He also sold or rented Remington typewriters at school to make extra cash. In the spring of 1941, he and a friend went down to the RCAF recruiting centre at Sackville. The friend was not accepted. Bill was, but the recruiting officer insisted that he finish his exams before joining. Bill's brothers George and Bob both trained as air gunners with the RCAF later in the war, but neither saw overseas service.

On seeing him off overseas, Bill's mother uttered the immortal cautionary advice: "Now, Billy, you fly low and slow." Both parents were proud that their son had joined up, as there was a tradition of military duty in time of war in the family. It was simply expected. After crossing the Atlantic Ocean on *Queen Elizabeth* out of New York, Carr languished in Bournemouth, England, for a period, but then took his photo reconnaissance training on Spitfires at No. 9 Operational Training Unit (OTU) at Dyce, Aberdeen, Scotland. Lord Douglas M.A. Hamilton was the wing commander in charge at the OTU. Bill then went onwards to RAF Station Benson, which was near Oxford and commanded by Schneider Tro-

phy winner Air Commodore (later Air Chief Marshal Sir) John Boothman. Bill did a couple of milk runs over the coast of France with 542 Squadron, and then was assigned a new Spitfire PR Mk XI. He was told to check it out thoroughly, and then fly it to 683 Squadron in Malta. No other advice was forthcoming; he was expected to make his own plans.

As Pilot Officer Carr of the RCAF serving in an RAF squadron, he received 13 shillings, 6 pence a day. His monthly pay was $187, at a time when a British pound was worth $4.87. The balance of his pay was put in a bank account. This customary practice meant that Canadians received no more month to month than their underpaid British or Canadian counterparts who had joined the RAF directly.

The Spitfire Mk XI had no armament; the space where the guns and ammunition were installed on other models of Spitfires was replaced by fuel. This model of Spitfire was a joy to fly—"the Cadillac of that unmatched breed," as Carr recalls. On one occasion he took his Mk XI up to 49,000 feet over Malta, and routinely operated between thirty thousand to forty thousand feet, flying to targets hundreds of miles behind enemy lines, on flights that sometimes took more than five hours. The closest he came to being shot down was by a box barrage over Perugia, Italy, where anti-aircraft gunners placed rounds below, above, behind and in front of his aircraft. Shrapnel penetrated from below, shredded the parachute on which he was sitting, and sliced a nick in his bum, drawing blood. He could not bail out, yet the engine oil pressure and temperature were off the clock. He set up a shallow descent, expecting that the Merlin would seize at any moment, and made it back to a safe landing.

No Luftwaffe fighter pilot ever damaged his plane, but he was once followed by an Me262 jet over Munich at thirty-one thousand feet. Bill did not know that the Germans had jet aircraft capable of overtaking a Spitfire at any speed or altitude. He was unable to escape by climbing to forty thousand feet, and a rapid dive to the deck did not work either. The German pilot did not attack; his Me262 was probably an unarmed experimental prototype. Carr dropped to a few feet above the terrain to make himself a difficult target as he escaped through the Brenner Pass between Austria and Italy. The intelligence officer had been briefed on this secret German aircraft, but it was not the policy to tell pilots about it because they might blab about it to their German captors.

Many challenges face the reconnaissance pilot, and Carr has written that boredom and overconfidence sometimes led to fatal accidents—for example, when a pilot finishing his tour wanted to perform an impromptu air show, or was so self-assured that he fatally botched a routine landing on the unforgiving terrain of Malta. The loneliness of the work meant that bonding on the ground was not as common as in a fighting squadron. If you disappeared on an op but made it home the next day, you might find that your mates had already divided your personal belongings and resented your wanting them back.

One challenge which Bill Carr and Brick Bradford have both noted is bladder control on long flights. Brick recalls an occasion when, having been airborne for several hours, he was obliged to urinate in the cockpit. Some of the yellow liquid froze to the cockpit instruments, including the compass, and had to be scraped away so Brick could navigate home. In Bill's case, he was diverted to the Anzio beaches to photograph the amphibious landing. When he landed at San Severo, Italy, the newspaper reporters were waiting to interview him about what he had seen. Bill was reluctant to get out of the cockpit because he had urinated in his flying suit and over his seat parachute. He might have got away with them not knowing except for an insistent photographer who wanted a hero shot, and an obliging mechanic who decided he was going to carry the hero's parachute, soaked in urine.

Not too long after arriving in Malta, Bill Carr was promoted to acting flight lieutenant in charge of "A" Flight of 683 Squadron, which had ten pilots, seven of them Canadians. "A" Flight was detached from 683 to San Severo; from that airfield its pilots excelled at bringing back great photographs during the Italian campaign. Bill was awarded the Distinguished Flying Cross and his citation observed that he had displayed

most outstanding skill, enthusiasm and dogged determination on all operational missions. His own achievements were worthy of the highest praise in that every one of his missions lacked nothing in so much as determination and accuracy were concerned. He displayed such a fine example that all the pilots in his Flight not only showed the greatest enthusiasm for their work, but also produced results of the greatest accuracy, thereby contributing much towards the success of the intensive programme of destruction by Desert Air Force to German lines of communication in Italy, prior to the advance to Florence from Cassino.

In addition to this, Flight Lieutenant Carr's flight flew all air cover for the 8th Army prior to the attacks on the Gothic Line. The accuracy of the work by this Flight was responsible to a great degree for the successes of the 8th Army.

For his rank, Flight Lieutenant Carr is outstanding, and for his achievements whilst serving with this force I strongly recommend him for an award of the Distinguished Flying Cross.

Brick Bradford received his DFC for a year of operations with 681 Squadron RAF and a particularly hairy op to a romantic-sounding place called the Salween Gorge. He recalls:

They wanted a picture of this bridge over the gorge. It had not been photographed for months, but supposedly had been bombed in the spring. The bridge was between Tengchung and Paoshan [China], and it was critical to the Japanese supply line for their campaign in Burma. The Salween River flows out from Tibet south and east along the spine between Thailand and Burma [today contentiously also known as Myanmar], exiting into the Andaman Sea at Moulmein. It was the hairiest flight of my career and took place on June 7th, '44, out of my home station of Alipore on the south side of Calcutta.

I was above cloud at thirty thousand feet, so I had to come down through a hole to fourteen thousand feet to photograph the bridge. I found the bridge visually, photographed it, and then realized that I had to head home from low altitude, burning four times as much fuel in the climb than in cruise. There had been thunderstorms I had dodged going to the target, and coming home I penetrated a monsoon thunderstorm, lost my artificial horizon due to turbulence, and

Wing Commander Fred D. Proctor, DFC, CO of 681, chats with Brick Bradford (in cockpit).

was flying on the turn and slip indicator without an airspeed indicator or altimeter because I was all iced up. I was using the sound of the slipstream to determine my pitch angle and speed. Eventually, abandoning all thought of fuel economy, I climbed at full power to get above, popping out between two saddleback thunderheads at forty-two thousand feet. I now had thirty gallons of fuel remaining, and didn't know where I was. But I was saved when I recognized the sun glinting off the mouth of the Ganges River between a break in the clouds. I now knew I was far past my refuelling stop. I checked my fingernails for lack of oxygen, and started down.

When I landed empty of fuel, and had a debriefing, Group Captain Bill Wise, officer commanding of RAF Element Photo Reconnaissance Force, listened in. I later overheard Wise muttering to the intelligence officer: "The bloody fool could have killed himself." Wise did not realize, perhaps, that I had over two thousand instructional hours and could fly well on instruments, which he probably couldn't. I dismissed the disparaging comment from my mind with the satisfaction of knowing that I had gotten the pictures of the bridge.

After 269 hours of operations, in April 1945, Bradford finished his tour. Wise strongly endorsed Wing Commander Proctor's citation for the DFC, which read:

This officer has carried out 53 high and low level photographic reconnaissance sorties over enemy-occupied Burma since April 1944. He has at all times, even in the worst possible monsoon weather conditions, shown outstanding determination, tenacity and courage to bring back the required photographs which have given invaluable information.

Flying Officer J.W. Bradford is a born pilot and by his excellent personal example of perseverance and devotion to duty he has set a very high standard, in his capacity as Flight Commander, which has always been a great source of inspiration to his fellow pilots. He has always been the first to volunteer for any task involving more danger or flying skill than is normal, and has carried out the special sorties in a most distinguished manner. Flying Officer Bradford is a most brave and gallant officer.

Both Carr and Bradford stayed in aviation, the former in the military and the latter in commercial airlines and corporate aviation. At the end of his military career, Lieutenant General Bill Carr was commander of Air Command and later became vice-president of international marketing for Bombardier. Brick Brad-

One of the Spitfires Bradford flew on operations in India is now on display at the USAF Wright Patterson Museum in Dayton, Ohio.

Courtesy of the John "Brick" Bradford Collection

ford, among many flying positions, was chief pilot of training for Overseas National Airways. He did not stop flying commercially until age seventy-seven. At that age he was flying solo instrument flight rules (IFR) nighttime cargo operations in a Cessna Caravan turboprop for the FedEx Corporation. A story in the company magazine about FedEx's oldest pilot brought his career to a close, after the corporation's CEO realized to his horror that he was legally responsible for a former Second World War photo reconnaissance pilot flying alone at night. As Brick observed to the author, "Truth to tell, I have been a loner all my life, which is why photo reconnaissance in the war and solo flying in a cargo aircraft suited me so well."

John "Brick" Bradford in retirement at age eighty-one.

Hurricane IIC in flight.

CANADIANS IN THE RAF AND FLEET AIR ARM, 1939–40

At the outbreak of the Second World War, more Canadians were flying and serving with the Royal Air Force in Britain than with the Royal Canadian Air Force in Canada. Historian and author Hugh Halliday estimates from his studies that more than 1,800 Canadians of all ranks were with the RAF. More than 750 were killed in action or died, and more than 400 were decorated. During the Depression, RCAF training was limited and few pilots received their wings. Moreover, the educational standard for acceptance as a pilot in the RCAF was higher than the RAF and the Royal Navy Fleet Air Arm. The RAF offered medically fit young men with a high-school education a chance for a short-service commission and a career as a flyer. What a great adventure it was for a nineteen-year-old Canadian to cross the ocean, be accepted on an almost equal footing by the British, receive those coveted wings and fly state-of-the-art 1930s fighters and bombers. The RCAF could offer nothing like it.

In addition to the flyers, many fifteen- to seventeen-year olds from Canada enlisted to become mechanics, referred to according to their speciality as fitters, riggers or armourers. These apprentices received three years of training in Buckinghamshire at Halton's No. 1 School of Technical Training. They graduated from the school with the rank of aircraftman first class (AC1) or leading aircraftman (LAC), and were typically known as "Halton brats" or "Trenchard's brats," the latter in honour of the father of the RAF, Marshal of the Royal Air Force Hugh "Boom" Trenchard, who founded the apprenticeship scheme in the 1920s. Two of the interviewees for this book, Squadron Leader Bill Cartwright and David Roberts, are graduates of the No. 1 School at Halton.

Very few of those Depression-era Canadians who crossed the Atlantic Ocean by ship to serve are still with us in 2005. Because they went abroad in peacetime, and were the first Canadians to train for war, they were in the front lines in 1939 and 1940. They served in England, in France, in Norway, in the Mediterranean theatre and the Western Desert. The first fighter aces of Canadian birth were RAF personnel; they also were the first to be decorated, as well as the first from our country to die in battle.

Profile – WILLIAM LIDSTONE MCKNIGHT
Born – Nov 18, 1918, Edmonton, AB
Died – Jan 12, 1941, in the English Channel
Father – "Mac" McKnight, buyer for a grocery company
Mother – Died circa 1920s; stepmother Hazel was from Nanton, AB; brother Raymond
Decorations & Medals – DFC and Bar
Marital status – Unmarried

One of the most distinguished aces of that early period, William Lidstone "Willie" McKnight, was born in Edmonton and grew up in Calgary, Alberta. He had enlisted in February 1939 and started flight training in England at No. 6 Flying Training School (FTS), Little Rissington, Bourton-on-the-Water, Cheltenham, in late April. McKnight's letters to friends back home (held by Library and Archives Canada in Ottawa) reveal a self-confident, argumentative scrapper, sure of himself and his flying abilities and forthright in his opinions of those around him. Typical of many future fighter pilots, he conflicted with RAF authority. Despite or because of his obvious potential, he lacked the appropriate humility expected of a novice. He was confined to barracks for fourteen days at least twice, and he and a classmate were put on open arrest for "being perpetrators of a riot."

Willie McKnight had left behind a girlfriend named Marian in Alberta whom, in his own opinion, he had treated badly and whom he missed very much. Even though she might never see him again or even want to talk to him, Willie believed that he was changing and hinted in a letter home that perhaps Marian, with whom he had had a tumultuous relationship, would approve of the new person he was becoming.

After September 1939, life became much more serious for McKnight and his classmates. The RAF stopped being akin to a flying club and went on a seven-day-a-week work schedule that allowed limited sleep, bad food, and stomach upsets. The latter were caused by the bad food to which the Canadian fellows were more susceptible, or so McKnight declared.

In November he arrived at 242 Squadron, a newly formed, predominantly Canadian-staffed RAF squadron commanded by an RCAF squadron leader on exchange with the RAF. During the quiet period of the so-called Phony War, 242 trained for operations, not flying sorties until March 1940 and not fighting its first successful battles until May 1940 in the skies of France.

McKnight scored the first victory for 242 Squadron on May 19 over Cambrai, France, in a region much disputed by Canadian fighter pilots during the First World War. All through the Battle of France and the Battle of Britain, he demonstrated again and again his natural talent for aerial combat, achieving about eighteen victories flying a Hurricane. He became an ace with five victories in a mere ten days, between May 19 and 29. His friendly rivals for top score at 242 were, first, Stan Turner, and then, with his arrival to command 242 on June 20, Squadron Leader Douglas Bader.

Bader was quoted in *Reach for the Sky* (Paul Brickhill's biography of Bader) as saying that McKnight was a great fighter pilot, with "flinty eyes." In Bader's opinion, he was characteristically Canadian: fearless and aggressive. Bader recalled that McKnight had a taste for romantic music, and insisted on playing and replaying his large collection of Bing Crosby records in the evenings in the officers' mess.

There is no doubt that the realities of war, combined with his drive to excel, aged Willie in a few burning months. Operations in France and over the English Channel eliminated his lighthearted banter in letters home. In February 1940 he complained to H.F. "Mike" Pegler of 1221 5th St. in Calgary about night formation flying in the Hurricane:

It's the most hair-raising thing I've ever done. Before the war you could use the navigation lights of the leader as a mark to formate on but as we're not allowed to use navigation lights we have to use the exhaust flames as a guide. Most of us have grown half a head of grey hair since we started and we hope we never have to do it again once we've got it "buttoned up" ... I've been made a section leader which means I lead one formation of three machines in the flight (there are six in a flight) and it sure is good fun except I'm not so keen on the responsibility. It's alright but I'd sooner be No. 2 in a formation any day where you've got the best position and only half the responsibility.

The first time that McKnight saw a corpse up close was at RAF Station Church Fenton, Tadcaster, Yorkshire:

We had a rather unfortunate accident here the other day—one of our new Canadian corporals was leaning against the wing of one of the machines when an armourer inside the cockpit pushed the gun tit and blew the top of his head off. It sure made a mess of him, so now they've fitted a few more safety devices to our remote control button just to make it harder for us. Every time some dumb airman pulls a trick like that they make it harder for the pilot to use the guns when he needs them. I was the first officer around after the accident and got one perfectly good tunic spoilt with blood and brains splashed all over it.

McKnight's letter is by no means unique. Young men writing letters home from the war often had an impulse to shock. The same can be seen in letters of pilots in the First World War. It likely is a method to dissipate the horror of being a witness to wartime events.

In the few weeks of the Battle of France, McKnight lost twenty-seven pounds. He recounts in a letter to his childhood friend Mike Pegler that "I almost looked like an overgrown kid when we arrived back in England." In addition to fighting, McKnight found time to have a short affair with a young woman who had escaped Paris ahead of the German army and, like thousands, was a refugee on the run to an unknown future:

The brass hats pulled out so fast we all had our own private cars. This girl and I, her name was M_____, took a flat in Nantes and had a hell of a time for about two weeks. All the boys kept dropping in every night and we'd all B.S. and listen to the radio and eat then bog off to bed (after the lads had gone). It was sure marvellous and I certainly miss it now—I tried to smuggle the girl back on one of our bombing planes but one of the few big noises left in France caught me and raised merry hell. It was too bad because she was certainly one first class femme—she had been to university and was a modiste until the Hun started to-ward Paris when she had to evacuate and then I ran into her. Oh well, I suppose I must have been fated for a bachelor—I can't fall in love anymore like I used to; I get all worked up for about an hour then I just lose interest.

After the battles in France, he was admitted to hospital in July 1940 for a rest. While recuperating he wrote:

I've been sick in bed for four days now and today is the first day I've been allowed to do anything at all and the MO even put a time limit to writing letters. Everything seemed to go wrong with me all at the same time, stom-ach, ears, throat, eyes, etc., or in other words I was more or less useless to anyone. The Doc says it was almost two months of no sleep and less food that did it then sort of coming back to a civilized life just floored my system and I was left sucking a hind tit. I should be out in another four or five days though I hope so as the "Blitz" is just starting again and I've got

to keep Turner from hogging all the fun. We two are the high scorers in the squadron so far, having got twenty-three between us—nine for Stan and fourteen for me—as we have a pretty keen competition going on and neither one of us likes to be off duty when the other one is on and we're both afraid we'll miss a chance to get something … It's a funny thing this fighting in the air, before you actually start or see any of the Hun you're as nervous and scared as hell but as soon as everything starts you're too busy to be afraid or worried. We've had several fights with Colonel Schumacher's squadron—its sup-posed to be in the same class as Richthofen's was in the last do—and I don't mind saying that they're about the finest pilots I've ever met … some bloke who must be the personal ace of the Luftwaffe jumped me and succeeded in shoot-ing away nearly all the machine except where I was sitting before I managed to dive into a cloud. Well anyway after we got home (three out of five) we found out that about eight Jerry squadrons had pooled their resources for the morning and we'd tried to jump about eighty machines. We laugh like hell when we think of it now but it wasn't so funny then … We've only got five of the original twenty-two pilots in the squadron left now and those of us who are left aren't quite the same blokes as before. Its peculiar but war seems to make you older and quieter and change your views a lot in life—you also find out who are the blokes worth knowing and who aren't and I haven't met one yet who wasn't worth knowing.

By September 1940, now with a DFC and Bar, Willie had developed a sophisticated insight into how war had changed him inside and also separated him from his past. It had mutated him into a war-rior with little connection to what he left behind in Alberta. He mused about his future:

I suppose I shall remain here until the end or until the other end. I've got so used to the thrill and the, I don't know how to express it, final feeling of victory that I'd feel lost and bored by a quiet life again. This war business changes people a lot and I'm sure you'd never believe that people were one and the same if you meet them again after a year or so's constant "dicing with death."

On January 12, 1941, Willie McKnight went missing near Gravelines while on a low-level "Rhubarb" attacking a German E-boat in the Channel. Rhubarbs were typically two pilots, two aircraft, flying at low altitude and high speed to coastal areas of France or Belgium looking for targets of opportunity. Rhubarbs were dangerous and not every fighter pilot did them (as one veteran observed to the author, "It appealed to pilots light on brains and heavy on courage"). Willie and his wingman, Marvin Brown, were fired on by very accurate anti-aircraft gunners, and then apparently bounced by an Me109. McKnight and Brown were separated. Brown made it home; McKnight disappeared. His body was never found, and the circumstances of his death are uncertain. We don't know whether he was killed by a flak gunner or one of the Luftwaffe's finest aces, the kind Willie wrote about in his letter to Pegler. Had he lived McKnight might very well have been Canada's highest-scoring fighter pilot of the Second World War. Today, a boulevard near the airport in Calgary is named for him.

* * *

Profile – ARTHUR HENRY DEACON
Born – July 22, 1916, Invermay, SK
Father – George Henry Woodford Deacon, postmaster, hardware store owner
Mother – Ruth Symmonds
Decorations & Medals – Golden Jubilee Medal
Post-war occupation – Hardware store and gas station owner
Marital status – Wife Geraldine O'Brien of Kuroki, SK; sons Dennis, Brian and James; daughter Chally
Hobbies – Hunting and fishing

One of Willie McKnight's friends at 242 was Arthur Deacon, who before the war had worked as a labourer at the Chicago airport to pay for flying lessons with a barnstormer named Pierce O'Carroll. When barnstorming ended in Chicago one fall, Pierce asked Art

to drive a car to Miami for him. Once in Miami, Art washed dishes to finance his flying training.

A United Church minister named Reverend Bowles of Invermay, Saskatchewan, had paid $2.00 for Art's first flight in an aircraft and ignited his love affair with aviation. Art had started out life in Invermay because his father, George Deacon, had come over from Ireland to visit his brother Fred who was homesteading ten miles south of the Prairie community. George stayed and became postmaster and owner of the hardware store, marrying Ruth Symmonds, daughter of the town's druggist. Art was born in July 1916, the first boy following two girls, Florence and Aileen. He attended Invermay High School and played the saxophone with the Invermay Boys Band.

It was difficult funding his own flying training, so when the RAF agreed to pay his passage to Britain in January 1939, Art jumped at the chance and travelled on SS *Montclair*. First, while still a civilian, he qualified on Tiger Moths at Prestwick, Scotland. Then he was sent to Uxbridge, England, for formal induction into the RAF, then onwards to the FTS at Brize Norton to train on Airspeed Oxfords. Like McKnight, he finished his training as the war broke out. He arrived along with eleven other Canadians at Church Fenton in Yorkshire on November 6, 1939, to join 242 (Canadian) Squadron.

A year later, 242 had a fine combat record—albeit with a casualty rate near 75 per cent—but its first few months were not always happy. It was a squadron that had been created more for propaganda and public relations than operational needs, at a time when the RCAF could not offer Britain even one properly trained and equipped day fighter squadron. The idea for such a squadron got its start in the early stages of Canadian-British negotiations about the British Commonwealth Air Training Plan (BCATP).

It did not really gain momentum until the British Foreign Office realized the propaganda value of a Canadian-designated unit of the RAF fighting in France for the French people; the Foreign Office hoped that as many French Canadians as possible could serve in such a squadron. The political motivation for and the evolution of this unique RAF unit of Canadians is told in detail in Hugh Halliday's *No. 242 Squadron: The Canadian Years*; it is an invaluable reference book.

Arthur Deacon at home in Vancouver, in 2004.

Courtesy of the Wayne Ralph Collection

The early training for the pilots, virtually all of whom were "pipeliners" fresh from the RAF training system, was on a mixed fleet that included some Miles Magisters, a Fairey Battle, a Bristol Blenheim and a North American Harvard. But in December 1939 it was decided that the propaganda value of an all-Canadian squadron flying single-engine fighters was better, especially if it was equipped with Hurricanes, the designated RAF fighter with British forces in France. The squadron started receiving Hurricanes in January 1940. The fighters arrived in the middle of a particularly harsh winter, when there was far more snow than England was accustomed to. Naturally, this slowed down the training.

Squadron Leader Fowler Gobeil, one of eighteen RCAF officers on exchange duties with the RAF at the outbreak of war, had been chosen to command the unit. At the age of eighty-seven, Deacon candidly recalls his memories of this period:

Gobeil was in no way an inspirational leader … the squadron was a bullshit squadron … it provided propaganda value for the Canadian and British governments, helping also to promote the BCATP, and decisions were driven by that political motivation. The quality of our tactics and gunnery training, and gunnery practice, was inadequate for the challenges that faced an average pilot in France in the spring of 1940.

Deacon flew on operations from March 25 through to May 28, 1940, but the most intense combat for him was when he and other seconded pilots from 242 moved to France on May 10 to serve with 85, 607 and 615 Squadrons. All the RAF pilots were stressed and fatigued; it was quite common for two sections of eight Hurricane pilots to be fighting against twenty-five German pilots in their higher-performing Me109s.

On May 19, Art Deacon had flown four ops with only two hours' sleep the night before. He destroyed a Heinkel (He) 111 bomber near Arras, France, on his second sortie, but it wasn't an easy victory for him. An inexperienced fighter pilot has difficulty gauging his aircraft's closing speed on a target. It is a typical rookie mistake to attack at such a high speed that there is no time to aim accurately. This happened to Art on his first pass. But he was fortunate to get in a second attack on the He111, with the tail gunner out of action. The bomber went down smoking and one member of the crew bailed out. In the Battle of France there were cases of German fighters strafing British pilots in their parachutes, and Art was tempted to fire on this descending German airman. He thought to himself that the German might have killed other British pilots, maybe even Art's friends. But he could not force himself to be that ruthless.

Four days later Art lost his closest friend on the squadron, Joseph "Bev" Smiley from Wolseley, Saskatchewan, who was shot down and captured. Two other colleagues were killed that day, Garfield Madore and John Graafstra. This brought the total number of killed, wounded or POW to six. By the end of May it was thirteen. Of the forty Canadian pilots originally assigned to the squadron, twenty-four (including one pilot from Newfoundland) were killed, and three others became prisoners of war (see Halliday, op. cit., for lists of personnel.)

In a confused action on May 28 over the Channel near Ostend, Belgium, against at least twenty-five enemy fighters flying a defensive circle, Deacon scored a second victory. One of his wingmen, Bill Waterton, had gone back to Biggin Hill with a radio problem, a problem that, in Deacon's memory, Waterton seemed to have too often. After six decades, the memory of his disappointment and conflict with Waterton is still fresh for Art. He does not forgive him for leaving since, shortly thereafter, his other wingman, Dale Jones, was shot down and killed.

Cutting across the defensive circle of German machines, Art managed to score hits on one 109; looking over his shoulder, he could see it belching smoke. Deacon was hoping to regain the safety of the rest of his section as quickly as possible. However, he was alone and was quickly bounced by another 109; his aircraft was severely damaged. When he put on full boost to get the Hurricane to accelerate, the Merlin engine vomited large quantities of oil. It was as Art surveyed this damage that the incongruous thought came into his mind: "Today is my sister Aileen's birthday and I was going to send her a telegram." Unknown to Art, older sister Florence was telling her family in Invermay on that very day that she had had a premonition that Art was in some kind of trouble.

He was just able to turn back from the Channel towards the coast but, after he had shut down the engine, his crash landing was so abrupt and severe that he was thrown out of the cockpit and knocked unconscious. He came to crawling on his hands and knees in a potato garden behind a Belgian hospital. He was taken inside by a nurse. Shrapnel was removed from his legs, and his eye was patched up. The attending physician advised Art that Belgium had surrendered to Germany that day. The doctor's son had recently been killed in the war. He escorted Art to his home and provided him with a brown suit and hat that had belonged to his son.

Art decided to walk to the French port of Dunkirk, where the evacuation of the British forces was underway. After some frightening adventures, including being shelled by British ships and, while under arrest, digging a grave for a German soldier,

he was deposited back at the same hospital where the same doctor loaded him aboard a bus headed for Antwerp, Belgium. The US Consulate in that city wanted no part of a British fighter pilot with bandages over his eye who was on the lam from the Germans. Art asked the Americans if they could at the very least get a message to his family but, despite assurances that they would do so, no message was sent.

Within a few days of hiding out with a Belgian family, Deacon was apprehended when he sought medical care for his wounds at a local hospital. His short fighter pilot's career was over. As with many other fighter pilots captured in the war, the first English words spoken to Deacon by his German captors were: "For you, the war is over. If you attempt to escape we will shoot you."

Deacon spent 1940 to 1945 in POW camps, including the North Camp at Stalag Luft III where he assisted in the planning and execution of The Great Escape. One of his duties was to play the saxophone in the camp band—the band provided a distraction for the guards at the appropriate time when the noise of tunnelling or other activities needed to be muffled. At Stalag Luft III were several ex-242 pilots from the Battle of France, including Bev Smiley, Lorne Chambers and the legendary second squadron commander of 242 with whom he had never gotten to fly, Douglas Bader, who was taken prisoner in August 1941.

* * *

Profile – RICHARD EDWARD BARTLETT

Born – April 21, 1919, Ft Qu'Appelle, SK

Father – Christopher Pennyciuck Bartlett, dairy farmer

Mother – Margaret Smales, died in 1931

Decorations & Medals – CD and Clasp, Golden Jubilee Medal

Post-war occupation – Naval officer, Lieutenant Commander, RCN

Marital status – Wife Margaret Falconer, son James, daughter Anne

Hobbies – Gardening, reading and travel

In 1938 the Royal Navy Fleet Air Arm broke away from the unsatisfactory interwar practice of using RAF pilots aboard their ships. It placed advertisements in newspapers in Britain and throughout the domin-

Courtesy of the Wayne Ralph Collection

Dick Bartlett at home in his garden in Victoria, in 2004.

ions inviting young men to join up for seven years as pilots or observers. Christopher P. Bartlett, a British-born dairy farmer who was a native of Winchester, England, and a graduate of Winchester College, was living just outside Fort Qu'Appelle, Saskatchewan, but subscribed to *The Times*. Two of his six children, Christopher and Richard ("Dick"), both wanted to fly, and they read *The Times* for any news about aviation in Britain. The elder boy, Christopher, trained at the Regina Flying Club and, after obtaining his private pilot's licence, left to join the RAF in the spring of 1937.

In 1938 Dick spotted the advertisements in the British newspaper for Fleet Air Arm (FAA) flyers. Always wanting to do something that involved both ships and airplanes, he sent in his application. Unlike the RAF in 1939, the FAA did not provide a paid passage to Britain; it invited you to come over from Canada for an interview, after which it decided if you were suitable. Dick Bartlett needed several hundred dollars to make his way to England and live until he was accepted.

During his four years of high school, Dick had an arrangement with a fox farmer, George McNeil, to take care of two female silver foxes and their litters, in exchange for half the offspring. By the time Dick had graduated from high school in the summer of 1938, he owned fifty fox pups, each of their fur pelts worth about $30. He sold them to pay for his ship's passage to Britain.

Friends of his father met Dick Bartlett at Southampton and took him home to Winchester. His induction interview at The Admiralty in London was a kindly affair that included questions similar to those posed in the First World War (*Can you ride a horse? What sports do you play? Oh, you know how to ski!*). The panel encouraged Dick to become an observer, but since his brother was a pilot with the RAF, which was still recruiting, he threatened to walk around the corner to the RAF office. He was asked to leave the room. Shortly after, he was called back in and told that he was accepted as a pilot with the rank of midshipman.

The first two months of training were on an aircraft carrier, HMS *Hermes*, with a group of sixty, evenly split between pilots and observers, and the third month on HMS *Courageous*. Training in England by ex-RAF short service commission instructors followed, first fifty hours on Tiger Moths at Gravesend and then one hundred hours on Harvards at Netheravon. Several students were killed in training and, in a Fleet Air Arm ritual whether one was at a shore establishment or aboard ship, the belongings of the dead were auctioned and the proceeds sent to the bereaved families. The training culminated in August 1939 when Dick became a qualified pilot, and his logbook, like that of all newly graduated flyers, was stamped and endorsed. There was no wings parade. He simply went to Gieves & Hawkes, the renowned military tailors at 1 Savile Row, London, and purchased a pair of wings to sew onto the left sleeve of his uniform.

Operational training of fifty hours followed on the Fairey Swordfish, a torpedo bomber of biplane construction with a cruising speed of 115 mph, a service ceiling of 9,500 feet and a 500-feet-per-minute climb rate. His course of twenty operated on HMS *Argus* in the Mediterranean to accomplish their six deck landings for qualification on type.

The main smokestack of the carrier was just in front of the round down of the deck, so landing over top of it meant ashes in the mouth and soot on your flying gear.

Rather than being assigned to an operational Swordfish unit, Dick was sent to Northern Ireland to a unit training air gunners flying Fairey Swordfish and Blackburn Shark biplanes. Shortly after his arrival a new monoplane was sent to this squadron. It was called the Blackburn Skua. Despite a crash by the senior pilot on the first new Skua to arrive, Dick volunteered to fly the next one, in part because he had flown the Harvard in training, and the adage was, "If you can fly a Harvard, you can fly anything." He thought he was well prepared to handle a beast like the Skua. As he explains it, in those days he was "both dumb and young."

Within the Royal Navy, the Blackburn Skua was an unlikely hybrid of competing needs for both a modern fighter and a modern dive bomber. In the experimental testing of the Skua, it was determined that releasing the bomb off the fuselage centre line while in a steep dive knocked the propeller off the machine. As an expedient solution to this problem, the engine was extended eighteen inches forward on a tubular frame. This created a new problem, a heavy 830-horsepower Bristol Perseus engine suspended on a longer and more flexible mount. The senior pilot who had flown the first Skua to arrive at Dick's squadron, being a bit unused to monoplanes, made a hard landing, and the engine promptly fell off the machine.

The initial deck-landing trials of the Skua were dramatic; the first aircraft to land blew a tire and narrowly missed going over the side of the carrier; the second came close to tipping up on its nose; the third hit the carrier island, cartwheeled and dropped over the side. The Skua had other eccentricities. It would not recover from a spin. So the manufacturer put a large parachute inside the tail, deployable by the pilot if he was so foolish as to enter a spin. Usually when the spin stopped and the parachute was jettisoned, the Skua plummeted into the ground or water. In April 1940, sixteen Skuas attacked the German cruiser *Königsberg* at Bergen, Norway; each carried a single five-hundred-pound semi-armour-piercing bomb. The cruiser was sunk with the loss of only one Skua. This was arguably

the high point in the operational achievements of what was a stable, rugged dive bomber but a slow, poor-climbing fighter.

For Dick Bartlett the Skua seemed a more modern aircraft than the Swordfish, and he logged three or four hours in Ireland. It was this brief exposure that qualified him to attend the ten-day fighter/dive-bomber training course at Eastleigh, near Southampton. The course included flying on the Skua and the Gloster Gladiator biplane fighter that was being phased out in favour of the Skua. Unfortunately, the synchronizing gear that allowed the Gladiator's nose-mounted guns to fire safely through the propeller arc was unreliable. Shooting its guns was prohibited. Dick therefore started his operational career as a Skua fighter/dive bomber pilot with the modest total of eight hours flying time on the machine but without even eight minutes of practical gunnery training.

He joined 803 Squadron at the same time as its new commanding officer, Lieutenant Commander John Casson. They both flew out of Hatston, Scotland, and landed aboard HMS *Ark Royal*. Dick was the only Canadian with the squadron and his mechanics painted a Royal Canadian Mounted Policeman on the side of his Skua. It was aboard *Ark Royal* that he teamed up with his rear gunner, Lloyd Richards from Guernsey, Channel Islands. As a rookie fighter pilot and a colonial, Bartlett found himself in a culture and among men very different from anything he had ever witnessed. As he recollects today:

> Some of the pilots in the Fleet Air Arm were a surprise to me. Their hair was long, they smelled of cologne, and carried handkerchiefs that hung out of their sleeves. But they would come back from a rough operation saying things like "Wasn't that fun! Let's go for a drink." Meanwhile I was trying to regain my composure thinking to myself, "Gee, I better go change my underwear before I go for any drink."

It was daylight virtually all the time at the northern tip of Norway in late May and June, and operations were almost continuous. Dick did five bombing trips which also including strafing targets of opportunity such as German cars, tanks and headquarters, all in the area from Tromso to Narvik, Norway.

The Norwegian campaign conducted by the British forces suffered many deficiencies in planning and supply, and this significantly affected the Fleet Air Arm's effectiveness. For example, Dick recalls that, despite being support aircraft for the British Army in the field:

[The Skua crews] had no maps of Norway, yet we were flying over unknown territory for more than an hour looking for targets of opportunity. We had some coastal charts, quite inadequate, and we had to find a landmark on the chart from which a plot could be taken to get us home to our ship. When we left the carrier we were given their mean line of advance, and the goal was to set a course from a known point on the coast towards the projected point on the carrier's line of advance. We could fly for up to five hours, and the carrier could move quite a distance in that time. We started to realize over Norway that this must be about where the first war left off [because] our manner of operations was little different to that of the First World War.

Bartlett and Richards managed to shoot down an enemy aircraft during a patrol, but received no credit for it:

One day a German He111 came at us three Skuas, flying in Vic formation, head-on and our section leader apparently did not see it. I was on the right-hand side so I gave it a burst as it went by, and I swung in behind, firing at him with my four .303 wing guns. I ran out of ammunition and then pulled up alongside to let Lloyd shoot at the damaged bomber with his Lewis gun. I saw four of the crew get out of the bomber after it hit the water. I put in a claim, but my gunner was the only person to witness it crashing. They said after I told them where it hit the water: "Well, that must be the one that the section leader claimed." With the rank of leading seaman, the Skua gunners were not included in briefings prior to operational

flights and their opinions were of little consequence. It seemed unlikely they would credit me just on our own say-so.

When the British Army gave up fighting and started to evacuate Norway at Narvik, a couple of destroyers were used to shuttle men out to the troopships among the islands offshore. A typical air-cover sortie during the evacuation was two hours. If your ammunition ran out after thirty minutes, you were still expected to continue for another ninety minutes. Pilots were required to fake attacks even without ammunition, in the hope the Skua would be misidentified as a Hurricane and force the enemy to break away. This actually did work from time to time.

The standard of aircraft recognition among Royal Navy gunners during the early stages of the Second World War was universally regarded by airmen as dismal (many interviewees state that the Royal Navy never improved). Bartlett and Richards and other Skua crews became accustomed to being shot at by their own people after five-hour trips:

Often as you came out of the murk heading for the fleet, a destroyer, which might already have been bombed several times, let go a burst of gunfire. If you fired a Verey light to signal you were friendly, there was then a good chance that some other destroyer would then think you were firing at it and would return the compliment. On the other hand, if you didn't fire, some further vessel would just likely think you should have and would treat you as unfriendly. The result was that we often came back with holes in our aircraft caused by our own ships' guns as well as those due to enemy action. Our captain was the old-school type who innocently assumed you must have been really pushing home your attacks if you came back with holes in the aircraft, whatever the source.

According to historian Lieutenant Commander Stuart E. Soward, RCN (ret.), in *Hands to Flying Stations*, more than 100 aircraft and 150 aircrew, about one third of the entire cadre of the Fleet Air Arm, were lost in the abortive Norwegian campaign. Dick Bartlett recalls that senior naval officers who loved battleships had no respect for naval aviation, considering those who specialized in it as "a rabble." He and other trainees at HMS *Hermes* were told by the carrier captain that "as long as they continued in the Air Branch they would continue to be a rabble." In summary, aviators did not enhance the reputation of the Royal Navy and were considered entirely unsuitable for promotion.

Due to a deep-seated indifference or hostility to aviation, and a rather cavalier bloody-mindedness about threats of other kinds, the Royal Navy lost many capital ships during the war. One of the most tragic losses was the sinking of the carrier HMS *Glorious* on its trip home from Norway to Scapa Flow, Scotland, following a decision by its commander to proceed independently of the main convoy. Captain Guy D'Oyly-Hughes, DSO and Bar, a Great War veteran, had no lookouts posted and there were no aircraft airborne to provide long-range spotting to protect *Glorious*. The German battleship *Scharnhorst* and heavy cruiser *Gneisenau* came across the British carrier and in twenty minutes HMS *Glorious* went down with its two destroyer escorts, taking with them some fifteen hundred personnel. On board were also six RAF pilots and six RAF Hurricanes that these pilots had landed on the carrier just a short time before. Only a handful of men survived.

The German battle group was later found at anchor in Trondheim harbour at the end of a sixty-mile-long fjord that was defended by shore-based fighters, 109s and 110s and many shore batteries in the hills and mountains around the harbour. HMS *Ark Royal* was sent from Scapa Flow back to Norway and her commander was instructed by the admiralty to attack *Scharnhorst, Gneisenau* and *Hipper* at Trondheim. An order came down that fifteen Skuas from 800 and 803 Squadrons armed with five-hundred-pound semi-armour-piercing bombs should launch an attack in the early hours of June 13; six RAF Blenheims were assigned to bomb the fighter airfields as a diversion.

The pilots on *Ark Royal* knew that such an un-coordinated attack was pointless and near-suicidal. Knowing they were not coming back, many wrote final letters to their families the evening before the attack. There was no hope of success and little expectation of a safe return for the thirty pilots and gunners.

To compound the risks, the RAF bomber crews struck the German airfields too early. According to Bartlett, one Blenheim pilot, Joe Hill, told him later that the Blenheims had calculated the time for the operation based on statute miles versus nautical miles as in the Royal Navy. The early strike gave the single- and twin-engine enemy fighters ample time to refuel and be airborne to greet the Skuas as they turned up the fjord. On that particular Thursday, as the formations crossed the Norwegian coast at 2:30 a.m. the sun rose into a cloudless, crystal-clear sky, brightly illuminating the Skuas for the German forces. For the entire length of the fjord they were under attack. Donald Gibson (later Admiral Sir Donald Gibson) was a section leader and Dick flew as his No. 2.

Two Me109s repeatedly attacked Dick's Skua, blowing holes in both wings and damaging the main fuel tank. Pieces of the aircraft fell away as the enemy fired again and again. Several bullets struck Dick, opening up the left side of his body, and he felt as though he had been kicked in the side by a horse. He still managed to release his bomb, though not on target (of all the bombs dropped only one struck the *Scharnhorst* and it did not explode).

Complicating matters, Lloyd Richards had removed his chest-pack parachute to fire his Lewis gun and in the heat of the fight against the Me109s, the chute had fallen to the floor of the cockpit, out of reach. Dick learned this as they were flying up the fjord to drop the bomb. Afterwards he pointed his barely controllable machine towards the buildings of Trondheim rather than out to sea. Unknown to him the Germans had placed anti-aircraft gun batteries on the rooftops. He managed to fly past the town at low level without being shot down. From the comfortable armchair in his living room on Vancouver Island, Dick recalled:

By this time the engine was shaking so badly I could hardly read the instruments and to make matter worse I had lost a lot of blood and was quite dizzy. We may have clipped a tree, I'm not sure about that, but I do recall the engine fell off and we crashed ... Lloyd was uninjured and managed to burn the remains of the aircraft and fetch a mattress from a nearby farmhouse and lay me on it. I pulled down my suit to show him where I was wounded. According to Lloyd, my intestines and stomach were visible and this made him feel rather sick. However, at my advice, he headed off towards the Swedish border, a few miles away.

Not too long after, he returned under the escort of German soldiers, but I was unconscious by then. We were both taken back to Trondheim by car, during which, according to Lloyd, I bled freely and stained the seats with gasoline and oil. Lloyd was sent to a temporary prison, and I did not see him again for some forty years. I went into a hospital and while recuperating there the Me109 pilot who attacked me, a nice fellow, visited and told me how he had flown in Spain before the war.

At one point I was on a table being examined by a German surgeon and I could hear him say that he was going to amputate my left leg below the knee. I was distressed and picked myself up off the table and walked around it to demonstrate that the leg was just fine. The surgeon agreed and, at my request, handed me the bullets and bullet fragments taken from that leg and hip … I kept them for many years.

In a similar way to Art Deacon, but without the harsh interrogation since they were confident he was a carrier pilot not a spy, Dick was processed as an air force prisoner. He ended up like Deacon in Stalag Luft I on the Baltic Sea at Barth, Germany, for the rest of 1940. Bartlett was involved in several unsuccessful escape attempts both at Stalag Luft I and the much larger Warburg prison camp before arriving at the North Camp of Stalag Luft III at Sagan. He was paired with a Norwegian, Fugel Sang, to go out of the tunnel codenamed "Harry" in The Great Escape of March 24, 1944. A second Norwegian arrived at the camp, a friend of Fugel's named Hal Espelid, and it was mutually agreed that the two Norwegians would manage better together on the run given Dick's rudimentary Norwegian language skills. The decision saved Dick's life because both Norwegians were recaptured and executed along with forty-eight others by the Gestapo.

Four years to the day after his own near-fatal crash, Dick's brother, Wing Commander Christopher Smales Bartlett, DFC and Bar, by then commanding officer of 434 Squadron RCAF, was killed in action on his fiftieth operation, during a night attack of Arras aboard a Halifax. The sole survivor, a tail gunner named D.H. Crawford from Port Arthur, Ontario, eventually ended up at Stalag Luft III, and related to Dick what had happened. Two of the Halifax engines were on fire, so Chris ordered everybody to bail out. Shortly thereafter, twenty miles east of Lille, a German night fighter collided with the Halifax, and all Crawford saw was a large fireball as his parachute opened in the darkness.

Pilots of 416 Squadron. Front row, left to right: Bill Palmer, Dick Forbes-Roberts, Al McFadden. Back row: Pat Patterson, Bill Mason, Sandy Borland.

THE DEADLY YEARS:
RHUBARBS AND CIRCUSES
AND MANY, MANY WULFIES

By the time Willie McKnight went missing in January 1941, his squadron was a Canadian unit in name only. As Royal Canadian Air Force squadrons continued to be formed in Britain throughout 1941, the Canadians themselves eventually requested that references to 242 Squadron as all-Canadian be discontinued. It was not well known just how many Royal Air Force squadrons had Canadian personnel, pilots, fitters, riggers or armourers. In reality, the majority of the most experienced Canadians were kept within the RAF and away from the RCAF because they were so useful, even indispensable.

A good example was Wing Commander John Kent, DFC and Bar, AFC, born in Winnipeg in 1914 and the leader of 303 Squadron, itself a high-scoring Polish unit within the RAF. In a period of one year from September 1940 to August 1941, Kent led Polish and British pilots as both a squadron and a wing commander, destroying thirteen enemy aircraft. Despite a long and distinguished RAF career from the 1930s to the 1950s, Kent was little-known then, having never served with the RCAF. He has certainly not become a household name in Canada since the war. Wing Commander E.F. J. "Jack" Charles, DSO, DFC and Bar, Silver Star (US), is another example of a hero who has remained obscure outside military circles. Born in Britain but raised in the town of Lashburn, Saskatchewan, he was a pre-war RCAF officer who transferred into the RAF in 1939. He went on to be credited with the destruction of at least fifteen enemy aircraft, all of them fighters, plus many probables and damaged.

By the beginning of 1941, No. 1 (RCAF) Squadron—soon to renumber as 401 of the RCAF—had established a fighting presence. Three of the squadron's pilots, Squadron Leader Ernie McNab, Flying Officer Gordon McGregor and Flying Officer Blair "Dal" Russel, had received DFCs from King George at an October 1940 investiture for their combat achievements in the Battle of Britain. All three served throughout and survived the war, being promoted and decorated several times. All had successful post-war careers back in Canada.

If 1943 and '44 were the dangerous, grim years for bomber crews in Britain, the dark equivalent for fighter pilots was 1941 and '42. The RAF and the newly forming RCAF squadrons in Britain started to take the war to the enemy in France. Not everyone agreed with this policy of launching low-level "Rhubarbs" across the Channel, simply looking for trouble. "Circuses," with bombers and a fighter escort attacking French towns and industrial centres, often had mixed success.

The cost for the RAF in fighter aircraft and trained pilots was large in relation to the superficial damage that could be inflicted on German squadrons and airfields, ammunition dumps and factories. Moreover, the Luftwaffe was able to choose when and where it would fight and if it would fight. Frequently it simply chose not to engage, or waited for the last possible moment to attack enemy pilots, as they were running low on fuel and needed what was left in the tanks to make it home.

For an inexperienced pilot, a "sprog" with weak tactical and gunnery skills, flying in cumbersome squadron- and even wing-size formations over France, always near the limit of the range of his aircraft, 1941 and '42 was a frightening time. Battle damage, glycol leaks in engines or, worst of all, a fire frequently meant a bailout or a ditching in the English Channel. Many pilots who survived combat drowned or died of exposure in the deceptively narrow, cold, rough waters between France and England.

If a new graduate of the British Commonwealth Air Training Plan (BCATP) was to fulfill a childhood dream of flying a Hurricane or Spitfire, it was most likely to be in 1941–42. Later in the war, the rising casualty rates in No. 6 Bomber Group and the falling casualty rate in RCAF and RAF fighter wings meant that the majority of graduating BCATP pilots went to bombers. If you were going to become a fighter pilot, the best odds were at this point in the war, which was also the most dangerous period to be one, whether you were in Britain, the Mediterranean or the Western Desert.

The Luftwaffe had upgraded to the F model of the Messerschmitt Me109 and introduced a new fighter, the Focke-Wulf 190 "Würger" (Shrike or Butcher Bird.) It was fast, had a terrific roll rate and handled beautifully. The Spitfire Mk V could not match this new machine, and our pilots were, in 1941–42, in awe of it. Usually referred to in logbooks as "FW190" or "190," some wrote down "Wulfie," perhaps in recognition of the Luftwaffe's wolf-pack-like technique of hit and run.

The Spitfire Mk IX and the Packard-Merlin–powered P51B/C Mustang, which could fully match the FW190 and Me109F at all altitudes, were not available in 1941, coming into service only in the second half of 1942 (for the Spitfire) and the first half of 1943 (for the Mustang). For most RCAF squadrons the Mk IX or the P51B/C were a distant dream between 1941 and 1943; Canadian units had to wait their turn behind RAF squadrons to get them. However, if you were a BCATP gradu-

THE FOCKE-WULF 190 AND MOUNTING LOSSES

Throughout the rest of October 1941 the new Focke-Wulf Fw 190 was seen on many occasions and never failed to impress ... Although the Fw 190s' arrival came as a considerable shock to Fighter Command there should have been an aircraft available to deal with it...

It was clear that in the short term there was little that could be done to combat the threat posed by the Fw 190, and in the meantime Spitfire V squadrons would have to carry on as best they could. Circus operations were gradually wound down throughout October, the last raid being carried out on 8th November [1941]. The approach of winter flying was not the only factor, however as the whole policy of flying elaborate offensive operations over France had been called into question due to mounting losses.

Peter Caygill, *Spitfire Mark V in Action: RAF Operations in Northern Europe.*

THE RCAF 400-NUMBERED SQUADRONS OVERSEAS

It was in 1941 that the first significant body of graduates of the BCATP system started to arrive in the UK, and it was in this period that the RCAF formed its 400-numbered squadrons. Canada had been assigned a block of numbers from 400 to 449 for its overseas squadrons. For example, the following 400-numbered fighter squadrons of the RCAF were created that year: 110 Squadron was assigned Number 400, and No. 1 Squadron was assigned Number 401, and No. 2 Squadron was assigned Number 402, all three on March 1, 1941. Freshly created fighter squadrons included 403 formed in March '41; 409, 410, 411, 412 in June '41; 414 in August '41; and 416, 417 and 418 in November '41. Other fighter squadrons were formed in 1942, '43 and '44, and some Canadian-based fighter squadrons were assigned 400-series numbers when they arrived in Britain.

ate pilot sent to an RAF squadron, and about sixty of every one hundred BCATP graduates were, then your chances were good that you might fly the latest design or newest model: the Mk IX or XIV Spitfire, a Typhoon fighter bomber, a Mosquito night fighter and later on the Tempest air superiority fighter.

Profile – WILLIAM BARRY NEEDHAM

Born – August 8, 1920, Simpson, SK

Father – William Charles Needham, publisher

Mother – Bessie Adelaide Whitney

Decorations & Medals – Golden Jubilee Medal

Post-war occupation – Newspaper publisher and owner of a weekly newspaper

Marital status – Wife Martha Kerluke; sons Colin and Scott; daughters Denise and Debra

Hobbies – Fishing, reading

I called him from the pay phone in the beer parlour on the main street in Wynyard, Saskatchewan. He was just one of the names in the membership book of the Canadian Fighter Pilots Association. I was on my way east to Yorkton, Saskatchewan, and Grandview, Manitoba, and took a chance that he might be able to see me on short notice. It was a beautiful, hot afternoon in July 2001, a summer when many heat records were broken. I had been driving for a week from the west coast, doing interviews as I travelled eastward, and my white car was plastered with the green corpses of grasshoppers.

Many Saskatchewan villages have disappeared since last I flew over the province as a military flying instructor in 1973. In your automobile you can no longer spot your next village on the highway ten miles away, as they have torn down the grain elevators by the now-abandoned railway tracks. Driving at night, the blackness is more profound, the stars brighter, because there are fewer welcoming lights dotting the Prairies.

Barry Needham invited me to come over immediately; he was just a few blocks from the Wynyard Hotel. I said I was going to have my supper in the restaurant, and would see him in about an hour. He and his wife, Martha, live in a modest bungalow. They have a flower garden with a small pond and fountain at the back of the home. Needham was born in Saskatchewan at Simpson and, other than for

Photo of Barry Needham and wife Martha in the garden in Wynyard, Saskatchewan.

the war, has worked virtually all his life in Wynyard in the family publishing business.

He had signed up to fight in the RCAF in January 1940. He might have made it overseas quicker if the RCAF had not inadvertently categorized him as medically unfit (ATB) instead of the aircrew standard of A1B. Once this bureaucratic error was straightened out with the help of William Needham—Barry's father, who escorted his son into the recruiting centre—he was sworn in on September 30 in Regina, right alongside Rod Smith.

After elementary training at No. 15 Elementary Flying Training School (EFTS), Regina, on the Tiger Moth, Barry attended the first pilots' course at the newly opened No. 11 Service Flying Training School (SFTS) at Yorkton, in the same intake as James Edwards. He logged 150 hours on the Harvard and received his wings and sergeant's stripes on June 30, 1941. Like Smith and Edwards, he went overseas immediately. The ship Edwards was on diverted to Iceland and stayed for several weeks; also aboard was Ian Maclennan. Needham's ship made a quick passage, and he qualified by September on the Spitfire at the operational training unit (OTU) at Heston, England, logging just under 34 hours. One year since swearing in, and he was supposedly ready to join a squadron and fight.

As I sat listening to Barry describe his war career, I could hear crickets in the back garden. The heat of the day was still in the room even though the sky was dark. I asked him what he thought of his training to take on the Germans and he said: "When I look back on it now, I realize that we had bugger-all training. [It was] pitiful." With 180 to 220 hours of total flying time, most of one's attention is needed just to fly adequately. In many cases the rookie pilot is so absorbed in just keeping the aircraft at the right speed and altitude, and keeping his leader in sight, that there is simply no cerebral processing room left to notice what is happening in the world at large.

Barry joined 412 Squadron where Rod Smith was serving as a deputy flight commander at the age of nineteen. Barry remembers Rod as mature beyond his years, conscientious and no party animal. When Barry and his best friend, A.P.L. "Apple" Smith, from Cupar, Saskatchewan, went out to the pubs to drink with, flirt with and, he hoped, sleep with the young English girls at the pubs around Digby, Lincolnshire, Rod Smith stayed on the station. Since Barry was a sergeant pilot, whereas Rod and his friend John Gillespie Magee were pilot officers, socializing was limited, and conversation was confined to operational matters.

In London, Barry made his home at basement clubs like the Chez Moi, just around the corner from his favourite hotel, the Regent Palace. The owner of the club, Marie, had instructed her doorman to refuse entry to Americans. She hired a tiny, elderly lady, a fixture in the evenings, to tinkle away at the piano in the corner. When newcomer Barry told the owner that he was en route to join a squadron at Digby, Marie insisted that he "make sure and say hello to my boyfriend up there, 'Cowboy' Blatchford."

Needham knew that she was speaking of Wing Commander Howard Peter "Cowboy" Blatchford, DFC, newly appointed head of the Digby Wing. They would have to be out of their minds as green NCO pilots to approach him and extend best wishes sent by a boozy blond in a London bar. Blatchford

was the son of the mayor of Edmonton. He had joined the RAF in 1936 and had been the first Canadian in the RAF to shoot down an enemy aircraft in the Second World War. He was killed in action in May 1943; the Edmonton Municipal Airport in the city was named Blatchford Field in his memory.

* * *

Profile – GEORGE DENNIS AITKEN
Born – June 21, 1920, Edmonton
Father – Tempest Aitken, postal worker
Mother – Charlotte Collyer
Decorations & Medals – AFC, Centennial Medal
Post-war occupation – Civil servant, retired as director, admin services, Manpower and Labour, Gov't of Alberta
Marital status – Wife Daphne Burkett; daughters Deborah, Heather and Dorothy
Hobbies – Air force history

The interviews completed for this book took place over a period of more than three years. Most of the interviews were in homes, a few in coffee shops and restaurants and several in offices with men ranging in age from seventy-eight to eighty-three who were still thriving at their chosen careers. In almost every home I visited were mantel clocks or grandfather clocks that chimed the hours and quarter-hours. The generation that lived through the Depression and the Second World War inherited family heirlooms and keepsakes, and among these very commonly are clocks. If they were not inherited, they looked as though they might have been.

On the tape recordings the clocks can be heard chiming loudly, sometimes more loudly and clearly than the voices of the men, some of whom have had heart attacks or strokes or are living with cancer or conditions such as diabetes and macular degeneration, to name just a couple. Despite or perhaps because of these vicissitudes of aging, when asked, "How would you describe your childhood?" the answers are almost always the same and sound typically like this: "My childhood was happy"; "We didn't have much in those days, but I look back on my childhood as idyllic"; "I had a very happy childhood. My father was strict but fair, and how my mother managed to raise us on so little … well, she was a remarkable woman."; "In those days nobody had much, so you did not feel deprived. People helped each other."

I don't believe all fighter pilots had happy childhoods. Indeed, I sometimes found evidence to suggest the opposite. But perhaps there is something in the character of the fighter pilot that is deeply optimistic or at least accepting. As a result, most seem to view their personal history as a positive, upward climb through a busy, productive life, always starting with a happy childhood.

George Dennis Aitken of Edmonton is characteristic of this kind of fighter pilot. George is a soft-spoken, gentle and generous man with a keen memory and a learned demeanour that is indicative of his insights as a historian. He has a great sense of humour and an infectious giggle, and likes to spice his stories with an ironic touch. He has written extensively about his own life in the war, as have many of the other fighter pilots I have interviewed. George sent me many personal documents and photos and has also helped many other published authors in Canada and Britain to write the histories of the squadrons of the RCAF and RAF.

As a boy, Aitken frequently pedalled his bicycle up to the Municipal Airport in the middle of Edmonton to watch aircraft taking off and landing. He also made model aircraft and won a prize—a free ride in a real aircraft with local pilot Chris Moon, who himself was killed in action early in the war flying as a pilot. After a "very happy childhood" living on Clover Bar Road in the Forest Heights neighbourhood of Edmonton, and graduating from Grade 12 at Victoria High, George completed a one-year course at Percy Page's McDougall Commercial High.

In 1939 George volunteered to join the army. He wanted to get into the RCAF but ended up like many others waiting around for the call-up (George was typical of many pilots that I interviewed in spending time in the army while waiting). He enlisted in the 49th Battalion, and his typing skills helped clinch his assignment as a clerk at $1 a day with 130 Mobilization Training Centre. His boss, Colonel Jamieson, knew George wanted to fly and was the first to wish him well when the RCAF finally called in early December 1940.

In a pattern of training repeated, with minor variations, by thousands of young air crew of all types,

George went through the following: parade-square bashing at the Brandon Manning Pool; some weeks of useless guard duty while waiting to start training, in his case in Red Deer; followed by No. 2 Initial Training School ITS in Regina for aircrew *ab initio* indoctrination and assessment, then a short journey west to Lethbridge to No. 5 EFTS to fly Tiger Moths. He was then shipped east to Dauphin, Manitoba, to train on Harvards at No. 10 SFTS. He received his pilot's wings and sergeant's stripes on August 8, 1941.

His luck held. There was no assignment to instructional duties; the sea passage, aboard SS *Laconia*, was uneventful, followed by a train journey to Bournemouth, home of the RCAF in Britain. There he waited in pleasant surroundings with his fingers crossed that he was going to get fighters—not bombers, not target towing, but fighters.

After qualifying on Hurricanes at Crosby on Eden, England, George was sent to Peterhead, Scotland, to join a new RCAF squadron just forming there, 416. There was only a single Miles Magister to fly and all the pilots who were arriving to fill the squadron had just been trained on the Hurricane. George and the others soon learned that, despite their recent training, they were to be equipped with Spitfires. This was good news. As George explained it, "Behind every one of our dreams was the eternal hope that we would fly Spitfires."

The Mk II machines that arrived, however, were scarred old warhorses that had equipped a Czechoslovakian squadron of the RAF in the Battle of Britain—the Czech markings were still painted on the Spits. The engineering officer and his fitters and riggers worked overtime to make them serviceable, and the pilots began to check out on them. Still, there were brake failures, flap failures and damaged props and undercarriage as part of the learning process.

Heavy snowfalls in the north of Scotland as well as low overcast cloud kept flying restricted, even after operational duties were assigned in January 1942. In February a youthful-looking Flight Lieutenant Lloyd Chadburn, of Aurora and Oshawa, Ontario, arrived as flight commander, and in March he became the commanding officer. He is a historic figure in RCAF wartime history, not least because he was the first pilot graduate of the BCATP to take command of an RCAF fighter squadron in the field.

Lloyd Chadburn in his office in Britain.

Profile – LLOYD VERNON CHADBURN
Born – August 21, 1919, Montreal, raised in Oshawa and Aurora, ON
Died – June 13, 1944, Normandy beachhead in France
Father – Thomas Alonzo Chadburn died in 1925. He was an American businessman who owned a Ford dealership in Oshawa. Lloyd's stepfather was Frank Allen.
Mother – Florence Chadburn, from Quebec; she and her second husband ran a tourist home in Aurora
Decorations & Medals – DSO and Bar, DFC, Legion of Honour, Croix de Guerre
Marital status – Unmarried. According to biographer Robert Forbes, Lloyd's girlfriend, a WAAF named Nancy MacKay, gave birth to a son, Ian Nicholas MacKay, in September 1944. His adoptive family renamed him Andrew Cockshott. He met his father's wartime colleagues at a 416 Squadron reunion in Aurora in 1992.

Chadburn led George Aitken's first patrol in really bad weather, an op to provide cover for ships proceeding to Scapa Flow in the Orkneys. From the time the section left Peterhead en route to Skaebrae, they never saw the ground or the sea. In George's three hundred hours of operational flying, he cannot recall "flying again under such terrifying weather conditions. Other than Chadburn, none of us had that much Spitfire time or even air time in bad weather. It is still a mystery to me that we all survived that trip. I have no idea how Chadburn managed it."

A gifted leader who seemed to be able to lead without the least bit of outward evidence of stress, and who grew rapidly in maturity as responsibilities were added to his shoulders, Chadburn was scarcely older than many of those he led, having been born in August 1919. He had that most ineffable leadership gift, the ability to inspire confidence in others while being self-deprecating about his own abilities and talents. He seemed ordinary and approachable, with a wicked sense of humour. He was so hilarious in his operational briefings that the non-flying personnel, men and women alike, sat in the back of the room and listened just for the entertainment value.

Lloyd had a lighthearted, rather offhand and fearless approach to life. The insecurities that he sometimes felt, particularly in his early days in training, were expressed in his letters home, but not to the world around him. Despite a rather self-deprecating opinion of himself when writing to his family, Chadburn had combat flying abilities of the highest order. His navigation instincts in leading formations were so awesome, as Aitken had witnessed, that in his three tours of operations there were pilots who half suspected he had a secret frequency on his radio on which he spoke with his own personal radar controller.

Bill Mason, 416 Squadron in 1943–44, recalls that "Chad always seemed to know where he was geographically and on numerous occasions when returning from an operation short of fuel and full of concern as to our whereabouts, Chad would unerringly lead us down through several thousand feet of cloud almost on top of our strip." Richard "Dick" Forbes-Roberts, who served with Bill, states unequivocally that of all the wing commanders of the time, "Chad was the finest general in the air." When I interviewed the men who knew and served with Chadburn, perhaps the finest accolade I was offered about him in this regard was from Robert "Dagwood" Phillip: "He could take you through your girlfriend's back door from any point in England."

* * *

Profile – ROBERT DULMAGE PHILLIP

Born – April 5, 1921, Toronto

Father – John McLean Phillip, chartered accountant

Mother – Amy Edna Ketcheson

Decorations & Medals – DFC

Post-war occupation – Corporate pilot, senior pilot, Ontario Government Air Service

Marital status – Wife Margaret Vincent, son Edward, daughter Judith

Hobbies – Motorcycles, anything mechanical

Born and raised in Toronto, "Dagwood" Phillip paid $5 for his first twenty-minute flight to Leavens Brothers at Barker Field, located on the west side of Dufferin Street north of Lawrence Avenue. Later it was the Leavens Brothers Company that would complete his *ab initio* training on the Fleet Finch at London, Ontario. He enlisted in the RCAF in October 1940, received his wings in August 1941 and was discharged in September 1945. He had a long and successful post-war commercial aviation career, retiring in 1983 as a senior pilot for the provincial government of Ontario.

He served his fighting career interchangeably with 416 and 421 Squadrons of the RCAF, completing two tours of operations, shooting down two Focke-Wulf 190s and two Messerschmitt 109s and damaging six other enemy machines. He logged 777 hours on the Spitfire. After completing his Hurricane OTU at Crosby on Eden, he and Arthur John Moul, of Port Alberni, BC, and five other newly graduated pilots joined 416 at Peterhead, Scotland, as part of a second draft. They arrived just before Christmas 1941, bringing the squadron up to a full strength of thirty-two pilots.

Robert and Margaret Phillip at home at Gravenhurst, ON.

Profile – ARTHUR JOHN MOUL
Born – November 20, 1920, Vancouver
Father – Arthur John Moul, head sawyer at a sawmill
Mother – Wilamena Jensen
Decorations & Medals – MiD
Post-war occupation – Bush pilot, airline founder and co-founder, VP Charter and Contract, Pacific Western Airlines
Marital status – Wife Patricia Bishop died in 2004; sons William, David and Robert; daughter Lorraine
Hobbies – Reading

Arthur John "Jack" Moul had been born and raised in the Vancouver area before finishing his commercial courses and junior matriculation at Port Alberni District High School. His hobby as a boy was hunting and competitive shooting, and he won the Canadian Dominion Marksman Championship in 1938–39. After leaving school he worked in the sawmill where his father was head sawyer.

He wanted to be a pilot when he walked into the RCAF recruiting centre in the old post office building in downtown Vancouver. But he lacked the educational requirements of 1940 for that trade, and was sent in a draft as an air gunner to Manning Pool in Toronto, followed by ITS at Toronto's Eglinton Hunt Club. Due to the casualties of the Battle of Britain, the RCAF advised all the air gunners in Jack Moul's class at ITS that they were going to train as pilots at the EFTS in St Catharines. Jack was thrilled to get the opportunity to show what he could do and graduated with his wings in June 1941 at Uplands, Ontario, along with Bob Buckham.

Jack Moul, Bob Buckham, George Aitken, Dagwood Phillip and twenty-eight other pilots from Canada became charter members of 416 Squadron, training in Scotland over a miserable winter. The lack of operational activity encouraged many on the squadron to volunteer for higher-risk assignments in a warm climate: the Middle East and Malta. By late May at least eight pilots had left for the Mediterranean theatre of war.

There was no contact with the enemy in Scotland until May 27, 1942, when Flight Sergeant Moul and his No. 2, Sergeant Anderson, were scrambled just before 11 p.m. They intercepted a He111 bomber flying at about fifty feet over the water and, around midnight, Moul set it on fire over the North Sea. Moul and Anderson claimed and were credited with either a probable or a damaged ("What else could it be than probable," says

Jack, "on fire at midnight at fifty feet over the North Sea!"). From its formation in November 1941 until May 1942, this was the only harm inflicted directly on the enemy by 416 Squadron. A new squadron stationed in a northern location in winter conditions had very few opportunities to engage the enemy.

Jack Moul flew the first Rhubarb for 416 over France with Bob Buckham in October 1942. As he was strafing a train its steam engine blew apart, sending debris through Moul's aircraft, destroying one of the ailerons and the aircraft radiator. Moul was forced to ditch in the Channel; what saved his life is that the Merlin engine completely separated from the fuselage. The rest of the Spitfire floated. Unconscious after the impact for several minutes, Moul came to, dived over the side, inflated his life raft and rowed towards shore. He was taken prisoner shortly after.

He arrived at Stalag Luft III on November 11 and was interrogated by Pilot Officer Wally Floody of 401 Squadron. The aim: to determine whether Jack was a bona fide prisoner of war or a German plant. Moul's bunkmate was Jimmy Sinclair, from Prestwick, Scotland, son of an undersecretary of the RAF. Jack's speciality during the planning and execution of The Great Escape was tunnelling. On the night of March 26, 1944, he was assigned No. 77 of those selected to escape, that is, next to go up the ladder. As No. 76 climbed out of the hole, a German guard shouted an alarm, and Moul never got to find out if he could have made it home to England. That may well have saved his life, as the Gestapo later executed two-thirds of the men who had scrambled out of the tunnel and ran in the darkness across the snow-covered ground to the forest beyond.

* * *

George Aitken was promoted to flight sergeant in the spring of '42, and orders arrived posting him to North Weald, England, to join 403 Squadron, RCAF. He was not disappointed, for though he liked the fellows at 416, 403 Squadron had newer Spitfires and North Weald was in the south, much closer to the action. Action is what George got, and the trying days of doing nothing and seeing little in Scotland were past. In June he was to engage in the fight of his life and wish, perhaps, he had stayed in Peterhead.

Profile – MICHELL JOHNSTON
Born – February 29, 1920, Selkirk, MB
Died – March 8, 2004, Edmonton
Father – Merritt Johnston died in 1925 at age 45 after being severely wounded with the Cameron Highlanders in the First World War
Mother – Melinda Grace, seamstress, owner of a boarding house
Post-war occupation – Entrepreneur, founder of Michell Johnston Building Products in Alberta and Saskatchewan
Marital status – Wife Sigurlaug Thorey Johnson, daughter Jo-Ann, son Dale
Hobbies – Curling, bowling, golf

Michell Johnston at home, holding his framed medals in Edmonton, in 2003.

Michell Johnston's mother raised him, his brother Merritt and his sisters Ethel and Nellie in Selkirk, Manitoba, by running a boarding house and working as a seamstress. She had a widow's war pension, by no means large, because her late husband had served in the Cameron Highlanders overseas in the First World War. When a barnstormer landed his aircraft at Selkirk and invited young boys to go up, Michell could only watch as others went flying because he did not have the necessary $2. But he remembered the pilot and the biplane: it was an indelible, romantic image.

After graduation from Grade 11 at Devonshire Collegiate in Selkirk, he worked for two years as a delivery man for Epstein's General Store. He went down to Winnipeg on a Thursday afternoon (the store being closed on Fridays), to the RCAF Recruiting Centre in the Lindsay Building on Notre Dame Avenue near Fort Street. After a six-month wait he was enlisted in February 1941 and received serial number R95034. It is a rare airman who cannot remember his enlistment number sixty years later, and Michell could rattle off his R number (R for Reserve) as a recruit and his J number as an officer.

His mother, Melinda, had raised Michell by herself and she did not want him flying in the RCAF. Occasionally, with the most loving of intent, mothers wrote to their sons asking that they fly very slowly and carefully, not very high and never at night—advice that always amused their sons in training and on operations. Melinda Johnston, like thousands of mothers, had to spend the war years reading between the lines of quickly scribbled letters from overseas and dreading that familiar face coming up the front walkway, telegram in hand.

In quick succession Johnston went to Brandon to the Manning Pool, then spent some weeks of guard duty at Dauphin, followed by initial indoctrination and assessment at No. 2 ITS at Regina, then No. 18 EFTS in Boundary Bay, BC, on Tiger Moths, finishing with No. 15 SFTS at Claresholm, Alberta, on twin-engine Cessna Cranes. His wings were pinned on his uniform in October 1941 by the Duke of Windsor, the abdicated King Edward VIII. Edward, the Prince of Wales, as thousands of adoring Canadians had known him from his youthful days, was in High River, Alberta, visiting the large ranch that he had owned for some years. In one of the unexpected twists that sometimes happened to individuals in the war, everyone on Michell's twin-engine course went to twin- or multi-engine aircraft except him. Sergeant Johnston got what he did not ask for and so many others coveted and did *not* get—Spitfires.

Michell Johnston joined 403 Squadron at North Weald on March 18, 1942. After a few convoy patrols over the Channel, he was assigned to fly a fighter sweep over France on April 13 as No. 2 to Squadron Leader Campbell. About as inexperienced as one might expect with the small sum of 220 flying hours, Michell lost control of his Spitfire the first time they spotted the enemy:

A Spit could not fly upside down, it had carburetors that did not run when inverted (until the Spit IX and later models). At some point in the patrol there were some enemy aircraft in the area which we had to evade … Due to the carburetors you must not bunt the stick forward [and I did]. Well, the motor quit, and by the time it recovered there was no one around. There I was all alone. Halfway back to my home aerodrome I saw a bunch of Spitfires, caught up with them, and they were my own outfit. After landing, Squadron Leader Kenneth Campbell said to me: "You did a fine job." Since he hadn't noticed my absence, I never said a bloody thing!

On April 27, while flying as No. 2 to Campbell and one of his flight commanders, H.P. Duval, Michell witnessed them colliding in the air after Duval's Spitfire was heavily damaged by anti-aircraft fire. Campbell was captured and Duval was killed in a high-speed dive into the sea. Four other pilots—Argue, Munn, Wood and Zoochkan—had also been casualties in April. Having experienced nothing with which to compare such traumatic and frequent tragedies, Michell concluded that on a fighter squadron, this "must be an everyday event."

A little more experienced after nearly two months at 403, Johnston flew an evening patrol on June 1 with Larry Somers and came through a dogfight unscathed. The following day he had a rest while Somers and other pilots flew on two ops. The first was uneventful, but the second at mid-morning would set a record for losses by an RCAF squadron on a single offensive patrol: seven pilots shot down. Weather played no part; it was a clear, sunny morning with scattered clouds.

Alan Deere, DSO, DFC and Bar, AFC, a distinguished New Zealand ace from the Battle of Britain, had replaced Campbell as commanding officer. No.

OF FIGHTER PILOTS VERSUS BOMBER PILOTS AND THE FATE THEREOF

It was frequently the case in wartime that talented pilots did not get what they wanted. Exigencies of the service determined the fate of thousands, leaving many frustrated that the system did not appreciate their talents.

For example, in December 1941, Sergeant Kenneth Brown was the only graduating member of his multi-engine course at No. 4 SFTS, Saskatoon, to be recommended for fighters. But he was assigned bombers anyway. He went on to establish a legendary reputation with 617 Dambuster Squadron, taking part in the famous raid against the German dams in May 1943, for which he was awarded the Conspicuous Gallantry Medal, second only to Wing Commander Guy Gibson's Victoria Cross. If Ken could have changed his posting to fighters he would have done it in a flash. It was only after the war that Brown got his hands on a fighter aircraft.

The bomber pilot who wanted to fly fighters and the fighter pilot who would have been happier on bombers was by no means an unusual situation in the Second World War. There are examples of frustrated bomber pilots killing themselves and their crews doing a "beat up" of their home aerodrome, determined to show what great fighter pilots they would make if only they had their chance.

Paradoxically, in the event one was recommended for or forced into the occupation of fighter pilot, there was no predicting how one might succeed or fail in combat. Promising young men had to be taken off operations for lack of performance, and unlikely figures with no self-evident talent or motivation excelled.

403 launched in three sections, with the typical call signs "Blue," "Red" and "Yellow." Deere led the four machines of Red section, with Walker in charge of Yellow section and Darling in charge of Blue. The twelve Spitfires of 403 RCAF teamed up in the air with 222 and 331 Squadrons RAF for a large, wing-size sweep over France. Crossing the coastline at Cap Gris Nez, France, above twenty thousand feet, this wing of fighters flew east towards St Omer then turned out towards the Channel at Le Touquet. No. 403 was the rearmost squadron in the wing as they turned towards home.

The Luftwaffe quickly made a decision to attack and was already airborne with forty Focke-Wulf 190s. The stories differ about what exactly happened next and, in particular, what radiotelephone (RT) exchanges had taken place between the squadrons and the radar controller, call sign Banjo. Banjo had been picking up large enemy formations on radar and

sending messages to the wing and squadron commanders, which could be heard by all the pilots.

When Banjo reported a large, large number of "hostiles," he or she recommended exiting the hot zone as soon as possible. The leading and middle RAF squadrons made it out of range of the enemy. But Deere was back on operations after months away. He had not previously had a dogfight with an FW190. Perhaps keenly motivated to fight, he may have delayed a crucial thirty seconds too long. Perhaps there was insufficient time remaining for 403 to exit the Le Touquet coast, even with the RT warning from Banjo. Some pilots feel there was ample advance warning; others say it would have made no difference.

Red, Blue and Yellow sections flying at twenty-four thousand feet over the French coast were cornered. The twelve pilots had to fight their way out of France. They were opposed by at least two squadrons of FW190s attacking from different

ACCOUNT IN THE OFFICIAL HISTORY OF THE RCAF, ABOUT THE SPRING OF 1942

"You are terribly short of fighter aircraft," noted the prime minister [Winston Churchill], early in March, "but it pays to lose plane for plane. If you consider CIRCUS losses will come within that statement, it would be worthwhile. But beware of the future." In the event, the pace quickened earlier than expected, with an average of 826 sorties a day between 13 and 17 April 1942 and over a thousand on the 16th. (Coincidentally, a month later Bomber Command would launch its first thousand-bomber raid.) The Germans responded selectively, as they had in 1941, intervening only when they felt circumstances favoured them. Fighter Command lost thirty-four aircraft in March and ninety-three in April, while claiming a total of 114 enemy machines destroyed. In fact, between the beginning of March and the end of June the Luftwaffe lost only fifty-eight machines in combat, while Bentley Prior [RAF Headquarters], claiming 197 victories, lost 259. As for the five RCAF squadrons, they lost twenty pilots while claiming to have shot down nine enemy machines.

Once again it is impossible to determine the number of enemy aircraft they actually destroyed, but this time the Canadian proportion was probably close to the overall Fighter Command ratio of over four lost for every one actually shot down. Nevertheless, since no one at Bentley Priory—or, indeed, in the Air Ministry or the War Cabinet—knew at the time how bad that ratio was, morale did not suffer unduly. Individual pilots who lost friends and colleagues were usually consoled by the belief that their squadron or wing was giving as good as it got.

That was not the case on 2 June 1942, however, as No. 403 Squadron lost six pilots in the course of a single disastrous sweep. At the time the squadron was under the command of a New Zealander, Alan Deere, DFC and Bar, the unit's sixth non-Canadian commanding officer in the thirteen months since its formation.

Greenhous, Harris, Johnston, Rawling, *The Crucible of War, 1939–1945: The Official History of The Royal Canadian Air Force.*

quarters, likely some forty to fifty German pilots flying a considerably better aircraft than the Spitfire Mk V.

Deere was an aggressive ace who had himself crash-landed, bailed out or survived imminent destruction nine times. He finished the war with more than twenty victories. He seemed indestructible; like George Beurling, he could boast that he had the nine lives of a cat, and that was the title of his 1960s autobiography: *Nine Lives*. He and his wingman, Sergeant Murphy, though separated in the battle, made it home to England.

However, the other experienced section leader, an ace named Flight Lieutenant E.V. "Mitzi" Darling, DFC, who was a close friend of Alan Deere, was shot down in the Channel and did not survive. Of the remaining pilots, all Canadians, five became prisoners of war, and one, George Aitken, bailed out in the Channel but was picked up.

Profile – NORRIS EDMUND HUNT
Born – September 13, 1920, Ottawa
Died – October 19, 2004, Huntsville, ON
Father – Septimus Hunt, Dominion Land Surveyor
Mother – Amy Tabor
Degrees & Awards – BM, published author, *Muskoka: Change of Seasons*
Post-war occupation – MD, family physician
Marital status – Wife Maureen Hardie; sons Geoffrey (deceased) and Fraser; daughter Jane
Hobbies – Photography, music

One of the five pilots taken prisoner that day, Norris Edmund "Joe" Hunt, was actually on his first full day of operations, on only the second op of his career. In his personal memoir written in 1996, Dr Hunt wrote that as he left the coast of France at sea level he was congratulating himself for getting clear of the battle above, when "tracers again came flying by—awfully close to my aircraft. More defensive violent manoeuvres were called for and in the process of doing so I found to my dismay that three FW190s had followed me down."

Flying very close to the water as he had been told to do in training if under attack did not help because the 190s could outrun his Spitfire, forcing him to turn repeatedly into their attacks to save his life. His fuel

was being burned up at a high rate as he was forced to keep turning yet maintain precious speed and manoeuvre his way across the Channel. Norris Hunt wrote about the terror of no avenue of escape:

I realized that my situation was getting rather desperate and the thought suddenly came to me that "this was it"—that my final moments on this planet were drawing to a rapid close. It may sound strange but the thought that flashed through my mind at that time was a vision of the "Sky Line Trail" in the Gatineau Hills, north of Ottawa. It was my favourite place to hike in the fall. "Would I ever see it again?"

… They had got smart and left one of the three out in front of me so that when I turned towards them I presented a nice target. I felt the impact of bullets hitting my engine and another whizzed by my head through the Plexiglas of the canopy. I guess it is a subconscious movement but during a steep turn I turn my head towards the direction of that turn. If I had not done so the bullet would have gone through my head! I was also lucky that it was not a cannon shell instead. Smoke began billowing from the engine and it began spluttering and I could feel the loss of power. I was not far from the French Coast so I elected to try to make it to shore … I suddenly became conscious of two FW190s flying in formation with me as a sort of escort. I was touched that there still remained some "esprit de corps" in the German Luftwaffe.

Hunt was assisted by a soldier with a Luger in his hand as he was extricated from his inverted Spitfire, now lying in a muddy field. He was escorted by the Germans to the receiving centre for captured Allied aircrew, the so-called Dulag Luft. It was there that the physical shock of what had happened gradually was replaced by feelings of guilt at having let the RCAF down. He also felt great bitterness and anger towards Alan Deere. Put in isolation at the Dulag Luft to soften him up for questioning, Joe felt very alone, and very sorry for himself because of how he had come to be in German hands. He felt even worse when the German interrogator said confidently: "Oh, you must be a new member of 403 Squadron—we haven't heard about you!"

He found some measure of comfort after he learned that others in the squadron had also gone down to defeat, so at least his failure wasn't unique. On the way to the bathroom under German escort one day he passed the cell of Jack Parr, who had been leading George Aitken in the second element of Blue section. After the war he learned the full scope of the losses, how the pilot who had been leading him in the second element of Yellow section, Larry Somers, was severely burned on his face and scalp and had to be cared for in a German hospital. Also "in the bag" was Darling's No. 2, Don Campbell, and Red section's second element leader, Doug Hurst.

GARDINER AND MONCHIER KILLED AT DIEPPE

Ed Gardiner and his No. 2, Norm Monchier, were killed in action on August 19, during the Dieppe Raid. Their remains were removed from their Spitfires by the villagers of St Aubin de Caulf, and buried in the church cemetery. Photos of the two in a glassed-in case are mounted on the church wall, and the villagers put flowers on the graves of the two Canadians on Sundays. The villagers have resisted any attempt by authorities to remove the bodies to a British Commonwealth War Graves cemetery. Their response is simple: "They are our heroes, and they belong to us."

Profile – ROMAN ROY WOZNIAK
Born – June 29, 1919, Saskatoon
Father – Stefan Wozniak, maintenance subway, CNR
Mother – Anna Shibiki
Degrees & Awards – BSc Pharmacy
Post-war occupation – Pharmacist
Marital status – Wife Margot Martin; daughters Gail, Lynne and Lee; son Graham
Hobbies – Curling

Flight Lieutenant Brad Walker and his No. 2 in Yellow section, Ed Gardiner, son of Minister of Agriculture James Gardiner in the Mackenzie King government, got home intact. Red 4, Roy Wozniak, had his elevator cables almost entirely severed and his right tire blown out, but still managed to get his Spitfire down and walk away intact. Wozniak is a youthful-looking eighty-five-year-old retired pharmacist in West Vancouver. His voice is full of enthusiasm as he describes his escape to me:

I got hit by a cannon shell in the fuselage. It felt like being hit by a sledgehammer. The armour plate saved me, the shrapnel hit the armour plate behind my seat, but one piece lodged in the heel of my boot … I was thrown into a spin; by the time I pulled out there were three on my tail … they had me off to one side all to themselves … I slowed down, waited for them to close in, and I whipped around in a very tight turn, and I almost got the leader head-on … for whatever reason, they broke it off and I headed for home. I noticed there was a lot of play in my stick, and my throttle did not respond.

Blue 4, George Aitken, had attempted to protect Jack Parr but he was bounced from behind. Bullets struck but did not penetrate the armour plating behind his cockpit, and a second FW190 fired cannon shells through his wings. George was fortunate to evade these pilots by spiralling downward in a very tight left turn from ten thousand to five thousand feet. But flames from the engine exhaust and leaking fuel directly into his cockpit forced him to bail out at around one thousand feet. George couldn't swim a stroke and was gratified that his Mae West and dinghy inflated properly. His recollection today is that:

Deere circled me when I was in the water, and so did another pilot. I was cold and shivering, but along came a torpedo boat. They took me on first, to mid-Channel, and then transferred me to air-sea rescue boat No. 147 to take me back to Dover. That particular boat was lost a while later at Dieppe … Michell

Roy Wozniak of 403 Squadron, with Susie, and Sgt. Del DeLong, Roy's crew chief.

Johnston picked me up at Hawkinge … I was in a navy rolled-neck white sweater, and still shivering uncontrollably.

In my discussions with George about that day and the resentment of Joe Hunt and the other casualties who were captured, he does not hold a grudge against Deere for what he did or, more importantly, failed to do. Aitken felt then and still does that the job of a fighter pilot is "to fight, not run away!" Roy Wozniak expresses the view that the circumstances, with 403 being the high-cover squadron, trapped them. Given that there were four Luftwaffe squadrons in an up-sun position waiting to attack, there was little chance for 403 to outrun the FW190s.

In conversation with Michell Johnston, I learned that George Aitken was all in when Michell picked him up, and that both young men were glad of a rest period at Martlesham Heath. On June 22, the day after George's twenty-second birthday, he and Michell celebrated their commissioning with a few drinks. They were no longer NCOs; they were now "officers and gentlemen."

Deere protested the decision by headquarters to withdraw 403 from the line of battle, saying his pilots were still highly motivated despite the events of June 2. Whatever the feelings of the pilots, Air Vice-Marshal Trafford Leigh-Mallory was having none of Deere's arguments. According to the RCAF official history and Deere's own autobiography, Leigh-Mallory, who had seen action as a young pilot in the Great War, felt that Deere should carry some burden of what happened because he was "rather too fond of a fight" and took "unnecessary risks."

Courtesy of the George Aitken Collection

George Aitken, 403 Squadron, of Edmonton, AB, 1942.

Courtesy of the Dr. Norris Hunt Collection

Norris "Joe" Hunt, 403 Squadron, of Ottawa, ON, 1945.

Profile – DOUGLAS WARREN

Born – May 28, 1922, Nanton, AB

Father – Earl Warren, farmer

Mother – Marie Gullig

Decorations & Medals – DFC, Air Medal (US), CD and two Clasps, Centennial Medal

Degrees & Awards – TP—graduate test pilot, Empire Test Pilot School (ETPS)

Post-war occupation – Air force officer, Wing Commander, RCAF/CAF

Marital status – Wife Melba Bennett

Hobbies – Lay chaplain of the Royal Canadian Legion Branch in Comox, BC

During the period that 403 was resting and rebuilding after the debacle of June 2, a newly graduated pilot from OTU on Spitfires arrived at their station, Digby, Lincolnshire. He had just turned twenty and was eagerly looking forward to starting his operational life as a fighter pilot. He had hoped to serve with his brother, but at the OTU there had been a British flight commander who had had bad experiences with brothers on squadrons. He told Douglas Warren that he would not recommend any such pairing. This was all the more distressing for Douglas because he was an identical twin to his brother Bruce. In their entire life since their birth at Nanton, Alberta, in 1922, they had been in each other's company.

Their American-born parents (from Indiana and Missouri) did not endorse the twins' decision to volunteer, but Bruce and Douglas loved their country and loved aviation. They joined together and were assigned enlistment numbers R93529 and R93530. They bought identical Rolex "Victory" wristwatches ($32.50 each) just before they began training at No. 5 EFTS, High River, Alberta.

As twins they each had a preternatural ability to know what the other was doing or thinking, even at a long distance. Douglas once reported to his EFTS flight commander that Bruce was missing on a flight,

Courtesy of the Douglas Warren Collection

Bruce and Douglas Warren were born on May 28, 1922, and are shown here at age four in Nanton, Alberta, with Topsie and the new wagon made for them by their father Earl.

saying he had not landed. The paperwork suggested otherwise, but Douglas knew as only a twin can that his brother was not on the ground. He was proven correct a short time later when Bruce and his instructor, delayed by winds, finally came in to land.

The two farm boys, ecstatic to be flying and especially happy to be off the farm, graduated as pilots after performing equally well in their flying on Harvards at No. 34 SFTS, Medicine Hat. Well, almost equally well. Bruce was slightly better in ground school. There was just enough difference in their marks that Douglas ranked ninth and Bruce eighth. This was characteristic of their entire schooling, Bruce usually being slightly above Douglas in marks. Since only the first eight of the thirty-seven graduates on the Harvard course were commissioned, Douglas received sergeant's stripes. The hierarchy of officer versus NCO now separated them.

Pilot Officer Bruce Warren was so concerned about this that he talked the other commissioned officers with

him on S.S. *Stratheden* into smuggling Douglas into the same cabin. Since Bruce and Douglas were absolutely identical, they could swap uniforms and change rank without anyone knowing, eating at will in the dining rooms aboard ship that catered separately to NCOs and officers. This was true throughout their wartime careers, because the only people who could ever reliably distinguish between them were their family.

Before leaving Canada they went to see the personnel administration of RCAF Western Command in Calgary, pleading their case for Douglas to be made an officer. In due course after arriving in Britain, he was commissioned retroactively and given the same seniority date as Bruce. But in the meantime they were separated for the first time in their lives. Bruce took his OTU training ahead of Douglas and was posted to 165 Squadron RAF at Heathfield, near Ayr in Scotland. It now looked as though, due to one man's arbitrary hostility to brothers on squadrons, they might never serve together.

Bruce Warren, J9286 (left) and Douglas Warren, J9735, at 165 Squadron, Gravesend, part of the Biggin Hill Wing, just before a sweep in September 1942. White bands on the left forearm contain vital information about radio frequencies, course to fly, and so on.

However, the commanding officer of 165 was more sympathetic to the Warrens after he heard from Bruce how much he wanted his brother with him. Squadron Leader Archie Winskill pulled strings at Fighter Command HQ to get Douglas plucked from 403 after only two days. Douglas Warren recalled his departure from 403 on very short notice: "I had never mentioned my desire to join 165 to S/L Deere, but, when I chanced to meet him just before my departure, I explained why I was so pleased about the change. He said very little, but seemed quite understanding, and wished me luck."

Douglas and Bruce were the only Canadians serving on 165. The twins served two tours of operations on Spitfires with the RAF in the same units. After 165 Squadron, they moved to No. 58 OTU as instructors and onwards to 66 Squadron in July

1944 for their second tour as flight commanders of "A" and "B" Flights. Their nicknames on squadron were Duke I (Bruce) and Duke II (Douglas), and their Spitfires were so named.

When they flew in parallel with separate sections in combat, they had a habit of whistling briefly on the radio in a distinctive way so each knew the other had come through safely after a dogfight. They could and occasionally did replace each other on operations and other pilots never concerned themselves as to whether it was Duke I or Duke II leading them—they were identical in looks and identical in their leadership.

Neither young man drank alcohol, smoked cigarettes or prowled the London bars looking for stunning British showgirls from the Windmill theatre. Their hobbies were photography and miniature models. Such clean-living habits are sometimes an impediment to advancement in a fighter squadron. The twins were adopted, as many young men were, by British families—in their case, by the Archie Pratt family of Gravesend.

There were many brothers serving in arms in the RAF and RCAF, including a set of twins who served tours in Bomber Command and were decorated. Their names were Eric and Allan Sherlock and they became good friends with the Warrens after the war. The story told here of Jerry and Rod Smith at 126 in Malta is that rare case of brothers flying together as lead and wingman on fighters. But to the best of my knowledge the Warrens are the only example in the Allied air forces of the Second World War of identical twins serving within the same fighter units at the same time and assigned similar duties throughout the war.

King George awarded Distinguished Flying Crosses to Bruce and Douglas in March 1945 at the same investiture, murmuring as he did so that he could not recall a medal event with twins before. Bruce logged 248 sorties (336:15 hours), and Douglas 254 sorties (342:50 hours) on Spitfire operations between 1942 and 1945. Both chose RCAF flying careers after the war, Douglas on fighters, and Bruce graduating as a test pilot at the British Empire Test Pilot School. Tragically, Bruce and his navigator were killed in 1951 while testflying the CF-100 all-weather fighter at AVRO Canada in Toronto. Douglas was devastated by his loss and credits his wife Melba with getting him through the grief of losing the other half of himself. His religious faith helped as he believes that he will rejoin Bruce someday soon and they will carry on their interrupted conversation.

In late June 1942, in anticipation of the assault on the beaches of Dieppe, Chadburn's 416 got to move south to Sussex. Enemy encounters increased and one experienced pilot named Archer, a flight commander born in Bridgetown, Barbados, shot down the first enemy aircraft for the squadron on July 17; on August 2, pilots McKendy and Gates teamed up to shoot down a Dornier 217 bomber.

The Dieppe Raid, postponed in July, was back on for Wednesday, August 19, and in the course of that historic event hundreds of RAF and Luftwaffe aircraft would fly on operations. Douglas and Bruce Warren flew on three of the four ops that day for 165 Squadron. On the second sortie as No. 3 and No. 4 to Colquhoun and Pederson, both in Scotland, they shared in the destruction of a Dornier 217 bomber. No. 416, led throughout by Lloyd Chadburn, had its most distinguished fighting day since being founded. Four ops were flown, at 0720 hours, at 1050, at 1320, and finally at 1800 hours. Some twenty-one squadron pilots took part in the day's operations, flying a total of forty-seven sorties.

In the operation after lunch, Flight Lieutenant Russel and Pilot Officer Buckham each shot down an FW190; both German pilots bailed out. Then Flight Sergeant Dagwood Phillip attacked the first enemy aircraft of his career, an FW190, from underneath with little or no deflection, and after several bursts the pilot bailed out. These were the three confirmed victories that day for 416, along with one probable and another seven damaged, remarkably without any squadron pilots or Spitfires being lost.

This was not typical of RAF operations, however, for the squadrons and wings as a whole. In fact, aerial support to the Dieppe Raid inflicted serious casualties on the RAF. According to Peter Caygill in *Spitfire Mark V in Action*, twenty-nine Spitfire pilots were killed and eleven taken prisoners of war. Duke Warren says:

Pilots taking part in the combined Operation on the 19th of August knew it was a "big show" as such episodes were described then. Only later did we learn how big it was, for the RAF had flown almost 3,000 sorties, the Luftwaffe 945. At the time, it was thought losses were about equal, 100 aircraft on each side, but it was later found the Germans had only lost 50, whereas the Allies lost 106.

* * *

Profile – ALLAN ROBERT MCFADDEN
Born – December 11, 1918, Ft McLeod, AB, raised at Lacombe
Father – Archibald Robert McFadden, agricultural worker at the Experimental Farm
Mother – Mattie Louise Taylor
Degrees & Awards - BSc
Post-war occupation – Agricultural engineer
Marital status – Wife Marjorie Lenore "Lennie" Wilson, son Murray, daughter Brenda
Hobbies – Golf, curling, skiing

I first met Allan and Marjorie McFadden in January 2001. I was just starting out on my project to interview fighter pilots, and a call had come from my friend Bill Arbuthnot alerting me that the McFaddens were moving from Lethbridge and had arrived to reconnoitre. I immediately went over to visit, hoping that Allan would consent to an interview. He sat on the couch and spoke in a soft voice, pausing from time to time to rest and chuckling as thoughts came back to him. He had an oxygen tube running from a portable tank to a line around his head. Sometimes in my interviews, the wife of the pilot is present, or perhaps a child or grandchild. They usually hear stories that have that comfortable quality of well-worn repetition, but there are the other stories that have never been told inside the family until I ask my question. On this occasion Dr Murray McFadden, Al and Lennie's son, sat next to me as I asked Al about his early military life.

On many occasions when I interview, the veteran's wife leaves the home so we can have privacy—they know that once their husband starts talking about those days, hours will fly by. I get to meet many wives as I am packing up my briefcase and they are coming home; some consent to be

Photos courtesy of Allan and Lennie McFadden

Allan McFadden during the war years.

Allan McFadden with his wife Lennie on their honeymoon.

photographed with their husbands, some do not. The overwhelming majority of these wives are the women that the veterans met during the war or shortly thereafter.

Some of the wives are also war veterans, and may have met their husbands while serving in the RCAF or RAF at or near the same station. For example, as previously mentioned, Beaufighter ace Carl Fumerton married Madeleine, a fighter controller; also, Mosquito navigator "Kirk" Kirkpatrick married Barbara, a fighter controller. Spitfire pilot Roy Wozniak married Margot, the assistant adjutant at RAF Station Peterhead; Spitfire pilot Frank Hubbard married Shirley, who worked in RCAF Headquarters in London.

Sometimes a wife will sit in and remind her husband of events, correct the dates and names in stories being told, serve coffee and lunch and find photographs from the war. One wife endeared herself when she took me aside in private and said that her husband's mind was not what it used to be, and

that I should telephone her if I needed further clarification on her husband's answers.

Al McFadden sometimes was moved as he recalled episodes of escort duty in 1943, particularly with torpedo-carrying Beaufighters on anti-shipping strikes. An escorting fighter pilot providing top cover to any attacking force is sometimes a powerless witness to horrific slaughter. There were occasions when only two-thirds of the attacking force came home, and the escorts turned back after they had protected nothing and defended nothing, but been marked by the experience forever.

It is often these memories that are the most indelible throughout a fighter pilot's life. This was the case with Al McFadden, and also other fighter pilots I have met. Al wiped tears from his eyes as he remembered the bravery of Beaufighter crews, exploding in flames, crashing in the Channel as they attempted to launch torpedoes against German ships. At this stage, I was new to the business of interviewing fighter pilots of the Second World

War, so I did not know what to make of his feelings, or my own. As it was unexpected, I felt embarrassed that I had upset him by my question, or somehow caused the event. I was to learn through subsequent years of interviews that I was simply the conduit for the veteran's experience.

McFadden told me that his assignment as a fighter pilot had been interrupted at its inception when he was taken prisoner in 1942 in Africa by the Vichy French. The story of how he became an internee of the Marshal Pétain regime is worth re-telling, since it illustrates the surreal world that a fighter pilot might encounter en route to combat or in its aftermath.

Within weeks of receiving his wings at No. 10 SFTS, Dauphin, in October 1941, Pilot Officer McFadden crossed the Atlantic on SS *Warwick Castle*. He trained on Hurricanes at No. 55 OTU at Usworth in Durham, England, graduating in February '42. His hope was to immediately join a British-based squadron but, alone among his class of graduates, he was posted to the Middle East. He went aboard HMS *Adamant*, a submarine depot ship, on March 21 for the long trip to Africa, to Freetown, Sierra Leone. It was one month later when he arrived on a rusty coastal steamer at Takoradi, on the Gulf of Guinea. This was the assembly location for the RAF to ferry single- and twin-engine fighters and bombers across the vast expanse of northern Africa to Cairo. Like all ferry operations in the war, there were casualties. People

and aircraft vanished without a trace along the four-thousand-mile stretch of mountains, deserts and jungles.

In a formation of six heavily laden Hurricane IICs, each with two external fuel tanks under the wings and four 20mm cannon in the wings, McFadden took off at dawn on April 27 bound for Cairo. There were eleven stops along the way at places whose names echo in history—places such as Fort-Lamy, Khartoum and Luxor. The formation was led by a pilot/navigator who carried the group's only maps and charts; since there was no radio contact between aircraft, each subsequent leg was briefed in the evening on stopovers.

Tropical storms in Africa are among the most powerful in the world. When the formation entered one, Al was on the outside right as the leader entered a left-hand turn with his six fighters. The severity of the turbulence in the cumulonimbus cloud put his aircraft completely out of control; then his Merlin engine stopped. He managed to recover at just two hundred feet above ground, and spotted a beach through the torrential rain. He set down heavily on the sand and:

> The aircraft flipped over on its back so I grabbed the stick and pulled myself as deep as possible into the cockpit. The canopy was torn away, and I ended up with the back of my head and shoulders on the wet sand. The smell of gasoline was very strong and I was

From an Interview with Derrick England, 416 Squadron in 1943–44

I felt that the boys who flew Beaufighters were probably the bravest men who ever lived. I have never witnessed such brave acts as twelve Beaufighters attacking a German convoy just off the coast of Holland. This twelve went straight at the convoy and the anti-aircraft fire coming from that convoy was absolutely horrendous … I watched three of the Beaufighters go into the sea … we as the escorts were helpless to do anything, other than just watch …

I will always remember this particular sortie as it was so vicious … I always admired anyone who flew the Beaufighter.

fearful of fire. I could not locate the lever for the breakout panel on the side of the cockpit and I panicked for a moment or so, then finally found it. The panel dropped away, letting in fresh air. About the same time the tip of a bayonet appeared, and upon looking up I saw a large black soldier holding the rifle and bayonet. Behind him were a white man and more black soldiers.

After Al released his harness lock, the soldiers were able to haul him out of his Hurricane and escort him to the hospital at Contonou, Dahomey (today the country called Benin). As he later recalled, "other than a scratch on my knee I was okay. Mentally I was very upset and worried about my folks back home as well as being out of the war."

He learned from an English merchant who visited him in the hospital that he was now under the control of the Vichy French government. His next journey was like something out of a Joseph Conrad novel. A sergeant in the French army, using a French-English dictionary to communicate, escorted Al first by train, then bus, and lastly in a thirty-foot metal boat. For twenty-three days they lived in the boat, with two bunks and an open roof, while four natives with long poles and rope pulled the boat up the Niger River from Gao to Timbuktu. To relieve the monotony, McFadden's guard lent him his rifle to take shots at a pelican. The terrain he surveyed was alien to a young man who had grown up at the Dominion Experimental Farm at Lacombe, Alberta:

We passed many villages of mud huts. Wild ducks, geese and pelicans were abundant on the river along with the odd crocodile basking on the banks. Our food was purchased from the villagers along the way—mostly fish, wild waterfowl, chicken and couscous. One of the boatmen did the cooking; we ate reasonably well and I survived the trip in good health.

He arrived at the internment camp in Timbuktu on May 29. There were quite a few Allied prisoners in the camp, primarily Merchant Marine as well as one Royal Navy officer. The diet in the camp was couscous with gravy and peanuts in the shell. By summer McFadden had been moved to a military camp at Koulikoro, located between Timbuktu and Dakar. There he met other Royal Navy officers and one Royal Australian Air Force officer, Dusty Rhodes, who became his best pal.

In the civilized manner of the French, each internee at Koulikoro was paid in francs, their rate of pay based on their equivalent rank in the French army. The internees combined their pay and hired cooks, who bought the food and prepared meals; beds were made each day by the hired help. As long as they did not attempt to escape, life was relatively hazard-free and comfortable. The French guards were sociable and provided news about the outside world. On the whole they were favourably disposed towards their internees, even though, in theory, they were allied with Germany. With the surrender of the Vichy regime after the invasion of Tunisia, McFadden was transferred to Dakar in December 1942 and shipped home to Britain, where he arrived in late January '43.

After an intelligence debriefing at RCAF HQ, Al was advised that he was entitled to a month's leave in Canada. He turned it down, saying he had done nothing to deserve it. Al's response was: "Go back, hell! I haven't done anything in this war yet. I want to stay here and fight." Shortly afterwards he was sent to Dundee, Scotland, for refresher flying training, and met up with Dick Forbes-Roberts, who was from Arcola, Saskatchewan, and had been educated in Regina.

Dick recalls his Prairie childhood as idyllic, akin to the fictional boy in W.O. Mitchell's novel *Who Has Seen the Wind?* ("though I didn't lose my father like that boy"). He had escaped to Dundee from his instructional duties in Calgary as "A" Flight Commander at No. 3 SFTS on twin-engine Ansons and Cranes. Forbes-Roberts had received his wings in the summer of 1940, after graduating in December 1939 from the Royal Military College (RMC) of Canada in Kingston, Ontario. His entire RMC class was graduated early with wartime certificates to hasten their entry into war service. Dick had entered the RMC in 1937 with the intention of making his career in the RCAF.

Profile – RICHARD DRUMMOND FORBES-ROBERTS

Born – July 18, 1918, Arcola, SK

Father – Herbert Forbes-Roberts, electrical engineer

Mother – Melissa Jefferson

Decorations & Medals – CD and Two Clasps

Degrees & Awards – Royal Military College, RMC No. 2568, Class of 1937 (war certificate December 1939)

Post-war occupation – Air force officer, Wing Commander, RCAF

Marital status – Wife Dorothy Innes Hopkins, son Ronald, daughter Jacqueline

Hobbies – Golf, model railroading

When Al and Dick joined 416 Squadron RCAF at Digby it was June 1943, and Squadron Leader F.E. "Bitsy" Grant was the commanding officer. As they arrived at the squadron, a long-time member, Dagwood Phillip, was preparing to leave. Dagwood was called into Wing Commander J.F. "Johnnie" Johnson's office and asked to consider a transfer over to 421 Squadron as a flight commander. No particular explanation was provided to Phillip. This would allow another pilot at 421—a flight commander named Arthur Sager—to move over to 416. While low flying in a Tiger Moth with one of the ground crew, Sager disturbed a sports day in progress at St Thomas School. A formal complaint by the school's chairman of the board ultimately affected Sager in three ways: he was reduced in rank, lost his flight and was sent off to 416 Squadron.

Sager was a little older than the average Canadian fighter pilot, better educated and more sophisticated. He had received a BA degree from the University of British Columbia in 1938, and says of himself that as a student he was definitely "a pacifist." A childhood friend of Sager during two summer vacations spent in Crescent Beach, south of Vancouver, was Robert "Hammy" Gray, future Royal Navy Fleet Air Arm fighter pilot and Victoria Cross recipient. In the year before the war Sager had been making a meagre living in Britain as a junior reporter with *The Daily Mirror* and as an actor on the stage (the Gaiety in London, the Theatre Royal in Margate).

He returned to Canada to enlist in the RCAF, being called up in February 1941, and his SFTS training at Saskatoon was on twin-engine Cessna Cranes, which did not bode well for single-engine

fighters. The son of a medical missionary working with the First Nations in the north of British Columbia, Sager emphasized in conversation: "I wanted to be a fighter pilot so as to kill fewer people, so as to be responsible for my own killings." In his memoir, *Line Shoot: Diary of a Fighter Pilot*, he recalls being asked by the examiner after his final test on the Crane:

> "Sergeant Ruppel tells me you want to be a fighter pilot?" "Yes, Sir!" I replied, trying not to shout. "That's why I joined the Air Force!"
>
> He smiled, said nothing. But I found out later that he'd given me an "Average Plus" and recommended the precious S.E., Single-Engine rating. As far as I knew, I was the only one in the class to go on to fighters.

Profile – ARTHUR HAZELTON SAGER

Born – October 22, 1916, Hazelton, BC

Father – William Sager, medical missionary with First Nations, northern BC

Mother – Ethel Mary Duckers

Decorations & Medals – DFC, French Legion of Honour (2004)

Degrees & Awards – BA at the University of British Columbia (UBC) in 1938

Post-war occupation – Public relations executive, UBC, CBC Radio; chief of Africa section, Bureau of Technical Assistance Operations, United Nations; Food and Agricultural Organization, Rome

Marital status – Divorced; son Eric, daughters Ann and Susan

Hobbies – Writing and reading

Dagwood Phillip knew nothing of the circumstances of Sager's faux pas, but he was happy to move to 421 as "A" Flight commander, particularly at the request of someone he liked and admired. While at 421 over that summer, Dagwood shared in the destruction of one Me109, destroyed a second and damaged an Me108, an Me109 and a FW190. His DFC citation noted:

> This officer has shown marked ability in leading his flight over enemy territory. His exceptional keenness to seek out the enemy and destroy him has been an outstanding example to those flying with him. During these offensive operations this officer has destroyed two

Arthur Sager in Victoria, BC, in 2003.

enemy aircraft, shared in destroying others and damaged six.

Al McFadden served with 416 until August 1944 under four squadron commanders. Of Lloyd Chadburn, who had been promoted to wing commander in January 1943, McFadden declares: "He was a superb leader and I would follow him to hell and back." R.H. "Kelly" Walker followed Bitsy Grant, who within a week of moving over to take command of 403 was killed on operations. Walker was replaced in October by F.E. "Freddie" Green, DFC, who had been born in Petersburg, Virginia, of a British father. Educated in Canada, Green enlisted in the RCAF in 1940 and is one of the most memorable characters of the war for those who flew with him. Arthur Sager served with Green first at 421 and then at 416, and recalls him in his memoir as ebullient:

The unquestioned pace-setter of the squadron was the C/O Freddy Green, "Da Chief"

as he was often called. Speaking in a drawl, walking with a slouch, pipe constantly in his mouth, always grinning. Freddy had a charismatic air about him. A good storyteller, he was the author of the squadron's most colourful expressions, mostly off-colour. He exuded calmness and good cheer, led without making an effort to do so, and enjoyed the loyalty of pilots and ground crew.

Profile – RICHARD DOUGLAS BOOTH

Born – July 4, 1920, Vancouver

Father – Richard Booth, manager at American Can Corporation

Mother – Blanche Whitworth

Degrees & Awards – BComm, CGA

Post-war occupation – Accountant, Benson Bros. Shipbuilding Co., Ltd., Vancouver

Marital status – Wife Joy Rathie died in 2001; sons Rick, Donald and Jack

Hobbies – Crossword puzzles, lawn bowling

When McFadden joined "B" Flight at 416, one of the section leaders in the flight was Richard Douglas Booth, of Vancouver. He was the only child of British-born parents, Blanche Whitworth and Richard Booth. His father worked as a supervisor in American Can Corporation, taking care of the canneries along the British Columbia coast, and had met his wife in Britain during the Great War while working as a dispatch rider in the Army Service Corps. They married shortly after Richard returned with Blanche to an east Vancouver neighbourhood in 1919.

By his own admission merely an adequate student at King Edward High School in Vancouver but a pretty good athlete, especially at lacrosse, Doug Booth had no interest in aviation as a boy. A chance encounter in the RCAF Recruiting Centre in Vancouver's Merchants Exchange Building sent him down a path he neither planned for nor coveted. He successfully completed his pilot training at No. 2 EFTS, Fort William, Ontario, and No. 13 SFTS, St Hubert, Quebec, graduating as a sergeant pilot and immediately going overseas. During his OTU training at Aston Down northeast of Bristol, with the confidence of 250 flying hours, Doug took his Spitfire under the Severn Railway Bridge. This

Courtesy of the Douglas Booth Collection

Doug Booth at three stages of his youth, in Vancouver, BC, and with 416 Squadron in Digby, Britain.

long nineteenth-century bridge, about eighty feet above the water, had a space of forty-eight feet between vertical supports; the Spitfire has a wingspan of about thirty-seven feet.

When Doug arrived in September 1942 at Martlesham Heath, Suffolk, as a new member of 416 Squadron RCAF, one of the squadrons of 11 Group RAF, Lloyd Chadburn was his commanding officer and Hugh Russel his flight commander. Hugh, from Westmount, Quebec, was the younger brother of Blair "Dal" Russel, a Battle of Britain No. 1 Squadron RCAF veteran. Wing Commander Russel survived the war with seven gallantry awards.

Hugh was killed at age twenty-one on D-Day plus ten in a dogfight against a much larger Luftwaffe formation. The section of four Spitfires from 443 Squadron also included Squadron Leader James Hall of Toronto, twenty-two, along with Luis Perez-Gomez, twenty, of Guadalajara, Mexico, and Donald Walz, twenty-six, from a farm at Quincy District, Saskatchewan. Only Walz survived the dogfight; he bailed out of his burning aircraft and evaded capture through the help of a French family.

The NCO pilots at Martlesham Heath were accommodated in little houses around the perimeter of the aerodrome. In Booth's house were also some Polish pilots serving in 11 Group. It was unsettling to watch the Poles get up in the morning because "they wore a silk stocking on their head when they slept to keep their hair in place … apparently it was a European custom. But it was astounding to a Canadian kid like me." As part of the usual indoctrination for all rookie pilots, he was taken up for aerobatic and formation evaluation, in his case with Flying Officer R.J. "Bob" Turp:

He really wrung me out … we were doing tail chases, loops and rolls, tight turns, formation at low level down at two hundred feet with me on the inside of the turns … I guess I made a pretty good account of myself, because I heard later that Turp was razzed by his colleagues in the officers' mess for not being able to lose the rookie … Bob was lost on operations in February '43.

Doug Booth had been rated as an above-average pilot at the Advanced Flying Unit (AFU) at Watton,

England, where he trained on the Miles Master II, the usual RAF transition aircraft for those moving from a Harvard up to a fighter. He was rated average on graduation from 52 OTU on the Spitfire. While he did not at first glance fit the stereotype of the fighter pilot on the ground, being quiet-spoken and almost intellectual, in the air he could be quite impetuous. He was also quite lucky, as he readily admits; his Spitfire was never damaged by flak or bullet holes despite many close escort sorties with bomber formations.

On one occasion he decided to show his flying skills to a passing Lancaster by executing a stern attack followed by a barrel roll around the bomber. It was not, as Booth admits today, a smart thing to do since one of the gunners could easily have shouted to his pilot, "Hard port, skipper," resulting in two fireballs and the deaths of eight flyers. Such is "the callowness and stupidity of youth," declares Doug. On the matter of flying versus gunnery, the latter being the critical skill of a fighter pilot, he observes:

I couldn't hit the ass end of a bull with a shovel, whereas Chad could hit the enemy in a single head-on pass … and Danny Noonan, boy, could he shoot! Our main duties at this time were to escort bombers, primarily US Army Air Corps B26 Marauders and RAF Beaufighters. If we stopped the enemy from shooting them down, we accomplished our primary job, and justified our reason for being there …

I recall the first time I had a crack at an enemy aircraft. We got into a real dogfight one day, and I was up behind an Me109. He was doing a port turn, and I could see all these splashes on his port wing root. Then the pilot bails out. So I think, "Hey, I got one," but back on the ground, I find that the C/O had had a crack at him, plus somebody else experienced, then me, and I was number three on the totem pole …

On a later occasion we were vectored by radar to a perfect bounce against enemy aircraft. Just as we are closing in to the perfect kill, from up-sun, an entire squadron of Polish pilots came screaming straight down into the middle of our attack, fucked everything up and, on top of which, shot down our targets. Boy, our wing leader that day—I can't recall whether it was Johnnie Johnson or Lloyd Chadburn—was he livid!

I had the good fortune to meet Doug Booth in 2001 at a Vancouver Island reunion of the western branch of the Canadian Fighter Pilots Association held at CFB Comox. I did not know that he was a neighbour living only two blocks away from my residence in White Rock, BC. His wife, Joy, had recently died and the reunion was his first social event since her death. As the reunion drew to a close he asked me, "Well, have you heard enough bullshit for one weekend?" Taken aback by this assessment, I realized he might be an entertaining interview and asked if I could visit him.

THE DIGBY "TRAVELLING CIRCUS," JUNE 1943–JAN. 1944

Although the Squadron (and Wing) called Digby "home" for most of the time from June 1943 to February 1944, it was "home" only in a restricted sense, a rear base to which the pilots returned after operations to grab a change of clothing, collect their mail, and have a brief rest while the ground crews serviced the aircraft. For operations the pilots flew to advanced aerodromes along the coast, moving from one to another as orders required; often they were away from Digby for days at a stretch. As a result of these peripatetic activities 416 became acquainted with many of the coastal airfields in England from Coltishall around to Exeter and it also became familiar, from a different point of view, with the enemy-held coast from Texel to Brest, particularly the section between Den Helder and The Hague.

416 Squadron production, *416 Squadron History*.

Due to physical proximity, strength of character, independence of thought and for all-round irascibility and entertainment value, Doug Booth is the fighter pilot I have come to know best. He is one of the most self-deprecating men I have ever met and one of the most self-deprecating of fighter pilots. Given the clichés about the occupation it is not a quality one expects in a fighter pilot. Yet repeatedly in interviews I found men who were exceedingly modest about their strengths and honest about their weaknesses.

Booth had no campaign medals in a drawer and had never gone through the process of applying for them. When I asked why, his response was, "What would I do with them?" His wartime pal Al Mc-Fadden has his campaign medals and wings framed and hanging on the wall, as do many veterans. But until he was cajoled into doing so at age eighty-one, Doug had nothing on his walls to mark his wartime history. He coveted one badge from the war that had gone missing, and for which a replacement was being sought. It was the 3.5-centimetre-wide gilt and silver wing worn on the left pocket by aircrew who survived a tour of operations. Moreover, Booth, though entitled to them, had never received his Caterpillar Club lapel pin or Goldfish Club cloth badge (see page 105), both of which he valued more than any medals. It was one of my first tasks after meeting Booth to set the wheels in motion to obtain his campaign medals and the three badges that declared *Been there, done that!*

Badges of Recognition
and Achievement
Official and Unofficial

The "Operational Wings" was a badge unique to the RCAF; there was no counterpart in the RAF. The US Army introduced a Combat Infantry Badge (CIB) during the Second World War for the Corps of Infantry. It is worn above the left pocket above medal ribbons by an infantry officer, warrant officer or enlisted soldier who has served satisfactorily in an infantry regiment, battalion, rifle company, platoon or squad while such unit is in ground combat with an enemy. The period of assignment must be at least thirty days. The CIB is a much-coveted award in the US Army Corps of Infantry and was retained for the wars in Korea and Vietnam. For RCAF aircrew, the Operational Wings badge was akin to the CIB but was unique to the Second World War.

The "Ops Wing" on your pocket meant you had been there for a long time, probably been shot at and had survived a period of operations against the enemy—a period measured in trips flown, hours flown or years of duty. The winged device was conferred only after completing a tour, not simply for starting one. Men who completed two tours received a bar attached below the outspread wings, and a second bar for those rare individuals completing three tours.

Other than the "gongs," i.e. the British Empire gallantry awards such as the Conspicuous Gallantry Medal (CGM), the Distinguished Flying Medal (DFM), the Distinguished Flying Cross (DFC), Distinguished Service Order (DSO) and the Bars on the ribbon indicating additional *Gazetted* awards, at least two unofficial awards had cachet.

They were the Caterpillar Club lapel pin and the Goldfish Club cloth badge. The first declared that you had used an Irwin parachute to save your life, the second that you had been rescued from the ocean after a bailout or a ditching. They were not official military awards and wearing them on uniforms was not an approved practice. These marks of recognition were for all aircrew, but fighter pilots in particular might bail out several times in a tour, sometimes on fire, and then survive in the ocean for days and come back to fight again and again.

There is a third badge for the Guinea Pig Club, those who have been burned or crushed and then reconstructed at the Queen Victoria Hospital, East Grinstead. No one covets this badge, but many fighter pilots, flying fighters with fuel tanks directly in front of the cockpit or beneath it, have become members of the club, its badge being a guinea pig with wings.

Royal Canadian Air Force

This is to Certify that, on the authority of
the Chief of the Air Staff,

Squadron Leader J.F. Edwards, D.F.C. & Bar, D.F.M.

has been awarded a Bar to the Operational Wings of the
Royal Canadian Air Force, in that he has completed a
second tour of operational duty in action against the enemy

A.M.

Signed this Eighth day of January 1945

Caterpillar Club
Certificate of Membership

F/LT. R. I. A. SMITH. D.F.C.
is a member of the CATERPILLAR CLUB
having saved his life by parachute.

SIGNED
HON. SEC. EUROPEAN DIVISION

IRVIN   IRVIN

THE GOLDFISH CLUB
was formed in 1942

*Membership is available only to aviators
who have 'ditched' or 'baled out'
over the sea*

*The design of this card is based on the
unique 'waterproof' card issued during world war II.*

Membership Card

This is to Certify that

F/LT. R.D. BOOTH   R.C.A.F

*Qualified as a member of the Goldfish Club by
escaping death by the use of Emergency Equipment on*

22nd OCTOBER 1943

Signed ....

CHARLES A. ROBERSTON

**THE
GOLDFISH CLUB**

**MEMBERSHIP
CARD**

1942

When asked about his officer-like qualities or lack of them at age twenty-one, Booth is candid. "I was not a mature individual, I had a rather limited outlook. Young men in the RCAF had differences in education, in *savoir faire*, poise, whatever you want to call it … not everybody is suited to be an officer [at that age] and I certainly wasn't. But as for flying the aircraft, that is a physical skill. I was reasonable at it because I had lived an athletic youth."

He admits landings were not his strong suit in flying the Spitfire. In 1943 he and other pilots were sent north to train with the Fleet Air Arm on Seafires. The thought was that Spitfire pilots could travel from aircraft carriers in the English Channel to the continent after the invasion. The Seafire was a Spitfire that had been "Navalized," fitted with an arrestor hook and an airspeed indicator measuring in nautical miles per hour. They were well-used airframes and had been thumped on hard many times.

One day while practising carrier landings ashore, Doug noticed a Seafire ahead of him that had tipped up on its nose after landing. Distracted by this, he set down heavily; one of the oleos gave way and he slid to a halt wing down. The station commander, visiting the Seafire that was on its nose, witnessed Doug's arrival and drove rapidly over to the machine. He asked: "Are you all right?" Doug, thinking he was about to be yanked off 416 Squadron to tow targets for the rest of the war, replied, "Yes, sir." The station commander, who Doug appraised as having had "a liquid lunch," simply replied, "Well, that's great. Carry on, laddie." Fifty-five years later, while comparing logbooks, Doug learned that Al McFadden had been the offending pilot up on his nose that day in Scotland.

Despite his callow qualities, as he describes them, Booth was assigned increasing responsibilities at 416. He rose to section lead while still an NCO, and then to "B" Flight commander. His promotions to flight sergeant and warrant officer second class—pro forma in the RCAF at six months and one year—never seemed to arrive:

So here I am leading officers around as a sergeant pilot, and I am commissioned in the field. Well, I got my back pay as flight sergeant and WO2, even though I had not worn those ranks. Les Pow and I were both WO2s and were both commis-

sioned. I was happy to be commissioned because it gave me more money, and better quarters … you attract the ladies when you have a little better rating … being a flight lieutenant was better for that than being a flight sergeant.

Booth, who claims his bad memory is lifelong rather than a sign of old age, says he is able to remember his officer's number (J17416) to this day because it ends in 416. On occasion his memory works well and he recalls anecdotes and episodes with great clarity, later forgetting them all over again. Booth recollects that he, and many pilots at 416, as well as throughout the Allied air forces, had a ceremonial pee on the tail wheel for good luck before going on a sortie. Eventually, a formal notice was posted by the wing commander prohibiting this superstitious act because it damaged the rubber wheels.

When Doug Booth and Les Pow were commissioned, they pooled their two £50 uniform allowances to support a grand-style "piss-up." Les had a girlfriend in London who worked at an "off-licence shop." They showed up in a taxi with a big carton and left with ample supplies of Scotch and beer. They sent out word to everyone they knew and a four-day party ensued at the Regent Palace Hotel, with the hotel staff dropping in frequently to see that their "Canada" guests were well cared for. Canadian flyers were known to be generous to waiters and waitresses, busboys, bartenders and barmaids.

When Booth ran out of money he sent a telegram to his mother and father, who were living at 2746 Trinity St, Vancouver. The telegram read: "Urgent, please send 50 pounds." But his mother was terrified to open the envelope, believing her only child was no longer. Since Doug and Les had spent all their allowance on the party, they simply signed the tailor's invoice for the uniforms and had it put on their account.

On another occasion Doug, having drunk too much in the mess, took a swing at fellow pilot Karl "Lucky" Linton, DFC, for some imagined slight. He tripped and fell and Linton took advantage, getting in several hits while Booth was on the floor. The female serving staff were horrified at this scuffle. They were mystified the following morning as Doug and Karl amiably exchanged sections of the daily newspaper over breakfast. Neither could remember the reason they had fought.

BOOTH'S BAILOUT OVER THE ENGLISH CHANNEL

On Friday, October 22, 1943 Booth's favourite Spitfire, marked on the fuselage "DN-R," the R in Doug's mind stood for "reliable," sprang a glycol leak over the Channel. He was warned earlier about the leak by his No. 2, but did not want to appear cowardly on the outbound leg of an escort do, so he ignored the warning. As he and his section returned from the aborted op due to weather, the leak became serious, the engine temperature rose steeply, and fire was visible under the engine cowling. Doug advised his squadron commander, who hollered three times: "Bail out! Bail out! Bail out!"

It is a fact that Spitfire pilots were never taught how to bail out of a Spit, yet the handling notes for the fighter advised against ditching due to certain adverse characteristics on water (i.e., we won't tell you, but this machine will sink like a Simonized manhole cover). Doug believed it was self-interest by the air force to encourage pilots to stay put for the sake of His Majesty's valuable aircraft. He had read about Squadron Leader Jack Charles bailing out over the Dutch coast using the bunt method. This required plenty of forward trim plus a sharp push forward on the stick. The technique generated enough negative G on the aircraft to eject the pilot up and out and well clear of the machine's tail. That was the theory.

Doug slid back his coupe top and put the side door on what was called "the half lock." This was a customary procedure on most landings in the Spit to avoid being trapped if the aircraft flipped upside down. He remembered to unfasten all harness straps, including his radio cord and oxygen hose (pilots in the anxiety of getting out sometimes forgot the attachments). However, as he popped out on the bunt his parachute hung up on the finger pull for the coupe top. Half in and half out of the machine, he struggled to free himself as the grey waters rapidly approached, briefly sitting down almost calmly on the canopy, then unhooking himself. He recalls covering his face with his arms as he whistled past the tail.

Coming down in his parachute, he felt terrible hanging there helpless. He desperately wanted that phase of his survival to end. Thinking ahead, he kicked off his heavy sheepskin boots. But the wind was so strong that he could not control his direction or drift and smacked the water hard on his back. With the chute billowing, the wind dragged him along and he struggled to collapse it. When he finally managed to release the lock on the parachute harness he found that the carbon-dioxide cartridge on the Mae West had not worked and that the dinghy cord was gone. So Doug had no life vest and no raft, and he was in rough half-gale seas. His head kept slipping below the surface. The fact that he was a very strong swimmer tempted him to try for the beach.

Fortunately, Al McFadden and others were watching Doug's predicament from the air and had called air-sea rescue with his position. He was a mere one mile off Beachy Head, England, but far enough out to drown quickly or die of exposure. He was pretty much all in by the time air-sea rescue boat 513 managed to pluck him out by snagging a boat hook in his Mae West. He declined a tot of rum: he was too exhausted and sick to stomach it.

He shivered through a sleepless night in a rest home at Beachy Head and the following morning caught a truck and then the train into the south side of London. As the bedraggled pilot came up out of the tube station, a London bobby spotted him. Booth was wearing his white woollen roll-neck sweater stained with yellow dye marker, and he had a Mae West over his shoulder and a pair of bedroom slippers in place of his flying boots. The policeman took Booth aside (calling him "laddie"), flagged a cab and told the driver to take this young pilot to the next train station.

After a year of operations and then a bailout that damn near ended him, Doug Booth admits today that his nerves were more keenly drawn from then on. He listened more carefully for variations in the roar of the Merlin and always breathed easier when the Channel was behind him. After his bailout that Friday, the fog rolled in and stayed for more than a week. This allowed Doug and the rest of the squadron to rest.

RAMROD 290: NOVEMBER 3, 1943

Doug and 416 did not fly again on operations until Wednesday, November 3, as part of a close fighter escort assignment codenamed "Ramrod 290" (the word "Ramrod" indicating a few bombers escorted by many fighters, with the hope of enticing the Luftwaffe to fight). This do was one of the most remarkable in the history of RCAF fighter operations. Squadron Leader Freddie Green, his flight commanders Flight Lieutenants Doug Booth and Art Sager, and nine other pilots of 416 (City of Oshawa) Squadron teamed up with twelve pilots of 402 (City of Winnipeg) Squadron to attain a measure of immortality. In national Canadian press coverage they were credited with shooting down nine enemy aircraft in nine minutes. Post-war research has suggested that the figure may be eight not nine, with five of the German pilots killed in action. Nevertheless, it was still a record for an RCAF wing to that point in the war.

An article in *The Star Weekly* on New Year's Eve, 1943 was mistakenly illustrated with a Hurricane. The headline shouted "We Bagged a '109' a Minute"; the author was nominally Wing Commander Chadburn, though it is likely that the public relations personnel at RCAF HQ, Lincoln's Inn Fields, were involved.

Freddie Green had the Malta veteran Gordon Farquharson, now fully rested and recovered from his gunshot wounds, as his No. 3. Freddie's No. 2 was Derrick "Dyke" England, a pre-war provisional pilot officer of the RCAF and a graduate of Wartime Course No. 1. England, the younger son of Valerie de Bury, had been born in England at Coverack in 1921. His mother divorced his British father, an army officer, and returned to Canada where Dyke and his older brother Peter were raised in Quebec City. Dyke and Peter's grandfather, a Belgian count, was the superintendent of the Dominion Arsenal, an ordnance depot. Colonel de Bury, a career officer of the British and Canadian armies, hoped that his grandsons would attend Royal Military College at Kingston as he had done. Dyke's mother moved the family to St

Petersburg, Florida, from 1936 to 1939, and Dyke graduated from high school there, but returned to Canada to join the RCAF in September 1939.

Flight Lieutenant England was a new arrival, with more than two thousand twin- and single-engine flying hours behind him. But he had had no gunnery training before joining the squadron and only a hasty one-week course on the Spitfire. Ramrod 290 was to be his first operational do as a day fighter pilot; England recalls that the only order from Freddie Green was: "'Don't leave me, stay right on my wing.' So I just stayed right with him. Freddie had the sense to know that I was green as grass as a fighter pilot."

Profile – WILLIAM FRANCIS JOSEPH MASON
Born – February 5, 1918, Owen Sound, ON, raised at Smith Falls
Father – Thomas Mason, insurance salesman for Metropolitan Life
Mother – Veronica Baker
Degrees & Awards – BComm
Post-war occupation – Comptrollership, Canadair
Marital status – Wife Madeleine Downs; daughters Ann, Patricia and Joan; sons Thomas and John
Hobbies – Golf, bridge, fishing

Booth was leading his usual White section that day, with J.C. "Wulfer Bait" McLeod as his No. 2 and Bill Mason, who grew up in Smith Falls in the Ottawa Valley, as No. 3. Mason had his first flight in a Curtiss Jenny in 1928, at age ten, when a barnstormer offered to take him and his pal up for $10; the boys were not strapped in, and when the barnstormer did a slow roll, the boys fell halfway out of the cockpit. After graduation from pilot training, Bill Mason served at Dartmouth, Nova Scotia, flying Hurricanes on air defence duties with 126 Squadron. He had been with 416 since July and served till October 1944, destroying one, damaging one and getting, in his opinion, another probable that was never credited.

Doug Booth's pal, Art Sager, was leading Green section, Sager's No. 2 being William Jacobs of Toronto (also, like England, on his first operational trip), and his No. 3 was Danny Noonan, from Kingston, Ontario. Danny had graduated first in his class of fifty-two at No. 4 SFTS, Saskatoon, in March 1941. After being chosen to instruct, he spent eighteen months teaching on twin-engine machines at No. 12 SFTS,

Courtesy of the Wayne Ralph Collection

Bill Mason at home in Victoria, in 2001.

Brandon. As an ex-instructor arriving in Britain, he was offered his choice of any type of aircraft. When he arrived at 416 in April 1943 he was keen to show what he could do on single-engine day fighters.

Noonan had excellent gunnery skills and finished the war as an ace with the DFC. But he had a fright early in his fighting career that could have exiled him to a target-towing squadron had he been with a less amiable leader. On an op flying as No. 2 to Chadburn, he was encouraged to take out an FW190 that they had both been chasing in and out of cloud. In my conversation with Rev. Noonan at Sidney, BC, in 2001, he recollected:

As Chad opened his throttle, I heard him say, "Go get him, Danny!" Then I saw a plane emerge from the cloud, and I hit the gun button—just for half a second—then saw the round wingtips. It was Chad's Spitfire! My heart sank because I hoped I hadn't hit my leader ... Soon we were on our way back

across the Channel; and I heard Chad say, "My engine's a bit rough, but I'm okay." Again, my heart sank; but we got back all right. When I landed, I went over to Chad to apologize—by then they had spotted one bullet hole in his radiator. Chad just laughed, and said, Never mind, Danny—you're not the first one of my gang to take a shot at me."

The Digby Wing had been escorting US Army Air Force bombers long enough that the American Eighth Air Force inquired as to who had led the Spitfires that protected them. The Americans sent congratulations to the commander of the Digby Wing, Lloyd Chadburn, nicknaming him "The Angel." Just after 12 p.m., The Angel led his wing of Spitfires from 402 and 416 to protect B26 Marauders across the North Sea. Their target was an airfield at Schipol, Holland, and this is how Art Sager recalled the inbound run:

We rendezvous with the Marauders as they climb over the North Sea. Chad, leading 402, takes position slightly above and to starboard of the two leading boxes while Freddy Green with 416 covers the last two, also on the right. When light flak appears at the Dutch coast the extra fuel tanks are released. On the way into the target the flak intensifies and the sky is full of black and dirty grey blotches, some showing red as they explode. They bracket the bombers and it seems impossible that any will get through without being hit, but they plough steadily on, the boxes remaining intact.[1]

Two bombers were blown up by flak over the target. The remaining seventy bombers were spread out in four box formations; as they turned towards Ijmuiden, Holland, and the journey home, some fifteen German fighters came in to attack. The spread-out formations were nearing the coast as the enemy fighters moved in. The Germans selected a box of eighteen machines being watched over by 402. The front box, farther away out over the Channel, was being guarded by RAF squadrons of the Coltishall Wing. Chadburn was with 402 and quickly shot down in flames two of the attacking Me109s. Flight Lieutenant John

[1] Correspondence with British author Peter Caygill as quoted in *Spitfire Mark V in Action*.

109

Mitchner, a twenty-nine-year-old from Saskatoon, shot down two more, and 402's Squadron Leader Geoffrey Northcott, DFC, a Malta veteran from Minnedosa, Manitoba, destroyed one.

The pilots of White and Green sections of 416 knew from the RT chatter that there was a major scrap taking place ahead of them. Sager's Green section, with Noonan and Jacobs, attacked two separate elements, damaging one, then a second Me109. When Sager's guns jammed, Noonan carried on firing and the German machine went down. Jacobs and Noonan became separated from Sager, and Noonan destroyed a second Me109 after a tight turning fight. Jacobs may have been hit by one of the other enemy machines, and he was last seen streaming glycol. He was the only casualty on Ramrod 290. His body was buried at Zandvoort by his enemies.

Doug Booth spotted three enemy fighters coming inland from the Channel at one thousand feet below. He dove to attack and fired several short bursts as the enemy pilot attempted to evade him by getting closer to the water. The German levelled off briefly, then rapidly rolled inverted and dove into the sea. Bill Mason and "Wulfer Bait" McLeod both watched the fighter splash into the Channel. Doug later wondered if the German pilot had simply run out of ammunition and was taken by surprise seeing Spitfires coming towards him from the land.

Shortly after the pilots landed, a press conference was set up on the airfield at Coltishall, complete with movie and still cameras. The seven pilots credited with victories were lined up, and Chadburn had them practising for their radio interviews. Their wingmen were standing in the background. Unwisely Chad told his boys to lobby for better "shooting irons" (i.e., the Mark IX Spitfire). He wanted them to be sure to say how much better the RCAF would have done if it had not been stuck with the old machines (i.e., Spit Vs).

Whatever news source did the interviews— possibly the BBC or RCAF Public Relations—the broadcast was never aired. It is possible to find photos that bear Imperial War Museum serial numbers and show the smiling pilots, but the movie footage has apparently not survived. Was it because every pilot complained about his Spitfire, instead of being

modest and grateful? Many who flew on Ramrod 290 certainly thought so.

Doug Booth left for a rest as a training pilot at a group support unit (GSU) in February 1944, and Danny Noonan took over his flight. Bill Mason, Gordon Farquharson, Al McFadden, Dick Forbes-Roberts and other pilots such as G.R. "Pat" Patterson and Sandy Borland served through the spring and summer. After months of little enemy contact, on May 22, six 416 pilots fought six German pilots over a Luftwaffe airfield at Entrepagny, France, scoring five victories without a loss. One of the German pilots was driven down without a shot being fired by Bill Mason, as he was out of ammunition. The squadron history book stated:

> F/L Mason (Red 2) … could fire only a short burst before his ammunition was exhausted. (All pilots had expended much of their ammunition in the previous attacks on the trains.) Although he was now unarmed, Mason continued in a tight turn behind the enemy until the rear one began to level out just above some trees and then swooped down into a large field at over 250 mph. The Spit was right behind the Messerschmitt on the deck, but when Mason pulled up again only one enemy fighter remained; the other had not come up from its swoop. A little later P/O Palmer saw the wreckage of an aircraft in the middle of the field, with some smoke or dust rising from it.

In those days, a story of such high drama was declassified by the RCAF for Canadians back home.

After a War Bond tour in Canada and many interviews, Lloyd Chadburn had returned to start his third tour of operations as Wing Commander (Flying) of 127 Wing. He wrote a letter to his mother on May 24 boasting that the boys of his old squadron "who are with me, got five Huns yesterday. It was a very good show … Well, Mom, must run now as it is lunch time. Probably write my next letter in French. Bye again. Love, Lloyd." On Tuesday, June 13, D-Day plus seven, while leading 416 Squadron at about 5:30 in the afternoon, Wing Commander Chadburn collided at twelve thousand feet with Flight Lieutenant Frank Joel Clark, of Toronto, a

Wing Commander Lloyd Chadburn, microphone in hand, asks Doug Booth a question after Ramrod 290. Art Sager, at right, awaits his turn at the microphone, while Bill Mason and Derrick England, supporting wingmen, watch with amusement

pilot with 421 Squadron. Both aircraft crashed in the area of Benouville, France, and that is where the bodies of both pilots were buried at the time; they were moved after the war.

On the evening of July 14, Dick Forbes-Roberts was involved in a dramatic dogfight off the end of the runway at his own airfield, a fight that was witnessed by many from the squadron, including the fitters and riggers. Dick had led a section of four Spitfires, including Borland, Patterson and Mason. The radar controller advised of a large formation and said they were friendly aircraft. By the time that was recognized as a serious error, Bill Mason's Spitfire was riddled by bullets and oil, and glycol had coated his windscreen. Unable to see clearly, he headed for his home strip and was entering the traffic pattern when an FW190 climbed up directly in front of his nose; the FW pilot bailed out and the aircraft promptly exploded. The Luftwaffe pilot had apparently followed Mason to his home aerodrome. Forbes-Roberts, unseen by Mason, shot down the FW190 in plain view of all the fitters and riggers, who were most impressed to see the war brought to their doorstep in this dramatic way. Mason's most vivid memory of this period of his life is the terrific explosion directly in front of him.

The pilot of the FW190, a Hungarian, was taken prisoner by the army in the vicinity of the airfield, but the aircrews, including Wing Commander Johnnie Johnson, asked that he be released to them for a period. Dick asked the Luftwaffe pilot if he could have his Mae West; he agreed and it was subsequently autographed by all on the squadron, making its way ultimately to the Canada Aviation Museum in Ottawa.

On July 16, Al McFadden, leading a section out of B9 aerodrome, came across a German vehicle on the road heading south from Lisieux, France, through Livarot to Vimoutiers. When McFadden recalled this operation for me, his tone was sombre and reflective: "When you come down to strafe a vehicle like that, you are a one-man execution squad. There is no escaping." It was not work that many fighter pilots relished. Rod Smith, for example, could not continue shooting at soldiers once they started running from vehicles on fire. He found it too repugnant.

McFadden strafed the jeep and killed the occupants near the intersection of the east-west road from Boissey. He gave no more thought to the events at the time but wrote the particulars in his logbook. Decades later, while watching a television documentary on Field Marshal Erwin Rommel, he learned that the famous Desert Fox had been taken to a French hospital at Livarot after being badly wounded by strafing Spitfires (as Rommel's staff officer recalled later).

The German commander was wounded on the 17th, and Al has always wondered whether his entry of the 16th for the op was incorrect, and whether the op he flew actually took place on the 17th. His memories of the vehicle, the location, the crossroads and the time match closely the events surrounding Rommel's wounding. However, just as there were many rival claimants for the killing of Manfred von Richthofen, the Red Baron, in April 1918, there are many claimants for the wounding of Erwin Rommel in July 1944. American, French and Canadian pilots have all, since the war, put forth claims, including Charles Fox of 401 Squadron and Bill Weeks of 442 Squadron. It does not appear that any researcher has found the German records that can corroborate the time, place and entry into hospital of Rommel. Without such records the wounding of the Desert Fox remains one of the unresolved dramas of the war.

Vern Williams, navigator, and Rayne "Joe" Schultz, pilot, aces with 410 Squadron.

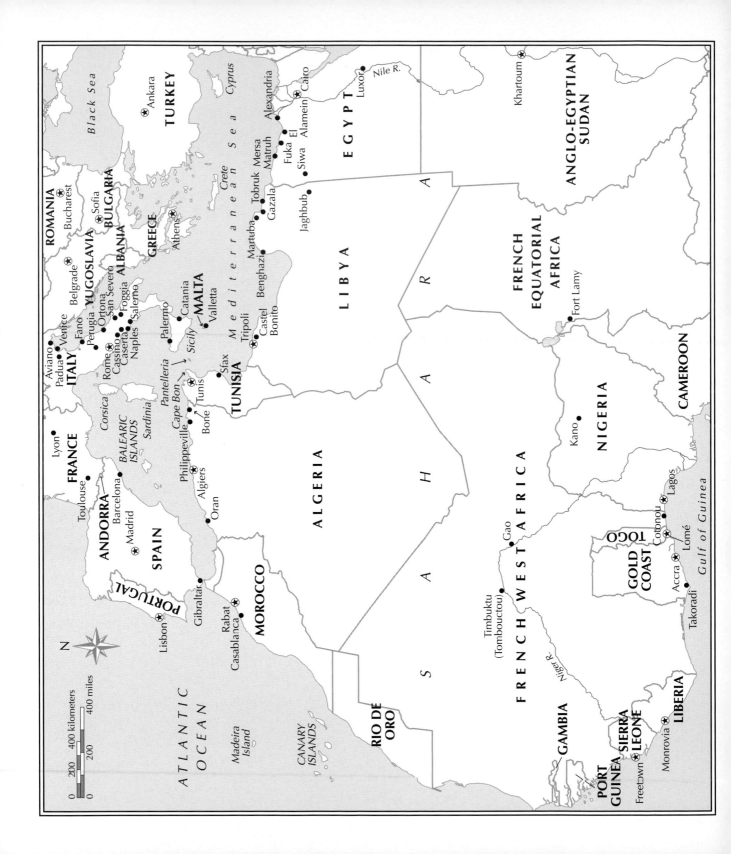

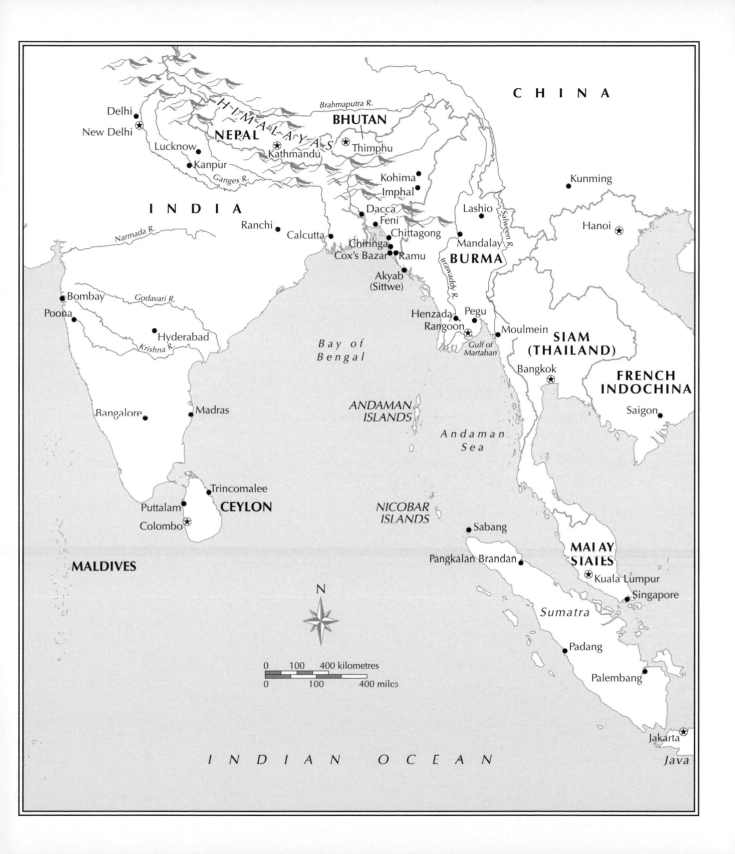

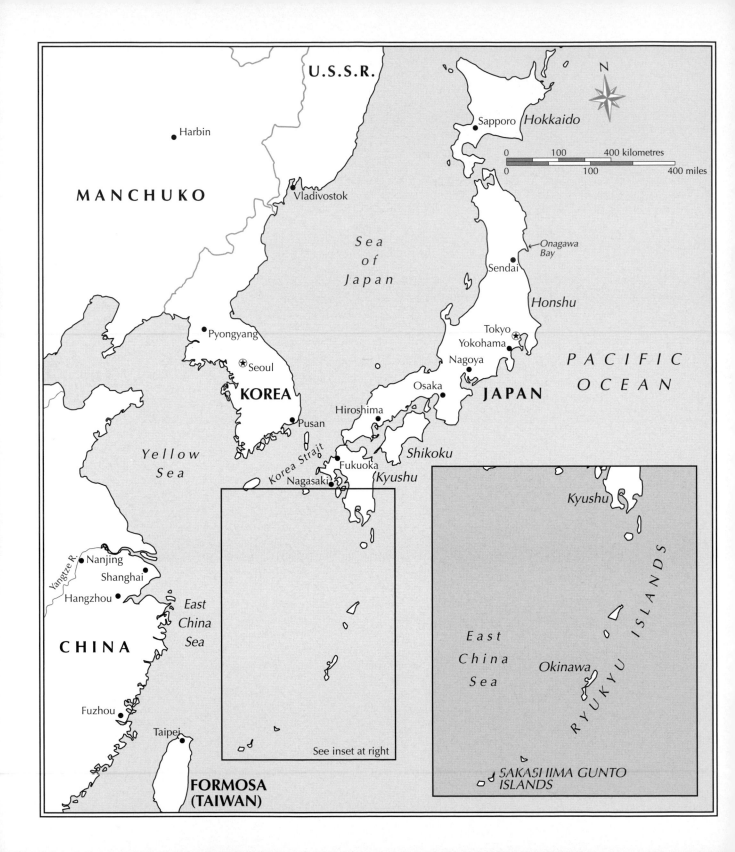

U.S.S.R.

MANCHUKO

Harbin

Vladivostok

Sapporo   *Hokkaido*

N

0   100   400 kilometres

0   100   400 miles

Sea
of
Japan

Onagawa
Bay

Sendai

Honshu

Pyongyang

⊛ Seoul

KOREA

Tokyo
Yokohama
Nagoya

⊛

Osaka

Pusan

Hiroshima

JAPAN

PACIFIC
OCEAN

Yellow
Sea

Korea Strait

Fukuoka

Shikoku

Nagasaki

Kyushu

Kyushu

Nanjing

Yangtze R.

Shanghai

Hangzhou

East
China
Sea

CHINA

East
China
Sea

Okinawa

RYUKYU ISLANDS

Fuzhou

Taipei

See inset at right

SAKASI IIMA GUNTO
ISLANDS

FORMOSA
(TAIWAN)

THE WORLD OF THE BEAUFIGHTER AND MOSQUITO IN BRITAIN

Some of Canada's most decorated Second World War fighter pilots served their tours of operations at night. They may well have started their careers on the slow and wrong-headedly designed Boulton Paul Defiant; the pleasant, forgiving, but equally slow Bristol Blenheim; or the very capable but demanding Bristol Beaufighter. Many Canadians had outstanding fighting careers in night operations on the Beaufighter, yet we most often remember those who flew the Mosquito. Somehow it is this machine, like its single-engine counterpart, the Spitfire, that conferred immortality. Second only to the Spitfire as a legendary aircraft, the Mosquito did everything well in its multi-role career, but excelled at night-fighter and night-intruder operations.

I was fortunate to meet and interview several Beaufighter and Mosquito night-fighter pilots, and I tracked down three navigators who flew in combat with three of those pilots. They were able to tell me of the special relationship that existed between navigators and pilots, a symbiotic relationship that made it all possible.

Night fighting in the war, either shooting enemy machines down or intruding into enemy territory to seek them out, was mostly a solitary occupation. Typically it involved just a single aircraft with pilot and navigator and the guidance of a ground radar controller. On intruder operations the pilot and navigator were hunters sent to look for prey in the dark, hoping they did not, through inattention,

THE PILOT'S PERSPECTIVE

Rayne Schultz
Group Captain
RCAF (ret.), DFC and
Bar, OMM, CD

I found the Beaufighter cockpit to be very well designed—a world of improvement over the Blenheim. The view out the front was fabulous ... the instrumentation was marvellous and all the other controls were easy to hand. The comfort level and heating were also good ... In some ways, the Beaufighter cockpit was better than the Mosquito. The view from the cockpit was similar to a single-seat fighter ...

I flew the Mosquito for well over a thousand hours ... The view through the canopy was superb, but it wasn't as good as in the Beaufighter. The compass was down low by your left knee and was difficult to see, but the instrument panel was excellent. The engine instruments were well placed, but the whole throttle quadrant was not very good. The comfort level was about the same as in the Beaufighter, but the heating in the Mosquito was superior to both the Beaufighter and the Blenheim.

Frankly, there's not a lot that I didn't like about the Mosquito. I am prejudiced to this day, and consider it one of the finest airplanes I ever had my hands on.

THE NAVIGATOR'S PERSPECTIVE

Vern Williams
Flight Lieutenant,
Navigator, RCAF, DFC

I flew in the Beaufighter and the Mosquito, but I preferred the Mosquito. I found the Mosquito to be relatively comfortable, but because I looked after the airborne radar, I was too busy to take much notice. I didn't like the navigator's position in the Beaufighter. It was located in the middle of the aircraft, apart from the cockpit. It was cold and drafty and you didn't know what was going on. You could only talk to the pilot by intercom. In the Mosquito, you sat right beside the pilot, which gave you a ringside seat. I preferred that because I felt more confident and more like a member of the team.

You also felt safer getting out of the Mosquito, with the door right beside you (in the fighter version). In case of emergency, the navigator would be the first one out. That was a comfort. The Mosquito was a great aircraft.

Donald Nijboer, with photos by Dan Patterson, *Cockpit: An Illustrated History of World War II Aircraft Interiors.*

become prey. Their success might light up the night sky, but a sharp-eyed Ju88 rear gunner, or an enemy night-fighter aircraft, could result in oblivion, a crash into the ocean, a missing aircraft, no radio call, no other word. They could be gone for a burton, as the British say.

For my first swing across the southern Prairies in 2001, I left Grandview, Manitoba, on July 31 heading southwest towards Regina, following Highway 10 through Yorkton and Melville. The local radio station was broadcasting a news special about a grain elevator fire at Melville, so I stopped to look. The fire trucks were just packing up, the grain still smouldering, the spectators heading back to their homes and offices.

The night before, I had telephoned a pilot who had flown Defiants, Beaufighters and Mosquitoes. I told him I was arriving in his hometown the following day and asked if it would be possible to meet and interview him that day, and only on that day, as I was moving westbound to other appointments (or so I hoped).

I had learned by trial and error that getting appointments with retired fighter pilots was most successful if I provided as little notice as possible. Their lives are normally so full of activities that it was pointless for me to attempt to mastermind a schedule two months ahead with ten pilots scattered across three provinces. My early efforts to do so had been unsuccessful because no five people on my list could see me in sequence in an economical fashion. I frequently heard a variation on the following: "Well, I have a medical appointment that week, and the following week my daughter and grandchildren are coming for a visit. Can you come in September? It's quieter then."

Complicating my scheduling was the fact that almost none of the veterans I telephoned knew me or had read anything I had written. Why should they meet a stranger on such short notice? In fact, it was gratifying that most could and would if it was at all possible, just on the strength of a telephone call.

Robert Ferguson had never heard of me, but was pleased that I could stop and see him. When I arrived at around 4 p.m. at 334 Pasqua Ave, Ft Qu'Appelle, he was waiting for me outside his bungalow. He was dressed in a grey tweed sports coat and RCAF tie, with grey slacks. We shook hands and he said, "Call me Bob." We sat in his dining room, where he had spread out his memorabilia from the war. Knowing I was coming he had handwritten a biographical summary to help my project.

As I walked into the foyer of his house I glanced at the certificates on the wall. They were of a kind I had never seen before—one was for the Order of Canada, a second for the Saskatchewan Order of Merit and a third for an honorary Doctor of Laws degree. Bob Ferguson had been a night-fighter pilot in the RCAF, and that was why I wanted to interview him and why I had driven to Ft Qu'Appelle. But his family history and post-war achievements were completely unknown to me. All my interviews begin with family history, and the story of Ferguson's history was characteristic of nineteenth-century Canadian immigration.

Bob's great-grandfather, James Ferguson, was from Moy in County Tyrone, northeast Ireland. He boarded a ship bound for Canada in 1839, his final destination being Upper Canada. His wife, Frances Ellis, and their three daughters died of cholera on the voyage. James then married Frances Hunt, with whom he had eight children. After the death of his second wife, James, now aged sixty-four, married a seventeen-year-old named Frances Jordon, a hired girl on his farm, with whom he had seven more children. He died at Glen Huron, Ontario, aged eighty-eight in 1902. Bob Ferguson is descended from the oldest child of James's second marriage.

Bob's father, Robert George Ferguson, was born in 1883 in South Joliette, North Dakota. George, as he was called in the family, graduated second in his class as a medical doctor in 1916 from the University of Manitoba. He married the woman he had been engaged to for four years, Helen Ross, a nursing student whose grandfather was a medical doctor, as were two of her four brothers. A third brother was a pharmacy worker and the fourth a veterinary surgeon.

Robert Ferguson at home in Ft Qu'Appelle, SK, in 2002.

Courtesy of the Wayne Ralph Collection

Profile – ROBERT ROSS FERGUSON

Born – May 13, 1917, Winnipeg; grew up at Ft San, near Ft Qu'Appelle, SK

Father – Dr Robert George Ferguson, superintendent of "Fort San" sanatorium, SK

Mother – Helen Florence Josephine Ross

Decorations & Medals – MiD

Degrees & Awards – BA, BSc Agriculture, Order of Canada, Saskatchewan Order of Merit, honorary Doctor of Laws (Regina)

Post-war occupation – Farmer; member, Board of Governors and Senate of University of Regina.

Marital status – Wife Norma Cecilia Johnson, sons Martin and George, daughters Laura and Colleen

Hobbies – Golf, curling, tennis, swimming

Dr George Ferguson became a leading researcher and treatment specialist in the fight against tuberculosis. He was invited to become the medical superintendent of the Ft Qu'Appelle Sanatorium, "Fort San" for short, at Echo Lake, two miles west of Ft Qu'Appelle. A few weeks after their first child, Robert Ross, was born in Winnipeg, George and Helen moved to Fort San on the north side of Echo Lake and it was there that they worked and raised their six children.

After graduation from Regina College and the University of Saskatchewan, Bob Ferguson started farming in the Edgeley district in 1939. There was no exposure to aviation in Bob's childhood, but he did know the Bartlett family whose sons Chris and Dick enlisted before the war. He had been mightily impressed that these young men, farmers just like him, crossed the ocean in peacetime to join the RAF and the Fleet Air Arm of the Royal Navy. They stayed in his mind as role models when he went through

Elementary Flying Training School (EFTS) in Ft William, Ontario, on Tiger Moths, and later at the Service Flying Training School (SFTS) in Dauphin, Manitoba, on Harvards. He graduated on September 24, '41, with 180 hours, was commissioned immediately and headed overseas on SS *Akaroa*, a New Zealand sheep hauler that served a daily diet of mutton, and plenty of it. The ship arrived in Belfast after a stormy crossing and Bob went onwards to Bournemouth, where he stayed a mere ten days.

While others waited months in Bournemouth, Ferguson decided to immediately ask for night fighters, based solely on a *Maclean's* magazine article that reported night-fighter crews flew all night and slept all day. Bob had been a night owl throughout his childhood, so he thought he was perfectly suited for such work. He arrived at No. 60 Operational Training Unit (OTU) at East Fortune, twenty miles from Edinburgh, Scotland, on December 10, 1941 and was checked out on the Miles Master, then the Boulton Paul Defiant: "The Master had a big motor and was off the ground very quickly, like an extra-powerful Harvard ... the Defiant was much more sluggish."

During the Defiant course, Bob was paired with his wireless operator/air gunner, a Sergeant Doleman, who was an Australian. As a result, both were sent to a Royal Australian Air Force (RAAF) squadron, No. 96, at RAF Wrexham, Wales. Bob was the only Canadian flyer at 96, but there were some Canadian ground crew (see sidebar for Harris

account). Ferguson's stay there was short, from February 17 to March 26, because 410 Squadron of the RCAF was flying Defiants at Drem, Scotland, and needed Canadian pilots. During the twelve months of 1942, 410 operated in succession—and with some overlap—the Defiant, the Beaufighter and the Mosquito at stations in Scotland and England.

When Ferguson arrived at RAF Station Drem, a renowned Battle of Britain ace named Peter Townsend was the commanding officer. Townsend took a personal interest in training his new pilots in the squadrons, which was not a customary duty of a station commander. Townsend felt that the Beaufighter was a hot machine that did not forgive sloppiness. It dropped out of the sky if not flown just so—it was no Blenheim. One piece of advice Townsend gave all the trainees was to keep the Beaufighter at 115 mph on final approach, not 105 as recommended by Bristol, or they might become a smoking hole in the ground.

Ferguson was impressed with the station commander's practical streak and his insistence on flying with each and every pilot who was in transition: "In two days he had everybody safely through their conversion. Townsend was a leader of men; he saw the things that had to be done and did them." It was this war hero, and Ferguson's course mate at No. 60 OTU, John Aiken (later Air Chief Marshal Sir John Aiken), who served as his role models in the war for leadership and integrity.

Ferguson was paired with Donald Creed, airborne interception (AI) navigator, an exceptionally

ALAN HARRIS, RDF TECHNICIAN, 96 SQUADRON

Posted to Wales, he learned to test, service and repair the identification friend or foe (IFF) equipment of Boulton Paul Defiants in 96 Squadron. Four other Canadian airmen worked with him: Clifton Butler, Irving Kornblum, Sandy Sanderson and an LAC Lesarge.

Harris was with the unit only a short time, but a manufacturing error in a newly delivered aircraft almost ended his career. Secret airborne equipment such as radar and IFF were coupled with explosive devices that would destroy them, either in the G-forces of a crash or manually, so that the technology would not fall into the enemy's hands.

While performing a functional check of the new Defiant's IFF system (located behind a panel on the left side rear fuselage), the detonator for the IFF exploded. Investigators found that factory workers had wired the detonator switch to turn the power on and off, while the power switch ignited the explosive charge. Al's face was slightly burned and healed quickly. However, he still has a tiny scar on his eyeball caused by the explosive debris.

capable man who had a degree in geology from the University of Saskatchewan. They were paired by the commanding officer of 410, Wing Commander Maurice Lipton, because they had attended the same university. At this period of the war there were few Canadian navigators and, therefore, it was common for a Canadian pilot to have a British navigator.

Squadron members never successfully downed or damaged an enemy machine with the Defiant in the twelve months they flew it—it had no radar, relying on vectors from ground radar controllers and good eyesight. When they started operating the Beaufighter Mk IIF (the less popular, underpowered Merlin-engine model), their record improved and the first successful attack by 410 was on the night of September 6/7, 1942, flying out of Scorton, Yorkshire, when Bob Ferguson and Don Creed damaged a Ju88 over Whitby. Unknown to them, the gunner of the Ju88 put a bullet into one of the engines of the Beaufighter, so that could have ended up being their first and last attack.

Reviewing his performance, Bob today regrets his lack of speed; had he been a little quicker he could have destroyed the Ju88: "He got so far ahead of me and went through cloud. We had a long time when no enemy aircraft were coming north of London, so we had few shooting opportunities. Eventually the squadron shifted to free-lance intruder work in France, shooting up barges and trains … and I did some damage attacking trains."

One of the finest accounts about night-intruder operations is by the late Dave McIntosh, in *Terror in the Starboard Seat*, where he describes destructive forays into France, Denmark and Germany. David Norman McIntosh, from Stanstead, Quebec, and his pilot, Sid Platt Seid, from San Francisco, flew and fought hard, but also, as McIntosh wrote, partied hard and chased women. His memoir makes great reading, but the casual reader might think that McIntosh and Seid's activities were universal. When I asked Bob Ferguson about his social life as a night-fighter pilot, compared with the experiences of McIntosh and Seid, he reveals a different world:

I was a pretty quiet sort of guy. I went to movies quite a bit. I looked up distant relatives, both of my own family and that of my friends in Canada, due to which I was adopted by

DAVE McINTOSH RECALLS THE WOMEN OF LONDON

We'd duck down to the Chez Moi for a couple of drinks while waiting for the next train. And there went another leave passed entirely in London …

The Chez Moi was a basement bar halfway down Denman Street, a little side street starting at the Regent Palace Hotel. It was the hangout of Canadians in Fighter Command … Few women came into the place. The only woman around regularly was Old Sylvie who acted as a barmaid while she drank up the profits and played a drunken piano for glasses of gin until she fell over and was carried away to a little cubby hole in the back …

Sid was always inordinately lucky at the Regent Palace. He not only got a room but nearly always one on the ground floor just off the main bar lounge. He could sweep the lounge with a glance … pick out the service girls on leave who were wearing their old civilian clothes and trying to look like women again …

Unless they were already registered themselves, it was tough getting girls into London hotel rooms. The hotels would close all doors at night and leave one narrow opening, at which was posted a wise old bellman who kept intoning, "Residents only, please, residents only…"

It was possible to meet girls in the pubs. But the best place was the Palais de Dance in Hammersmith at the end of the underground. But it was no place for a slowpoke because the last train back to the West End was about 2220 and if you didn't make it you had to dig deep for the price of a cab, if you could find one.

Dave McIntosh, *Terror in the Starboard Seat.*

several British families who treated me wonderfully, including the family of the member of Parliament for Sheffield who lived at Sunderland. Some fellows on the squadron played poker, lost all their money, and could not go anywhere when leave came their way … I did not approve of poker, but I played bridge for points rather than money. It helped while away the hours and days when we were grounded due to thick fog, or parked up north at some alternate waiting for days for the weather to clear at our home station near London.

During the latter part of his tour of operations at 410, Bob was sent to an Air Firing Course to improve his gunnery skills. Many pilots who went into action without training found that the course, belatedly, opened their eyes and immensely improved their accuracy. There Bob met the most skilled pilot of all at air gunnery:

I was on the Air Firing Course at King's Lynn, near The Wash, my first [gunnery course] since joining the RCAF, and Beurling was on my course to become an instructor. He did not want to be a gunnery instructor. He had the highest scores they had ever seen at the course, but he simply refused to write the final exams and therefore did not qualify as an instructor…

One day it was real hot, and the boys were out in deck chairs beside the flight, and I watched Beurling take off to do his air firing. He goes right to the farthest end of the aerodrome, he did not have to go that far down, half that distance would have been ample room … he became airborne, and stayed with the prop at three feet above the grass, there was hardly a wiggle, he was changing [height] about two inches. The precision of that guy's flying was unreal, just so stable. He is heading straight for these guys in the deck chairs [Ferguson chuckles]. They see he is not climbing. So they rolled off the chairs and lay flat on the ground. He pulls up and waves to them and does a roll off the deck. But his ability to follow a straight line, I just didn't believe it could be done that accurately.

COMPETITION AT WEST MALLING

In October 1943, 410 Squadron moved to West Malling in Kent. While stationed there, the RCAF unit ran into a problem that was characteristic of night-fighter operations in Britain. Competition was understandably keen among the various RAF, RAAF, RCAF and Royal New Zealand Air Force (RNZAF) night-fighter squadrons to find targets and destroy them. Early nightfall and just before dawn were less desirable launch periods. The launch times and patrol periods each squadron were assigned from nightfall to dawn determined just how target-rich the skies were going to be for them. To build up a high score as a night-fighter ace, you had to have shooting opportunities and that could happen only at certain hours of the night.

It was common for squadrons with high-scoring crews to be favoured by higher command. The highest-scoring night aces sometimes expected preferential consideration. Moreover, "poaching" became an issue. There was another night-fighter squadron at West Malling—not an RCAF unit—and on this squadron's nights "off," when the pilots were not assigned for interception duties, they launched aircraft and listened in on the radio for contacts. If they could intercept an enemy target ahead of the duty squadron, they considered that fair game. Inevitably this generated rivalry and distrust between night-fighter units.

As Ferguson recalls, "they figured they owned the skies in that area, and were very put out that the Canadians had arrived on their station." This friction came to a climax after 410 had been at West Malling for a couple of weeks. A 410 crew had been vectored to a perfect, line-astern position on an enemy aircraft. Abruptly, over the radio, the Canadian pilot, Bud Green, was ordered to move aside by an RAF wing commander, one of the best-known of the night-fighter aces, so he could shoot the target down. Green, who was in a perfect position to effect a kill, refused, and promptly shot down the enemy machine. Green's disobedience resulted in 410 RCAF being unceremoniously moved to Hunsdon, where it could offer no competition to the rival air forces.

Bob Ferguson completed his two-year tour of operations with 410 without any further successful encounters with enemy aircraft. This was not an uncommon situation for night-fighter crews; many completed forty operations without a single successful interception. There was no precisely defined number of operations for a tour on night fighters—it was dependent on the individual, the squadron and the period of the war.

In the spring of 1944, Ferguson became officer-in-charge of the Air Firing Flight at Winfield, England, near the Scottish border, teaching air gunnery to pilots. The flight was part of the Training Wing of Charterhall, within No. 9 Group.

By this time he had been promoted to squadron leader (twin-engine night-fighter squadrons, unlike single-engine day fighters, were commanded by a wing commander, and the flights by squadron leaders). He received written commendations for his leadership in the training of pilots, and in particular for dramatically improving the average gunnery scores of graduates. Ferguson was bothered that twin-engine pilots had to take gunnery training on single-engine Spitfires. He lobbied for a change. This led to an invitation by the RAF's Central Gunnery School to set up a twin-engine flight.

After he did so, the norm was for squadrons of all air forces, including the Americans, to bring their twin-engine fighters to the Central Gunnery School with their own armourers and fitters. In that way, crews could train on the aircraft they would fly in combat, a much more efficient training method. Ferguson received a Mention in Despatches (MiD) for his insight and diligence in improving gunnery training and standards.

One of the most talented pilots that Bob Ferguson knew at 410 was Rayne Dennis "Joe" Schultz from Alberta, who arrived at the unit at the beginning of December 1942. When Ferguson checked Schultz out on the Mosquito, he felt that the Albertan's technique was so smooth he could fly the machine better on his very first trip than Ferguson could after many months.

Someone who helped Rayne Schultz become an outstanding pilot was his first instructor at EFTS, a Great War flyer named Harley Godwin. He had been a pharmacist in 1939, but volunteered to serve as a civilian flying instructor for the British Commonwealth Air Training Plan (BCATP). Godwin was sick with cancer, and Schultz was his second last student before the Great War veteran was forced to resign and, shortly afterwards, died. Godwin taught Schultz aerobatics in a way that was not on the syllabus. In a very short period of time, Rayne was performing advanced manoeuvres such as the inverted falling leaf. He went on to SFTS and received his wings in April 1942.

Profile – RAYNE DENNIS SCHULTZ

Born – December 17, 1922, Bashaw, AB

Father – Albert Schultz, railroad fireman

Mother – Phyllis Victoria Roberts Dench

Decorations & Medals – DFC and Bar, OMM, CD and two Clasps

Degrees & Awards – Member, Canada's Aviation Hall of Fame; McKee Trophy; Honorary Member of USAF Hall of Fame; received Flight Safety Foundation Certificate of Merit

Post-war occupation – Air force officer, Group Captain, RCAF/CAF

Marital status – Wife Mary Elizabeth Butler died in 1993; daughter Kathleen

Hobbies – "Procrastination"

After receiving training on the twin-engine Airspeed Oxford in Britain, he was advised that he was being posted to Wellington bombers. Six months short of his twentieth birthday, Rayne marched into the wing commander's office at the Advanced Flying Unit (AFU) at South Cerney, England, and said, "I am not going!" The wing commander replied, "No one ever has said that to me before, and furthermore your salute was terrible. Come back at 2 p.m. and I'll see what I can do for you."

At 2 p.m., the answer was surprising: "I can't get you Spitfires, but I have got you Beaufighters, night fighters. If you haven't got a DFC and Bar within a year, I will bring you back here on Wellingtons." Rayne did not quite meet the one-year deadline, offered only partly in jest, but by war's end he had his DFC and Bar and eight enemy aircraft destroyed. He had the highest number of aerial victories for 410 Squadron in the war.

After an operation in December 1943, in which he and his navigator Vern Williams of Oakville, Ontario, destroyed three Dornier 217s in an intense few minutes, they were recommended for immediate DSOs. Immediate awards, as opposed to non-immediate, were intended to recognize exceptional and rare fighting achievements. In their wisdom, higher authority issued the pair immediate DFCs, one level below a DSO. But, from the moment they landed, Schultz and Williams became the talk of the night-fighter squadrons, especially among those crews who had flown night after night, month after month, and seen not even one enemy aircraft let alone shot any down. Sitting in his Ottawa home, I asked Group Captain Schultz to tell me his memories of this op:

I was playing poker, making money for a change; we were seventh or eighth on the patrol list. Nearly all the Mosquitoes in 11 Group were grounded due to flame-trap troubles. Most of our airplanes had not been modified, but mine had. With a full moon, I was grumbling about having to go. Vern says there is a flashing light on the Dutch coast. He says the intelligence report said the Germans were using these lights for the bomber stream. I said nonsense. The controller then said, "I may have some trade for you." They vectored us onto the first bogey [an unidentified aircraft], a Dornier 217, and we shot it down. Then Vern said "I have another contact" … but our speed was too high, so I fired a short burst, and it blew up, the bomb load must have gone off, I never had a ride like that, just one *ga-whump*. Then Vern says "I have a third one." On his Mk 5 radar, no less! A punk piece of junk, but it was working this night …

We had an awful battle; we fought him from twelve thousand feet down to the sea. We hit him in his engines, he hit us with one HE [high-explosive] round. It took out the instruments. It blew out our port radiator, but I did not know this at the time, and then after we shot him down, we had to feather the port engine. We recovered at Bradwell Bay where my buddy in OTU training, Doug Robinson—a New Zealander who was part Maori—was serving at 488 Squadron RNZAF on Mosquitoes.

Heart-stopping though the battle with this third Do217 was, it could not compare with an interception two months later, on the night of February 13/14, '44. It was Schultz's most stressful by a long margin for the whole war:

It was heading home very fast, a 188, in thin cloud, well out over the North Sea … we hit it badly, and it was flaming, two-three hundred yards [of] flames streaming behind … My navigator being a serious-minded individual said "Let's get in closer and take a good look at it, as it is a different type of aircraft and I can report on it when we get down." So I closed in, which was the *stupidest* thing I ever did …

The mid-upper gunner was not dead; he was sitting inside of the flames. The next thing I saw the gun traversing down towards us. I broke as fast as I could, but he put forty to forty-four 13mm cannon shells into us. The 188 went in, and it was confirmed the next day. However, if the German gunner had been firing high-explosive or semi-armour-piercing rounds, instead of ball ammunition, there is no way we would have gotten back. We would have gone into the sea right there next to him. I had pistons blown out of one engine, and the constant speed unit blown out in the other. We were bailing out! We jettisoned the door and the navigator was halfway out when the chap came back from the Ground Control Intercept (GCI) and said, "There is a Force 9 to 10 sea and we will never be able [to rescue] you."

So we brought that aircraft back to Bradwell Bay and I can tell you it never flew again. My navigator was wounded, bleeding from the face. I could see the engines running red hot, one was actually running on molten metal … the whole thing glowing inside. As long as they were at full power they ran on molten metal (that is a Merlin for you) … as soon as I reduced power they quit. The air bottles were shot away and I had no brakes for landing. The Mosquito was in ribbons. The C/O at Bradwell Bay provided three Scotches and between that and the adrenalin I was well on the way to success by the time our ride home flew in to get us.

Rayne Schultz was one of several pilots trained by Bob Ferguson who went on to have successful night-fighting careers. One decorated pilot whom Bob remembers vividly and recommended I interview is Ian March, a Newfoundlander. At the time of the Second World War, Newfoundland was an independent country with its own long-standing connections to the British Army and the Royal Navy. In addition to those services, many hundreds of Newfoundlanders joined the Royal Air Force.

NO. 125 (NEWFOUNDLAND) SQUADRON ROYAL AIR FORCE

During the Second World War the Newfoundland government asked the British government if it could sponsor an RAF fighter squadron. The RAF reactivated a dormant unit, No. 125, designating it 125 (Newfoundland) Squadron. Originally equipped with Defiants, it later flew Beaufighters, then Mosquitoes.

According to Royal Cooper in Gander, Newfoundland, who served a tour of ops with 125, the squadron was credited with forty-four destroyed, five probables, and twenty damaged. In 1943–45 somewhat more than 50 per cent of the ground personnel and about 15 to 20 per cent of the aircrew personnel were Newfoundlanders. In his autobiography, Royal recalls the happy and stressful moments on his night-fighter unit:

"One of my favourite characters on the Squadron was an old scruffy dog, the unofficial mascot … Scruffy loved to fly … I would take her up on training flights and she would sit on some equipment directly behind me with her head resting on my shoulder, looking out the left window. She would spot an object below—a boat or a house in the country—set her eyes on it, and follow it with her eyes until it disappeared under the wing. As it disappeared she would go 'woof' and start looking for another object. Nobody knew where she came from, but I think a former commanding officer had left her with the Squadron.

"One thing that always amused me was some of the code words used by the RAF such as 'angels' for thousands of feet altitude. Bandit, which I have already mentioned, is an enemy, while a 'bogey' is an unidentified aircraft. Radar was 'weapon.'

"Many of the radar controllers were WAAF (Women's Auxiliary Air Force). When they wanted you to use your airborne radar, you were told 'to flash your weapon.' You had to reply 'my weapon is flashing.' Or if it was unserviceable, 'my weapon is bent.' You can imagine some of the unrepeatable comments heard on the radio …

"[After an unsuccessful 30-minute chase of an Me410] we climbed to 4000 feet and contacted control. We were immediately told that 'our tail was dirty' meaning we were being followed at fairly close range, probably by the same night fighter we had been following ourselves … With the throttles wide open, we headed for the treetops, as low as we estimated we could safely get. We shook him off our tail and arrived home at Middle Wallop with little more than fumes left in our tank …"

"… The FIDO operation was located on a very long field with pipes parallel to and about 200 feet from each side of the runway. Fuel was pumped into these pipes under high pressure and ignited like a giant blowtorch. The result was two walls of flame rising about ten feet in the air which would burn off the fog near the runway and also provide visual reference for pilots when no other options were available. There were six or seven of these units in England. This saved a great number of aircraft which would otherwise have been lost. I got to use it once or twice at Bradwell Bay, and it was the most eerie feeling, to be running between two walls of fire. I could feel the heat in the cockpit and got out of it just as soon as I could."

Royal Cooper, *Tales From a Pilot's Logbook.*

Profile – IAN ANDERSON MARCH
Born – July 11, 1921, Aberdeen, Scotland; raised in St John's, Newfoundland
Died – January 24, 2005, Deer Lake, NF
Father – Major J. Wesley March, MC, Croix de Guerre, owner of the S. March and Sons shipping company of Newfoundland
Mother – Helen Brownley Taylor
Decorations & Medals – DFC
Post-war occupation – Airline pilot, TCA/Air Canada, retired as captain on Boeing 747 in 1981
Marital status – First wife Dorothy Downs, second wife Yvonne Brown; sons Robert and Stephen (deceased)
Hobbies – Aircraft owner

It would have been natural for Ian to have joined the Royal Newfoundland Regiment, given that his father, Major J. Wesley March, had served in the Great War as one of the original five hundred "Blue Puttees" and received the Military Cross and Croix de Guerre. However, as a five-year-old, Ian had seen Charles Lindbergh fly low over St John's harbour and out through the Narrows in *The Spirit of St Louis* en route to Paris and worldwide fame. That image was indelible and motivated him to fly.

While attending Memorial College in St John's in 1939, he applied to attend and was accepted for Cranwell, the RAF College, for the spring term of 1940. With the outbreak of war that intake class was cancelled and he was asked to join the RAF Volunteer Reserve. The catch was that he had to pay his own way to England. About this time, the *Montreal Standard* had a feature on RCAF pilot training at Camp Borden, Ontario, pointing out, among other things, that RCAF students received more than $2 a day, while their counterparts in the RAF made less than half that.

Ian wrote a letter to a famous Newfoundlander in the RCAF, Group Captain Roy Grandy, commanding officer of RCAF Station Dartmouth, asking if the RCAF accepted Newfoundlanders for pilot training. Grandy's answer arrived in a short mimeographed slip of paper: "come on ahead." On board SS *Baccalieu* to Halifax, March met an older fellow traveller named Robert Hayward who was enlisting as an RCAF equipment assistant. Ian asked him: "Why not try out for pilot?" Hayward had been out of school a few years but was persuaded by March

to go into pilot training with him. They bunked together for a month in Halifax while waiting for the RCAF to process them, and at month's end had seventeen cents between them. In desperation with the waiting around, March and Hayward enlisted as air gunners though they really wanted to be pilots.

Ultimately the two Newfoundlanders were remustered from the air gunner trade and received their pilots' wings in late 1940. This was a time when virtually all graduates were being streamed into instructing or staff flying for the BCATP. Pilot Officer March went to 8 SFTS at Moncton, New Brunswick, while Sergeant Hayward went to No. 2 SFTS at Uplands, Ontario. In the fall of 1942 both went on embarkation leave, crossed the Atlantic on *Queen Elizabeth* and trained as fighter pilots, Hayward on the Spitfire, March on the Mosquito.

Both rose to the rank of squadron leader, and Hayward became the most successful day-fighter pilot from Newfoundland, destroying at least five enemy aircraft and damaging another five. He received the DSO and DFC for his fighting and leadership ability commanding 411 Squadron RCAF.

When Ian March arrived in Britain he trained on Beaufighters, and then received a squadron conversion to the Mosquito from Bob Ferguson at 410 Squadron in March 1943. His first few months of ops with navigator Kristjan Eyolfson were uneventful. After D-Day the two men destroyed three enemy aircraft in less than four weeks. On the night of June 13/14, 1944, they destroyed a Ju88 and on the night of June 17/18 they overtook a fast-moving Ju188. The latter was a memorable victory because Ian March fired only six or seven rounds per gun. The RCAF Air Historian wrote in a 410 Squadron history:

> March and Eyolfson had a long 15 minute chase after their bogie before they caught up to it southwest of Caen. Night glasses showed it to be a 188. A short burst from 200 feet astern made debris fly from the cockpit, port wing and engine. The enemy pilot made a violent break down to the left, but a second burst caught his aircraft again in the port wing. After a great explosion the wing collapsed and the Junkers, flicking over on its back, went straight down in flames. March pinpointed

the burning wreckage on the ground before heading for Hunsdon.

On the night of July 7/8, Ian chased an Me410 for thirty minutes, his engines overheating; he just managed to catch and shoot down the fastest piston-engine twin in the Luftwaffe.

After approximately fifty-five ops, March and Eyolfson were repatriated as a crew back to Canada to instruct at the OTU at Debert, Nova Scotia. Ian March's DFC was sent to him, as with many other flyers, in the mail. Following the war he joined Trans-Canada Airlines (TCA), flying Lockheed Lodestars from Moncton. He retired from Air Canada in 1981 as captain of a Boeing 747.

In 1942, nineteen-year-old Rayne Shultz(p.119) was one of the youngest pilots to graduate at No. 54 OTU. Another Canadian, Bill Vincent, was only a few months older than Shultz. They were both sergeant pilots, Rayne at 410 Squadron, Bill at 409, and both were commissioned on December 9, receiving closely adjacent serial numbers, J16359 for Rayne, J16356 for Bill.

Profile – WILLIAM HORACE VINCENT
Born – January 31, 1922, Winnipeg, raised in Vancouver
Father – Horace Vincent, travelling salesman
Mother – Alice Leaderer
Decorations & Medals – CMM, CD and Two Clasps
Degrees & Awards – NORAD Certificate of Achievement as senior director of the battle crew, Seattle Sector; Commendation Certificate, USAF Air Defense Command
Post-war occupation – Air force officer, Air Vice-Marshal, RCAF/CAF
Marital status – Wife Margaret Harrison, sons Peter and John, daughter Anne
Hobbies – Municipal politics

William Horace "Bill" Vincent had been born in Winnipeg, but grew up in Vancouver, attending Lord Byng High School. His father, Horace, was of United Empire Loyalist stock from Canning, Nova Scotia, and worked for Fletcher's Ham and Bacon as a travelling salesman. A wounded war veteran of the 27th Battalion, Winnipeg Rifles, Horace suffered from deafness caused by a head wound. His oldest son, Bill, watched the RCAF aircraft flying around

Jericho Beach, BC, and says: "I knew I wanted to be a pilot in the air force from 1937 on."

Bill's younger brother Peter, born in 1924, served as a tail gunner on a Halifax bomber at 192 Squadron RAF. He was shot down on April 22, 1944, while returning home from a bombing mission over Karlsruhe, Germany. As Bill recalled, "It was quite devastating. My sister said it almost killed my mother … My youngest brother Carl was too young for the Second World War, but he later joined the army and served in the Korean War."

Vincent liked flying the Bristol Blenheim and Beaufighter and de Havilland Mosquito. He recalls that the cockpit of the Beaufighter machine was pilot-friendly:

The Beaufighter was a nice comfortable aircraft, lots of visibility. The Bristol engine on the Beau VI was quieter than a Mosquito. The cockpit was better laid out, the controls for fuel, the undercarriage lever, the flap lever were nicely positioned … nice quadrant in front … the radio had a row of push buttons, eight buttons, eight fixed frequencies, all on one box. In the Mosquito they had sixteen buttons on more than one box and it was harder to remember and the cockpit was more cramped so you could not see.

The Blenheim preceded the Beaufighter in the training, and in my conversation with Air Vice-Marshal Vincent he recalled an episode from a night trip on the Blenheim:

At 54 OTU flying the long-nosed Blenheim, we were sent out for a practice vector at seventeen thousand feet, simply flying outbound, turning around and coming back inbound. As we commenced the let down, my navigator and I heard a machine-gunning sound. We were warned that the Luftwaffe might have intruder aircraft around that could shoot us down. What it turned out to be was the ice on the propellers breaking off as we descended into warmer air, and hitting the long nose of the Blenheim … I can tell you my mouth was pretty dry when it happened.

Alice Vincent came close to losing two sons in the war when Bill was training at the Beaufighter OTU. As he recalls:

It was called "banging heads" when you are up doing radar, you go in pairs, where each can practice an intercept on the other. We finished our intercept. When I was the target my navigator was telling me where he was … he said, "He is right underneath you here, he is coming in kinda fast. He should be breaking away pretty soon." Then he shouts, "Christ, he is right underneath you." The next thing I know the Beaufighter is right in my face. When he came up he was just a little starboard. My starboard prop chopped his port elevator off. The props on the Beaufighter II with Merlin engines were variable pitch wooden … I heard a hell of a clatter and a bang, and wood was flying everywhere, the props being broken. I hit his slipstream and flipped upside down, and we were at ten thousand feet. I got the aircraft back under control at four thousand feet. The engine mounts were just hanging there, the props gone …

The New Zealand pilot and RAF navigator did not get out in the other Beaufighter. They did a big investigation and I was exonerated, and they learned through the investigation that the other pilot had been in the habit of doing this.

Vincent's first tour at 409 was uneventful. His navigator David Thorpe and he had a great working relationship and they chummed around between flights. But there was simply no enemy action at Acklington, Northumberland, and the two men flew month after month of standing patrols without enemy contact. However, he had one intercept that reveals how difficult it could be on a black night to separate friend from foe. He and Thorpe came close to shooting down a British bomber piloted by a Canadian whom Bill Vincent had joined up with:

The op took place in February 1943 while our 409 Beaufighters were located at RAF Station Acklington north of Newcastle on Tyne. The Germans had decided to make a

bombing raid on Newcastle and Sunderland in northeast England. We were scrambled to meet the incoming bombers, and my navigator and I were vectored onto a "bogey" at twelve thousand feet … We approached our target with caution from below and astern, feeling sure that it must be a German bomber advancing towards the target area.

At minimum radar range I had to drop some flap and use full fine pitch on the engine props, to slow down safely without having the Beau stall out. I was surprised that if it was a German bomber approaching its target, it would be going so slow. It was a very dark night and the target was just a black blob at minimum target range. I initially decided that it was a Do217 because I could detect twin rudders, but his slow bombing speed made me suspicious. I reasoned that it could be a slow Whitley bomber which also had twin rudders. It was too dark for me to see any fuselage marking such as a German cross or an RAF roundel, nor could I determine if there was any mid-upper or tail-gunner position. I was careful to stay out of sight of these positions whilst avoiding the possibility of stalling out the Beau.

I asked my nav if he could see anything from his bubble window in the rear of the fuselage. I also asked him to come forward to see through my windows to determine if he could see any better than I, but he couldn't. We decided not to open fire because we could not definitely identify it as an enemy though it was obvious that a bombing raid was taking place in front of our position …

On return to base we encouraged the intelligence officer to call the bomber OTU at Inverness in northern Scotland to see if they had any of their aircraft out on training missions over the North Sea, making landfalls on this area of England. Indeed they did. So I was glad that I had made the decision not to open fire.

There is a postscript to this story: about forty-five years later I was in contact with my World War II friend "Punch" Thompson [Walter R. Thompson, DFC and Bar, MA, LLB, QC], who joined the RCAF the same day as I …

Punch was streamed into bombers whilst I was streamed into night fighters. I then learned that he had been a student at the Inverness bomber OTU and on checking his logbook he indicated that he could possibly have been airborne that night on a training mission on Whitley bombers over the North Sea making landfalls in that area of England. We could not determine exactly, as I did not have my logbooks, which were stolen, along with a lot of my clothing and war souvenirs, when we had to overnight at RCAF Station Lachine in Montreal after offloading from the ship which brought me home from UK in August 1945. (Welcome home!) I was a bit shook up when I learned that he could have been our target that night!

Squadron Leader Walter Thompson, ex-Pathfinder pilot, observed during a conversation with the author that he is relieved Bill Vincent erred on the side of safety. Had he not, it would have abruptly and unfairly ended Walter Thompson's war career and his post-war life as a lawyer, author, husband and father.

Vincent's second tour was with 410, after D-Day, flying as a night fighter from temporary fields in France with his navigator "Red" Heinbuck. When the war ended, in common with many flying veterans, Bill was relieved but his feelings were mixed:

I was quite confused, and thinking "What am I going to do now?" It was a blank feeling of what's next, what the hell is going to happen now, the war is over and we have to go home and make something of our lives.

The "we" was Bill and his wife, Margaret Harrison, from Sunderland, England. While stationed at Acklington in 1943, Bill had gone to the Navy, Army, Air Force Institute (NAAFI) Club. A Women's Auxiliary Air Force (WAAF) "ops" assistant, who worked in the control tower, got off her shift that night at 11 p.m. and decided to bicycle in the pitch black around the aerodrome perimeter track to listen to the band at the club. As soon as Margaret walked in the door Bill spotted her and asked her to dance. The attraction must have been mutual as they were married in November 1943. Bill stayed with 410 Squadron, and

the RAF sent Margaret to another station. When Bill's second tour was over, the RCAF sent him back to Canada in August 1945. Margaret was released from the RAF in November '45 and joined her husband in Canada the following February. As she recalls:

It was not a hard adjustment … from the moment I put my foot on Canadian soil I was happy. I went to Toronto where Bill was on course; the wife of one of Bill's navigators (Betty Heinbuck) took me in hand, and we shopped, which was wonderful. I was able to buy all this new clothing without using my family's clothing coupons, required in England. I had already used so many of their precious coupons when I purchased my wedding gown.

As Bill advanced in rank from flight lieutenant to air-vice-marshal in the RCAF, Margaret raised their children. Over thirty years, she and Bill lived in thirty-two different homes. Later assignments included Canadian air attaché in London and commander Air Defense Command/Air Defense Group and 22nd North American Aerospace Defence Command (NORAD) Region, at North Bay, Ontario. Margaret reminded me what the 1940s protocol for an officer's wife had entailed when her husband reported in for his new job:

When your husband was transferred to a new station the wife would wait until she knew when the Station Commander's wife was *not* home, call upon her and leave her calling card. The station commander's wife would then entertain all the newcomers for tea. It was also the custom that to be an officer's wife was to be a member of the Officers Wives Club. Needless to say, this is a far cry from present protocol! I enjoyed moving, it was easy for me to adjust to the move to different parts of Canada, USA, England and meeting new friends. I actually miss this in retirement. It was a wonderful life.

After retirement in 1977, Bill wished to contribute to the community in which he lived. He was elected alderman in the town of Comox and served in the capacity for eighteen years. Among many other charitable and community activities, Vincent has been the chairman of the Comox Valley Association for Mentally Challenged People for twenty-five years. Now eighty-three years old, he is an immediate past president of the Canadian Fighter Pilots Association Western Region and the Comox Valley Association for Mentally Challenged People. He is also committee chair for the BC Special Olympics Summer Games, scheduled to be held in the Comox Valley in June 2005.

* * *

Courtesy of the Wayne Ralph Collection

Doug McNabb at home in Sun Lakes, Arizona, 2001.

Profile – HAROLD DOUGLAS MCNABB

Born – August 9, 1920, Winnipeg

Father – Donald James McNabb, railway mail clerk, CPR, north Winnipeg

Mother – Gertrude Elizabeth Birthman

Post-war occupation – Representative, Transo Envelope Company, Chicago, IL

Marital status – Wife Phyllis Wynn, son Waid, daughter Brenda

Hobbies – Golf, curling

Douglas McNabb, who grew up on Albany Street in the city of St James, on the west side of Winnipeg, received his wings and his sergeant's stripes at the end of February 1942 and sailed to England on SS *Cape Town Castle*. Doug's brother, Donald, also received RCAF pilot's wings and commission and followed Doug to England, then served his operational tour on Dakotas in India.

When Doug's eyes were routinely tested again in Britain, he was told his night vision was above average, so he thought, "Why don't I ask for night fighters?" His training was completed at Brize Norton, England, and then Charter Hall, flying Oxfords, Blenheims and then Beaufighters in September 1942. It was at "Slaughter Hall"—as the aircrews referred to the OTU—where he met his AI navigator, RAF Sergeant Brian Tindall, from Truro, Cornwall. McNabb joined 406 when Wing Commander Wills of the RAF was in charge at Predannack, Cornwall. It was a fallow period, with no enemy aircraft being seen for many weeks at a time. McNabb had to wait until March '44 to have his first successful encounter with an enemy aircraft.

When asked if he was ever afraid flying around at night, Doug McNabb observed that he looked forward to the darkness—it felt comforting, like home. The only experience at nighttime that spooked him a little was a natural phenomenon of ships and aircraft in certain atmospheric conditions; it was St Elmo's Fire coursing up and down the Beaufighter's windscreen.

Reported by sailors since ancient times, St Elmo's Fire is named for the fourth-century patron saint of Mediterranean sailors, Saint Erasmus. It is caused by what is known as corona or point discharge. When the electrical field potential strength reaches about one thousand volts per centimetre, electrons are generated. It is most common around thunderstorms and in highly charged atmospheric conditions. In the darkness (it cannot be seen, though is still present, in daylight), the tips of a tall building, the masts of a ship or an aircraft's propellers, tail surfaces, wingtips, nose and canopy deflect the electrical forces, causing bluish-white or green light.

If a flyer touches the canopy or windscreen with his finger, a spark or light will follow the finger as it moves. Radio communications are sometimes hampered, and there is a hissing sound in the radios that

Courtesy of the Doug McNabb Collection

Doug McNabb and John Hall after their night victory against a Ju88, March 27, 1944.

changes in pitch and tone moving up and down the scale. The first time a pilot encounters St Elmo's Fire it can be akin to a religious experience; it is unlike anything in the ground world. Sailors felt that the gods were sending a good omen since it was most apparent after storms, and it was seen as a sign of a safe passage.

Doug McNabb is retired now, and he and his wife, Phyllis, are living in Sun Lakes, Arizona, about twenty miles south of Phoenix. Looking out at the brilliant yellow sun, I asked Doug to describe how he and his navigator achieved their first victory. He told me that he was not scheduled to fly on March 27 and was having a social evening in Exeter. Doug's NCO navigator Tindall was not in town with him, but another navigator named Pilot Officer John Hall

was. As they got off the bus bringing them home from Exeter, they got word that all available squadron personnel were to scramble.

Doug and John high-tailed it to the aerodrome and went through the strap-in and start-up procedures. It was now after 11 p.m. There was quite a bit of fog at the aerodrome, but Doug's Beaufighter (s/n KW981) was cleared for takeoff. "Derek 21" was Doug's call sign, and he climbed on instruments to sixteen thousand feet in the vicinity of Bristol, a city under attack that night by German bombers. They started hunting between the broken layers of cloud, in darkness with no moonlight.

John, after picking up the radar contact at twenty minutes before midnight, kept up a stream of verbal directions to Doug. Doug knew in the dark what the exhaust flame of a Ju88 looked like, but he asked John to confirm by looking out from the bubble observation dome halfway back on the upper fuselage that it was not a friendly aircraft. German night fighters followed bombers back to England to their home aerodrome, shooting them down in the circuit or even as they touched down. One of the jobs of the Allied night fighters was to catch these German intruders. It was necessary to distinguish them from bombers, particularly damaged stragglers limping home with engines out. There were quite a few cases during the war of friendly fire from Allied night fighters over Britain and the North Sea. Various Allied bombers, mainly the twin-engine types, were attacked in error, being misidentified as German intruders.

Once he was sure that the bogey was a Ju88, Doug McNabb opened fire with his four cannon and eight machine guns, setting the aircraft alight. With the flames streaming behind from both engines, John and Doug could see the German markings on the fuselage. The Ju88 remained in level flight for two or three seconds, and then spun down. The wreckage of the aircraft fell near the town of Berkley in the county of Gloucester. Doug was elated that he had finally scored, though disappointed that his navigator Tindall, despite all the uneventful flights they had made together as a crew, did not share in his first big success.

Doug landed his Beaufighter at St Eval and did not get home until the next day. In the dark the pilot and navigator had not witnessed the four crew members bailing out of the Ju88. One wounded crew member later had his leg amputated by American surgeons at the local military hospital. (Several decades after the war, as part of historical ceremonies for the Bristol region, McNabb learned that all the German flyers had survived the war—he and they were invited to participate in unveiling a historic marker.)

On May 14, 1944, McNabb and Tindall were credited with a probable and a damaged in attacks over the Channel. McNabb today believes that it was a certain victory not a probable because:

When you hit something and follow it down as low as you can go, and you are five hundred

[feet] above the water with a fog bank below, and the other plane goes off the radar screen, well, we figured we got it because it had to go in the water. Then we started for home and we found another [target] and we hit it, but then we lost it. I said to Tindall, "We got to get home, we are a hell of a long way from shore, and we are down to our auxiliary fuel" … Well, we managed to land straight in on the runway at Bolt Head right on the coast … and the man on the fuel pumps told us our aircraft had no fuel in the tanks. It was then that I began to shake a bit.

On June 5, while they were patrolling at night near the airport at Morlaix, France, their aircraft was damaged by flak. They were in that area because they had been briefed that afternoon that their efforts on the night of the 5th were in support of the D-Day landings the next morning.

No. 406 Squadron was commanded in succession by three of the RCAF's most exceptional night-fighter aces, R.C. "Moose" Fumerton, D.J. "Blackie" Williams and R. "Russ" Bannock. By the time Bannock arrived, McNabb had completed his tour and been sent for "a rest" to fly Hurricanes with No. 6 Bomber Group doing fighter affiliation, but he remembers Fumerton and Williams with affection mixed together with chagrin and awe.

Fumerton was "quite a guy … very easygoing, very likeable," who particularly impressed McNabb by demonstrating a low-level slow roll in the Beaufighter. Williams was "a frighteningly fast driver who slowed down for nothing on the narrow English roads." The one occasion that Doug McNabb hitched a ride to and from town with Blackie he vowed was his last; McNabb insists that the drive was far more frightening than anything that had happened to him in the air. Blackie Williams recalled to the author that his first vehicle was a three-wheel Riley, which was rather unstable, especially with many people on board. He later purchased a 1924 Rolls-Royce so that the squadron members could ride in greater comfort and safety to the pubs, rather than hanging off the sides of the Riley.

Photos courtesy of the Warne Ralph Collection

George "Red" Sutherland, 2001, Chilliwack, BC.

Profile – GEORGE "RED" SUTHERLAND

Born – July 2, 1918, Calgary, raised in British Columbia

Father – George Sutherland, stone mason, garage mechanic and owner

Mother – Mary Williamson

Decorations & Medals – CD and Clasp, Centennial Medal

Post-war occupation – Air force officer, Group Captain, RCAF/CAF

Marital status – Wife Marion Phyllis Bennett, daughter Bonnie, son Jim

Hobbies – Golf, downhill skiing, gardening

David "Blackie" Williams, July 2004, Richmond, BC.

Profile – DAVID JOHN "BLACKIE" WILLIAMS

Born – January 6, 1919, Vancouver

Died – August 20, 2004, Richmond, BC

Father – John Williams, ship's master, CP Ships in British Columbia

Mother – Anne Williams

Decorations & Medals – DSO, DFC, CD and Clasp

Post-war occupation – Air force officer, Group Captain, RCAF/CAF

Marital status – Wife Helen Jackson died in June 2004; sons David and Richard; daughter Jane Ann

Hobbies – Golf

George "Red" Sutherland had been sweet-talked by an RCAF recruiting officer into training as a rigger. The recruiting officer promised Sutherland that later on he could transfer into pilot training, but at least he would be getting useful training and a daily wage in the RCAF. George graduated as a rigger from the Technical Training School at St Thomas, Ontario, and was subsequently promoted to sergeant. But every time he requested to remuster to pilot, there was some excuse. Frustrated, Red wrote a scathing memorandum to the commanding officer (CO) of the repair depot at Calgary, saying how he had been lied to and screwed over by the system.

When Sutherland was instructed to show up at the CO's office, he figured his goose was cooked. But the group captain, memo in hand, looked up at Red and said: "You know, Sergeant Sutherland, I think you have a point. I think you have been misled. Go get yourself an aircrew medical. If you pass, I'll have you remustered today."

Red dropped back to Aircraftman 2nd Class rank to train as a pilot, but later his stripes were reinstated. When he graduated second on his course on Ansons at No. 7 SFTS at Ft McLeod, Alberta, he was immediately commissioned. He arrived at Bournemouth in November 1941 after a fast passage, with seventeen thousand others, on the ocean liner *Queen Elizabeth*. He was posted as a Beaufighter pilot to the RCAF's first night-fighter squadron, 406, in the spring of 1942 and served with the unit until January 1945.

Group Captain Sutherland lives today in Chilliwack, BC, where he graduated from high school in 1935. I met him at the Chilliwack Airport Coffee Shop, so famous for its homemade pies that pilots are known to fly in just to have a piece. Over coffee and pie he told me his life story. Serving so long on one squadron, and a renowned one, Red had the privilege of knowing and flying with many great leaders. Two of the most memorable for him are Robert Carl "Moose" Fumerton and David John "Blackie" Williams. His eyes lit up as he told me story after story about these two legends of the RCAF.

Red recollects that the whole squadron was greatly buoyed up to hear that one of the originals of 406, Moose Fumerton, was returning from the Middle East to take command in August 1943. The RAF commanding officer that summer had limited rapport with the Canadians; Fumerton, however, was not only the highest-scoring Canadian ace on Beaufighters at the time, but he had scored the first victory for 406 back in September '41. Fumerton's personality was a breath of fresh air for the aircrews, and his flying abilities were awe-inspiring.

On one occasion when Red complained about his Beaufighter, Moose offered to fly it, with Red standing in the well behind the pilot's seat. When the aircraft behaved perfectly, Moose turned to Red and said, "I don't see much wrong with this machine." He then commenced a flawlessly executed slow roll: "God, that roll was smooth, smooth as a baby's bottom. And I thought to myself, *Jesus, he's a better pilot than I am.*"

Blackie Williams had done a tour in Bomber Command with 408 Squadron RCAF flying Handley Page Hampdens in 1942. Sutherland says that put Williams in good stead with the pilots at 406 because the Hampden "was called the flying coffin, and he was one of the few people I ever knew to survive a Hampden tour. They were terrible machines."

Williams told me that the aircrew losses for Hampden bombers at 408 Squadron RCAF in the 1942 period were 77 per cent over a tour of thirty-two operations: "You didn't get to know anybody on the squadron because the losses were so high, many being lost on their first trip fresh from the OTU." He was one of the first pilots, if not *the* first RCAF BCATP-trained pilot to complete a tour.

An independent thinker like Moose, Blackie had a habit of attacking German targets from the east, which was not the typical direction from which German fighter pilots expected to intercept enemy bombers. Williams and his Hampden crew had been credited with the destruction of an enemy Ju88 on their way inbound to the Kassel marshalling yards on August 28, 1942. Although their plane was damaged in the Ju88 attack, they went on to bomb the target, drive off an Me109 on the homeward leg and get back safely. It was such a rare accomplishment that Williams received the DFC, and his crew, Flight Sergeant Turner and Sergeant Leech, each received the DFM.

Blackie Williams arrived at 406 as a flight commander in June 1943, just before Moose Fumerton arrived. Blackie describes Moose as "a fine chap and a fabulous pilot," who was happy to delegate responsibilities. Still fiercely independent at age ninety-two, Wing Commander Fumerton observed in my first conversation with him, "I have my own ideas. I have always had them." On one occasion he flew his Beaufighter to North Africa without telling anybody; no particular reason—he just wanted to go. The RCAF HQ took a dim view of Moose's inspiring but casual methods of command and sent him home to Canada in August 1944, promoting Williams to command 406.

With Fumerton sent off to No. 7 OTU at Debert, Nova Scotia, where he would add an Air Force Cross to his other decorations, Red Sutherland was now promoted to squadron leader and took over Williams's flight. He became for Williams what Williams had been for Fumerton, a second-in-command. Their relationship would stretch across a thirty-year RCAF career and both would retire as group captains.

Red and Blackie liked to tell stories about each other's escapades. If I asked for clarification of what happened, each separately would say, "Yeah, that's true, but let me tell you what *really* happened." So I would go back and forth fine-tuning the details, each fighter pilot adding to, or correcting, the latest version I had heard from the other. The first escapade I heard from Williams involved Red and his wartime love affair with a beautiful woman named Barbara.

Blackie had ordered Red to take command of the squadron while he went to London for the weekend. Red was angry at Blackie for picking that particular weekend, his own weekend off, to go into London. As his anger mounted he called up his WAAF girlfriend, a fighter plotter, and said, "Let's go to London." As luck would have it, Williams could not get a room in his favourite hotel, the Park Lane, and was in the same lineup as Red and his girlfriend at the Strand Palace Hotel.

Blackie was so furious at what Red had done that he immediately ordered up a Mosquito from the squadron to pick the two up and take them back to the station. Due to a meeting of senior commanders involving none other than Prime Minister Winston Churchill, there was a concentration of high-ranking officers at the London airfield. One transient air vice-marshal (AVM) of the RAF watched in amazement as the pilot of the Mosquito, dressed in the uniform of the US Army Air Force, got out of the machine.

The American was an RCAF-trained night-fighter pilot who had transferred to his country's air force but carried on flying with the RCAF. The American then assisted the British WAAF to sit on Squadron Leader Sutherland's lap, in the navigator's seat, for the trip home. Nobody offered a word of explanation, and the AVM decided he didn't want to know.

No. 406 Squadron was the first night-fighter unit on the order of battle for the D-Day invasion on June 6. They were assigned from dusk on the 6th to provide a standing patrol over the beachhead for that night, and Sutherland led the section that covered the beaches. A few weeks later, Red's section of Mosquitoes was grounded with an unserviceable machine very near Paris. He took the opportunity to visit the city and was so swept along by the recent liberation of Paris that he stayed for a full twenty-four hours. On this occasion Red was such a good promoter of what Paris had to offer that Blackie decided to visit on his own.

Despite Sutherland's occasional insubordination, Blackie enjoyed flying on operations with him. On one particularly dirty night, January 20, '44, the two volunteered to go hunting German E boats in the Channel. "They said we didn't have to go as the weather was so terrible," recalls Red. E boats were very capable seaworthy vessels and three of them were attempting to attack under the cover of foul weather the Allied ships at Lyme Bay, England. The Beaufighter's radar had the ability to pick up surface targets, but with the cloud ceiling at only one thousand feet above the water, it required Williams and Sutherland to stay quite low. They found the three boats on radar and picked them up visually due to their phosphorescent wake in the black void.

Williams told me that Sutherland's efforts that night deserved a DFC, as his Beaufighter was badly damaged by the gunners on the E boats on each of his attacks. To Williams the attacks were a wonderful demonstration of Red's courage and tenacity. Sutherland remembers:

One of us dropped a parachute flare, and the other made a strafing pass with the four 20mm cannon, and eight .303 Browning machine guns. We chose the starboard boat. I dropped the first flare, Williams attacked, then he dropped a flare, and I attacked … We got that first boat. It stopped dead in the water. Two turned back towards France. They could not find wreckage the next day, but we figure we got it. I received seventeen hits on my machine including one incendiary … this was a volunteer op, as we did not normally attack E boats.

No medals came to either crew. But a short message from the Royal Navy read: "Good show."

Sutherland and his navigator, Geoff Jones, were scrambled in miserable weather on April 1, 1944, on vectors to find a B24 Liberator that was lost and running low on fuel. Jones was able to get close enough using the Beaufighter radar, and Sutherland got the attention of the Liberator captain. The B24 had flown out of North America, and there was no common radio frequency that the bomber and the Beaufighter could talk on, so sign language had to suffice. They led the B24 down to a safe landing at Winkleigh, Devon. A short while later the squadron received a telephone call thanking them for a job well done; one of the passengers on the B24 was President Franklin Roosevelt's son, Elliott, a colonel and P38 pilot in the United States Army Air Force.

Accompanied by his navigator, Clarence Joseph "Kirk" Kirkpatrick of Saskatoon, Blackie Williams shot down five enemy bombers. Perhaps the most dramatic episode involved an attack against three bombers in the Bay of Biscay on July 21, '44. Sixty years after that attack I met Group Captain Williams for the first time; it was only five weeks before he died, and a month after his wife Helen had died. He had moved to Richmond, British Columbia, from Ocean Shores, Washington, to be closer to his son David. His RCAF buddy George Sutherland urged me to go see Blackie Williams, as he was not in great health.

I listened intently as he described what happened over the Bay of Biscay, the two of us sitting at his kitchen table. Blackie was using supplemental oxygen to help him breathe, but that did not stop him from chain-smoking. We were both drinking what he always drank during his long RCAF career, dark rum and Coke. Williams credits Kirk Kirkpatrick with getting them home safely from the operation:

The destroyers were being attacked off Bordeaux by Dorniers and we flew down under the weather at night. Because the weather was so thick they told us we could come back at low altitude and bail out once we got over England. When we got down there, we picked up the Germans. I shot the first Dornier down into the water; on my second Dornier, two of my cannons jammed and I had to feather the starboard engine on my Mosquito because they had damaged it. But on one engine, my machine was still better than a Dornier, so I pulled up alongside as they were starting to bail out. [After they got out] a Mosquito from Coastal Command came in and shot at the empty aircraft … so I ended up having to share that claim.

We came home at under one hundred feet and as we approached the Cornwall coast at Predannack, Kirk recognized the aerodrome … how the hell he was able to do that I do not know. So I pulled up over the top of the hill, but was heading directly for the hangar, and I didn't want to crash into it. I had the gear and flaps down, so I pulled up the gear and turned left into the good engine and went over the top of the cliff, through the trees. I had about one hundred feet to the water to gain speed, so I pulled it back around, came back over the top of the cliff and managed to land it on the runway … you were not supposed to do that with a Mosquito, but it was just fine.

This effort and many others resulted in Blackie receiving the DSO and Kirk the DFC. The citation for Blackie Williams's DSO reads:

This officer has completed a large number of sorties, including a number during which he has successfully attacked a variety of targets on the ground. In the air he has destroyed five enemy aircraft at night. He is a brave and resourceful pilot whose fine fighting qualities were well illustrated one night in July 1944, when he destroyed two enemy aircraft in one sortie. In the fighting his own aircraft sustained damage but he flew it safely to base in the face of extremely adverse weather. This officer is a most efficient and inspiring flight commander.

THE
PERSONALITIES
OF PILOTS AND
NAVIGATORS IN
NIGHT-FIGHTER
OPERATIONS

The author has interviewed the following Beaufighter and Mosquito specialists: Bannock, Bing, Edwards, Ferguson, Finlayson, Fumerton, Hope, Kernaghan, Kirkpatrick, Marr, March, McNabb, Phillips, Schultz, Shulemson, Sutherland, Sutherland Brown, Vincent, Williams

and Wright. All have emphasized in their conversations the symbiotic relationship that was essential for a night-fighter, intruder or ground-attack/anti-shipping crew to prosper. A navigator had to be confident that his pilot was competent not only to fight but also to fly well in all circumstances and bring the aircraft and crew safely home. As navigator Dave McIntosh wrote of Sid Seid in *Terror in the Starboard Seat*: "I liked the way that big hairy right hand gripped the stick and how the big hairy left hand gripped the throttles."

In turn, the pilot had to be confident that the navigator knew how to navigate if they were an intruder squadron, or had the finesse to handle the often finicky radar set if they were a night-fighter squadron. Then there were the other radio aids, like the secret equipment code-named "Gee," to be

Courtesy of the George "Red" Sutherland Collection

The wedding of Geoff Jones, Red Sutherland's navigator, 406 Squadron, 1944.

Blackie Williams and Kirk Kirkpatrick at 406 Squadron in 1944.

mastered. But, above all, a navigator had to have the steady nerves to tolerate violent events without even murmuring. Dr Ross Finlayson says of his navigator from Winnipeg, Alan Webster:

> [He] was just perfect, completely unflappable, it didn't matter what happened there was never a peep out of him. He never swore. If I made a good landing, he said, "Good landing." If I didn't, and there were some pretty wonky landings, he never said a word. Only once, when I was in a dive after an enemy aircraft and I was slow to recover, did he say, "Pull out, man, pull out!"

The importance of trust in each other was so paramount that, in the absence of one or the other, the remaining person very often could not or would not continue. For example, Bob Ferguson asked Don Creed to entertain a second tour of operations with him. When Creed turned him down, Bob realized he did not want to go on operations with anyone other than Don, and knew his war was now over. Similarly, Sutherland's navigator, Geoff Jones, an erudite ("he used words that I didn't know what they meant," says Red), university-educated RAF sergeant, got married in 1944, and told Red that he had had enough of operational flying. George was upset with him and said so. He still agreed to be best man at his wedding, but didn't really forgive him.

He still has regrets today that his sympathy and understanding came too late—long after the trail of his navigator had gone cold. During the war he knew that without Jones his own future on operations was in jeopardy. When he was assigned an experienced navigator who was an alcoholic and completely hopeless in the air, someone foisted off from another squadron, he knew his tour was over.

Social compatibility sometimes had little to do with airborne success. Since Flying Officer Doug McNabb's navigator, Sergeant David Tindall, had a family nearby at Truro that he visited frequently, Doug did not socialize a lot with his navigator. Yet their rapport in the air was excellent. Blackie Williams recalled that Kirk Kirkpatrick was a Saskatoon-born accountant before the war who was "very solid and secure; a very fine chap." But Kirk, unlike Blackie, had a serious girlfriend in Britain, Barbara Phyllis Copper, whom he later married, so the two men did not chum around with each other. Kirkpatrick says of his two accomplished pilots:

> I had utmost confidence in Williams and Bannock in the air. It was like sitting in a movie theatre. Blackie Williams was a real hero, and he never promoted himself, always the other person. He was a man that we all said at 406 Squadron in an earlier age would have been a pirate. He was boisterous on the ground, but once in the air, he was a cool customer, nothing fazed him.

When Blackie Williams died in his sleep on August 20, 2004, his son David asked me to telephone Kirk to let him know. I had encouraged Kirk to speak to Blackie as soon as possible as he was not well, and Kirk had reconnected by telephone after a long interval just the night before Blackie died. Kirk was very sad to hear the news, but glad that he had made the connection one last time. Two months later I received a telephone call from Phyllis Kirkpatrick in Saskatoon to let me know that her husband Kirk had died on October 7.

Profile – CLARENCE JOSEPH KIRKPATRICK
Born – August 7, 1918, Kindersley, SK, educated in Saskatoon
Died – October 7, 2004, Saskatoon
Father – Robert Franklin Kirkpatrick, farmer, died in 1941
Mother – Mary Helena Sproule
Decorations & Medals – DFC
Degrees & Awards – Bachelor of Accounting, Saskatoon, 1939, CA
Post-war occupation – Chartered accountant, partner Price Waterhouse
Marital status – Wife Barbara Phyllis Copper, daughters Louise and Heather, son Neil
Hobbies – Charitable fundraising, community affairs

Profile – JAMES DAVIDSON WRIGHT

Born – August 28, 1921, Rosthern, SK

Father – Frank Wright, farmer

Mother – Agnes Thomson

Decorations & Medals – DFC

Degrees & Awards – BSc Chemical Engineering, Fellow of the Canadian Mining Institute, PEng

Post-war occupation – Metallurgical engineer in the mining industry

Marital status – Wife Laurice Ferris, sons Frank and Robert, daughter Ellen

Hobbies – Music and carpentry

Profile – ROSS HUNTER FINLAYSON

Born – February 22, 1921, Hamilton, ON

Father – Hunter Gray Finlayson, manager of Sam Manson Sporting Goods, Hamilton

Mother – Mercaline Ross

Degrees & Awards – BA, 1942, DDS, 1949

Post-war occupation – Dentist

Marital status – Wife Betty Smith, son Donald, daughters Joan and Nancy

Hobbies – Model planes, reading

James Wright, navigator for Donald MacFadyen, one of the RCAF's highest-scoring night-fighter aces, learned early that he had an extremely experienced pilot with more than two thousand flying hours to his credit, compared with his modest four hundred. Wright himself was unquestionably a very bright person who excelled academically and graduated as the top student of his navigation course at Portage la Prairie, Manitoba, in March '43. He was a good match for his pilot. But his pilot had an unpredictable personality and was heartily disliked by many around him. By his own admission, he was "a compulsive perfectionist, appallingly egocentric," as Hugh Halliday has written in *The Tumbling Sky*. This likely inhibited his promotion upward.

In today's psychological language he might be labelled as deficient in emotional intelligence, a deficiency probably not uncommon in young wartime fighter pilots. Jim Wright and Don MacFadyen made a terrific fighting team and became aces at 418 Squadron RCAF. Wright was credited with seven, and MacFadyen seven, plus five V1s (the pilotless planes also known as buzz bombs), and many others destroyed or damaged on the ground during intruder missions over the continent. They performed well in combat, but Jim and Don were not in any sense close pals; they bunked together in the same room, but sometimes not, particularly on those occasions when MacFadyen felt hemmed in. On some squadrons, crews roomed together, but it varied according to units and individuals. In general, within twin-engine night-fighter and intruder squadrons, men socialized with those with whom they felt compatible; flying together had little to do with that feeling.

Finlayson and Webster flew as a crew with 409 Squadron RCAF from July '44 until the war ended. Despite flying forty-four operational trips and destroying two enemy aircraft, actions that in some squadrons might have resulted in a "gong" (a medal for gallantry) or at least an MiD, Finlayson received no official recognition, and did not qualify for the Operational Wings. At night-fighter squadrons there was no defined standard for the number of ops required to finish a tour (the expression of the time was "tour expire"). Just as portrayed in Joseph Heller's novel *Catch-22*, the number required to be relieved of combat duties in the RCAF increased as the war progressed. Dr Finlayson retired from his Hamilton, Ontario, dentistry practice at age eighty in 2001 and his knees give him plenty of grief from the years of standing. He recalls the two successes he had in eleven months of combat operations:

> There were fellows on squadron who spent the same time I did or longer and never saw an enemy aircraft. I was on two chases and I got two aircraft, one in October, one in December … there was a big dry spell from December 1944 until the end of the war …
>
> I shot down a German night-fighter pilot named Feldwebel R. Koch of 5 NJG1 Squadron at Dusseldorf. His aircraft was an Me110 and I shot him down October 6th in the Sittard area; I was flying a Mossie, the serial number was MM560. Koch was taken prisoner of war and sent a note to me, telling me he had shot down five four-engine bombers, and had flown hundreds of hours on operations (far more than we had) and been shot down many times.
>
> [In my attack] on December 18th, the enemy crew of the Ju88 were all killed. The radar

PILOT'S PERSONAL COMBAT REPORT

From : ~ No.409 R.C.A.F. Squadron.

To : ~ H.Q., R.C.A.F., H.Q., A.E.A.F., H.Q., No.85 Group,
2nd T.A.F., No.24 Sector, R.A.F.

STATISTICAL.

Date:	(a) Evening October 6th/7th, 1944.
Unit:	(b) No.409 Squadron, R.C.A.F.
Make & Type of A/C.	(c) 1 Mosquito XIII Mk. VIII A.I.
Time of Combat:	(d) 23.20 hours.
Place of attack:	(e) Sittard area.
Weather:	(f) Hazy — Visibility poor below 4000 ft — good at 8000 feet.
Our casualties — personell:	(g) N/A.
Our casualties — aircraft:	(h) N/A.
Enemy casualties — air combat:	(j) 1 Me.110 destroyed.
Enemy casualties — ground and sea targets.	(k) N/A.

GENERAL REPORT.

F/O Finlayson (Pilot) F/O Webster (N/R)
Airborne from base 2300 hrs returned 0005 hrs.

Under 15119 control we were informed of a bandit 18 miles away and given a vector 100° and told to make 12,000'. During climb G.C.I. confirmed the height as 12,000' and told us to investigate with caution. Successive vectors toward 180° were given and the target began to cross from port to starboard at a range of three miles. F/O. Webster discovered the weapon was partially bent since no contact was obtained at two miles on a vector of 240°. G.C.I. controller gave us an excellent run in to approximately ½ mile in a stern chase on the same vector and we obtained a good contact and took over. F/O. Webster brought us into 1000' through a gentle weave and I got a visual on the target 30° above, 11 o'clock. Closed to 50 feet while the target turned onto a reciprocal course before we could positively identify it as a Me.110, with drop tanks and radar aerials in the nose. The target was at 12000'. We dropped back to 400', gave it a short burst and strikes were observed about the port engine. A second burst struck the fuselage and starboard engine. The bandit went into a descending turn to port and caught fire after a third burst, strikes observed all over the aircraft. It continued in a steep dive and we saw it strike the ground and burn. G.C.I. controller also saw it fall and explode in the Sittard area. We gave canary immediately and G.C.I. fixed the position. No return fire.

We claim 1 Me.110 destroyed.

Pilot. B H Finlayson ....

.... W.H. Whipp .... F/O.
Squadron Intelligence Officer,
No.409 Squadron, R.C.A.F.

was wonky on this trip. Webster was giving me miles to go, and it was actually just feet to go. Next thing I knew I was right under him; in fact, I nearly ran into him. I put down gear and flaps to slow down. I pulled ahead slowly, had a good look at him … we were so close we could see the outline of the pilot and navigator. Being directly below they had no chance to pick us up on their radar. We did not see him hit the ground, so I claimed a probable, but the army called it in to their HQ, which called Air Force HQ, and it was confirmed.

But on VE day—May 8, '45—Webster went to Finlayson and said: "I am not going up flying in a Mosquito ever again." Alan Webster's war was over and he wasn't putting himself unnecessarily in harm's way. From then until 409 Squadron disbanded at the beginning of July, Ross Finlayson flew either alone or with the airmen in the office on the unit. Ross says his fitter and rigger were happy to maintain his Mosquito but were not by any means anxiously standing in line to go flying.

In the fluid border situation in the weeks after the war, Russian fighters patrolled on the east side of the ceasefire line, and British, Canadian and American fighters flew on the west side of the line. The Mosquito was assigned to low-level patrols, and some of the most exhilarating flying Finlayson ever did was cruising down the German autobahns at fifty feet. All the single- and twin-engine fighters on daily patrols were showing the flag to their Russian counterparts, who were eager to dogfight if anyone penetrated the lines, and not just for fun, but for real. It is a little-known chapter of the war that Allied pilots patrolling the east-west line sometimes fought against each other after May 8, 1945.

Profile – WILLIAM LLOYD MARR

Born – July 4, 1917, Bramshott, England

Father – Dr Benjamin Butler Marr, medical doctor, Ft Langley, BC

Mother – Isabel "Drew" McIntosh

Decorations & Medals – AFC

Post-war occupation – Airline pilot, TCA/Air Canada, captain DC8, retired 1977

Marital status – Wife Henrietta McAteer, son Richard Flynn, daughter Katherine Ann

Hobbies – Flying, fishing

The experience of William Lloyd "Bill" Marr at 409 is one that illustrates the operational challenges of finding the enemy and shooting him down. He was the only son of a Boston-trained medical doctor, Benjamin Butler Marr, who was United Empire Loyalist stock from New Brunswick. Bill Marr was born on July 4, 1917, in Bramshott, England, where his father was stationed at the Canadian Army base hospital. His mother, Isabel "Drew" McIntosh, had joined her husband at Bramshott, leaving behind the family home in Fort Langley, British Columbia. Dr Marr registered his son's birthday as July 5, not wanting any child of his to be born on the United States' date of independence from Britain.

Bill grew up in Canada near the Hudson's Bay post in Fort Langley where his father had become the village doctor. He spent most of his childhood on horseback and never owned a bicycle. Unlike many Depression-era boys, he could afford one or two flights, in his case in a Curtis Robin that barnstormed off a friend's farm. His mother died in 1937, and in 1939, while Bill was in his third year of pre-medicine at the University of British Columbia and flunking his French, Latin and Biology courses, his father died. This left Bill and his nineteen-year-old sister, Katherine Isabel, without immediate family.

He had joined the Canadian Army in 1939 just before his father's death, enlisting in the Royal Westminster Regiment on September 3 (he had attended their summer camps in the 1930s), and was made corporal before the RCAF sent him word that he could start training. He joined the RCAF on June 6, 1940, and after receiving his wings around Christmas of 1940 he became an instructor on Ansons with No. 8 SFTS in Moncton, New Brunswick, then, a few months later, a Central Flying School (CFS) instructor at Trenton, Ontario. He married eighteen-year-old Henrietta McAteer while at Moncton and they had a six-month-old son, Flynn, when, with fifteen hundred flying hours behind him, Bill escaped from the BCATP to start his operational career in Europe.

In November 1942 he completed AFU training in Britain, receiving a rare "exceptional" pilot-rating stamp in his logbook. He joined 409 Squadron RCAF stationed at Acklington, north of Newcastle, and ultimately paired up with J.L. "Joe"

Carpenter, who was his navigator throughout all but the early stages of his tour. Carpenter refused to fly with anyone but Marr. In learning to fly the Beaufighter Mk VI, Marr did a checkout by looking over the shoulder of the "B" Flight commander for an hour (there was no dual-control Beaufighter). He then went solo for an hour, practising landings and engine-out procedures:

My next three flights were with my first navigator, a man named S_____, who did not work out and whom I asked to have replaced. We did an air-to-air test with the camera gun, a night-flying test, then a camera-gun test in a two-plane formation. The last flight was intended to test the Beaufighter's 10-centimetre radar out to its ultimate range of nine to ten miles. We were now ready to fly operations. My call sign was "Gravel 31" when I was first there, and later "Kitchen," the squadron code on the side of some 409 aircraft being "KP."

Marr described the process of closing on an enemy aircraft in cloud, and the frustrations that could occur:

Navigators have a tobacco auctioneer's singsong chant, talking all the time. As the pilot I never respond, just listen to him as he is talking range and position of target: "2,000, 2,000, coming in 1,900, 1,900, check left, go left, slightly up, he's up above us, I think he is turning left, go left, go left, go hard left, climb, climb, 20 degrees up ..." and so on. Joe gave me one interception entirely in cloud and eventually the first vision I got was of the tail, I couldn't even see the wings; it was exceptional navigation. I pulled the nose up to fire on this Heinkel 177 and the cannons would not fire. I could not fire a shot. I was so mad I considered putting my propeller through his rudder.

I called GCI and told them it was a Heinkel 177, and a British voice said, "We are on frequency ... we have contact." So I turned about forty five degrees to the right and then pulled up with full power. Well, as I looked over my shoulder I could see this other Mos-

quito. I shouted, "Not me, not me. Turning my landing lights on now." The British voice in the other aircraft came back, "Sorry, old boy." I would never have known what hit me!

Marr received an Air Force Cross (AFC) for his flying skills during his operational tour with 409 because of the many mishaps that he handled well. The citation states in part:

He has always been a tower of strength in Squadron affairs since arriving here and though he has had bad luck in contact with the enemy (on two occasions his guns jammed when in position to make a kill), he has never lost interest and has shown exceptional and outstanding keenness at all times. During his long tour he has had five successful single-

Bill Marr by his Mosquito.

Bill Marr at the annual Dawn Patrol, Vancouver, BC, 2003.

engine landings at night and during his entire service career at no time has he had the slightest mishap or damaged his aircraft.

As the war was ending, Marr was pleased that he had been granted an AFC, but he never knew why he got it:

After I finished my tour and was instructing at an OTU, the adjutant of the station, a woman I think, advised me that I had an AFC but I never saw the citation and I had no investiture. She gave me a bit of ribbon to sew on my uniform. The medal came in the mail long after the war, about 1950 …

As veterans we had to make application to get our medals, and many of the boys did not. I think that was terrible, that you had to apply for your own campaign medals. When I joined TCA we could not wear our ribbons on our airline uniform, like they did at BOAC. The original civilian pilots at TCA had no medals, and it seemed that they did not want us wearing ours.

In a flying career that spans six decades he has had no accidents that caused death or injury, but Marr recalls that in wartime there were plenty of ways to kill yourself and your navigator other than air combat:

We had a few crashes. When we got into France after D-Day, we were operating off primitive and bombed-out fields, and for night flying all we used was seven or so "Glim" lamps, hooded lights on a long string, each separated by 150 to 200 feet, with about a 40-watt bulb in each light. At this one airfield they had managed to put in two rows of these lamps, one for each side of the runway. Now we were like the airlines. Unfortunately, one set, the left-side string, burned out. Our usual procedure with one set of lamps was always to land with the lamps on the left side, i.e., the captain's side of the aircraft. In this case, by landing with those Glim lamps on their left, they were landing off the runway. One aircraft hit a bomb crater in the dark, collided with another aircraft: they were both written off with all four men killed. So that is how easy these things happened.

We had another one, during our move up to Lille, and B_____, our commanding officer, had been awake and flying for thirty-six hours, and he disappeared. We later learned that he had most likely drifted off to sleep as he was seen to fly into a hill and blow up … those are the stupid things in wartime that happen.

We lost S_____ and N_____ when they were shot down by one of our Lancasters. They came in far, far too fast, off-track, in and out the cloud tops, with about one hundred knots of overtake speed. Most of my intercepts were on Lancasters or Halifaxes, but as soon as you see the four-engine exhaust pattern you break off, and right away. If you look in Joe's logbook, you see these intercepts marked as "friendly," and there were lots of them.

One night I had just returned from patrol and had taken over the remaining portion of the night's operation ... I offered S_____ and N_____ my aircraft that night as it was now fully armed, fuelled, ready to go. They just wanted another aircraft up, it seemed routine, and they would be back soon. We heard nothing, until we learned much later that they had been shot down by one of our own. It was a moonlit night, cutting in and out of cloud, and the tail gunner in the Lanc had a type of rear-facing radar detection system, called "Duckpond" as I recall, and as soon as they popped out of cloud the tail gunner, who knew from his radar they were closing quickly, just nailed them. S_____ and N_____ became prisoners of war. Sadly, B_____ was shot down and killed by a P61 Black Widow [US Army Air Force night fighter], though we never proved it. They claimed a Heinkel, but we on the squadron thought it was him.

I asked Bill Marr if he resented tail gunners on friendly machines firing at him. He replied:

It was all part of the game ... and a fair game provided we know that is the way the game is played. I know he is going to fire as soon as he sees me, so I know to be very careful—I don't need to find out if it is a Lanc or Hallie [Halifax]. I don't care, it is a friendly. Four exhausts, it is obviously a British airplane, so you break off.

[If you are] a gunner on a Hallie, a Lanc or a Stirling and you see a twin-engine airplane coming in you can't wait. The Germans had 30mm cannon with much longer range and greater hitting power than their .303s, and we had 20mm. If you are a tail gunner you are not going to wait, you are going to fire.

On their last operational trip, a Dunkirk patrol over the Channel, November 2, '44, Bill and Joe almost got shot down by a Royal Navy ship. They were flying at seventy feet above the water, using the green, amber and red lights on their radio altimeter to gauge height above the water, red being fifty feet.

At one point Joe looked back and, by the moonlight, he could see their propeller wake on the surface of the water.

On the sixth turnaround, they drifted too near a ship equipped with a tethered kite balloon. The cable attached to the balloon could shear through an aircraft wing, and this discouraged any pilots wanting to make low-level attacks against ships. Perhaps nervous about who was out there in the darkness, the ship's crew flicked on their searchlights and started firing their Pom Pom guns. Joe hollered, "Ship dead ahead, hard starboard." Marr replied, "We're close enough to patrol end. Let's go home."

Marr bitched to the intelligence officer (IO) about the Royal Navy and, getting no sympathy, said "Well, it is all very well for you to sit there ..." The IO gave him a big grin and said, "Relax, Bill, you're finished ops, you will be off home soon." Marr was finally taken off operations on November 10. He then served for six months as a flying instructor in Britain on Mosquitoes. Asked how he felt about the war ending on VE Day, he reflected:

I was happy because I had a future. I had Etta, I had a son, I had a job with TCA. I had a whole new future. My feeling was one of release. I was excited. I was not sad, certainly no sadness at all ... I don't think there is any person who went through the war that isn't a peacenik. We're the greatest peaceniks in the world, the veterans of war.

There were 240 wartime pilots hired by TCA—most were bomber and transport types. Bill Marr is one of only six RCAF fighter pilots to have a post-war career as a commercial airline pilot with TCA. The company's name changed to Air Canada in 1965. When Marr retired in 1977 as an Air Canada captain, he had had sixteen years on the DC8, and twenty-nine thousand hours' total flying time.

* * *

No. 418 Squadron, formed in November 1941, was an RCAF squadron primarily dedicated to intruder operations, taking the war to the enemy at night and also by day in so-called Day Rangers, attacking

Luftwaffe airfields and hunting for enemy aircraft in the air, or taking off or landing at their airfields in occupied Europe and in Germany. On November 21, 1944, No. 406 replaced 418 in this role, and 418 carried on as a close air support squadron with the Second Tactical Air Force.

Its record of 79½ buzz bombs and 178 enemy aircraft destroyed makes 418 "City of Edmonton" Squadron the leading RCAF fighter squadron of the war in terms of total enemy flying machines destroyed. No. 418 was also the fighter squadron of the RCAF with the highest casualties—72 aircraft written off; 143 personnel lost on ops, killed, missing or POW; plus 31 killed on non-operational duties. In comparison, No. 401 Squadron RCAF, with 195 enemy aircraft destroyed, was the highest-scoring single-engine day-fighter unit and highest of all the squadrons in the Second Tactical Air Force.

Profile – JOHN HAROLD PHILLIPS

Born – April 23, 1923, Toronto

Father – George Hector Reid Phillips, commercial pilot Ontario Provincial Air Service

Mother – Lorna Maria Cruickshank

Decorations & Medals – DFC, CD and Two Clasps

Degrees & Awards – BA, TP – graduate test pilot, Empire Test Pilots' School (ETPS)

Post-war occupation – Air force officer, Wing Commander, RCAF/CAF

Marital status – Wife Olga Kathleen Papas, son John Barry, daughters Barbara Louise and Dianne Kathleen

Hobbies – Sailing

The only pilot I interviewed who grew up in a flying environment was Wing Commander John Harold "Jack" Phillips, DFC. He was the first child of George Hector Reid Phillips and Lorna Cruickshank. He was delivered in Toronto by his Great-Aunt Hanna Reid, a.k.a. Dr Hanna Reid, who practised medicine in the city with her sister, Dr Minerva Reid. Jack's father had served in the trenches of Ypres, Belgium, been wounded by mustard gas, and was commissioned in March 1917 at Mont St Eloi, France. He volunteered for the Royal Flying Corps, serving as an observer in the last weeks of the war with The Independent Air Force of the RAF.

While farming near Orangeville in 1922 he was invited to be an observer with the newly formed Ontario Provincial Air Service (OPAS) and soon thereafter trained as a pilot. In 1931 George was awarded the Trans-Canada Trophy, better known as the McKee Trophy, for his contributions to Canadian aviation and the development of OPAS. He retired from aviation at age sixty-five in 1959, having flown fourteen thousand hours, and was inducted into Canada's Aviation Hall of Fame in 1973.

While growing up in Sault Ste Marie, Ontario, the home of the OPAS, Jack occasionally went flying with his father. George demonstrated spins directly above the house they lived in at 124 McGregor Ave. To let his wife, Lorna, know that he was on his way inbound, George buzzed the home at low altitude, routinely and with great finesse touching the floats in the tops of the trees on the property.

After graduating from Toronto's Lawrence Park Collegiate with his senior matriculation in June 1941, Jack Phillips visited the RCAF recruiting centre. He was eighteen, but looked about fifteen, and the recruiting officer noted in his assessment that "Phillips is a doubtful candidate as a pilot." When Jack arrived at No. 1 SFTS at Camp Borden for Harvard training, his night-flying solo checkout was completed by his father, who was one of the squadron commanders at the SFTS.

To Jack's disappointment, having placed second highest in his training course, just behind his pal Jack Frizelle, he was made an instructor on Harvards. He tried to argue that at the tender age of nineteen he was too young to instruct, that his students would find him lacking in credibility. It didn't work, and he received the following advice: "Keep asking to go overseas on fighters, but do a good job as an instructor." A senior staff officer spoke with Jack's father about pulling some strings to keep Jack in Canada and away from the war. Squadron Leader George Phillips took great exception to this kind of preferential treatment. He declared to his well-meaning colleague: "In the Phillips clan, one is either by his shield or on it! If my son wants to serve in combat, don't you dare stand in his way."

After fourteen months at No. 14 SFTS in Aylmer, Ontario, Jack Phillips finally got his wish. He completed OTU training on the Mosquito at Greenwood,

Mosquito in France in August 1944.

Nova Scotia, in November 1943, and it was there that he met Bernard Job, his British-born navigator, who would fly with him in combat in 1944–45.

Jack and Bernard arrived at 418 Squadron in April '44 and started their operational career doing night-intruder work. The unit was experimenting with intruding in daylight, and it was these very successful Day Ranger operations that soon made 418 a famous fighter squadron. It was also in this period that the unit became known for its success in destroying the pilotless buzz bombs falling on London and other urban centres. Some of the most successful fighter aces of the RCAF served with 418, most notably John Caine, Donald MacFadyen and Russell Bannock. Jack Phillips remembers all three men vividly, but his first encounter with the perfectionist MacFadyen was unfriendly:

He was a strange fellow, came from a wealthy family living in Rosedale in Toronto. His mind was meticulous, very sharp. He embarrassed me when I first joined the squadron, when I made some offhand comment about the speed of an aircraft. He put me right and said I was mistaken; it was 385, not what I had said. That was the way he was … but I did not know him well; he was just one of the people I looked up to in the squadron. After the war, when I was demobbed, I was attending university in Toronto, and one day I am walking along and he drove by and stopped his car, saying, "Jump in." He took me to his home in Rosedale, they served me tea in a very proper manner, and he couldn't have been nicer. And yet, I didn't think he even knew I existed.

Jack took a great liking to Johnny Caine, of Edmonton, who by the end of the war had destroyed twenty enemy aircraft—five in the air and fifteen on the ground—seventeen of which were jointly shared with his navigator Earl Boal, from Weyburn, Saskatchewan. This made Caine one of the most successful fighter pilots in the RCAF and top gun at 418; on just one Day Ranger intruder op, on May 2, '44, he destroyed six seaplanes and landplanes on the water and on a German airfield, and he also damaged two others.

Phillips remembers Caine's modest demeanour and how it concealed a ruthless and professional approach to war:

> Johnny was a very quiet, unassuming fellow at 418; he had brown eyes and was a terrific shot. He was the last guy in the world to step into the limelight. Not long after I joined, he destroyed a number of aircraft on a single op. The German crew scrambled out of the BV137 or Do18, not sure of the type, and Johnny came by and killed them all … The big discussion in the mess was should one or should one not have killed them. Johnny, during a pause in the conversation, said, "I'd do the same thing again." …
>
> I bought Johnny Caine's motorcycle, a Triumph Speed Twin, from him when he left the squadron in May. My ground crew looked after it when I was on ops, and when I returned it was always full of fuel; I never asked where they got the fuel, but they took good care of it.

For twenty-eight of Jack Phillips's forty-four ops trips he flew one Mosquito, serial number NS991, with a L'il Abner cartoon on the side since the cartoon characters of its creator, Al Capp, were used on all 418 aircraft; 409 used Walt Disney characters. Phillips summarized his tour of operations in the following way:

> The letters were TH for the squadron. My machine was TH-T, hence T-Tommie. My call sign was, if memory serves, "Credo 21." Mammy Yokum from L'il Abner was painted on the portside of the nose.

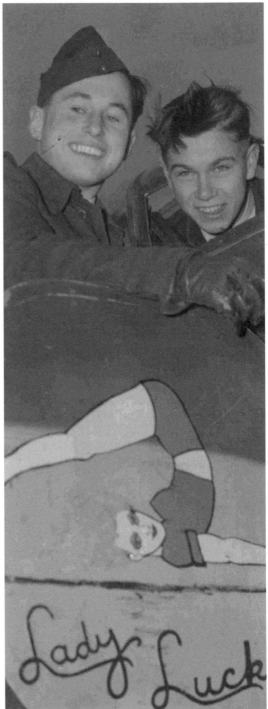

Bernard Job, left, and Jack Phillips, right, with their Mosquito .

Courtesy of the Jack and Sunny Phillips Collection

Olga Papas and Jack Phillips at their wedding after the war.

I shot down one buzz bomb, but I never saw a German aircraft in the air in my tour, except one night on the other side of Munich I saw the lights of one … Stan Cotterill came to us from instructing, and on his very first trip he shot down four aircraft. The aerodrome he had been sent to patrol I had patrolled several times and seen nothing. The Germans were up to something the night he visited, and he got four of them … Nevertheless, I thought, *holy smoke, this guy is good* [he was killed in October 1944] …

I strafed and bombed. If you saw a light on their side, the German side, you would shoot at it. It could be just a farmer carrying a lantern to the outhouse … that was the way it was. So you could see why the German people felt the way they did about us. If you got caught by civilians who were not too happy about being strafed every night, it might not turn out well … I sometimes carried a neat Smith & Wesson .38-calibre revolver that I could put in my flying boot, but I stopped carrying a weapon as it was considered riskier having one than not …

I was badly wounded in the hip over Denmark on my twenty-fifth trip, a Day Ranger, where I was No. 2 to Ross Gray, my flight commander. We were supposed to make landfall to the south of Esbjerg. The lead navigator was navigating, and my navigator knew that we were off track to port … with radio silence we couldn't say anything. We were north of Esbjerg. There is a lighthouse about 10 miles north of there that is the only significant landmark. When Ross Grey spotted the lighthouse he immediately turned south. However, the coastline changes with tides there, and there was no solid checkpoint for the navigator to know when to turn inbound towards Copenhagen. We were flying very low, and we got no fire from the ships we passed … My leader turned inland, and we immediately got accurate anti aircraft fire. With the Mosquito they almost always fired behind, not knowing how fast we were cruising (about 260). They were more likely to hit number two than the lead … Ross radioed to me, "Do you know where you are?" I replied after talking to my navigator: "We are not certain."

We had been told that we would have cloud cover at the Dutch coast, and that was accurate. Grey started turning, and I began to lose sight of him, and I pulled up in the clouds, but it was not solid, more broken. I had lost speed by pulling up, and as I turned towards the sea, I saw this aerodrome, and told Bern [Bernard Job]. At that point they hit us with flak—bang, bang, bang, three hits … then, bang, they hit us in the aileron. I said to Bern, "We have been hit, bail out." As he was getting out down below I grabbed him, and said, "Hold on." I gained speed and headed out over the sea …

I had a hole up through the port wing, the starboard aileron had been damaged, one round had come up through and hit me, and the other had come up through the cannons and hit Bern. He asked, "Have you been hit?" "Yes," I said. "So have I," he said.

The engine control knobs had been damaged, but I was able to adjust the engines to smooth them out. That alone improved our morale. I looked at the instruments, which were badly smashed. My main concern was would they scramble fighters after us? ...

Bern gave me a course to steer ... It was a long ride home and I had to keep pressure on the stick to the right to compensate for the damaged aileron, which got very tiring. I approached the coast near Coltishall, and offered Bern a chance to bail out, but he declined ... We fired off a red flare, did a normal approach, and just as I was rounding out, the control column jammed. I taxied in, shut down ... They lifted me out in a sitting position and took me to hospital ... got my uniform off ... the doctor picked up these two chunks of metal caught in the cloth, and handed them to me for a souvenir. The fragments had gone completely through my leg.

I was in hospital at Ely from the 11th of August to the 3rd of November and was operated on twice. No. 418, in the meantime, had moved from Middle Wallop to Hunsdon. When I rejoined them I was given light ground duties while I was convalescing. One day they sent me up to Coltishall to pick up a repaired Mosquito. I did not know, and it was quite by accident that I was assigned to pick up T-Tommie, NS991, which had taken all this time in the repair depot.

The man handing me the maintenance documents saw that my name was Phillips, and asked if I was the pilot of this particular machine that had landed there the previous August. I said I was. He said, "I never thought we would see you alive. There was blood outside of the aircraft all the way back to the tail. "Here," he said, "let me give you the inspection report about the many items that needed repairing." His name was Baker and he was really quite excited to meet me again. As head of the repair party he had seen the machine when I parked it months earlier. He couldn't quite believe that I was the same pilot that had flown it in there after the ops to Denmark.

For his operational contributions to 418, including the safe return of NS991, Phillips received the DFC, his citation noting that:

This officer has completed a number of varied missions, during which he has proved himself an enthusiastic, skilful and determined pilot.

JOHN TODD CAINE
EDMONTON, ALBERTA
CITATION FOR A SECOND BAR TO HIS DFC

Flight Lieutenant Caine has completed many operational sorties since the award of a Bar to the Distinguished Flying Cross. In May 1944, whilst on a patrol in the Barth area, he inflicted much damage on the enemy's lines of communication and destroyed several enemy seaplanes at anchor. In April 1945, while over southeast Germany he destroyed one enemy aircraft and damaged a further two. Despite the fact that on this sortie Flight Lieutenant Caine's aircraft was hit by anti-aircraft fire which damaged the flying controls, a successful return to base was made. His indomitable fearlessness and skill have merited the highest praise. Since his previous award he has destroyed a further eleven enemy aircraft, bringing his total victories to at least twenty enemy aircraft destroyed.

His fine airmanship and high courage in the face of danger have won the admiration of all members of his squadron.

Jack heard he had received a gong while standing at the urinal in the washroom of the officers' mess. Someone passing by hollered, "Hey, Jack, you got the DFC." Wing Commander Anthony Barker, RAF, the commanding officer at the time, arranged that Jack and some other aircrew who were decorated go to an investiture, rather than receive the medal in the mail. Jack was instructed at Buckingham Palace not to squeeze King George's hand very hard.

After leaving the RCAF in 1945 to go back to university, Phillips was not entirely sure what his future held. His father was so proud of him that he insisted they smoke cigars on his first morning home, just to celebrate the occasion. George Phillips also insisted on bringing him around to his place of work, introducing him to the OPAS flying crews. He even asked his son to lower his pants and show the war wounds on his hip that had been inflicted by German gunners over Denmark. Jack obliged his fifty-two-year-old father—who had his own wounds from the Great War—to the amazement of the OPAS crews, some of whom were happy to remind Jack of this episode decades later.

About a year out of the RCAF, Jack was contacted by the service, which invited him to rejoin with his wartime rank of flight lieutenant. He accepted and went on to have a successful and varied career, flying with the first jet aerobatic team of the post-war RCAF, the Central Flying School de Havilland Vampire team, at the 1948 Canadian National Exhibition, and attending Course No. 8 in England of the Empire Test Pilots' School along with Bruce "Duke I" Warren in 1949. He later attended and taught at RCAF Staff College and one of his last military jobs was as air attaché in Moscow. Retired now, he can sit on his balcony overlooking Semiahmoo Bay, BC, and admire the Gulf Islands. Jack likes to sail and most years he charters a boat for a month in the Caribbean.

* * *

Two of the most famous and successful of all the RCAF pilots on the Beaufighter and Mosquito in northwest

Europe are Wing Commander Russell Bannock, DSO, DFC and Bar, of Edmonton, and Flight Lieutenant Sydney Shulemson DSO, DFC, of Montreal. Had the war not intervened, it is interesting to speculate on the lives these two men might have led. They showed such exceptional talent in everything they did over a relatively short period that they are almost without parallel in the history of the RCAF. In addition, however, both have made exceptional contributions since the war, Bannock in the world of flight testing and aircraft sales, and Shulemson in the foundation of the state of Israel and the birth of the Israeli Air Force.

The depth and scope of their talent and leadership could not have been foreshadowed by their childhoods. They were good students with a talent for mathematics and were hard-working sons of immigrants. Any upward mobility in the society of the 1930s would have been determined by their work ethic and their intelligence, not their position in Canada's social register. Without the war, however, they might never have had an opportunity to demonstrate how capable they were. There are both parallels and contrasts in their childhood that present a particular irony in the context of the Second World War.

Profile – RUSSELL WILLIAM BANNOCK
Born – November 1, 1919, Edmonton
Father – William Bahnuk, supervisor of railway yards, Grand Trunk Pacific, CNR
Mother – Julia Jarmen
Decorations & Medals – DSO, DFC and Bar
Degrees & Awards – Canadian Aviation Hall of Fame
Post-war occupation – Aerospace executive, test pilot, president and CEO of de Havilland Aircraft of Canada, on company's board for twenty-two years; business entrepreneur after leaving de Havilland
Marital status – Wife Nora Quinn; sons Paul, Michael and John; daughter Anne Josephine
Hobbies – Flying, aircraft owner (finally sold his de Havilland Beaver in 2004)

Wing Commander Bannock was christened Russell William Bahnuk in 1919 and grew up with that name, until his father anglicized it to Bannock in 1938. Russell's father, William Bahnuk, and mother, Julia Jarmen, were both born in Austria, and were immigrants to Canada in 1905 and 1911 respectively.

Members of the Bahnuk family in Austria on his mother's side were inducted into the Austrian army in the Second World War and were subsequently killed. William Bahnuk was a supervisor of construction for the Grand Trunk Pacific Railway (which went from Winnipeg to Prince Rupert), and later the CNR.

Russell and his older brother Albert trapped muskrats in the Depression, making $100 each spring selling the skins at $2 apiece. Russ had his first long arm, a single-barrelled shotgun, at age twelve, and was an excellent duck hunter. Growing up in Edmonton in the 1930s was to be imbued with the romance of bush flying. The city was the southern terminus for all flying into the north right up to the Arctic Sea; it was the crossroads for every famous Canadian and American pilot—men like Clennell Haggerston "Punch" Dickins, Charles Lindbergh and Wiley Post. Bannock routinely bicycled to the Cooking Lake seaplane base and to the municipal airport in the city, made model aircraft and just knew that someday he too would become a pilot.

After he graduated from Eastwood High School in 1937, Russell worked that summer as night bar steward aboard SS *Distributor*, a Hudson's Bay Company ship that serviced all the posts up to Aklavik on the Arctic Sea. The following year he made $125 a month swinging an eight-pound sledgehammer in the gold mines of Consolidated Mining and Smelting not far from Yellowknife, at Gordon Lake. Most of the gold miners were experienced Finnish hard-rock miners who taught Russ how to swear in their native tongue.

The whole purpose of this back-breaking work was to pay for flying lessons, and in the winter of 1938 Bannock flew the Gypsy Moth on skis at the Edmonton Flying Club. He qualified for his private pilot's licence under the tutelage of flying legend Maurice "Moss" Burbidge.

In 1939 Bannock was back at another mine at Moberly Lake, northern British Columbia, working eight-hour shifts, blasting with dynamite and then breaking the quartz with sledgehammers. By the summer Russ had his commercial licence and was hired as an apprentice mechanic with Yukon Southern Air Transport in Edmonton. This allowed him to get co-pilot time with another aviation legend: Grant McConachie, founder of Canadian Pacific Airways.

Every commercial pilot in Canada received a telegram from the Department of National Defence in the fall of 1939 inviting them to become provisional pilot officers in the RCAF. Russ's mother, Julia, when seeing him off to pilot training in the RCAF, *actually* uttered the immortal lines, "Now don't you fly too high or too fast." Wearing civilian clothes, Russ attended a two-month course at the Vancouver Flying Club on instrument flying and then took the train to Trenton, Ontario, for a one-month officers' course. Joining so early in the war, before the BCATP was formalized, his officer's number was C1086. The rest of his flying training was on Harvards, Battles and twin-engine Ansons at Camp Borden, where he graduated with Wartime Course No. 1 on February 28, 1940.

For a brief period it seemed that Bannock might go overseas to help defend France with the Lysanders of No. 112 "City of Winnipeg" Squadron, stationed at that time in Rockcliffe, Ontario. But with the fall of France, he was sent to instructors' school at Trenton and from 1940 through 1943 served in the BCATP, latterly as chief instructor at No. 3 Central Flying School (CFS), Arnprior, with the rank of squadron leader.

After four years in the BCATP training system, Bannock became desperate to get overseas and fearful that he might never experience combat. He had a classmate at Uplands, John Sully, the son of Air Vice-Marshal Sully, Air Member for Personnel. John said, "Russ, go see my dad." AVM Sully invited Russ into his Ottawa office and listened as Bannock explained that he had three thousand hours' instructing and testing and deserved to go overseas. "What do you want to fly?" asked Sully, sitting behind his desk. "Mosquitoes," answered Bannock. Sully pushed an intercom button on his desk, spoke with some squadron leader at the other end and barked an order: "Send Bannock to Greenwood."

When the group captain at No. 3 Training Command in Montreal learned that Bannock had gone over his head, he threatened to court-martial him, but the charges were never laid. At Greenwood, Bannock completed Mosquito training and met his Scottish-born navigator, Robert Roy Bruce, an accomplished pianist and composer in peacetime, who flew with him for his first tour of operations. By June 1944 when Bannock and Bruce

Bannock (right) in Britain with Barker and Gray, 1944.

arrived at 418 Squadron, it had a well-established reputation, and a large majority of the squadron was made up of ex-instructors like Bannock, each typically having fifteen hundred to two thousand hours' minimum experience.

It was intensely energizing when a fighter pilot scored a victory early in his operational career. The examples of James Edwards in the Western Desert and Rod Smith in Malta have previously been noted. Bannock and Bruce destroyed their first enemy aircraft less than a week after arriving on 418. They were doing a night intruder to a Luftwaffe aerodrome at Avord, near Bourges, one hundred miles south of Paris, on the evening of June 14/15. They were able to destroy an Me110 on the runway, and in Bannock's memory it stands out as one of his most memorable and frightening operations, a close-run thing that almost killed him and Robert Bruce:

I spotted a tail light on final approach, and started to follow it, but the Germans, knowing my Mosquito was in the vicinity, turned on a searchlight, and anti-aircraft batteries opened fire. This forced me to break off the pursuit to one side of the airfield … but as he touched down he turned on his landing lights, and as he was rolling down the runway, I turned towards him and fired. In the light from the explosion I could see it was a Messerschmitt 110 and Robert said, "Good shot." Immediately the other side of the airfield lit up like the 4th of July, it was a solid wall of ack-ack … I did a sharp, tight, tight turn, and my instructing experience is what saved me. I pulled so tight, probably at over three hundred mph, it flicked, I did a high-speed stall, it literally flicked and at that point they coned me in searchlights. I could see, below me, the trees. As I would in train-ing, instinctively I let go of the stick, and the Mosquito sort of shook and righted itself, and I stayed just inside the wall of ack-ack … I think I shook all the way home.

It was during this same month that Bannock and Bruce witnessed one of the very first pilotless V1s en route to England. He assumed at first that it was a burning aircraft travelling at high speed, as the pulse jet engine of the V1 trailed a fiery exhaust plume. Russ called up Sector Ops and explained that a burning aircraft was heading inland. The controller came back and said: "What you have just seen is one of Hitler's new secret weapons."

The Mosquito squadrons on intruder ops were immediately assigned to "Anti-Diver" patrols to shoot down the V1s. The Mosquito, though a very fast air-craft, could not cruise at the 390- to 400-mph speed of the V1. Don MacFadyen and Russ Bannock put their heads together and calculated a profile that could catch the V1. Their first attempts were to dive from ten thousand feet on the V1, reaching a limiting speed of 440 mph, and overtaking the vehicle from behind. This provided a brief, thirty-second shooting oppor-tunity, but at rather low altitude and with the danger of over-speeding the propellers of the Mosquito.

MacFadyen and his navigator, James Wright, had the first success on the night of June 16/17 and Bannock and Bruce on June 19/20. They learned af-ter a couple of line-astern attacks that a thirty-degree off-deflection shot provided a better chance of suc-cess. They decided the best way to intercept the buzz bombs at night was to watch the French coast for the fiery plume of the V1 launch. Sitting up at ten thou-sand feet, they followed the V1 across the Channel and started a dive as they were halfway across.

On Bannock's first line-astern attack, his aircraft was damaged by debris caused by the intense explo-sion of hydrogen peroxide and kerosene fuel. The radiators on the Mosquito were vulnerable, and if damaged could result in a loss of coolant and engine fire. In addition to debris, the explosion destroyed a flyer's night vision. Bannock had a habit of cover-ing up one eye as he was firing, so that at least one eye retained its night adaptation after the explosion. Failure to protect your night vision was believed to

be the cause of some fatal accidents on Anti-Diver ops. To ratchet up the stress of these missions, the Germans sent over accomplished night-fighter pilots to attack the Mosquitoes while they were preoccu-pied, turning the hunters into the hunted.

The destruction of V1s by MacFadyen and Wright and Bannock and Bruce were the first times that jet-powered aircraft were destroyed in combat in air-to-air attacks; these were also the first V1s to be destroyed by pilots. In the space of less than two months, Bannock and Bruce destroyed nineteen V1s, including three on one op (July 3/4) and four on a second op (July 6/7), a record for the RCAF and also the RAF.

Bannock and Bruce continued to do night- and day-intruder ops on the continent. In mid-July they flew a long mission to an airfield at Altenberg, 100 miles south of Berlin, where they destroyed one Focke-Wulf 190 and damaged a second one, both in the air, before the flak became too intense. At the end of August they, with Sid Seid and Dave McIn-tosh as No. 2, attacked an airfield in daylight near Copenhagen and destroyed a Ju88 and an Me110 on the ground; Seid and McIntosh damaged a 110 and a 190. In September three more enemy aircraft were destroyed, including two German trainers at a German flying school that Bannock had decided to visit. What seemed like easy targets turned into something more sinister:

The name of the airfield was Parrow, on the Baltic straight north of Berlin, where the Germans had an OTU. I planned a solo Day Ranger (in hindsight it might have been safer to go with two Mosquitoes) where I took off at 0400 and arrived at first light … Sure enough, when I arrived there the circuit was full of airplanes, at least eight or ten. They used an Me108 as their equivalent to our Harvard. It was a four-seater, and I shot down one, then another. But rather foolishly I hung around trying to shoot down one of those Bucker Jungmeister biplanes. I saw the instructor take control of the aircraft and pull up to evade me, but then I tried to take a crack at another. Bob Bruce called out to me: "Russ, we have an Me109 shooting at us." I dropped my hundred-gallon external fuel tanks and accelerated, and fortunately for us he was flying an older model Messerschmitt. But he put two bullets in our left wing, and not long after, flying at just above the trees, Bob shouted, "Our left engine is on fire." Sure enough it was ... and I pressed the prop feathering button and the engine fire extinguisher.

So here we were over northern Germany on one engine; we were supposed to have cloud cover and it was blue skies. Bob said, "The only way we are getting home is if we head for Sweden." That was not palatable to me to spend the rest of the war in Sweden. We flew across the Baltic at low level to southern Denmark ... we bypassed a couple of Ju52 transports that apparently did not see us. I was, just momentarily, tempted to shoot them down. Anyway, cruising at 190 on one engine we made it home across the North Sea, and I kept reducing the mixture on the right engine. We had plenty of fuel and overflew Coltishall and landed at Hunsdon, a long seven hours and fifteen minutes in the air. Later, the engineering officer showed me the thumbnail-sized chunk of Perspex from one of the Me108s I had shot down that had penetrated the radiator, causing me to lose all my coolant—that was what caused the engine fire, not the bullets from the Me109.

In October, Bannock was promoted to wing commander and took over 418 Squadron. In November he was called in and asked to take command of 406 Squadron and convert the unit to intruder operations from night fighting. Bannock was viewed as an outsider to 406. Navigator Joe Green (after the war an accomplished politician and Liberal cabinet minister) shouted disparagingly to his friends at the bar that Bannock wore "a band inside his hat." Bannock, as a new commanding officer, wanted to set a good example, hence he wore a regulation hat. The crushed cap, dirty and oil-stained, without any reinforcing band, and the battledress with the top button always undone, were hallmarks of experienced fighter pilots. Only headquarters types and rookies dressed in accordance with regulations, hence the ridicule from Joe Green at the bar.

Russ Bannock at home in Toronto, 2002.

Courtesy of the Wayne Ralph Collection

Bannock quickly put his own stamp on 406. He was obliged to send three disobedient flyers home to Canada; this action, he says, made the other members of the squadron pay closer attention and he had no further complaints. Since the navigators at 406 were experts at radar interception and the navigators in intruder squadrons were experts at map reading and dead reckoning, Russ brought Bob Bruce with him to be squadron navigator at 406, now that Bob's tour at 418 was over.

Bannock flew at 406 with Clarence L. "Kirk" Kirkpatrick, who had been Blackie Williams's navigator. Between November and April, Bannock and Kirkpatrick destroyed another four enemy aircraft and damaged several others. At war's end Bannock had nine victories in the air, nineteen destroyed V1s and many other aircraft destroyed or damaged on the ground, making him the premier RCAF intruder ace of the war.

He felt happy to survive the war and confident that he was going to be successful either in the RCAF or the civilian world. While figuring out his options, he attended and graduated from RAF Staff College and was selected to become the first post-war RCAF air attaché in Moscow. Fatefully, he was also recommended to Geoffrey de Havilland as a good candidate to be hired by that famous company, in particular, as operations manager to Phillip Garratt, president of de Havilland Canada, himself a former Great War and 1920s bush pilot.

Geoffrey de Havilland checked out Russ on the first de Havilland Vampire jet fighter, and Russ spent his extensive back-leave learning the workings of the manufacturing company that had invented the Mosquito. Ironically, he was talked out of staying in the RCAF by the commander of the Overseas Headquarters of the RCAF in London, Air Marshal G.O. Johnson, CB, MC. Unbeknownst to Russ, George Johnson was himself personally unhappy with how the RCAF was treating him.

In hindsight, although perhaps given for the wrong reason, the air marshal's advice was sound, because Bannock went on to be the test pilot for some of de Havilland's most successful aircraft, including the Beaver and the Twin Otter, and later became president and CEO of de Havilland Canada. He was inducted into Canada's Aviation Hall of Fame in April 1984. With his son Michael Bannock as captain, Russ still gets to fly in the cockpit of his beloved Twin Otter. Russ sold his last Beaver in April 2004, at age eighty-four; he had owned the aircraft for twenty-two years.

Bannock keeps in touch with his navigator Bob Bruce, who lives in England. Bruce had a successful artistic life after the war, becoming a professor of music at Cardiff University. He had always promised his pilot, as he sat at the piano relaxing and unwinding after their sorties, that one day he would compose an original work based on their experiences at 418 Squadron. Twenty-five years after the war, the *Bannock-Bruce Symphony* was completed by Bruce and delivered to his pilot as promised. It has since been played by several symphony orchestras and recorded by Warsaw's symphony orchestra.

Profile – SYDNEY SIMON SHULEMSON
Born – October 22, 1915, Montreal
Father – Saul Shulemson
Mother – Rebecca Rosenberg
Decorations & Medals – DSO, DFC, CEM and Clasp
Degrees & Awards – Inducted into the Quebec Air and Space Hall of Fame and the Veterans Hall of Valour.
Post-war occupation – Salesman, business executive in the printing business, consultant in the mergers and acquisitions business. Shulemson assisted in recruiting military personnel and acquiring military equipment for the Israeli War of Independence.
Marital status – A bachelor till age 74, when he married Ella Lozoff; sons Rick and Jerry Lozoff
Hobbies – Golf

Sydney Simon Shulemson was born to Saul Shulemson and Rebecca Rosenberg in 1915, in a stone house on de Bullion Street not far from the corner of Rachel Street in Montreal. Sydney's paternal grandparents came from a town called Baku in southern Romania and arrived in Montreal in the late nineteenth century when Saul was seven years old. Grandfather Harry Shulemson had a store that sold kosher chickens. Sydney's maternal grandfather, Tobias Rosenberg, was from Russia via Romania, and later, when Syd was a teenager, lived with Syd's parents.

Syd attended Commercial High and Baron Byng High School, where he played basketball and dreamed of becoming an aeronautical engineer. He was an army cadet through the 1930s and cadet commander of the army unit at Commercial High. He was also a member of the Non Permanent Active Militia (NPAM) as an army signaller—though several years short of his eighteenth birthday—through the collusion of a friendly regimental sergeant major of artillery who needed a signaller. The closest he got to real aircraft before the war was the time his sister Roslyn took him to RCAF Station St Hubert for an air show, where he watched transfixed as the RCAF's Siskin team performed their aerobatic routine.

In the 1930s, McGill University had a quota system to restrict the number of Jewish students, but Syd managed to get in, having an average out of high school of over 85 per cent. He was sixteen years and ten months old when he started at the university. Syd recalls that a professor directed him towards aeronautical studies at the Jesuit school in Detroit:

> It had a degree course in aeronautical engineering, giving courses for three weeks at a time and then adjourned for three weeks during which time one could work in the many auto and engineering plants in the Detroit area (and get paid) and then resume classes for another three weeks, year round. But during 1932–33, Depression years, no paid work was available. So although I had been accepted, I declined to register.

Neither Syd nor his family had the money for tuition in the absence of paid work, and Syd gave up his dream of aeronautics to work in New York City in the advertising business. In 1939 he returned to Montreal to work at his Uncle Ted's printing company. On September 10, the day Canada declared war on Germany, he went down to the Westmount headquarters for the RCAF Auxiliary Squadron to join up:

> The line-up was all the way down the block at nine o'clock. By noon I was at the front door. In an otherwise empty hallway, an RCAF corporal of 401 Squadron was seated at a "trestle" table. He asked me my name, followed by "Can you cook?" "No," I said, "I want to be a pilot." "Outside, outside," he said, "we need cooks." It took me a while to get over that ...
>
> Then I heard about the Gatehouse Building in downtown (where CIL House is today). On the first floor up there was a nice set-up, an officer of the RCAF, girls typing. I said I wanted to join the air force as a pilot ... he starts flipping through a book. "What are you doing?" I ask. "I can give you an appointment in three months," he says. I walk out.
>
> Later, I heard of another recruiting office in the Post Office Building on Bishop Street ... I meet the recruiting officer who is, in fact, someone I used to do business with before the war. So I say to him, "I want to join today, but I will come in three months, as I have business to wrap up." He agrees, arranges for

my medical immediately and even gives me a day's pay, $1.70.

> I report on Labour Day 1941 to the Manning Depot at the CNE Grounds in Toronto. I joined on my own, but, you know, we had some eight thousand Jewish people from Montreal and seven thousand from Toronto who joined up in all branches of the service. I knew that Hitler and the Nazis were extremely anti-Semitic, and I was very motivated to fight for that reason.

Shulemson graduated on July 3, 1942, at Aylmer, Ontario, and was immediately commissioned. He was sent to Charlottetown for his advanced pilot navigation training, slated for Coastal Command. In July 1943, having checked out on the Merlin-powered Mk II Beaufighter, he joined 404 Squadron RCAF, stationed at Wick in Scotland ("Some guys in the bar commiserated with me. 'Gone to Wick!' they said, like it was a life sentence," Shulemson laughs). The primary job of the squadron was to attack shipping along the Norwegian and Dutch coast.

The rest of Shulemson's OTU class ferried Beaufighters out to India. He missed going with them because he was in hospital to have a cyst removed from his spine. When he was discharged, all his course mates were gone—he alone was sent up to 404, his combat career determined by a routine surgical procedure.

Shulemson and his navigator, Al Glasgow, had a dramatic success on an early do, one that established Syd as an aggressive and talented Coastal Command anti-shipping expert. Ironically, though Syd does not today consider himself a fighter pilot, on his first proper operation he destroyed one Blohm und Voss BV138 flying boat and assisted in the destruction of a second over the Norwegian Sea:

> They had lost six new crews quickly one after another, and they were loath to send me out on operations ... I believe we had the highest losses of any RCAF squadron.[1]
>
> They sent me out on practice reconnaissance flights, and just local flying ... Some time later there was a big raid going on in the south, a commando raid, and a diversionary

[1] According to Kostenuk and Griffin in *RCAF Squadrons and Aircraft*, of the twin-engine RCAF fighter and fighter bomber squadrons, 418 had the highest total casualties for the entire war, with 404 second. Each unit flew between 3,100 and 3,500 sorties. However, virtually all of 404 Squadron's operational casualties were fatal, only two being taken prisoner of war. According to the Hugh Halliday files, more than 50 of 418's 176 casualties occurred on the Douglas Boston in 1942–43, before the arrival of the Beaufighter.

153

force was launched some two hundred miles north of the Shetlands … It was a naval task force moving towards Norway, an aircraft carrier force, and a cruiser force led by HMS *Belfast*. They sent me up to the Shetlands with Al De la Haye, who was my leader, with me as his No. 2.

[We had a rocky start to the trip] when he signalled me, so I mistakenly thought, to take off on the short runway. This runway was only six hundred yards long, and I bounced the aircraft on the road off the end of the runway, but just kept it up in the air. Al took off on the long runway, and I formatted on him and we headed north.

As soon as we got in sight of the *Belfast*, they radioed, "We have a bogey for you." Al transmitted to me that he could not hear the *Belfast* controller, only me. So in effect I took over the leadership, me on my first trip! I immediately turned onto the vector they gave me, applied full throttle. De la Haye was nowhere to be seen at this point. I found the bogey, chased it up to six thousand feet alone and lost it in cloud. When I turned onto the reciprocal to return to escort *Belfast*, I received another message about another bogey and when I approached, in a dive at full throttle, I saw De la Haye turning away because he was being fired at by the rear gunner with a 20mm cannon. I then descended down to sea level and came up underneath the BV138, and shot it down. But I got hit, a panel of my aircraft was blown out and there was a lot of noise … I asked my navigator what happened and Al said, "I can take a drift sight now just looking down between my legs!" [Drift sights were used by navigators to determine wind velocity and direction.]

Belfast gave us another contact, and De la Haye and I intercepted this BV138 and we shot it down. A Beaufighter at full throttle burns 135 gallons of fuel per hour per engine, and we were a long way from home. Well, we got back to Sumburgh, in the Shetlands, from which we had departed, but I ran out of fuel as I turned off the runway … The admiral at the time up at Scapa Flow, was it Admiral Sir Bruce Fraser?

I am not sure. Anyway, the admiral sent a message to us saying "Good show."

Although this dramatic trip on July 28, '43, had been flown with Sergeant A.D. "Al" Glasgow, most of Shulemson's ops were flown with an RAF navigator named Peter Bassett, a former bank clerk.

Shulemson was a little older than the average age of flyers in the war. He had the courage of his convictions and seldom prevaricated. On an early operation that was led by a wing commander of an RAF squadron, the patrol was not completed as ordered. They flew to the coast of Norway, turned around and came back. Shulemson had an overheating cockpit heater that was burning his flying boot and so he flew on ahead, landing before the rest of the formation. As a result, the station commander presumed that the formation had been on a strike. When Syd was asked what had transpired, he told the truth and "there was hell to pay over it … I wasn't going to lie and say we had done the patrol."

On another occasion, having established a reputation for accomplishing tough ops, he was asked by the senior commanding officer of 18 Group, Air Vice-Marshal Ellwood, to lead a strike against a ship that was docked outside a Norwegian harbour. Shulemson exclaimed to the AVM:

"I was there a few days ago and that is an anti-aircraft ship, a Sperrbrecher … There is no point; I will fly up to take photos, but I won't take a squadron to attack that ship—that is suicide." To have done so would have killed a lot of people, and there was no strategic advantage to sinking it; in fact, you couldn't sink as it was full of foam. Well, he was very upset with me and asked "Are you refusing to fly?" "No," I said, "but I won't lead the squadron to sink that ship.

I met Syd Shulemson a few days after he had returned to his Cote St Luc, Quebec, apartment after his usual five-month winter sojourn in Florida. Looking tanned and fit, and nowhere near his age of eighty-eight, Syd has an excellent memory for the operational and technical details of the Beaufighter and Mosquito. He recalled some of his survival lessons of combat along the Norwegian coast and in the Bay of Biscay, one of which is to always fly very low:

Courtesy of the Sydney Shulemson Collection

Sydney Shulemson in the Second World War.

Courtesy of the Wayne Ralph Collection

Sydney Shulemson at home in Montreal, 2004.

We knew that our aircraft could not be picked up by German radar units on the coast if we stayed in the spray off the ocean ... at thirty-five feet above the ocean, the spray concealed us and they could not pick us up. Beaufighters always came home from operations with their windscreens coated with salt. I also developed a personal technique for dealing with anti-aircraft batteries. I knew that the time of flight of shells was quite long, maybe twenty seconds or more. I flew dead level, but as soon as I saw the muzzle flash, I changed altitude. It worked for me very well, though once I relaxed too soon ... I saw a gun flash, and I ducked, and they had a four-gun battery ... so I flew straight and level, then climbed. The explosion was below. Then he stopped shooting, I did not evade, and he put one final shot through my empty fuel tank (for some reason the tank did not explode) ... but I was stupid for relaxing.

After eliminating two BV138s, Shulemson later damaged a Ju88 and killed the rear gunner just as the aircraft entered cloud. A more frightening episode of dogfighting took place when his squadron was "bounced" by a formation of Me109s off the coast of Norway. Shulemson wanted to protect a less-experienced wingman:

[I] fired a burst to attract [the Me109 pilot's] attention, and he turned to attack me. We had a ten-minute dogfight at very low altitude over the water, where I was used to flying and he was not. But he put a whole lot of bullet holes in our machine; on the back of the armour plate behind the navigator's seat were many dents. There was very heavy icing in the clouds so I could not hide there ... when I came out of the clouds he was still there. An Me109 can out-turn a Beaufighter, so I started a steep turn at low altitude and did a series of flick rolls in

155

the opposite direction at wave-top height, and that is how I got away from him.

A gifted leader, Shulemson seems philosophical about not getting promoted above the rank of flight lieutenant, and particularly proud of how he looked after people:

I ran into very little anti-Semitism in the RCAF. The guys on my squadron would follow me into hell and back, they had a lot of faith in what I would do. I wouldn't do anything stupid or risky beyond reasonable limits. I was leading a wing or a squadron as a junior officer, but my boys expected me to stand up to the AVM or anyone else who demanded too much ...

I lost some people, and it weighs on me to this day; it is a monkey I carry on my back to this day, but I lost as few as I could. Perhaps I am a hero because I survived. But they are heroes, too, those who did not survive ...

We had a job to do, we had a task and it was important. We were sinking ships that were carrying supplies into Germany, so we were disrupting their war effort. These ships were always escorted in a convoy by many German warships, and destroying them was also an important function of ours ... I can state with some confidence that I personally sank or damaged thirteen ships.

Despite his unusual candour with senior officers, Shulemson was so self-assured and had such battle calm that he was recommended for his first decoration after a few months. He received a Distinguished Service Order, gazetted in the *London Gazette* in February 1944. Flight Lieutenant Shulemson was particularly unusual in getting a DSO ahead of his DFC, and getting both awards because he excelled at leading formations that customarily were led by squadron leaders and wing commanders. The citations for his DSO and DFC remark on this:

On numerous occasions he has led the squadron and the wing in a most competent and capable manner, once inflicting heavy damage on three enemy destroyers and on another sortie sinking

two heavily defended enemy vessels in the Bay of Biscay. *[Excerpt from his citation for the DSO.]*

On numerous occasions he had led not only this squadron, but the whole wing in a most competent and capable manner. On D-Day he led the squadron against three enemy destroyers in the Bay of Biscay inflicting heavy damage on them, and on August 13 he was deputy leader of this unit's aircraft which, together with aircraft from another unit, attacked and sank two heavily defended 8,000-ton enemy *Sperrbrechers* in the Bay of Biscay.

Flight Lieutenant Shulemson has always maintained the highest efficiency both on the ground and in the air, and his continued and untiring search for knowledge has made him one of the most well-informed and capable leaders on the most difficult Norwegian coast. His perseverance, devotion to duty and his courage and determination in pressing home his attacks in the face of very heavy flak from both ships and shore, are outstanding. *[Excerpt from his citation for the DFC.]*

Other scholars and writers have researched and written about the singular war record of 404 Squadron, most recently Stéphane Guevremont at the University of Calgary. He shows that 404 Squadron had the greatest success of any Coastal Command unit during the war at using unguided rockets fired from rails mounted under the wings.[2] The rockets themselves were three inches (7.5 centimetres) in diameter, approximately eight feet (2.439 metres) in length, and fitted with a twenty-five-pound armour-piercing head. The operational success using the rocket-equipped Beaufighter and later the Mosquito at 404 was so dramatic that RAF Coastal Command reversed its decision to eliminate the rocket from its arsenal. It ordered all the Mosquito squadrons in the RAF to be fitted with rocket rails and to train using the methods developed by the pilots of 404 Squadron, RCAF.

The main driving force and inspiration for the success at 404 was Squadron Leader Ken Gatward, RAF, and Flight Lieutenant Syd Shulemson, RCAF. By trial and error they developed the appropriate tactics to destroy vessels in a way that had previously been done,

[2] *Deadly Duo—No. 404 Squadron (Buffalo), RCAF and the Rocket Projectile, 1943–45 (paper).*

but at great personal cost, by torpedoes. Shulemson showed flair and accuracy with the rockets, and he and Gatward worked on refining their methods of attack. Many of the rocket-strike missions by 404 in 1944 were alternately led by Gatward or Shulemson.

Shulemson trained all the pilots to fire at exactly four hundred yards' range from the target, in a 12.5-degree dive at an airspeed of 265 knots, at which point the aircraft would be well below one hundred feet above the water. The two-hundred-foot-high steep cliffs near the aerodrome allowed the pilots to practise repeatedly diving down over the cliff at 12.5 degrees at a white target floating in the water. Why such precision? Syd explains:

We used a regular gunsight adapted for our use to give us exact range from the target. The gunsight had adjustable light bars to tell us exactly when we had four hundred yards' range. We developed a way of attacking a ship or convoy that proved very successful, whereby we fired at one thousand yards with our cannons. They were harmonized to give a range of fire, raking the deck. After releasing the rockets at well below one hundred feet, we had to climb pretty quickly to miss the wires and masts of the ship ...

The rockets were designed to hit the ship below the waterline. To hit the ship that way, you have to hit the water before the ship. When the rockets hit the water they tended to flatten out and strike the ship at ten to twelve feet below the waterline. If you fired at four hundred yards' range, the rocket motor would still be burning and it would cause havoc inside the ship, ricocheting around inside the ship, causing explosions, even though it was not an explosive head but simply a twenty-five-pound, solid, bullet-shaped head.

Shulemson flew the harmonization trials on the Mosquito. In the nose of his Mosquito, he had a specially fitted camera with an intervalometer. He had two people to help with the mathematics and the camera interpretation: a Newfoundlander who had been a professor of mathematics before the war, and a WAAF who was a trained photo interpreter. He deduced after undershooting his target consistently that the plywood wings of the Mosquito were warping when the plane was flying at high speed, which meant the rocket rails also were flexing (the Beaufighter did not have a flexing problem since it had metal wings).

In discussions with the squadron's armament officer, Shulemson learned that there is a master gun on a Mosquito, fixed in pitch but movable in yaw. So he asked the armament officer to realign the rocket rails relative to the master gun out-doors at their aircraft dispersals. With this realignment there was no more undershooting and no necessity to bring each aircraft into a hangar, lift the tail, make sure it was perfectly level and set the rocket rails at the proper angle. Shulemson also learned that three vics [a three-plane formation in the shape of a "V"] of three Mosquitoes per vic, a total of nine aircraft, were necessary to guarantee the sinking of vessels, and that is how operations were flown.

Coastal Command's Banff Wing in Scotland was founded in September 1944 and was headed by Lord Beaverbrook's son, Group Captain the Honourable J.W. Max Aitken, a successful Battle of Britain and night-fighter ace. In the last months of the war the Banff Wing became famous as an elite unit specializing in rockets. Aitken's rocket projectile officer for the Banff Wing was Syd Shulemson. His duties included setting the rocket rails properly on the aircraft, adjusting the gunsights for ship busting, training the aircrews in marksmanship on rocket projectiles, training as well for tactics, and finally briefing the crews for each operational trip.

Max Aitken thought very highly of Syd and gave him full support. However, Syd's training ability and knowledge were so important to the Banff Wing that Aitken refused to allow Shulemson to fly on ops after his forty-ninth trip. Much of the lustre of the Banff Wing's achievements as noted in history books can be explained by Shulemson's effort, an effort unrecognized and unheralded in the official accounts.

Flight Lieutenant Shulemson was selected by Air Vice-Marshal Ellwood to brief the head of Coastal Command, Air Chief Marshal Sholto Douglas, and his Coastal Command headquarters staff just outside London, just before D-Day. On another occasion, while attending the Fighter Leader School on Typhoons, Shulemson was asked to demonstrate rocket projectile firing on a target on the beach near the school.

The demonstration was for a group of American generals in a bunker. When asked afterwards by an

Aerial photo of the attack in the Bay of Biscay by Shulemson and his squadron.

Courtesy of the Airforce Magazine Collection

American general, who was impressed with his deadly accuracy using only two rockets, how many hours he had on the Typhoon, Syd confessed, "Less than two hours." In addition to completing the fighter leader course, Shulemson also graduated on Spitfires and Beaufighters from the RAF Central Gunnery School.

When the war ended Syd went back to his job working for Uncle Ted's company, Apex Press Limited. Just after being demobbed he was asked to serve as an air cadet officer with the Young Men's & Young Women's Hebrew Association (YMYWHA) No. 78 Air Cadet Squadron in Montreal. He later took command of this air cadet squadron and eventually retired after more than twenty-five years of service in the Non-Permanent Active Militia and RCAF.

In 1947–48 he recruited Second World War veterans and acquired military equipment for Israel's War of Independence. In a meeting with military reps from many places around the world in New York City, Shulemson recalled:

> I gave them my standard lecture on "victory through air power," saying that if Israel was to become a state, and they would certainly be invaded, then they needed an Israeli Air Force for defence and offence. I pointed out that with the Second World War just over [for] two years, there were all kinds of military aircraft sitting idle around the world and many military men whose skills were not that rusty and who would want to help.

Syd Shulemson's adventures also encompass the story of his contributions to the birth of the Israeli

Courtesy of the Airforce Magazine Collection

Rocket-firing Beaufighter of 404 Squadron RCAF.

Air Force; his reluctance to enlist George Beurling to fight for Israel; his deep regret after Beurling's death when he had to inform the fighter pilot's family that their child was dead; his surprise that George had been raised as a member of the Plymouth Brethren; and his decision to move the ace's body from what George's mother called the "unholy" city of Rome to Israel to rest in an honoured grave. Because of Syd Shulemson, Beurling rests in the military cemetery at Haifa, along with four other Christian veterans from Canada who died fighting for Israel.

After sitting in his apartment for several hours, Syd and I went out to dinner on Easter Sunday evening in Cote St Luc, to one of the landmark Montreal restaurants that serve roasted chicken. We sat in a booth at the back, and the young waitresses knew and fussed over him, an elderly man with a gentle manner. They asked me why I had a tape recorder. I said to interview this man about his time in the war. "What war? What did he do?" they asked. "He was a war hero in the Second World War," I replied. Their eyes widened a bit as they took in the man in the red turtleneck and blue pullover who had eaten regularly at the Cote St Luc BarBQ for years.

We were almost alone in the restaurant. The young women returned to discussing their shift schedule and what they were going to do on Easter Monday, as the restaurant was closed that day. Their voices seemed light and cheerful, far removed from the war stories I had been listening to. Perhaps because it was a religious holiday, I asked Syd about his beliefs:

I am not religious and I don't believe in an afterlife. You know, some of life is uplifting and some sad, but life goes on. I am an optimist because I am still alive. I should have been dead many years ago. I have lived another day ...

I have achieved the dream of being a successful military pilot. I did that! I was Jewish. Getting at the Germans—it does not make up for the six million—but I did my share. I killed my share of Germans. The RCAF got their money's worth from me. I trained many excellent crews, and I sank many ships. I did what was good and what was right and I did it well.

Squadron Leder Frederick Ernest "Freddie" Green, an American in the RCAF, in his Spitfire.

Two Americans in the RCAF

We live in an era now in which it has become fashionable to be anti-American, and especially anti-Republican. The majority of Canadians, it appears, do not favour foreign wars and especially wars started by the United States. It is not well known today in Canada that sixty-five years ago many Americans volunteered to fight in our foreign war, a war in which the United States started out as officially neutral. After the First World War, Canada erected a monument at Arlington National Cemetery to recognize the contributions of Americans in that war; the monument also acknowledges the American sacrifice on behalf of Canada in the Second World War and Korea. According to Spencer Dunmore in *Wings for Victory*, close to nine thousand Americans joined the Royal Canadian Air Force in the Second World War.

Many of the instructors of the British Commonwealth Air Training Plan (BCATP) were American-born. Without the assistance, in the early stages, of experienced flyers from the United States, and without the influx of well-educated young Americans, many with pilot licences, it is certain that our training system would have taken longer to reach full production. About 10 per cent of the RCAF's aces are American-born, including David Fairbanks, DFC and Two Bars, of Ithaca, New York, and Claude Weaver, DFC, DFM, of Oklahoma City, Oklahoma, each with about fourteen victories.

Almost every Canadian fighter pilot I interviewed trained with and/or served with Americans. By tradition, American students in the BCATP were nicknamed "Tex," no matter their place of birth. After the United States entered the war, considerable pressure was put on these Americans in the RCAF and RAF squadrons to return to the armed forces of their own country. Their air combat experience was recognized by the US Army

Air Force (USAAF) as invaluable. Some elected to keep serving with the British and Canadians, but the majority transferred. Two who stayed throughout the war with us are profiled below.

Profile – PHILIP GORDON (Bockman) VICKERS
Born – September 27, 1919, Michigan
Died – June 2003, Arizona
Post-war occupation – Sales pilot on Long Island with Commonwealth Aircraft; stage, radio, TV and movie actor in England; sculptor in Washington, DC, and Sedona, AZ

Of all the fighter pilots I have interviewed, American-born Philip Vickers had the most intriguing post-war career. He was one of only two fighter pilots I met who have made their living as artists, the other being Robert Hyndman of Old Chelsea, Quebec. Hyndman was a formally trained artist before the war and, after a tour of operations on Spitfires, was offered a position as an official war artist for Canada. For the past sixty years he has simply continued in his life's calling, and is still teaching art in Ottawa at age eighty-nine.

After the war, Phil Vickers flew for a couple of years for a manufacturing firm, Commonwealth Aircraft of Valley Stream, Long Island, which had corporate offices in New York City. But Phil lost his job when the company went under shortly after the death of its president. Phil lived in Greenwich Village, and his artist friends in the Village encouraged him to take acting classes at Columbia University. He had always hated his birth name, so he adopted the stage name of Vickers, in honour of the Vickers Supermarine Spitfire that he had flown in combat. The simple act of adopting a stage name was a huge boost, removing the burden of a difficult childhood from his shoulders.

Philip (Bockman) Vickers: fighter pilot, actor, sculptor, 2002. One of the thousands of Americans who came north to join the RCAF after 1939.

After some bit parts in off-Broadway productions and summer theatre, Phil Vickers received his Actor's Equity Card. He then decided to return to England, where he had served in 1944–45. Phil felt far more at home there than in New York or Oklahoma City. Due to his RCAF service on behalf of King George VI, as well as some legal pull facilitated by the actress Hermione Gingold, he was allowed to live in England on an indefinite work visa.

Philip Vickers made his living for more than nine years as a supporting actor in the British theatre, on BBC radio and television and in the movies. He worked with Bob Hope at The London Palladium and toured with Hope's company in England, was a member of the cast of *Damn Yankees* in the West End and also had supporting roles with Gregory Peck and Peter Sellers on the BBC. His movie credits in supporting roles included *No Highway* with Jimmy Stewart; *The Night My Number Came Up* with Sir Michael Redgrave; *The Whole Truth* with Stewart Granger and Donna Reed; *Joe MacBeth* with Paul Douglas and Ruth Roman; and *Mark of the Hawk* with Sidney Poitier and Eartha Kitt.

An actor he was dating during the making of *Mark of the Hawk* was being sculpted by a British sculptor. When Phil witnessed this artist at work, she invited him to try his hand, and he recognized that this was what he wanted to do with the rest of his life. He established a studio in Washington, DC, and later in Sedona, Arizona. His bust of Squadron Leader Wally McLeod, DSO, DFC and Bar, with whom he served, is on display at the RCAF Officers Mess on Gloucester Street in Ottawa.

Born Philip Gordon Bockman on September 27, 1919, in Michigan, Phil grew up in Oklahoma City. Uncharacteristic of most fighter pilots I have interviewed, he had no fond memories at all of childhood. Sitting in his artist's study overlooking the red mountains of Sedona, he described a Depression-era tale of conflict and struggle:

> My father did not do much [of anything]— my family life was a total absolute mess, all I ever dreamed about was getting the hell out of there and flying, into the skies, an escape from all that. My mother died when I was fourteen, and I left home. I saw my father once when I was sixteen, and we argued. I left and never saw him again. I hitchhiked to Ft Sill, Oklahoma, to try to join the Army Air Corps; I tried to get into the Merchant Marine in New Orleans; then I hitchhiked out to California. I thought I would try the Curtiss Wright [Technical] Institute [in California], but I had no money.
>
> I came home and enrolled at the University of Oklahoma in engineering school. After a couple of years I realized that I could not manage the math and science, so I switched to arts. The Civil Air Pilot (CAP) training program let me join in 1941, and I flew the Piper Cub. I got thirty-five hours and thought I was a pretty hot pilot. God, I thought, this is it, what I have always wanted. I met a guy who had come back from Canada, Cole Garrison. God, I wonder what the hell happened to him!

He had been up in Canada with the RCAF and got kicked out ... but he said he regretted screwing up and getting kicked out. So I hitchhiked to Windsor, Ontario. I had only a few dollars and the clothes on my back. I arrived in Windsor, went to the recruiting centre. [*Phil reached into a drawer in his desk, retrieving some newspaper clippings in a folder.*] The *Windsor Daily Star*, 10 September, 1941, wrote: "Americans off to avenge Hun attack..." but the picture is of Ivor Williams, who was not an American. He later became a newspaper editor in Regina.

Going to Canada really turned me around, it really did, and I think it turned around a lot of young guys, young Americans. It made a great difference in my life ...

I was posted to 126 Squadron at Dartmouth, Nova Scotia, and it was a big letdown for me because I wanted to go overseas. I got really frustrated and impatient and, after conversations with another American, a fellow named Mann from North Carolina, we decided to go AWOL and head for Peru. Well, I made it to Dallas and was going to cross over into Mexico.

I realized the Mexicans would arrest me, so I changed my mind and went back to face the music. I was one day overdue from leave, and when I complained that I was not in Europe, my squadron commander said, "Yes, well everybody wants to go overseas. You've got a job to do here and by God you will do it." Was he angry with me! He said, "You'll go overseas; you are going to 127 Squadron at Gander, Newfoundland." So that was where I went. I spent a lot of time there on Hurricanes (even had a crash in a snowstorm, but got rescued) and then we became 443 Squadron. Wally McLeod was our commanding officer, and we arrived in the UK in February 1944. We flew Spit Vs to start with at Digby. Then when we went down to Westhampnett in Sussex and got Spit IXs. I was commissioned not long after we got over there. I flew a bit longer than [the usual] tour of about 160 ops."

Phil looked on his squadron commander as a father figure. "Wally could have been anything he

wanted, he had unlimited possibilities," he said. "It was a great loss to your country of Canada when he died." Through the spring of 1944, Phil flew with Wally McLeod and with another pilot he admired, Donald Walz, who had grown up on a farm a few miles south of Moose Jaw. Walz had gone down in flames on D-Day plus ten but rejoined 443 after weeks of hiding in France. A popular and capable fighter pilot, Don flew with and scored a victory on the day Wally McLeod was killed.

It was on an op led by Walz that Vickers was hit for the first time by flak. His damaged Spitfire started to leak fuel: "I got back and landed in trees, tore the aircraft up, hurt my back and had lacerations, and spent that summer in a cast." After his return from convalescence to 443, following the death of Wally McLeod, Phil flew on occasion with Wing Commander Johnnie Johnson and came to appreciate his exceptional balance of aggression and prudence.

Johnnie Johnson wasn't going to play the macho type by flying into flak ... if he saw it coming up he would say, "Out of here." In my experience he realized what his chances were. He had to weigh things pretty carefully; he knew where he was good, where he had a chance and where he didn't. If he didn't have a great chance, he was out of there. Someone who has reached that stature or level of skill to be leading a squadron or wing understands that they are trying to achieve something that is bigger than themselves ... more important than themselves.

He liked flying with McLeod's replacement, Squadron Leader Art Sager, DFC ("a helluva nice guy, go see him"), and liked Sager's replacement, Tom de Courcy, DFC. He was devastated when de Courcy, having survived the war, was killed in an auto accident on a German road in June '45:

God, that was heartbreaking, Tommie was almost there. It was a great release for me to know that I had made it. I volunteered for the Pacific but they wanted me to convert to twins ... I had a German girlfriend, she was

163

a nurse, so I spent a lot of time hauling food from the officers' mess to her family. I wrote to her later after I left Germany, but I never heard anything. I knew the peacetime air force was not for me—sports, button polishing, parades—that was not for me ... I had no home to go to. I did not want to go back to Oklahoma. I had a sister but she had moved to Florida, married a US Navy fellow.

In need of a job, Phil visited the Civil Aviation Authority (CAA) in Washington, DC. On the strength of his RCAF logbook, the CAA issued him with a commercial pilot's licence, and he went looking for any kind of flying job—after all, that was what he knew, what the RCAF had trained him for.

Profile – HOWARD LYNN PHILLIPS
Born – October 12, 1914, Greenville, TX
Father – Chester Lee Phillips, cotton farmer
Mother – Lucia Delphinia Taggert
Post-war occupation – Farmer, manager of the Graham County Chamber of Commerce, land developer
Marital status – Wife Virginia Goode, daughters Susan and Sarah
Hobbies – Poker club, walking

Chester Phillips, father of Howard Lynn "Tex" Phillips, believed in keeping his three sons busy; this was not hard to do on a cotton farm in Greenville, Texas. Cows were milked early each morning; on Sundays you attended the Methodist Church in Greenville dressed in a suit, your shoes shined

THE DEATH OF S/L WALLY MCLEOD, DSO, DFC AND BAR, SEPTEMBER 27, 1944

Wally McLeod wanted to be the top-scoring Canadian fighter pilot and did not handle failure easily. He had complained to Squadron Leader Rod Smith on the evening of September 26 that he had missed a good opportunity and was going to make up for it on his next op. Perhaps he felt competitive with Smith, as they were both Malta aces, both from Regina and Smith had downed two Me109s on the 26th. Smith, newly appointed commanding officer of 401 Squadron, would repeat this feat on the 27th and 28th, adding six victories in a mere three days and setting a great example as head of this distinguished squadron.

On the 27th, Wing Commander Johnnie Johnson and Squadron Leader Wally McLeod led 443 Squadron, a total of twelve Spitfires. Don Walz was flying as Red 3 in this formation. Johnson recalled in his autobiography *Wing Leader* that it was a miserable day in the area of Nijmegen, Holland, which lay dark and ominous across the Rhine River, and he felt ill at ease. Then "the ever-vigilant Donald Walz" startled Johnnie by transmitting: "Graycap from Red Three. Nine 109s below."

No. 443 was in a good position to attack the enemy, a section of five and a section of four, in line abreast. As Johnson closed to destroy his selected target, soon to be his thirty-eighth and final victory of the war, he watched the leader of the other Me109 section pull up into the vertical. He cautioned McLeod that whomever this German pilot was, he was no rookie: "Watch that brute, Wally. He knows the form!"

McLeod went after this leader and pulled so much G that his No. 2 blacked out and fell out of formation. By the time McLeod's No. 2 regained his situation awareness and control over his Spitfire, he could no longer see McLeod. No one else witnessed what happened thereafter. Was there a dogfight? Was there a loss of control? Who was the German pilot? We do not know. The twenty-eight-year-old was found in the wreckage of his Spitfire [NH245] the following day. His remains are buried at the war cemetery in Rheinberg, Germany.

Donald Walz at home on his farm south of Moose Jaw, 2001.

and hair combed. Neither Chester nor Lucia put up with any backtalk, and as one of their sons you did what you were told. Howard, the oldest, attended St Mary's University in San Antonio, Texas, for three years, studying liberal arts:

> I wasn't focused on anything particular. I tried to join the Army Air Corps and was turned down, so they said, because I was colour blind. I took my transcript of marks from the university to the sheriff of San Antonio, and he wrote me a letter of endorsement. I took a car up to Detroit, stayed overnight, went to the recruiting centre at Windsor the next morning, and was on the train that afternoon for the Manning Depot in Toronto. On my first night in the "bullpen" at the CNE Grounds, I hear this military expression for the first time: "Is there anyone here from the West?" "Yes." "Well, f___ the West!" I thought that was so funny.

Howard graduated with his wings from the No. 11 Service Flying Training School (SFTS) at

Yorkton, Saskatchewan, in the fall of 1941 and was commissioned immediately, being assigned serial number J8653. Once he was in England, he asked at Bournemouth to go on single-engine fighters and volunteered to go to the Middle East. By the time he arrived at Abu Sueir, Egypt, the United States had come into the war, and he wrote a letter to the US consul in Egypt and went through the bureaucratic process to transfer to the US Army Air Force.

In the meantime, though, Howard's name was drawn out of a hat, and he was sent to No. 61 Operational Training Unit (OTU) in the Sudan to train on the P40 Kittyhawk. Other nationalities training alongside the young American included seven South Africans, four Greeks and two Free French (the Free French were organized under General de Gaulle and kept fighting with the Allies after the surrender of France). Howard recalls:

> I was not unhappy with the aircraft, but when you get the speed up it wants to roll one way and yaw the other ... you had to have a pretty good arm to fly the P40. They asked me where I wanted to go. The wing commander offered me 112 Squadron (called the Shark Squadron because of the painted mouths on the sides of the P40's nose area), commanded by Billy Drake, a great character and ace.

In his first few operations flying with Billy Drake, it all seemed so confusing to Howard:

> [Messerschmitt] 109s came through and shot some of us down and I didn't know it until I got back to the base. I wanted to fly every mission, I wanted to do well. I had three engine failures; the sand was hard on the Allison engine in the P40 ...
>
> Just as my transfer came through to move to the USAAF, Rommel started his push to the east. So I went to Billy Drake and said, "Hell, this is what I came here for. I'm not going to leave now. I don't want a transfer to the USAAF."

After the battle of El Alamein, while stationed in November in Sidi Barrani, Egypt, Howard Phillips and J.M.S. "Joe" Crichton scrambled during a sandstorm with the visibility on the aerodrome down to near zero. Howard is No. 2 and Joe is forced to bank to the right to avoid hitting a crane used for the recovery of armoured vehicles. Phillips's aircraft struck the ground while on the inside of the turn, and caught fire. He was badly burned on his face, losing his eyelids and parts of his ears, and his jaw was broken and his forehead was pushed in. At the hospital in Heliopolis, Egypt, an attempt was made to graft new eyelids, but they kept getting infected.

Phillips was shipped back to Britain; being an American he was designated as a "British protected person." He flew out via Lagos, Nigeria, on a BOAC flying boat on March 8, '43, and shortly thereafter was a patient at the Queen Victoria Hospital at East Grinstead West Sussex. There, Dr Archibald McIndoe and his surgical team removed scar tissue from his hands and grafted some new eyelids. Howard Phillips became a member of the "Guinea Pig Club," formed by the burned flyers who had

been treated by Dr McIndoe and Canadian surgeon Dr Ross Tilley and the other doctors and nurses at Queen Victoria Hospital. By war's end there were 649 Guinea Pigs, about 70 percent British; the balance were Canadians, Australians and New Zealanders.

After two months, Phillips was sent to what was called the Central Medical Board in London for aircrew assessment. They passed him as fit to fly; he requested Spitfires, and while at the OTU at Montford Bridge, England, he became good friends with Gordon Driver, who went off to 421 Squadron. (When Howard mentioned Driver's name in conversation with me, he paused momentarily, then said: "I never had a better friend than Gordon Driver. It was sad, he was vice-president of Noranda Mines after the war, but died in a commercial plane crash flying to Brussels.")

Howard was sent to 412 Squadron, commanded by George Keefer (later Wing Commander, DSO and Bar, DFC and Bar, Croix de Guerre); the flight commanders were Barry Needham and Ken Robb. Howard remembers Keefer as:

> A great guy and a superb leader, Keefer was every bit as good a leader and pilot as Buck McNair and Johnnie Johnson, I think, just not so outgoing. He says to me, "Let's go up and have a tail chase." After about ten minutes he radios that his engine is overheating, "Let's go home." I think he had had enough.

Question: "So you passed your checkout?"

Answer: "Oh, yes, I did. I can turn as tight as anybody."

Through 1943 and into 1944, Howard flew bomber escort sorties to the continent. Like many other Spitfire units, 412 in 1944–45 had a secondary role, dive-bombing with five-hundred-pound bombs. When I asked Howard what he thought of that role, he replied, "Oh, probably about the same as the other pilots. I didn't like it much."

In May 1944 he attended a fighter leader's course at Millfield, Northumberland, with Gordon Farquharson of 416 Squadron. The course served him well after he returned to his squadron, because

Phillips in his Spitfire in 1944.

Courtesy of the Howard Phillips Collection

he flew on D-Day and through the aerial battles inland from the beachhead into July and August. On July 2, he was leading a section with Don Laubman as his No. 3, and Don destroyed two Me109s near Caen, France, his first victories: "Don is a great person and certainly the greatest fighter pilot I ever knew. But he was a low-key guy, just hanging loose like the rest of us."

Howard let me look at his logbook. Like many a fighter pilot's logbook it has brief notes about what was happening day to day; who had been lost, who had survived: "7 June, damaged a Ju88; Lucky Likeness reported POW; 17 June, Larry Love missing; 6 July, very twitchy; 7 July, Needham shot down by flak; bounced three times by Mustangs and Thunderbolts."

I asked Howard to recall some of these events, including friendly fire incidents, and any details of the men he had flown with:

I saw Needham go down, and I never saw him get out. I didn't know till afterwards that it was him. You know, I never met anyone who didn't like Barry Needham ... Beurling, I liked him, and I can tell you he didn't have to chase the WAAFs very far, the women *really* liked him. But he was a loner and flying was his entire life ...

One of our guys shot down a USAAF Mustang, so the American pilots didn't have the market cornered on mistaken identity ... generally, if we turned into them they could see by our wings that we were Spitfires, and they would break off.

By the time of the battles over Nijmegen in late September, I had 201 operational hours at 412; I had one confirmed victory and nine probables or damaged. Altogether, I had flown 178 missions in the Western Desert and northwest Europe. I was ready to have a rest ... I was ready to go home.

My youngest brother, Chester, was a pilot on B24s with the 44th Bombardment Group, and he had been killed on May 14, 1943, leading his squadron on a mission to Kiel, Germany. He is buried at Wege, Belgium. My parents, they didn't pressure me, but they

wanted me to come back, and I went home as much for them as for me. Major Howard Moore, Chester's commanding officer, met me in London one time and he said, "Chester, if he survives, will make general." Chester was a great person.

When Howard was repatriated back to Canada he went to RCAF Station Trenton, where he resigned from the RCAF, and then headed home to Greenville, Texas, to see his parents. He is now ninety years old and living in a townhome community at Green Valley, Arizona. I was in Tucson when I telephoned Howard to ask for directions to Green Valley. He said, "It's on the road to Nogales. Take the road to Nogales, you can't miss us." After our interview he invited me to lunch with his wife, Virginia, and I asked how they had met.

I met her on the high plains of Texas, at Pampa, where my brother Harold had a finance business. She was a schoolteacher there. Down the hall from Harold's office, at another company, was a friend, a bit of a matchmaker, who introduced me to Virginia. When I saw her I was real impressed and I asked her for a date for the next day. She went out with me ... We farmed and Virginia taught school for thirty years, lastly with Eastern Arizona College [in Thatcher, Arizona]. For fourteen years I was the manager of the Graham County Chamber of Commerce [in Safford, Arizona]. Later on I bought acreage and developed it.

When I had spent several hours in conversation with Howard, writing many notes while tape-recording, I asked him to summarize his war. In one touching, evocative sentence he revealed the ineffable gulf that always lies between any writer and the subject of air war: "It is a greater experience than you can put into words."

Painting of Donald Laubman in 1944 by 411 Squadron Spitfire pilot and Official War Artist Robert Hyndman. Lieutenant General Laubman, age 83, lives in Red Deer, Alberta, while Robert Hyndman, age 88, lives in Old Chelsea, Quebec, still painting and still teaching art classes.

RCAF SPITFIRE
OPERATIONS FROM
BRITAIN AND EUROPE

Courtesy of the Wayne Ralph Collection

Kenneth Lett in his office at the Calgary airport, 2002.

Profile – KENNETH CHARLES LETT

Born – July 13, 1923, Carp, ON

Father – Leonard Hyde Lett, farmer

Mother – Nancy Lillian Reid

Decorations & Medals –CD and Two Clasps

Degrees & Awards – BS

Post-war occupation – Air force officer, Major General, RCAF/CAF, retired 1978; business executive/owner Executive Flight Centre, Calgary

Marital status – Wife Roma Lois Bowes

Hobbies – Golf ("more a passion than a hobby")

Most of the pilots that I have interviewed are new people in my life. I may have heard about them, or read about them, but often I am meeting them for the first and, sadly, the only time. However, Major General Kenneth Charles Lett is a Second World War fighter pilot that I have known for more than twenty-five years. Easygoing, always amiable and not one to stand on ceremony, he seems not to have a mean bone in his body. This is particularly remarkable given that he is a retired major general, a still-working business executive and a man who has spent a great deal of his adult life in peace and war in the fighter aircraft business.

Ken grew up on a farm at Carp, Ontario. His grandfather, Andrew John Lett of County Cork, Ireland, received a land grant to settle in the Ottawa Valley after the War of 1812. One of the many things Ken loved about the air force was that it got him off the farm and gave him a profession. Some Second World War fighter pilots went back to farming after the war was over; Ken Lett was grateful that he was not one of them.

After leaving Manning Depot in Brandon, Manitoba, he did some guard duty at Trenton, Ontario, and attended Initial Training School (ITS) just a few miles away at Belleville. At the Elementary Flying Training School (EFTS) St Eugene in Hawkesbury, Ontario, he was introduced to a memorable instructor named Wally McGuire who gave him his first flying lessons in the Fleet Finch. It was not part of the syllabus, but Wally taught Ken how to perform an inverted falling leaf.

When Harley Godwin had taught future Mosquito ace Rayne Schultz an inverted falling leaf in the Tiger Moth (see Part Seven), he said: "If you can master this, nothing that happens to your aircraft in the future will ever scare you." Wally McGuire, an old bush pilot, had the same belief, and showed Ken Lett how to fly the Finch inverted, just above the stalling speed, with the aircraft oscillating from side to side, while descending vertically with the help of gravity. McGuire climbed the Finch to eight thousand feet above ground, then shut down the engine and the aircraft fell to three thousand feet. McGuire recovered to level flight and restarted the engine. He then turned control over to Ken for his first attempt.

The control column is held forward throughout the manoeuvre. The alternating pressure on the left and right rudder pedals keeps the aircraft oscillating from one side to the other — first up on one wingtip, then the other, back and forth. The Tiger Moth requires much less rudder input than the Fleet Finch. To perform an inverted falling leaf requires finesse because the pilot must continually vary the pressure on the control column and rudder pedals to avoid a spin. At the same time, the pilot must keep the aircraft oscillating from side to side and also falling upside down at low speed.

Since this is the more challenging inverted rather than an upright falling leaf, the pilot's head is pointed downward towards the ground, and he is hanging in his straps. With the control column forward, creating negative "G" forces, all the dirt on the cockpit floor and any loose pencils or coins float to the top of the canopy. When viewed from outside, the aircraft is descending in an oscillating, lazy manner, rather like a dry leaf falling from a tree in the autumn. Demonstrated on lightweight biplanes in the early decades of aviation, especially by First World War pilots, and always considered a mark of fine airmanship, the inverted falling leaf is seldom performed today.

Ken Lett's first instructor at the Service Flying Training School (SFTS) at Uplands, near Ottawa, then introduced him to low flying—so low that the instructor was grounded, leaving Ken without anybody to teach him. This was distressing because for some time he did no flying and quickly fell behind the other students on his course.

There was a favourite watering hole for SFTS personnel called Standish Hall, located at the end of

the streetcar line in Hull, Quebec. There Ken met an instructor named E.G. "Irish" Ireland, later a well-known fighter pilot and Royal Canadian Air Force post-war senior officer. When Irish asked how it was going, Ken told him how worried he was that he had no instructor. Irish got Ken an instructor immediately, and by flying three or four trips every day he caught up with the others.

He graduated from the SFTS at Uplands in October 1942 and spent that winter at Bournemouth, England, waiting to go on a fighter operational training unit (OTU), in his case at Eshott, Newcastle. He was scheduled to go to Africa but that posting was rescinded, so by the time he finally got to a fighter squadron it was October 1943. His commanding officer at 402 Squadron RCAF at Lincolnshire was Geoff Northcott, who always took the rookies flying with him. After his first trip Geoff said, "You don't have to fly that close!"

At this stage of the war, in anticipation of the invasion of the continent, the Royal Air Force established the Second Tactical Air Force. Prior to D-Day this TAF trained as a self-contained fighting force, the pilots and mechanics living in tents, learning how to pack up and move at short notice. Its role after D-Day would be to support the land battle, following the troops as they advanced through France, Holland and Germany. Air cover, standing patrols, fighter escort duties and air-to-ground attack, as well as photo reconnaissance, were all part of the duties of the Second Tactical Air Force.

However, 402 Squadron was the only Canadian fighter squadron not transferred into the Second Tactical Air Force, but kept with RAF and Polish units for the air defence of Britain through the spring and summer of 1944. No. 402 was part of 11 Group, assigned to defend the southern half of Britain. In addition to air defence and bomber escort sorties, there were occasional night patrols. This was a miserable task in the Spitfire as the exhaust flames from the engine impaired the pilot's night vision.

Since the Luftwaffe was not much in evidence over Britain in 1944, Ken's first months as a fighter pilot were relatively uneventful. After D-Day the exciting air combat was over the Continent, not in southern England, and it was very frustrating for the pilots of 402 to see their colleagues at the centre of the war, while they were left behind. One advantage, however, was that London was not far away on rainy days when nothing was happening.

Lett's social life in London, like that of many fighter pilots, revolved around the clubs along Denman Street and the Regent Palace and Strand Palace Hotels. He enjoyed walking along Denman because Canadians were popular and welcome in the various clubs and bars.

There was not a lot of harm in the things we got up to socially, but they were not things we would have done if we had stayed home in Carp, Ontario. I liked Bobbie Page's Kimmel Club. (Page was an old First World War balloon pilot.) It had been a theatrical club, a hangout for pilots during the Battle of Britain looking to meet theatrical ladies of London. Page was a wholesale florist at Covent Garden...

There were lots of clubs along Denman, and many years later, I was walking along the street with my wife and saw the Copacabana Club. We went downstairs and the lady checked her membership list and I was still on it.

During the month of June '44, Ken flew a remarkable fifty-three hours; his ops involved flying from England up to the French beachhead, and a few miles inland. He recalls having three hours of sleep lying under the wing of his Spitfire before his first flight on D-Day, June 6. At the end of June he was on a rather ill-planned mission led by the wing commander, and he was lucky to make it home:

J.C. was leading our wing, and unfortunately he came out of France at low level and both German and friendly anti-aircraft fire did a lot of damage to us. It was not good leadership. I lost the three aircraft behind me, and he lost his No. 4. We had not done enough damage to the enemy to make it worthwhile to leave with twelve Spitfires and return with eight.

I never flew so low in my life—I didn't have any branches or leaves stuck in my Spit, but I ought to have.

On September 29, the pilots of 402 escaped the frustrating duties of British defence and flew to Grabe, Holland. The unit became one of the squadrons of 125 Wing RAF, and finally—in December—402 moved to 126 Wing RCAF, where it served for the balance of the war.

When I asked Ken to describe his state of mind in the first year of ops, he said:

I don't have any memory other than having a ball. I guess that is probably the wrong way to describe it. The reality was flying your aircraft and checking behind you. Beyond that I was unconscious of much of the rest of the universe ... I was doing something that I enjoyed doing, it was very exciting, *including* the flak. I was twenty years old, everything was new and different. You grow up fast, you learn something about your fellow man and a helluva lot about the guys that maintain your aircraft ... I used to help my fitter and rigger with work on my Spitfire (AE-X) — prop changes, things like that.

Spitfires in the Second Tactical Air Force did thousands of dive-bombing sorties, but it was not the best fighter for that role, and pilots, on the whole, did not like the work. During August 1944, Ken's squadron received the Spitfire Mk XIV, which was operationally a far different machine from the Mk V, on which he had started:

The model XIV did not have quite large enough a tail for that big engine, and you were fighting the torque when you dive-bombed ... We had 250-pound bombs, but even with a direct hit they did not do much damage, and the Germans quickly repaired whatever we had hit. But you could climb to forty thousand feet with a whole squadron faster than any of the early series of jet aircraft, much faster to altitude, for example, than the [post-war] de Havilland Vampire.

Ken had no confirmed victories during his tour at 402, and chuckles as he remembers the saying of another wingman: "I was one of those guys who kept you heroes alive." Ken's friend and course mate before going overseas was Richard Joseph "Dick" Audet, DFC and Bar, from Lethbridge, Alberta. Dick was one of Ken's favourite heroes from the war. Audet became an ace at 411 Squadron RCAF on one op on December 29, '44, by shooting down five enemy aircraft. He and Ken Lett celebrated the event at a casual gathering in the bar on New Year's Eve. Audet destroyed another six, including a couple of Me262 jets, before being killed on March 2, '45, while attacking a train.

Lett was saddened to hear he had been lost: "Dick Audet was a hell of a nice person, big, tall, dark and brooding-looking. He didn't smile a lot. He looked liked Victor Mature [the Hollywood actor]. He married about two weeks before he was killed." Fraser Campbell, who joined 411 Squadron RCAF in December, and George "Smitty" Smith, who joined in January, have similar recollections of Audet. Campbell, who flew with Audet the day he shot down five enemy aircraft in one trip, told me that he was "a very nice fellow who was no showoff."

Lett says that in the closing months of his tour, the day-to-day world of combat for every fighter pilot included many sights and sounds that were unlike anything that had ever been seen before in the history of war:

We experienced a lot of things that were a first time for us. We saw the first German V2 rocket launches, just the fiery plume. We reported them until the controller told us to stop; no one had briefed us on what they were. Also we could hear the buzz in our earphones when the German radar was tracking us, but we didn't know it was radar that was causing the sound ...

I had 143 ops when I and several others were called in by Geoff Northcott to tell us we were tour-expired. We all started protesting because we wanted to be there when the war ended. He said, "Get out of here before you get yourself killed!" I was in the city of Chester

when the war ended, teaching large-formation tactics at the OTU at Hawarden. A friend, Ritchie Richards, whose mother was dying in Canada, handed me the keys to his car and told me to sell it when I left the UK.

I came home and married my high-school sweetheart, Roma Lois Bowes, one year later. She played in a band, she had boyfriends; I never questioned her, she never questioned me. We had known each other since elementary school. I celebrated my twenty-second birthday at Paynton, England, while waiting to catch the boat, and I took my release from RCAF Station Rockcliffe. You had to be an instructor or have a lot of decorations to be able to stay in the RCAF, and I was put on a Class E Reserve list. I had my fill of farming, of milking cows, and was working in an automotive wholesale supply company, but I really wanted to get back in the air force.

In 1948 in The Belle Clair Hotel, just off Bank Street in Ottawa, a regular watering hole for RCAF types, Doug Lindsay and I were having a couple of beers—the old quart-sized tall ones. Doug was in RCAF HQ and he offered me an assignment in a Vampire squadron ... Bud Malloy ran the OTU on the Vampire, and then I met Don Laubman who was one of the flight commanders at 410 Squadron.

Ken Lett retired in 1978 as a major general; his last military assignment was as deputy chief of operations for the North American Aerospace Defence Command (NORAD). Still a young man, he went to Calgary and became president of Executive Flight Centre at the airport. In 1992, Lett purchased the company. Today it has fixed base operations (FBO) at eight airports across Western Canada, providing fuel and services to transient aircraft as well as hangar accommodation. Executive Flight Centre also builds and operates hangars. Except when he escapes to Arizona in the winter months, Ken goes in to work most every day at the Calgary airport. As he says, "I am more than twice as old as virtually all our employees. But I like being around young people, I always have. They keep me active and involved in life."

THE STORIES OF DONALD LAUBMAN AND DOUGLAS LINDSAY

Profile – DONALD CURRIE LAUBMAN

Born – October 16, 1921, Provost, AB

Father – Charles Francis Laubman, salesman for Caterpillar tractors

Mother – Charlotte Farquharson

Decorations & Medals – DFC and Bar, CMM, CD and Two Clasps

Post-war occupation – Air force officer, Lieutenant General, RCAF/CAF, retired 1972; business executive/owner Canadian Tire store, retired 1990

Marital status – Wife Margaret Gibson died in 2001; daughter Leslie; son Robert

Hobbies – Golf, fishing, woodworking

Profile – JAMES DOUGLAS LINDSAY

Born – September 16, 1922, Arnprior, ON

Father – Percival James Lindsay, woods manager for EB Eddy company

Mother – Jessie Caroline Watt

Decorations & Medals – DFC, DFC (US), Air Medal, CD and Two Clasps

Post-war occupation – Air force officer, Colonel, RCAF/CAF, retired 1972; business executive/owner Canadian Tire Store, retired February 1991

Marital status – Wife Anne Whelan; sons Robert, Graham and Michael

Hobbies – Golf, painting (watercolours)

In four years of interviewing Second World War fighter pilots, quite a few meetings came about through recommendations. One pilot would say of another, "You've got to interview him. He is a great fighter pilot. Make sure you go see him." Many times I heard this advice repeated to me about two well-known RCAF aces and senior officers, Donald Laubman and Douglas Lindsay. They are fully retired now and live in Red Deer, Alberta. They were famous not only in the history of the air force, for what they had done in war, but also for what they did when they retired. The Canadian Tire Corporation was indelibly connected to their names among their RCAF colleagues because, after removing their uniforms and donning business suits, they had cajoled their way into managing two franchises with little or no money. Lindsay observed, "I sometimes think he [Dean Muncaster, president, Canadian Tire] let us into the business just so we would leave the office and stop bothering him."

Lieutenant General Laubman and Colonel Lindsay had fairly typical Canadian childhoods. Both of their fathers had served in the Great War, Lindsay's being a regimental sergeant major and Laubman's a senior non-commissioned officer with the 49th Battalion. After the war, Laubman's father, Charles, sold Caterpillar tractors in Alberta, and Lindsay's father, Percival, was a woods manager for the EB Eddy company in Ontario. Don Laubman got his first flight in an aircraft because his school friend Dick Cull had a private pilot's licence—Don and Dick joined the RCAF on the same day, trained together, became fighter pilots from 1943 to 1945 and took their release on the same day in September 1945. Douglas Lindsay had a next-door neighbour and good friend named Moore Campbell, two years his senior, who had soloed on an Aeronca, took Doug for his first flight and let him fly the aircraft on several more flights.

Don and Doug received their wings in 1941, in May and September respectively. Both instructed in the British Commonwealth Air Training Plan (BCATP). Don Laubman managed to escape in September 1942 to 133 Squadron RCAF, where he flew Hurricanes at Lethbridge, Alberta, and later Boundary Bay, BC. Doug Lindsay continued instructing and had three thousand hours at the time of his arrival in England in 1943. Laubman was sent to 412 Squadron and Lindsay to 403. By war's end, Laubman had destroyed fifteen enemy aircraft and damaged three; Lindsay had destroyed eight, including three in a single sortie, and damaged five. Lindsay later flew F86s in the Korean War on exchange with the 39th Fighter Interceptor Squadron (FIS) of the US Air Force. In a short, fifty-mission tour in 1952—half that of American pilots—he destroyed two MiG 15s and damaged three, for which he received the American DFC and Air Medal.

Of the more than one hundred tape-recorded interviews that I did for this book, the personalities of Laubman and Lindsay were most similar. Embellishment is simply not part of their nature and, like many aces, they seem reluctant to spin a colourful story just because it might make good copy. Neither man seems prone to introspection or philosophical doubt. They have crammed a great deal of living into eight decades and seem almost surprised that anyone else considers what they did unusual. When I asked General Laubman if he had ever been scared going on ops, he answered this way:

I wouldn't call it scared. When you get into a close encounter, the adrenalin pumps you up, and it is the weirdest feeling you've ever had: your focus is intense, just incredible, it is unlike anything I have experienced before or since. It is like being in a different world almost. But there is a great letdown once the experience is over.

I asked Colonel Lindsay what had made him a great fighter pilot. He replied:

I really do not know why I should think of myself as better. Maybe there is a lot of luck in it, it is hard to say. I didn't get hit very often. I missed a few opportunities ... thinking, when perhaps I should have been more aggressive. Being in the right place at the right time [is important]. Knowing how to get out of trouble when trouble presented itself [is important.] You have to have some thought about your own survival. I can think of some individuals who went headlong into everything, and they didn't last more than three or four trips.

I asked whom he admired among fighter pilots he had met or served with, having known so many great figures. As an RCAF squadron leader serving on exchange duties with the 39th FIS of the US Air Force in Korea, his No. 2 was 1st Lieutenant Harold Fischer, who destroyed his first MiG on the day Lindsay got his second, and went on to destroy nine more before being shot down and taken prisoner of war north of the Yalu River.

The 39th FIS was also the home of Captain Joseph McConnell, who with sixteen victories became the highest-scoring ace of the United Nations air forces in Korea. But in the Second World War, Lindsay was introduced to combat by Canada's most famous fighter pilot. This is how Doug remembers it:

[George] Beurling was an influence. My first recollection of him was early one morning, a foggy morning. He was painting victory marks on the side of his Spitfire, twenty-seven of them ... Finally he said to me, "Do you see that tree over there?" Well, I could hardly see any tree through the fog. "Do you see that branch on the right hand side, four feet off the ground?" Yes, I replied, though I could not. "Well, if you go out about a foot and a half on that branch, there is a yellow leaf." He went back to painting crosses on the side of his aircraft. I went over to the tree, and sure enough there was a yellow leaf.

On the ground he was a peculiar chap. I really should say that I did not understand him. In the air he was great. The first four or five missions I flew with him were a joy. His flying was extremely smooth; he never wracked his aircraft around, and his eyesight was great. I was flying as his No. 2 when he got his twenty-eighth and twenty-ninth ... he called them out, and we were in a turn and he pulled the nose up and fired. I didn't see what he was firing at because I was busy watching him and doing a crossover turn. I didn't see anything else other than him firing. When they developed his film, and counted the rounds, he had fired only fifteen rounds.

Beurling was famous for destroying enemy aircraft with very few bullets. A less talented pilot might fire his full load of 120 cannon shells just to damage or destroy one aircraft. Johnnie Johnson admired Wally McLeod for being able to shoot the enemy down with just a few bullets, much less than Johnnie used, albeit to the same effect. Economy in the use of ammunition was one of the hallmarks of all exceptionally accurate gunnery.

Don Laubman had his first victory on March 23, 1944, flying with Barry Needham, the same pilot who had been at 412 back in 1941 with Rod Smith and John Gillespie Magee. The two were credited with downing a Ju88 near Creil, France. By August, Don had destroyed four more to become an ace. When I asked if he had ever been bounced by enemy aircraft, Laubman said no. But then he described an incident, during the battle for Nijmegen, Holland, in which he spotted two Messerschmitt 109s, just above a thin layer of cloud:

> I ducked below, they ducked below. We went back and forth above and below this cloud bank. As I got behind the leader, I looked out to see his No. 2 right off my wing tip. I don't know whether he thought I was his leader or what ... but he could have hit me with a stick! I was not aware of him until I looked over.

When Don reached fifteen victories, while on a fifty-hour extension, Dean Dover, the commanding officer, called him in and said he was finished. Don met Air Marshal Lloyd Breadner in London, had his portrait painted there by Robert Hyndman—official artist and former 411 Squadron fighter pilot—and was then sent to Gimli, Manitoba, for a rest at the Cold Weather Test Station of the RCAF. He pulled strings to get a second tour, and on April 14, 1945, while commanding 402 Squadron, he came very close to being killed.

A gas-filled vehicle he was strafing exploded directly under his Spitfire, burning it black, damaging the engine and forcing Laubman to bail out. He didn't make it out of the burning fighter until he was eight hundred feet above the ground, and then hit the tail in the escape—badly hurting his leg so he could not walk. He almost parachuted directly onto his own aircraft, which was cooking off rounds as it burned up.

He was captured by Hitler Youth soldiers armed with Lugers, while German civilians shouted at him that he was a baby killer. He ended up in a prisoner-of-war camp briefly, was felled by jaundice and put in hospital, but as senior Allied officer present accepted the surrender of the German general in charge of the camp and his staff, relieving them of their weapons and confining them to their barracks.

Doug Lindsay also talked his way back onto a second tour in April 1945 and served with 403, then 416, flying on the last day of hostilities, May 4. He stayed in the RCAF through the transition from war to peace and served for another twenty-seven years, retiring from the Canadian Forces as a colonel in 1972. His son Graham retired from the Canadian Forces as a colonel in August 2003.

Laubman was released from the RCAF in September 1945, and he and Dick Cull decided they were going to make a career as bush pilots. Don and some of his wartime friends agreed to a gathering in Banff, Alberta, two months down the road. At the appointed time and place in Banff, only Don and Wing Commander Dal Russel showed up. The two RCAF aces were walking along the street in Banff, in uniform, looking quite handsome, when five or six attractive young women strolled past in the opposite direction. Don knew one of the young women from school days and she introduced him there and then to Margaret Gibson.

Don and Margaret went on a hiking trip in the mountains with a picnic basket and a case of beer, kept chilled in the creek by the trail. Before he really knew it he had fallen in love with Margaret. However she made it clear to him that she did not want to be married to a bush pilot, so Don returned to the RCAF in January 1946. He served until 1972, retiring as a lieutenant general and the chief of personnel, Canadian Forces.

Laubman's and Lindsay's paths intersected during their peacetime years, as they were promoted and undertook new assignments, new challenges. They became good friends and, after retirement, business partners. Now over eighty, they visit each other frequently, play some golf and talk occasionally about the past, a past that seems incredible. They are true survivors.

* * *

The most heart-rending of deaths in war are those that take place in the last few hours or days before a peace treaty is signed. The intensity of the armed reconnaissance battles of fighter pilots over German territory in the last weeks of the war left little room for mercy on either side. Many German flyers and many German civilians died in those closing weeks without materially affecting the outcome of the war, and many of our most experienced Allied flyers were lost. One of the fighter pilots I interviewed who had reason to understand the wretched viciousness of battle in those closing days was Robert Bruce "Bill" Barker, DFC, whose American pilot friend went missing in action on the second last day of hostilities of the European war—May 3, 1945. The pilot's name was J9430 Flight Lieutenant Donald Mathew "Tex" Pieri, DFC.

Profile – ROBERT BRUCE BARKER

Born – December 4, 1918, Vancouver

Father – Robert Bruce Barker, payroll department of the CPR

Mother – Teresa Greer

Decorations & Medals – DFC, Coronation Medal, CD

Post-war occupation – Civil servant for the comptroller to the Treasury, regional administration officer for the Unemployment Insurance Commission in BC; Group Captain RCAF Auxiliary

Marital status – Wife Marjorie Waite died in 1999; daughters Rocky and Kelly; son Robert

Hobbies – Golf, painting

Courtesy of the Wayne Ralph Collection

Bill Barker and daughter Kelly at a Canadian Fighter Pilots Association reunion in Comox, BC, in 2001.

Bill Barker graduated from Yorkton, Saskatchewan's No. 11 SFTS in June 1941 with his course mate James Edwards. In ground school they had struggled with the mathematics, and the two crammed at night to get through the written tests. Their two war careers are instructive for anyone who wants to appreciate that beginnings in a war career often foreshadow nothing about what is to come; that success or failure in war so often seems to hinge on ephemeral events that have nothing to do with skill.

Unlike Edwards, Barker was commissioned immediately after graduation; when he first got word of it he thought someone on his course was playing a joke at his expense. In no way did he feel like an officer, and he had to be threatened with a charge before he bought his uniforms and put up his rank badges.

It then dawned on Barker that he could not even sit next to his buddy Sergeant Edwards on the train to Halifax, or bunk in with him on board ship. Someone he had chummed around with in training was now required to salute him. Barker remembers, shaking his head: "Edwards looked about twelve years old when he graduated, and that may have played a part in him not getting a commission." Bill and Jimmie could not drink together or even eat a

meal under the same roof. Bill Barker found the gulf created by his officer's rank awfully depressing.

Both pilots made it to Britain within weeks of graduation, but Edwards trained on Hurricanes and went to the Western Desert. Barker was selected to instruct, attended War Course No 28 at the RAF's Central Flying School and then returned to Canada for eighteen months.

When Bill finally got to a fighter OTU at Bagotville, Quebec, in March 1943, he crashed a Hurricane through failing to switch over from reserve to main fuel tank after takeoff. His logbook was endorsed with red ink, and he was exiled to Hurricanes at 130 Squadron, first at Bagotville, then at Goose Bay, Labrador.

It is notable that Edwards had a similar accident at his Hurricane OTU in England in 1942. He was spoken to by his understanding RAF flight commander, who offered the opinion that the young pilot had learned a valuable lesson and was unlikely to repeat it ("Carry on, Sergeant Edwards"). As a result, the RAF gained a future ace in the Western Desert. Anyone who has served in the military will recall episodes from their own service similar to that of Edwards and Barker, episodes that illustrate the arbitrariness of fate and military justice.

Barker was instructed in gunnery at Bagotville by Malta ace Wally McLeod and his logbook was stamped "Exceptional" in gunnery and "Average" in flying when he graduated. But he didn't get a chance to prove how well he could shoot until October 1944, when he joined 442 Squadron, and March 1945, when he transferred to 412 Squadron. He is credited with four victories plus two damaged. As Barker ruefully notes with a chuckle, just one victory short of being an ace—a common pattern in his life, so he says ("always a day late, and a buck short"). Barker is candid about his ignorance on the early sorties:

I was really frightened for about the first ten trips. The old tummy would just churn. Then you got used to it, and you could see better. For example, you learned that different calibre flak exploded in different colours—black smoke was 88mm, red and yellow was 40mm, the small-calibre was white ...

The first five or six ops trips I never saw an airplane. And everybody was saying there are Huns over there, break right ... my biggest problem at first was how am I ever going to find the aerodrome. On your first trips taking off in formation, you look back and the whole landscape looks the same. How will I ever get back? All the pilots that survived could say the same thing.

When I asked Bill if he worried about dying, he shook his head:

I never gave it a thought. By this time I had a wife and two children—a daughter and a son—and I was the only married fellow in the squadron. They didn't want married pilots in the squadron. But Geoff Northcott was fine with it, and kept me on, and I flew on his wing a lot because he liked a wingman with keen vision, and my eyesight was great. He had an expression: on a good-weather day he would come down to the flights and say, "I think I can smell Huns in the air. Barker, get your gear."

It is a terrible thing to say, but combat was fun. I had a ball. All you had to do was live. Seriously, what else! You can't go around moping, worrying about your girlfriend. My wife and children never entered my head during the day. I couldn't give it a thought. You couldn't dwell on your wife and children and do the job. But religiously every night I wrote her a letter, a blue airmail letter every night.

In March 1945, 442 Squadron was sent back to England to re-equip with Mustang IIIs, under the command of a popular and respected commanding officer, Squadron Leader Mitch Johnston, the same Johnston who had been serving during the aerial debacle of June 2, 1942 at 403 (see Part Six).

Wing Commander Northcott spoke privately to some of his best pilots—Bill Barker, Red Francis and Tex Pieri—and asked them to stay on Spitfires with his 126 Wing. He said to Bill:

"How would like to stay here on ops? If you go on Mustangs all you will do is fly five hours to Berlin and back. Stay *here* on ops." Geoff was such a great guy that we really liked to fly with him, so it was an easy decision ... Tex Pieri and I went to 412 ... Red went to 401.

On April 16, Barker's plane was damaged by flak and forced down in a field behind enemy lines. He was now on the run from both the military and civilians:

I landed in the worst-ploughed field you ever saw, grinding to a halt just by a farmhouse. I looked up and there was a fellow with a pitchfork by the farm ... I got out of the cockpit, but forgot my attachments, damn near broke my neck ... The fellow with the pitchfork was a Polish forced labourer. I gave him my Sweet Caps [cigarettes] and said he could keep my parachute. I could see a bunch of fellows running ... A German had got on his bicycle from this farm and rode away as I was crashing.

I was between the lines, and I started down the road. We were dressed in brown, no rank badges and no wings. If you were in blue they did not like you, they probably would shoot you because we were the ones doing the bombing and strafing. I walked down through the village, five or six miles ... the dogs were all barking at every house.

Then, out of nowhere, this guy had a Luger under my throat, and I said "I am a Spitfire pilot. *Parlez-vous français?*" It turned out that he was an escaping Polish prisoner of war. He and his companions picked me up on their shoulders ... they were all prisoners of war. It saved my life to speak those three words in French, because one of them recognized what I said.

After ten miles of walking I stumbled across tanks, and they didn't believe I was with their side. The town marshal was a brigadier and I got in to see him. He turned and said, "Captain Jones, take Barker back to his unit." So I got back after thirty-six hours—all fun and games. Returning to the squadron, I found that all my belongings, socks, underwear, everything, had been parcelled out among the pilots.

Barker took no notice that the war might end at any moment, and the flying continued into May 1, 2 and 3:

The war was winding down, but we did not have the feeling it was going to end. On May 3, I went down to ops and I had terrible stomach cramps. I was feeling sick and had a sore throat.

Tex Pieri drove me down to the flights. This was his day off. So I said, "Tex, take me to the hospital." I figured I could get some pills and still go flying. They put a thermometer in my mouth, and said, "You are going to bed." Since the MO [medical officer] grounded me, Tex said: "Well, I'll take your aircraft."

I had used his aircraft on April 16th and that was the one I had force-landed in a field. I guess he thought he would get back at me. Anyway, Tex took my trip ... and did not come back ...

Red Francis came into the hospital not long afterward and said, "Get out of bed, come celebrate, the war is over!" There was no word about Tex for a couple of days, so I decided I was going to go look for him ... I asked the commanding officer for a jeep and an interpreter. We visited several farms but found nothing; no one had seen a parachute or a Spitfire.

Many years later a friend in Ottawa found a report, with some sentences and names blacked out, and it said that Tex had walked into a farmhouse, and this German, the worst type of [Hitler Youth], shot this pilot and then ordered a fourteen-year-old boy to bury him in a shallow grave. When Pieri's wife received the telegram about him she telephoned my wife in Vancouver ... she was carrying his child and had been expecting Tex home now that the war was over. It was all very sad.

Mustang III of 442 Squadron RCAF in 1945.

Diving 6000 Feet Straight Down
Pilot's Body Weighs Two Tons at End of Descent

By GREGORY CLARK
Star Weekly Staff Writer

AN ADVANCED CANADIAN AIRFIELD IN NORMANDY

THIS is a story about what it feels like to dive a Typhoon with one 1,000-pound bomb eight feet to the left of you and one 1,000-pound bomb eight feet to the right of you, both of them as alive as the cannon-cracker you have just touched the match to, and in front of you a sort of fishnet of queer, clasping, red balls and small diamond spark-lers, through which you must dive, never deviating one hair's breadth from the straight-down vertical.

Flt.-Lieut. Roy Burden of Vancouver is sitting on the pine log opposite me here in this dripping, quiet forest and I am sitting on an-other log, listening. As we talk, the clouds overhead thud and mutter with an endless reverberation. I am an old soldier. I saw two years and three months of the front line of that old war and also I am a veteran of this war, for I spent seven months in Italy where I thought I had seen the ultimate. Italy is as far behind what we, Burden and I, talk through as Italy was ahead of 1918. Not one minute of the day, rain or shine, but the roof of cloud or sunlit sky over our heads, and it alternates every hour, shakes with the hatred of nations. In Italy we had some spectacular barrages. I remember before Ortona we fired 225,000 shells in one barrage. But that is chicken feed.

I hardly know how to describe it to you. Our horizon here on the beachhead is a sort of half-circle. Sometimes the whole half-circle is thudding at once. But for the most part, it comes in cycles all day, and all night. But never is it silent. Artillery, as I recall it in the old war and even as I recall it in Italy, was a recognizable effort of individual guns. In all these weeks I have never heard an indi-vidual gun; even up the line each ear-splitting crash of a gun right beside you was part of a pattern of sound, nearby and far off.

Young Flt.-Lieut. Burden says: "They tell you to yell when you dive. That is to tighten your muscles. You weigh about two tons at the completion of your dive, say from 8.000 to 3,000 or 2,000 feet, when you press the but-ton and let the bombs go. But I think you tighten up enough without yelling.

"As a matter of fact, you are all scrunched down on your stick, like a monkey hugging a football. You come over the target and you have time to tighten your straps and do any-thing you think you need to do. You are busy getting set and at the same time keeping the formation.

"The leading plane rolls over, and right in your turn you roll over, too. That brings the target right under you in a vertical dive. The ideal is the vertical. Straight 90 degrees down. Sometimes you have overshot or undershot and you have to alter the vertical a few degrees one way or the other. But it is a straight-down dive, whatever way you look at it. Of course, your engine is on full."

"And how do you feel in that dive?" I de-manded.

"Well," said Burden, "you have been through a lot of training, of course, and you know what to expect. You roll your plane over and then scrunch yourself over your stick, to hold it for a vertical dive and watching through your gunsights and at the same time watch-ing your altimeter and, if I may add, also watching your comrades to see when they let go. Commonly you black out—oh, just for an instant. Your body weighs so much—they say two tons—that if you let your hand off the control column it would fall to your side like a plummet and if you tried to lift your foot off the rudder bar you might as well try to lift 300 pounds of lead with your foot."

It is all part of the game. You hunch up. You try to be alert. You keep your mind cen-tred on the target. You press the button. There is a slight, almost imperceptible, jolt. They are gone. A 1,000-pounder on the right and a 1,000-pounder on the left, both gone by an electrical impulse. Then you draw the control column back two or three inches as everything grows black. And you feel the lovely lift. And you hoist up and off to one side to try to see the bursts . . . .

Harry Hardy in flying gear during the Battle of the Bulge, December 1944.

PART TEN
CANADA'S
TYPHOON PILOTS

Profile – HARRY JAMES HARDY

Born – May 30,1922, Verdon, MB, raised in Timmins, ON

Father – Robert Pancreas Hardy, sawmill worker

Mother – Evelene Mary Cliffe

Decorations & Medals – DFC, CD

Post-war occupation – Mechanical engineer, 32 years with MacMillan Bloedel

Marital status – Wife Hazel Claire died November 30, 2004; daughters Roberta and Christine

Hobbies – Aviculture, carpentry

His name is easy to remember. All I have to do is think of the Second World War big-band leader who played the trumpet with such clarity that it brings tears to my eyes as I listen to the soaring crystal notes of "Ciribiribin," or as the melancholy of "I'll Get By" or "These Foolish Thing" washes over me. The name is Harry James Hardy and he is a retired engineer, inventor and expert on endangered species of exotic pheasants. His avocation since 1954 has been to resurrect species that have been declared endangered under Appendix 1 to the Convention on International Trade in Endangered Species of Wild Fauna and Flora (CITIES)—species such as the Szechuan white-eared pheasant. Harry has bred 107 white-eared pheasants, for aviaries in the United States, Brazil, England and the Continent.

I toured his South View Aviaries in Burnaby, BC, and Harry's eyes glowed as he described to me how the two-week-old baby pheasants he was raising already had their flight feathers. It helps them "to hop up on branches, out of harm's way. They look kinda funny at this stage with only flight feathers. I will put them outside soon—the dry air inside is not good for their feathers." Harry Hardy has been

inducted into the Agricultural Hall of Fame for his forty-five technical papers about the raising of pheasants and waterfowl. Ten years ago, there were thirty-four Blyth's Tragopan pheasants in captivity around the world; there are now eighty-four, and thanks to Harry twenty-two of them were born and raised in Burnaby.

Since his retirement after thirty-two years as a mechanical engineer with MacMillan Bloedel Limited, Harry has also worked as an inventor with the Tetra Society of North America, which helps people who have disabilities. Harry has invented more than 160 mechanical or electrical/mechanical devices to help improve the daily lives of people with disabilities or those who are physically challenged. He has been nominated for the Order of British Columbia for his contributions to a better world and, more specifically, for his contributions to the citizens of the province.

All these life-nurturing, generous deeds come from a man who flew one of the most destructive fighter bombers in history, the Hawker Typhoon, in the most dangerous occupation for a fighter pilot in the war: close air support to the army. His personal Typhoon, the one he flew most frequently, was named Pulverizer I, and because of crashes, forced landings and bailouts, there were no less than three more in the series: Pulverizer II, Pulverizer III and Pulverizer IV. The last, serial number RB389, survived only to be melted down for scrap. It is the most famous Typhoon in the Royal Canadian Air Force, and its distinct profile, taxiing out to a runway while armed with two thousand-pound bombs, is probably one of the most frequently reproduced RCAF fighter images from the war.

Courtesy of the Martin "Pat" Peterson Collection

Harry Hardy's Typhoon, Pulverizer IV, 1945.

Harry is a renaissance man, knowledgeable on a vast array of subjects, and he can still tell you all the technical specs on the Typhoon:

Her armament of two 1,000-pound bombs and 480 rounds of 20-millimetre shells, a mix of armour-piercing and high-explosive, was one of the heaviest of any fighter. Twenty rounds from the end of the belt we had five tracer rounds and we stopped strafing ground targets when we saw the tracers. We carried 20 rounds per gun home in case enemy fighters jumped us. Our four cannons were harmonized to strike a single point 400 yards distant. You know, even when we dove at 400 miles per hour, the firing of the cannons slowed the Typhoon so much that we were pushed forward against our straps ... That seven-ton fighter kept me alive for 111 hours of combat flying ...

I flew my first op on August 12th, 1944, as a wingman to Blue section leader. He said, "Stick to me like glue and take no chances." We were fighting to close the Falaise Gap [in northwest France], supporting the Second British Army. The battle area was covered in smoke and dust and I could not see the tar-

get, but I stuck to his wing; when he released his bombs, I released mine. So much for my first operation—I never did see the target. I flew eleven more ops in support of the Falaise Gap battle. During those first ten days on 440 Squadron, four pilots were killed and I scarcely knew them. Their deaths made me more careful as to how I would attack my targets ...

Each op during Falaise consisted of one dive-bombing attack and about seven strafing runs. You lined up on your target about half a mile back, your speed was four hundred, your open-fire distance was four hundred yards, and you fired fifteen rounds from each cannon. This was a one-second burst. Every German soldier within range was firing back. Our Hispano long-barrelled 20-millimetre cannon fired 760 rounds per minute, 12 rounds per second per cannon, so the most you could fire per target was 60 rounds per single attack.

In August 1944, flying from airfield B9 at Lantheuil, France, Hardy's 440 Squadron was one of three in the RCAF's No. 143 Fighter Bomber Wing, the others being 438 and 439. The entire wing was equipped with Typhoons and it constituted one of four RCAF fighter wings within 83 Group of the Royal Air Force.

The Typhoon was a mediocrity as an air superiority or dogfighting aircraft, but when it was fitted with bomb racks and rocket projectile rails, it took on a fresh life working for the infantry. Once they overcame their skepticism that the air force could do anything useful for them, the infantry came to admire the Typhoon pilots for the way they defended them when their lives were on the line. Typhoon sections could orbit in what was called "Cab Rank"—waiting for the emergency call from the soldiers below. While the "Brylcreem Boys" of the air forces (as pilots in general were known) were the object of general derision, few infantry soldiers on the Allied side in 1944–45 had a bad word to say about Typhoon pilots.

When the Typhoon was assigned ground-attack duties, it became obvious that the rails for carrying rocket projectiles and the racks for bombs were not interchangeable quickly. Taking one off and putting the other on was several hours of work for armourers and riggers. Moreover, the techniques for firing rockets and dropping bombs were dissimilar.

Bombs were better against stationary targets, railway marshalling yards, railway embankments, bridges, troop concentrations, camouflaged heavy gun emplacements and, occasionally, a Gestapo headquarters. The RCAF Typhoons, being specialized on bombs, did not often attack armoured formations—that was for RAF rocket-firing Typhoons. If you fired rockets you were an RAF unit, if you dropped bombs, you were RCAF (there were, however, some RAF Typhoon squadrons that also specialized on bombs). It was the RAF Typhoon squadrons that provided close air support to the Canadian Army; No. 143 Wing RCAF used its Typhoons to support the British Army.

Harry remembers the attack profile for dive-bombing with two thousand-pound bombs, one under each wing, as if it were yesterday:

The dive itself was straight down. If you were not hanging in your straps, you were not straight down. If the target was heavily defended, we set our engine throttle for one-third open, dived from eleven thousand feet down to six thousand feet, released, and pulled hard. On the pullout the aircraft's airspeed indicator read 525 mph, the red line for the aircraft. If less heavily defended and we were feeling confident, we dove from eight thousand, released at four thousand. Now Roy Burden, over at 438, he told me he used to release at three thousand, but you'd be yanking pretty hard—me, I liked four thousand. If there was anti-aircraft fire coming up at us, we fired our cannons in the dive to keep their heads down. The typical delay on the bomb fuse was 1/25th of a second.

If we dropped bombs at low altitude in shallow twenty-five-degree dives or level flight, the fuse delay was eleven seconds, and this was set before takeoff based on the assigned target … When you release a bomb at four hundred mph, it is travelling at the same speed as you in the same direction, only separating from you in altitude. You don't want the bomb to explode until you clear the target. If we were assigned a railway embankment, for example, we would drop them so they buried themselves in the dirt below the rails, exploding when we were well clear. Bombs did a good job of curling up railway lines.

Harry Hardy invited me to attend the western Typhoon Pilots' Group lunch in 2001. A similar informal group exists in Eastern Canada. The groups have an exclusive membership, are by no means large, operate without any charter or rules of order and were not formed until the 1990s. At that first lunch I met about a dozen other Typhoon specialists, some of whom flew the aircraft with the RAF in air superiority or close air support, and one of whom flew a Typhoon in the photographic reconnaissance role. What these particular veterans shared was the bond that comes of surviving a tour of operations that the majority of pilots did not, and of flying the most powerful, heavily armed single-engine fighter of the British air forces.

It was customary in single-engine day-fighter squadrons to fly two hundred operational hours, typically 150 ops, to complete an operational tour.

Depending on when and where one served, this tour might take eighteen months to two years to complete. But the Typhoon's role proved so hazardous in 1944–45 that no Typhoon pilot on close air support duties could survive a tour based on the standards set for a Hurricane or Spitfire. After D-Day the rising number of casualties forced a reduction in the length of tour, first down to 125 ops, and when that proved too high, to 90 to 100 ops, typically one hundred flying hours.

Even with this restriction the tragic losses towards the end of a tour were unpredictable and seemed to happen more often on the Typhoon during or very near the last trip. As a result, commanding officers usually did not tell a pilot his next trip was his last. The jangled nerves a pilot might feel on his last strafing run could lead to a disastrous error. Moreover, some men could simply not complete ninety ops on the Typhoon. They were declared by their commanding officer to have completed their tour at sixty or seventy. At the end of the war any pilot with eighty or more ops on 143 Wing RCAF was considered in the operational language of the RCAF to be "tour expired."

After the heavy losses due to the Luftwaffe's Operation Bodenplatz on January 1, 1945, a call went out to all other fighter squadrons, soliciting volunteers to fly Typhoons. The elderly survivors of this fighter bomber recall ruefully that not a single fighter pilot on another type of aircraft volunteered. Typhoon pilots don't like being asked if they flew Spitfires; they want you to know, above all, that they were Typhoon pilots. It means a great deal to them when they say to you, "I flew Typhoons."

By the end of all hostilities in the Second World War, at least two hundred Canadian Typhoon specialists had been killed in action or in flying accidents, died of wounds or been taken prisoner of war, most in 1944–45. Many were lost in the last eight weeks of the war, and half a dozen died accidentally within a few months of war's end. Approximately one hundred of the Canadians who died on operations or in accidents were serving with RAF Typhoon squadrons, not with 143 Wing RCAF; some served as early as 1942, when the aircraft was still flying in air-to-air combat or close air support.

Profile – WILLIAM IVAN MOUAT
Born – July 16, 1920, Salt Spring Island, BC
Father – William Manson Mouat, an owner and secretary treasurer of Mouat Brothers Ltd, Salt Spring Island, BC
Mother – Effie Adelaide Wayne
Degrees & Awards – BA (UBC), BEd (U of Sask)
Post-war occupation – Teacher, principal, regional superintendent of education, NWT (Keewatin); consultant to Inuit Tapirisat of Canada; senior consultant (education), Dept of Indian Affairs
Marital status – Wife Susan Joy Greig, sons Greig and Jeremy, daughters Mary and Jennifer
Hobbies – Reading, writing short personal memoirs, walking

Ivan Mouat, who lives on Salt Spring Island, BC, as his family for over one hundred years, recalls that he and three other Canadians—Bob Deugo, Al Cluderay and Wally Coombes—were the first from Canada to check out on the Typhoon. This was in February 1942 when 56 Squadron became the first RAF squadron to receive the planes. Coombes later became a flight commander at 199 Squadron RAF, survived the war and now lives in Penticton, BC. Cluderay was killed in action with 56 on April 17, 1943; in the meantime Mouat and Deugo were sent to train new Typhoon pilots at 198 Squadron. While flying with 198, Mouat was shot down and taken prisoner on July 11, '43. His buddy Deugo was killed on July 20.

As Ivan explains, he preferred to fly "so low that I had to stand up to see over the waves," but his leader on July 11 had them up at five thousand feet, quite reckless in Mouat's view. The result was that flak from a barge destroyed his engine, and he was forced to bail out over Belgium. He was taken prisoner and was digging tunnels in the Centre Camp of Stalag Luft III when The Great Escape took place at North Camp on the night of March 24, 1944. The tunnel master for The Great Escape was a Canadian fighter pilot and former Ontario miner named Pilot Officer C.W. "Wally" Floody, shot down in October 1941 while flying with 401 Squadron. When it was later announced that fifty of the seventy-six escapees at the North Camp had been executed, Mouat recalls, the RAF group captain in charge at their camp, tears in his eyes, said that "if there are similar activities in Centre Camp, they shall not cease."

John Porter during the Second World War.

Profile – JOHN WALLACE PORTER

Born – November 12, 1921, Vancouver; raised in Prince George

Father – Herbert Isaac Porter, construction worker Grand Trunk railroad, fur buyer, prospector

Mother – Helen Stickney, Wisconsin

Post-war occupation – Helicopter pilot, Okanogan (1951), Canadian Coast Guard; Transport Canada civil aviation inspector

Marital status – Wife Aileen McDonald; daughters Christine, April and Jennifer

Hobbies – Musician, competitive ice dancer

John Wallace Porter had applied to become a wireless air gunner but the recruiting officer asked, "Why don't you want to be a pilot?" Porter had a Grade 10 education and was serving in the Canadian Army Artillery at Halifax when his call up came in August 1941. With his army discharge document in his hand, Corporal Porter was escorted by two captains into the Halifax RCAF recruiting centre. He felt certain his education would disqualify him from becoming a pilot, but as John recollects today,

the recruiting officer said, "If I pass you here as a pilot candidate, nobody will kick you out unless you fail. We have a houseful of air gunners this week. It is up to you." John's brother, Charles, had already gone through pilot training, and John jumped at the chance to follow him overseas. He struggled with the academics but was very happy when he earned his pilot's brevet and received his sergeant's stripes.

In February 1943, after John had arrived in England, he and Charles met up at Middleton St George, Durham, where Charles and his crew were flying with 419 Squadron RCAF, one of the squadrons of 6 Bomber Group RCAF. A month later John was training at No. 59 Operational Training Unit (OTU), at Millfield on Hurricanes when he was advised that Charles had been killed in action. Charles had been captain of a Halifax on a night mission to Berlin, and he had stayed at the controls of his bomber after it had been set on fire by flak, to allow all the crew to parachute safely. The survivors believed that he ought to have received a posthumous Victoria Cross; instead he was awarded the only other posthumous award, a Mention in Despatches.

Susceptible to the bends in the high-altitude pressure chamber, John Porter was restricted to flights below twenty-five thousand feet, which resulted in his posting—on Typhoons—to 247 Squadron, stationed at Bradwell Bay, Essex. It was a mixed-nationality squadron, with three other Canadians, a New Zealander, two Norwegians, a few Australians, a Welshman and a Scotsman. In mid-1943 the squadron carried two five-hundred-pound bombs and was assigned dive-bombing as well as escort to other Typhoons that were dive-bombing along the French coast: "By this time we know that the Typhoon is no match for an FW190 or Me109, but we could outrun the 109 in a dive ... we stayed up at eight thousand feet crossing the coast of France, which kept us clear of all but the heavy artillery." Re-equipped with rockets in 1944, 247 Squadron was assigned to ground attack on the continent.

* * *

Another Canadian who served with an RAF Typhoon squadron was George Martyn, from Welcome, Ontario. Shortly after completing his Initial Training School

(ITS) training at Eglinton Hunt Club in Toronto in early 1942, George broke his neck in a swimming accident on the farm and was rushed to the hospital at Port Hope. It looked as though his childhood dream of being a fighter pilot was over. The hospital reported his injuries to the nearest RCAF station, Trenton. Martyn remembered that a Wing Commander Noble, chief medical officer at Trenton, and Nursing Sister Montgomery took an interest in his case. They picked him up at the Port Hope hospital in an ambulance and took him to Trenton, where he spent four months in a cast and was nursed back to health.

Profile – DONALD EDWARD GEORGE MARTYN
Born – November 20, 1923, Welcome, ON
Died – September 26, 2004, Port Hope, ON
Father – Edward Howe Martin, farmer
Mother – Evelyn Rorke
Post-war occupation – Farmer for 10 years, construction foreman Stark Electrical, Oshawa
Marital status – Wife Olive Mason, son Larry, daughter Lynn
Hobbies – Golf

Dr Noble, seeing how heartbroken Martyn was, pulled some strings and got him on the Elementary Flying Training School (EFTS) course at Oshawa. No one questioned Noble's decision or did a second medical, which was a good thing for George because he could no longer rotate his left arm or lift his shoulder, and his left leg was permanently numb. He kept very quiet about the disability, flying eleven ops on the Hurricane out of Goose Bay, Labrador; twenty-one ops on Spitfires in Britain; and a further sixty-five ops on the Typhoon in northwest Europe. On his post-war discharge medical, the examining doctor was shocked to learn that George had been overseas on operations when, in his opinion, he was unfit for RCAF service of any kind.

There were very few Spitfire pilots who volunteered to go on Typhoons, but Martyn was one of them. He was bored with patrols in northern England, where nothing happened. He asked to go on the rocket-firing Typhoons and was posted to the RAF's 137 Squadron of 124 Wing at Eindhoven, Holland, in October '44.

When I asked George how he functioned in combat so physically disabled, he replied, "I could just curl my fingers around the throttle in the Typhoon, and I had full use of the thumb on my left hand, and that is all I needed to fire the rockets. My right arm and right thumb were normal. I did two forced landings in the Typhoon and walked away without a scratch; I never wanted to bail out because so many pilots hit the tail in that aircraft."

No. 137 Squadron was a multinational mixture of pilots from all parts of the British Empire, and, in the last eight months of the war, Martyn recalled, it suffered approximately 150 per cent casualties (i.e., all of the original pilots and 50 per cent of their replacements). According to George, No. 124 Wing RAF was strict about pilots completing one hundred ops, more so than at the RCAF's 143 Wing, which explains the horrific losses. "I was good, but I was also very lucky. You have got to have a lot of luck. Many good pilots didn't make it … My philosophy, which all of us had to have if we were going to fly rocket-firing Typhoons, was, 'It can't happen to me.'"

On January 1, '45, George's unit was airborne, attacking trains when the Germans struck at the Allied airfields. He and Flight Lieutenant George Clubley spotted and destroyed an He111 bomber west of the German town of Hamelin as they were returning home to their airfield. They could have destroyed two Me262s on the runway of a Luftwaffe airfield, but by this time they were out of ammunition.

His most vivid memory of the crossing of the Rhine in March, where 137 and the other squadrons were assigned to suppress the 88mm anti-aircraft batteries, was the wing commander's morning briefing: "I don't care how many of you boys I lose, as long we don't lose any of the Dakotas." Wing Commander North-Lewis was leading the wing and was the first Typhoon pilot shot down that morning. His "boys" could not help chuckling at the irony, but five days later they were glad to see North-Lewis walk home with German prisoners of war in tow. The soldiers who had captured him when he stepped out of his Typhoon later surrendered to him, and he marched them west.

On VE Day as Martyn was walking into the officers' mess to celebrate, he received a telegram from home saying that his mother had died of cancer. It meant a lot to George to know that his sister Doris had told his mother that the war was over and that George had survived.

In June he transferred from 137 over to 440 Squadron RCAF and flew with that unit till they disbanded in August. When he got home to Welcome, his girlfriend, Judith, advised him that she was marrying a fellow who had served in the Royal Canadian Navy. Having used up most of his luck, George decided he needed a safe job, and his father needed his son on the farm. He met his wife, Olive Mason, at a Wesleyville-versus-Welcome baseball game, and they have a son and a daughter and four grandchildren. George Martyn died on September 26, 2004, after a brief illness.

* * *

The nominal strength at 143 Wing was twenty-seven pilots per squadron, though Typhoon squadrons rarely had a full roster of pilots. No. 143 Wing commenced flying operations at the end of March 1944 and disbanded in August 1945. Of those who served in that period, more than eighty pilots died, and half a dozen ground crew. In the bomber campaign conducted by RAF Bomber Command between 1942 and 1945, total losses were about 58 per cent of those who served, and 44 per cent of Bomber Command personnel are estimated to have died. While the odds of surviving a tour were considerably better for flyers on single engine day fighters than for flyers on bombers, particularly in the last two years of the war, this was not true in the case of Typhoons providing close air support.

In addition to the Falaise Gap and the Battle for Arnhem, Harry Hardy participated in close air support to many other significant ground battles of the campaign in northwest Europe. He flew his final op, his ninety-sixth, on the first day of the crossing of the Rhine, March 24, 1944. By late October '44, after thirty ops, he had been promoted to Blue section leader at 440 Squadron. With about one-third of his tour over, seven of his flying mates had been killed. On November 2 he lost his long-time friend Ralph McDonald in a flying accident when Ralph struck a church steeple. On December 3, Derric Sugden died when he landed downwind with his Typhoon—bombs still hanging under the wings—then overshot the end of the runway and drowned in the canal beyond.

TYPHOON PILOTS MEMORIAL, NORMANDY

In June 1944 a ten-year-old named Jacques Bréhin witnessed a Typhoon crash and watched its wounded pilot parachute down onto his father's farm. In 1989 he started a fundraising campaign to erect a memorial to what the Typhoon contributed to the liberation of France. The Typhoon Pilots Memorial cost more than 554,000 French francs and was paid for over ten years by generous donations from the private citizens of Australia, Canada, France, Holland, Britain and the United States. It is located at Noyers Bocage, Normandy, not far from Caen. On the curved memorial wall are the names in gold of the 151 Typhoon pilots who died in the Battle for Normandy between May and August of 1944—42 of those being Canadian. There is also a second plaque with a dedication to the 666 Typhoon pilots and 21 supporting staff of all the Allied nations who lost their lives between May 1944 and October 1945.

The Typhoons supported the US Army in the forested Ardennes in December in what has become known as the Battle of the Bulge. When the weather cleared on Christmas Day, Hardy flew his fifty-eighth op in support of the American forces at St Vith. His Pulverizer II was so badly damaged by flak in the area of the rudder and rear stabilizer that he was unable to control the machine below two hundred mph. He bailed out from the right side of the cockpit, managed to miss the tail and was astounded by the beautiful silence as he floated downward towards the snow-covered earth. The British soldiers who saw him land in a tree took him to their mess and poured a glass of whiskey. Harry was shaking a lot and needed both hands to down his drink.

He ultimately flew six ops in the Ardennes. Though train-busting was dangerous, the Ardennes battlefield was more so, and Harry was glad to return to trains around the end of the month. He believes that his flying performance in the Battle of the Bulge had much to do with his later receiving the DFC.

On December 27 his mentor Donald "Buck" Jenvey, DFC, MiD, shot down an Me109. Jenvey was so excited about the victory that he performed a large victory roll around Harry Hardy and his wingman, Bill Clifford, before forming up to go home. Two days later his plane was damaged by the debris of an exploding train car on his ninety-eighth and final op. Harry watched Buck get out of his crashed Typhoon and run towards the trees; he turned as they flew by and waved to them. Harry says today that "during the two-minute silence on Armistice Day, I always see Buck standing there waving to me." Jenvey escaped and evaded for more than two months but was shot and killed by German soldiers while attempting to cross the Rhine in March '45.

With Jenvey gone, Harry was now in charge of "A" Flight and two-thirds of the way through his tour. Since his arrival seventeen pilots had been lost, and now Harry had to write the letters home to bereaved families. He describes it as a very difficult task which he took quite seriously. The following is just one of the six letters Harry wrote and the response he received from Mrs Passmore, from her home in Hensall, Ontario, where her husband was a minister:

HOLLAND
6 - 2 - 45

Dear Mrs Passmore:

It is with the deepest regret that I take pen in hand to add my sympathy in your hour of pain and grief. War is a terrible thing, it takes its toll of lives as it passes and whose turn it is next no one but God knows.

On the morning of his last trip Deke and I were kidding as usual as we dressed in our flying gear and prepared for the trip ahead. It was his first trip back off leave and he was keen to get back into the battle.

We were on our way home across Germany when we spotted a train. We peeled off and went down on it. I saw Deke's tail blow off, his Tiffie shudder and plunge into the ground. It all happened so quick he did not have time to think nor to feel any pain. It would not be right for me to give you any false hopes as I was only a few feet from him and I did not see him get out. I am sorry that it had to be Deke's turn so soon, he was well liked by all the pilots and his ground crew couldn't do enough for him. Please pass my feelings to Jonsy as he has told me much about her. If there is anything I can tell you further, do not hesitate to ask me.

Yours very sincerely,
Harry Hardy
Flight Commander
"A" Flight

MRS. PASSMORE'S REPLY

We cannot realize the effort it required of you to write that letter, but we wish to know that we surely appreciated your effort and we only wish we could repay you for what you have done for us. Before we got your letter we were worried about what happened—how it happened and where it happened—and we thought if someone could only tell us these things it would be a measure of consolation to us in our time of sorrow. We thank you for imparting this information to us.

If the rules of warfare will permit, we would like to know what became of the body. Do the Germans bury the dead and mark the place? Or does the Red Cross look after same?

Roy Burden (right) and his good friend Bert Chaplow circa 1935 at Lulu Island, Richmond, BC.

Profile – HERBERT ROY BURDEN

Born – November 15, 1919, Regina; lived in Richmond, BC, from age 11

Died – January 28, 2005, Port Moody, BC

Father – Ernest Burden, track repairman, CNR

Mother – Ada Shepherd

Decorations & Medals – MiD

Post-war occupation – Postal clerk, civil servant

Marital status – Wife Virginia Hampson, married in August 1941; daughters Carol Lynne (died in 2002) and Dianne Lee

Hobbies – House-building, camping, hiking

I had my first conversation with Roy Burden at the western Typhoon Pilots' Group luncheon to which Harry Hardy had invited me back in 2001. Many other conversations followed over the next four years.

But our first encounter was particularly vivid for me because Roy expressed so much rage and indignation at the kind of events that history books usually don't even mention. As we sat opposite each other eating our lunch he told me, unbidden, story after story. They were the sort of stories that darken with age but freshen in memory when retold.

He told of an administrative or engineering person from 143 Wing who, while out for a walk one day, came across a young German soldier and shot him dead. As Roy indignantly expressed it: "That wasn't his job, he had no right to do that. He could have taken him prisoner, he wasn't doing any harm. We pilots were appalled. He gave him no chance, and, in any case, it was we who were responsible for killing."

Roy Burden recalled with horror the Canadian Army lending rifles to German prisoners of war so they could execute two of their own following a court martial held by the German armed forces in Holland, this *after* the armistice had been signed. It was not a story I had ever heard, so I investigated.

The two men executed on May 13, 1945, were named Bruno Dorfer and Rainer Beck. They were transported to their execution in a truck driven by the Seaforth Highlanders of Canada, and the rifles used were German weapons that a Seaforth officer took from a locked room and handed to the Germans. The orders for execution came from a German general named Blaskowitz, whom the Allied commanders allowed to operate in Holland with full authority over his own army for weeks after the war had ended.

But Burden's deepest disgust was for the Holocaust deniers who were getting publicity in Canada, and the journalists who lent them credibility. Roy had walked through Bergen-Belsen concentration camp in April 1945, attempting to comprehend the incomprehensible. He wore coveralls that had been sprayed up the sleeves and down the legs with white disinfecting powder for protection. He photographed the mass graves, each holding a thousand or more bodies, all sprinkled with quicklime. As Roy approached the camp he stopped just outside the barbed wire to read the faded and chipped German signs, each marked with a skull and crossbones. They cautioned Germans to stay clear because of the danger of typhus. ("The people around there said they didn't know anything, but those signs had to have been up there for years.")

As ruthless as the air war had become in its closing months, as devastating as unbridled Allied air power had been against the German military and civilian population, the last operational days from April 15 and the liberation of Bergen-Belsen through May 4 were unparalleled. The German people had coined a word for the enemy fighter pilots: they were "Terror-Fliegers." If they caught one of them coming down in a parachute, they might stone him with rocks, pitchfork him to death or hang him from a lamppost. It had happened to Typhoon pilots who had had the misfortune to be apprehended by civilians rather than soldiers or airmen, and it had happened to Spitfire pilots on armed reconnaissance. Harry Hardy and other 440 Squadron pilots on their first operation out of Brussels into Germany were cautioned to surrender to a German soldier, not a German civilian, in the event they were shot down. Intelligence officers were aware of the civilian attacks on downed aircrew.

Roy was the first fighter pilot I interviewed who described his feelings of revenge, of his personal hatred against an enemy that seemed so remorseless. He saw many of his friends blown up, some while actually flying on his wing, and because of the proximity to the event, Typhoon pilots could often identify the anti-aircraft gun battery that had killed their friends.

The German four-barrelled 37mm cannons were particularly lethal, and Roy can remember on one occasion diving vertically on the gun crew to avenge what they had done to his pal. His four 20mm cannon could eradicate all sign of life with a one-second burst, but his action also gave the flak gunners a no-deflection shot on Roy's Typhoon. "Not so smart," Roy notes.

Burden had been in the war a long time when he flew the Typhoon, and had well over a thousand flying hours when he checked out on it. For many instructors who escaped the British Commonwealth Air Training Plan (BCATP), the Typhoon was their introduction to combat. Roy had done well in pilot training, soloing early with less than four hours' dual instruction on the Harvard. He graduated from Yorkton, Saskatchewan, in August 1941, and was immediately commissioned. He married his girlfriend Virginia Hampson that same month. After two years of instructing, in the summer of '43 he converted to the Hurricane at Bagotville, Quebec, and joined 118 Squadron at Annette Island, Alaska, where he checked out on the P40 and flew some reconnaissance patrols over the ocean. He recalls that the worst weather he ever flew in was at Annette Island.

But the RCAF decided to take three squadrons and all their personnel in Canada and send them to Britain—where they would then receive their aircraft and form an operational wing. This was the first time the RCAF had taken front-line squadrons serving on air defence duties in Canada and shipped them overseas. Roy's squadron, No. 118, became 438 under the wartime overseas numbering system, No. 123

BACKGROUND ON THE DORFER AND BECK EXECUTIONS

As scholar Chris Madsen, University of Victoria, has shown in his study of this appalling event, such actions to allow surrendered troops to execute their own were clearly a violation of the 1929 Geneva Convention. Canadian Army officers, from Lieutenant General Guy Foulkes downward to one Seaforth major, acquiesced to the principles of Nazi-inspired military laws.

According to Madsen, under the Geneva Convention, even assuming that a German court martial had any legal weight after May 7, no prisoner could be executed less than three months from sentencing. Bruno Dorfer and Rainer Beck were two of more than a dozen German soldiers summarily executed by their own military with Canadian Army cooperation.

In a final irony, the head of the court martial, Wilhelm Köhn, was acquitted in the 1960s of murder charges brought in a civil suit by Beck's sister. Köhn's defence, in part, was that the execution was the responsibility of certain officers in the Canadian Army.

Roy Burden in cockpit of Hurricane at OTU in Ayr. Scotland, 1944.

became 439, and No. 111 became 440. Congregated at Ayr, Scotland, the three squadrons transitioned to Hawker Hurricane fighter bombers followed by Hawker Typhoons and formed 143 Fighter Bomber Wing, a first for the RCAF overseas and also the RCAF's first fighter bomber wing.

The first wing commander (flying) for 143 was a popular British officer, Wing Commander Roy Marples. He had survived the Battle of Britain and was a veteran of the Western Desert plus the Greek and Crete air wars. (He told Roy Burden he had been "degreased and excreted" in both places.) He was very capable operationally; he had flown with Johnnie Johnson at 616 Squadron RAF; he had a great sense of humour, liked the ladies of the Women's Auxuliary Air Force and liked to party. Canadians from the Western Desert campaign of 1942–43 fondly remembered Roy Marples as commanding officer of 238 Squadron. He was considered a great leader with the ability to turn around a bad unit. Burdette Gillis, a graduate from Yorkton the same summer as Burden, still lives in his hometown of Rouleau, Saskatchewan. He recalls being No. 2 to Roy Marples in the Western Desert and trusting him implicitly.

But since one of the purposes of 143 Wing was to showcase the RCAF, whose senior officers had been denied most of the top positions in the Second Tactical Air Force, it was decided that a Canadian should be the commanding officer. Marples was gone in less than a month. Burden's disgust with this small-minded policy is still evident in his voice today: "They took Marples away from us because of 'Canadianization,' gave him to a Free French unit, and his No. 2 ran into him just after takeoff, cut the tail off his aircraft, and he was killed. It was a terrible loss ... any one of us would have followed him into hell." Johnnie Johnson in his autobiography remembers Marples for his "breezy nature and never-ending fund of spicy stories."

Burden flew his first op with 438 on March 20, '44, from an airfield at Hurn, located about four miles inland from the English Channel in Dorset. This was the first day of operations for the squadron in Europe, a routine sweep of the Cherbourg peninsula of France and the Channel Islands. Roy flew all the significant ops leading up to and including D-Day, and after D-Day was featured in the *Star Weekly* by the well-known journalist Gregory Clark.

Clark had been given a battlefield commission with the Mounted Rifles in the Great War, receiving a Military Cross for his actions at Vimy Ridge. (Among many other journalistic duties, he had offered Ernest Hemingway his first post-war newspaper job at the *Star Weekly* in 1920.)

It was Clark's first occasion to see a Typhoon and meet a Typhoon pilot. He let Roy talk about air combat, which included an embellishment by Burden as to the effect of "G" forces on the pullout from the dive. Roy's weight on a 7-G pullup was actually about a thousand pounds, not two tons (see reproduction of Clark's newspaper story, "Diving 6000 Feet Straight Down").

At the rate of attrition typical of a Typhoon pilot in that year, Roy Burden normally would have been finished his tour by the fall. But he and many other pilots liked to ride motorcycles, and he came a cropper in a shell hole in August. His injuries were so serious that he spent the next six months in Britain in hospital. Motorcycle riding was later prohibited for pilots in 143 Wing because so many were being injured. After his recovery it looked promising that he would get a month of home leave. However, someone noticed that he was about forty ops short of a full tour. They sent him back to 438, which was now stationed at Eindhoven, Holland, at airfield B78. He was, by his own admission, ambivalent about going back into action and certainly would have preferred to have gone home on leave.

No. 438 lost three commanding officers between late December 1944 and June 1945. Roy had been promoted to "B" Flight commander when his own flight commander was killed, and Bob Spooner was "A" Flight commander for similar reasons. According to Spooner the squadron was sent to England to improve its bombing skills, which operationally had been weak. In March 1945 at a bombing and gunnery refresher in Britain, Roy was witness to the death of his squadron commander, Jimmie Hogg, DFC. Roy was next in line after Jimmie to bomb a target floating in the water, and there was a crew on the ground to assess each pilot's performance. Burden recalls:

It was a nice clear day, he is ahead of me, and I can hear him talk to the people on the ground. There is radio chatter, then all of a sudden he has gone in ... a huge splash not terribly far from the target. I was thunderstruck ... I am sitting up there with my target bombs on, hardly knowing what to do; I could hardly go ahead and bomb after that ... it was a real shocker. When you are on these practice things there is nobody shooting at you, so you get in closer, slower, sneak on a bit of flap to get a good mark on the board. I am not sure but Jimmie probably went down too far, pulled out too tight ... You stall a Typhoon you are in deep do-do. If he had been doing it on an op he would have gone down faster ... It is a whole different ball game on operations versus the range when nobody is shooting at you. It was quite a shock and Bangs, the adjutant, advises me after I land that I am now squadron commander.

Burden, coming off his sick leave, refused the appointment, saying he had not been back on operations long enough and might commit errors that could kill people. In any case, there was a general feeling that being a 438 Squadron commanding officer was unlucky. Bob Spooner was slightly junior in rank to Burden. In the fall of '44 he had, from time to time, jointly performed the duties of an acting squadron commander along with the other flight commander at the time, Andy Lambros, DFC. When Squadron Leader Pete Wilson arrived to take command of 438 in late December, and then died of gunshot wounds in the German attack on Eindhoven on January 1, 1945, Spooner was acting squadron leader again. Despite not wanting the job as squadron commander Spooner inherited it as the next most senior officer in line.

Profile – ROBERT EDWARD SPOONER
Born – September 12, 1920, Victoria, BC
Father – Frank Spooner, chocolate and candy store owner, Victoria
Mother – Ruby Grosser
Decorations & Medals – DFC
Post-war occupation – Chocolate maker and Victoria manager with Welsh's Candy for six years, manager of Butler Brothers building supplies store for 30 years
Marital status – Wife Marie Graham, sons Roderick Norman and Robert Lawrence, daughter Kathryn Anne
Hobbies – Fishing, barbershop choir (four-part harmony)

One of three children of an American mother and a Newfoundland father, Bob was born and raised in Victoria, BC. Frank Spooner had served in the Great War with the Second Canadian Mounted Rifles and received a Military Medal; he refused a commission in that war, but he lied about his age in the Second World War and became a warrant officer 1st class in the Royal Canadian Army Service Corps. Both his sons joined the RCAF. Richard trained as a bomb aimer in 1944 and flew just one operation when the war ended in Europe. He volunteered for Pacific war service, but with the dropping of the atomic bombs at Hiroshima and Nagasaki, Japan, in August, Richard Spooner, like thousands of others, was quickly released from the RCAF, as the war was now over.

Bob Spooner put in eighteen months as an elementary flying school instructor before arriving in Bournemouth looking for a job on fighters. Due to the thousands of surplus pilots, he waited three months to get to an Advanced Flying Unit (AFU) and OTU. At the end of the OTU training, some of his course mates were posted to Spitfire squadrons and some, like Bob himself, were posted to the Second Tactical Air Force to fly Typhoons. His Spitfire course mates wished him luck and said in a pitying voice, "It has been nice knowing you." Typhoon pilots after D-Day were not expected to survive.

Spooner arrived at airfield B58 at Melsbroek, Holland, in mid-September '44 and was witness to the death of his own flight commander, Albert "Buck" Newsome, on October 7:

Newsome and I and two sections of 438 knocked off a train at a Y junction. I was green, and I knew only to drop bombs when he did and protect his rear. That is what he had instructed me to do. Buck decided to do a second pass, so I had to go with him ... The flak cars at each end of the train took a bead; they were ready for us on this second pass, and all hell broke loose. His plane oscillated vertically, his head was down and he did not respond to my calls, then his Typhoon rolled over and went into the trees. It was devastating at this stage, so early in my tour, when you have a lot of confidence in the experienced fellow ... but you press on and make the best of it ...

I soon became a flight commander, but my navigation abilities were not really good, being unfamiliar with the local area. Bob Fox, who knew the area, steered me towards targets if I seemed uncertain. But you smarten up rather quickly, because you can't afford too many mistakes. You can't be a sheep, you have to make up your own mind. Had I followed some other pilot's lead I could have been killed several times over ...

You really don't know until you do it how you are going to fare [as a flight commander] ... some guys stand up well to it and some don't. It was a treat to me to know that I could do it—a relief. I didn't ask to be a flight commander, and I didn't think I should be the one because I was a "newcomer" to the squadron with only nineteen operational trips. But they thought I had something, and they were happy with me. And that is all that matters, isn't it? ...

I think I had a guardian angel that looked after me, and that is why I am alive. For some period we were having problems with defective fuses on our thousand-pound bombs. Several pilots were killed instantly when the bombs exploded immediately upon release from the

Courtesy of the Wayne Ralph Collection

Bob Spooner in his home in Saanichton, Vancouver Island, in June 2001.

LAC FRED BERG, ARMOURER, 438 SQUADRON, REMEMBERS A CLOSE CALL

Leading Aircraftman Fred Berg and Leading Aircraftman Peter Moore were changing the barrels on a Typhoon at Ayr, Scotland. Peter assumed that Fred had already removed the belt-fed mechanism from the cannons. He sat in the cockpit and pressed the firing button. This was a routine procedure to release the breech block to the forward position. Instantly about seven 20mm rounds were fired. With the body angle of the Typhoon being fairly steep, the rounds headed skyward. One round struck a church steeple in the city of Ayr. Fred and Peter attempted to conceal the ejected casings, but were unsuccessful, and an inquiry and punishment followed.

This same kind of maintenance error happened at an airfield in France to Roy Burden and Bob Spooner as they were waiting to take off on a sortie. Fortunately, the body angle of the offending Typhoon ensured that the rounds passed over the top of their canopies and not through them. Nevertheless, it was a frightening episode to be sitting in the queue for takeoff and see tracers whistling directly over your head, with no way to evade.

Fred Berg recollected to the author that each Hispano-Suiza cannon barrel weighed 109 pounds, and was manufactured of the finest Swedish steel on a Swedish assembly line. Berg believes that 50 percent of those barrels were shipped to Britain, the other 50 percent to Germany.

aircraft. On one op I was delayed getting off because a wheel broke through the ice and by the time the ground crew got my plane back on the taxiway, the squadron had already set course for Germany. The squadron leader told me to stay put on the ground, rather than attempt to catch up. I left my Typhoon fully armed and later that day another pilot took it on an operation. He was killed when, due to the defective fuses, they exploded on release over the target."

Spooner held the acting squadron leader's position after Hogg's death for a couple of weeks until Jack Biernes, DFC and Bar, arrived on April 6—back for a second tour on Typhoons but his third tour in total, following P40s in Alaska. One of the most experienced fighter pilots in the RCAF, and one of the best-liked, Biernes died in a flying accident on June 1. Also on that day the *London Gazette* published Spooner's citation:

I got a DFC and I really can't tell you why because Roy did exactly the same job [and got only a Mention in Despatches]. I feel badly that he didn't get a DFC because I don't feel that I did anything heroic to deserve it. I think I got it for the squadron, because everybody did as much as I did and risked their lives just as much as I did ... I'm wearing it for them, for those who were lost. A lot of good guys went for the chop.

Roy Burden is one of the few Typhoon pilots, due to his interruption in tour, to have served before D-Day as well as in the Normandy campaign of '44, but also in '45 during the crossing of the Rhine. He flew his ninety-eighth op on May 4, the last day for combat on the German front, and had logged 112 hours, 40 minutes on operations. Not given to superstition or the notion of foreshadowing, Roy had heard that Flying Officer George Burden (no relation), a pilot from New Brunswick serving with 439 on the same airfield, had been killed in action on May 3.

Given his record as a flight commander, Roy Burden's logbook was endorsed by Wing Commander Frank Grant, DSO, DFC, Croix de Guerre as "excellent squadron commander material." When I asked Burden about this appraisal his only response was: "It is amazing what a bribe can do for you." Roy traded his well-worn flying jacket to an American soldier for a German Walther P38 pistol. He never flew again after the war.

MEMORIES OF BELSEN
MAY 5, 1945

Near to the incinerator a stack of shoes 12 feet high, 60 feet long, and 6 feet deep were piled as neat as cord wood. A girl of about twenty years of age showed us around. She looked bright and fairly strong. She explained that one of her duties was to serve food at one of the long tables. Anyone at the table who appears unable to survive the night got no food. She was strong enough to fight off the others and had the food for herself. She told us a guard was on the point of shooting her when the British arrived. She ducked as the guard raised his rifle and a soldier shot him ...

A small gypsy girl in a very threadbare cotton dress was a distressing example ... Her eyes had a vacant look, her frame so small and fragile; I knew she was going to die. The home for her and her mother was a shallow hole in the ground, covered by a ragged sheet. It was a graphic illustration of how low in the social scale the gypsies were when they could not get shelter in the long shabby barracks.

We passed out chocolate bars to our guide and other healthier-looking inmates, although a doctor warned it would do no good, but then he said it would do no harm. It might taste good.

It was days before we could get the smell out of our systems. It was a happy day near the end of June, to fly over Belsen and see the buildings going up in flames. The incinerator was left intact.

F/L Victor Le Gear, DFC, 439 Squadron

When he arrived back in Canada the newspapers wrote a story about his reunion with the daughter who did not remember him. At loose ends for a while, he was uncertain how to shape his life and decided to take a civil service test as a postal clerk. He achieved more than 90 per cent, perhaps not surprising for a veteran who had been rated above average at everything he had done in the RCAF. He joined the federal government and served for thirty-five years as a postal worker. When I asked him why he had decided to do so, Roy chuckled and said, "Well, I guess I just wanted a quiet job."

* * *

Bob Spooner completed his tour of operations seventeen days before Roy, flying his ninety-seventh op on April 17 on Typhoon F3V—"V for victory," he pointed out to me. He felt no great sense of elation. He was now left behind, irrelevant to the day-to-day functioning of the squadron, wanting to fly more yet not wanting to. He hitchhiked back from Brussels to Britain on a Stirling being used to evacuate casualties and celebrated VE Day in Scotland with a well-to-do Scottish family who had volunteered to put up veterans who were on leave or resting from operations.

He took his release at Vancouver, and the lieutenant-governor of British Columbia awarded Bob his DFC. His parents had run a candy shop before the war, Spooner's Chocolates, on Yates Street in Victoria, and because he had experience with the family business he decided with his veteran's credits to apprentice with Welsh's Candy as a chocolate maker. He remembers that his post-war adjustment took some time: "I didn't really know what I wanted. It was now a year after the war and I was bit lost. I had my medical with the RCAF, and it was fine, and they offered me a flying officer's rank, but then reneged and said I was too old. When they did come back later saying they had changed their minds, I said 'No, thanks.' But I came *that close* to an RCAF career!"

* * *

Profile – MARTIN JOHN PETERSON
Born – December 27, 1911, Vancouver
Died – December 23, 2003, Surrey, BC
Father – Martin Christian Peterson, born in Denmark in 1870, logger, also delivered bread with a horse and carriage
Mother – Louella Melinda Sprourt
Post-war occupation – Manager at the Shellburn Refinery, Burnaby
Marital status – Wife Minnie Margaret McIntosh died 2001; sons Douglas and Martin
Hobbies – Handyman, auto repairs, golf

After breakfast the maintenance crews had formed up in front of the NCO-in-charge who was reading out the day's orders. It was New Year's Day, 1945, at airfield B78, Eindhoven, Holland. With no advance warning, from four different directions, German fighters at low altitude howled across the field, strafing as they went. The airmen on morning parade scattered in all directions, looking for cover, any cover—a slit trench filled with icy water, a wooden bunk bed, even an oil disposal pool.

Leading Aircraftman Martin John "Pat" Peterson and his crew squatted down next to the blast wall at the back door of the nearest hangar. An FW190 came in from the south, directly over the hangar. The pilot looked down at the airmen and waved to them as he roared overhead. He didn't come back around. The attack was over in less than thirty minutes. Operation Bodenplatz, the German Luftwaffe's final attempt to cripple Allied air power on the ground, was a complete surprise but a military failure. However, at 10 a.m. at Eindhoven, with some seventy aircraft damaged or on fire and the wounded being carried into the medical tent, it looked anything but a failure.

Peterson wondered if any of this could have been foreseen. As he walked around the airfield, he remembered the German Me262 jet that had flown high overhead as the attack commenced. The wreckage of an FW190 that had been shot down was still smouldering as Pat peered in the cockpit. The German pilot was burned beyond recognition, and Pat's first thought was, *You poor bastard*. Leading Aircraftman Alf Raynor, Pat's best friend and a practical sort of man, nodded at the remains of a Typhoon he had overhauled in maintenance and complained, "Jesus Christ, Pat, all that bloody work gone for nothing!"

Later, Peterson discovered that the back of his battledress was shredded, and when he hung the jacket up, a bullet—a ricochet—fell to the floor. He could not remember when or how he might have been struck. He was luckier than Corporal Albert Eardley, Flying Officer Ross Keller and Squadron Leader Pete Wilson, who all died that day. The war now seemed as though it might go on forever, and he would never get home to Vancouver and his wife, Minnie.

Martin "Pat" Peterson had started life in Vancouver in December 1911. He dropped out of school in 1924 to help support his family. His first job, which paid $5 a week, was as a mechanic's helper at the Hornby Garage, on the corner where the Hotel Vancouver is now located. After ten years in the car-repair business, he was hired to work at Shell Oil's Shellburn Refinery in Burnaby and, apart from his war service in the RCAF, Pat stayed with Shell Oil until his retirement in 1973.

Because he was employed in an essential service, Peterson was not required to join the armed forces, but he enlisted in the RCAF in June 1942. At his age, with a Grade 8 education, he knew he could not become a pilot. Following the Wartime Emergency Training Program (WETP) at Vancouver—usually referred to by airmen as "Wet Pee"—and Manning Depot in Edmonton, he was shipped to St. Thomas, Ontario, to the largest technical training school in the BCATP. At age thirty-one, Pat was the oldest student on the fitters' course.

His first posting in April 1943 was back to the west coast, to No. 3 Repair Depot, RCAF Station Jericho Beach. But after only two weeks, Pat was sent by boat north to the US airfield at Annette Island, Alaska, where he was attached to 118, a P40 squadron. Peterson worked on the flight line servicing machines for daily air defence patrols, but a complaint he lodged with his boss, Sergeant Alexander, changed his career with the RCAF.

Pat—whose civilian job at Shell involved blending oils—complained that the oil drums on the airfield were not properly sealed. Dirt and sand were getting in through the bungholes of the drums.

Pat's casual bitching highlighted his extensive pre-war experience at the Shell Oil refinery. Alexander felt he was wasted in flights, doing the simple routines on aircraft between operations, and transferred him to maintenance, where engine overhauls were completed. For the rest of the war that was where Peterson worked.

Pat moved to Britain with 118 Squadron, re-numbered as 438, and from March 1944 to August 1945 worked in second-line maintenance (as opposed to flight-line duties) as the only leading aircraftman commanding an overhaul crew for the Typhoon's 2,200-horsepower Napier Sabre IIB engine. As a maintenance fitter Peterson despised the Allison engine on the P40, admired the Merlin of the Spitfire but was in awe of the brute power of the Napier Sabre. As a fitter he was on close, intimate terms with its shortcomings; it was complex, fouled its plugs easily and sometimes caught fire. Pat recalls:

> The Sabre was the hardest engine I ever had to start—it had twenty-four cylinders in banks of six, two horizontal-type engines [attached] to one shaft. It was a sleeve-valve engine that generated lots of friction as the sleeves moved. It was started by explosive cartridge, with each Typhoon having five cartridges. We used five sometimes and then sometimes more just to get it going. In maintenance we routinely put one mechanic in the cockpit, hand on the stick, with another guy on the wing reaching in to ram the throttle full forward when it caught ... If it did not start you had to pull the twenty-four spark plugs and inject oil into twenty-four cylinders, a time-consuming process.

On D-Day plus sixteen, 143 Fighter Bomber Wing moved to France. The first thing Pat noticed in France was the constant noise of artillery bombardment, as B9 airfield at Lantheuil was located only a short distance from the front. At night the pyrotechnic display from artillery fire rimmed the horizon in beautiful but deadly colours. Eight airmen slept in each tent on straw-filled *paillaises*, their Lee Enfield rifles propped against the centre pole. Food was served from a mess tent, but there were no tables. You took your food outside, sat on your helmet and ate.

Courtesy of the Pat Peterson Collection

143 Wing RCAF mechanics work on a Typhoon, winter 1944-45, Eindhoven, Holland.

The airfields were sometimes attacked by German fighter bombers scattering anti-personnel "butterfly" bombs, some of which hung up in trees and exploded later. Shrapnel literally fell from the sky, debris caused by anti-aircraft guns fired by the gunners of the RAF regiment protecting the airfield. This debris could and did injure airmen and, like everyone else, Pat always wore his helmet when anti-aircraft fire was intense.

Maintaining and servicing the Typhoons in a combat zone was hard, hazardous work. On July 16, Leading Aircraftmen John Holmes and Richard Wilman were killed when a Typhoon on takeoff collided with 438's dispersal area, and a bomb that should not have exploded did. The pilot, Flight Lieutenant Carl McConvey, was also killed in the explosion. Holmes's twin brother worked in maintenance with Pat and was inconsolable.

Death could arrive in many forms in the Second Tactical Air Force. A German 88mm shell could kill you as you rode in a three-ton truck from one temporary airfield to the next. You might, just for curiosity, poke around an abandoned German fighter and set off a booby trap. Friendly fire was a frequent risk, perhaps in the form of a US Army Air Force (USAAF) P38 pilot who thought that Typhoons were FW190s. During that summer an American pilot shot down a Typhoon pilot right over B9—he fortunately survived, but a complaint was lodged with the USAAF.

Leading Aircraftman Peterson was recommended for promotion by Flight Sergeant Leon Pedley, MiD, several times, but promotion never came. Pat had a speech impediment: he stuttered. It was felt by those higher up that this might place men at risk in an emergency. Pedley, who was just a year older than Pat, apologized that he couldn't get Pat his stripes. Pat comforted his boss by noting that Shell Oil was making up the shortfall of income while he served and sending the difference to his wife, Minnie. Stripes or not, Pedley put Peterson in charge of his own maintenance crew.

As a lowly Leading Aircraftman, Pat had more opportunities for leave and exploration. He liked being an eyewitness and carried a camera with him everywhere he went. But sometimes his adventures turned dangerous, and he gained horrific insights into man's inhumanity to man along with some bad memories that have lasted a lifetime. RCAF personnel were welcome guests in the towns and cities that were liberated in the summer of 1944. Pat was befriended during his first leave in newly liberated Brussels by Georgette Terrine and her family. Georgette's brother, Henri, fighting in the Resistance, had been captured and thrown into a concentration camp. He escaped but was recaptured, and the Gestapo executed him not long after Pat and Georgette met. Pat got leave to visit Georgette and attend the funeral (he hitched a ride on Air Vice-Marshal Harry Broadhurst's personal aircraft into Brussels).

The problem for a leading aircraftman on leave was finding the money to live well in expensive cities like Brussels and Paris. Out of necessity fitters, riggers and armourers learned to be expert scroungers. As the most successful entrepreneurs of the RCAF, they made up in ingenuity what they lacked in income. Fortunately, all RCAF personnel received a thousand cigarettes monthly, and cigarettes were as good as money in a war zone. With packs of cigarettes you could buy food, liquor, sex, guns and shelter. German booty, especially the coveted Luger or P38 pistols or the Leica or Contax cameras, fetched hundreds of dollars from well-paid American soldiers. Bayonets, badges and flags made up the smaller denominations in the wartime barter and black-market exchange system. Pat's photographs were so extensive and so good that, though illegally taken, they were used by 143 Wing for commemorative albums. The wing commander, knowing Pat's work and tacitly approving of it, negotiated to pay him in British pounds for reproductions. Pat made enough money from that venture to pay off the mortgage on his house when he got back to Vancouver.

Peterson's most daring extracurricular activity was stealing an abandoned Mercedes Benz, the keys still in the ignition. He and his friend Scotty were on a walkabout near the front lines. They strolled across a long steel bridge into a German town, a bridge that was patrolled at the far end by a German sentry. Scotty recommended retreat but Pat pressed on. Either the sentry did not want trouble or mistook

the RCAF uniforms for Luftwaffe uniforms (a not uncommon mistake). A German woman in an upstairs window waved at the two airmen until she took a closer look at their shoulder flashes and slammed the window shut.

Pat started the open-top military Mercedes, and he and Scotty drove past the sentry, back across the long bridge. They shortly thereafter encountered a Bren gun carrier; at Pat's polite request, its Canadian commander handed over a can of gasoline to help them make it back to their airfield. But he shouted at the airmen: "Are you two crazy? Hell, we haven't taken that town yet. We ran out of ammo. We are holding here for reinforcements to come up."

The popular commander of 143 Wing, Group Captain A. Dean "Father" Nesbitt, DFC, whom Pat had served under since their days up in Alaska, was impressed with the Mercedes, as were the Typhoon pilots. Pat was ordered by Alf Pedley to relinquish the vehicle for use as a flight-line taxi. He negotiated one more field trip before handing in the keys and wished later he hadn't. South of Hamburg he drove into a town that had just been taken by the US Army.

As Pat parked in the town square, he saw piles of bodies in various stages of decomposition being wrapped individually in white sheeting by civilians. An American officer, who was armed with a Thompson submachine gun and was greatly agitated in body and spirit, was dealing with the horrors of a mass grave. He had ordered the townspeople to wrap the corpses and give them a proper burial. Pat asked the officer: "What happened here?" The American shook his head. Nodding towards the townspeople, he said: "I don't know, but if it was my decision I'd shoot every damn one of them."

In the last weeks of the war, 143 Wing was stationed at B150 airfield, near Celle, about ten miles from Bergen-Belsen concentration camp. Pat Peterson could not bring himself to go inside the gate. His religious beliefs, his belief in mankind, were shattered by what he saw at the end of the war, and thereafter he could find no comfort in attending church. They had played "Ave Maria" at Henri Terrine's funeral in Brussels, and Pat was never able to listen to that song again. Even at age ninety, he could not talk about what he had seen and photographed in the war without tears flowing.

In 1944 Pat Peterson, at upper left, directs his maintenance crew during the installation of a Napier Sabre engine.

He had kept several German cameras and two handguns as souvenirs from his bartering in the war. He had the authorizing ownership permits from the 1950s, but had never fired the weapons. The year before he died, he walked the two weapons over to the local RCMP station in White Rock, BC, for disposal. He didn't trust that the RCMP, despite their assurances, would actually destroy them, given that one was a handsome Walther P38, a coveted collectible. Nevertheless, he was worried about house break-ins; that the German weapons might fall into the wrong hands. The smaller-calibre pistol, to his surprise, still had a full clip of ammunition in the grip, untouched since 1945. Once he knew he had a loaded weapon in the house, he told me, he became concerned that he might, in a despondent moment, turn the pistol on himself.

Looking back on his memories, Pat noted sadly to me, "You know, the whole damn war was the shits, but I wouldn't have missed it for the world. Isn't that the most peculiar thing?"

Typhoon being refuelled, location unknown, possibly gunnery camp in Britain.

Atholl Sutherland Brown in the Second World War.

THE FIGHTER PILOTS' WAR IN INDIA AND BURMA

Perhaps due to the dramatic entry of the United States into the war with the aerial attack by the Japanese Navy on Pearl Harbor on December 7, 1941, Canadians seldom immediately think of that war against the Japanese as "our" war. But Canadians played no small part in this phase of the war: more than 7,500 Canadian flyers served in the China-Burma-India theatre of war or in the Pacific theatre. A famous Royal Canadian Air Force pilot, Air Commodore Leonard Birchall, OBE, DFC—whom Winston Churchill labelled "The Saviour of Ceylon" for spotting the Japanese fleet in 1942—died in September 2004. His is one of the very few heroic flying stories from the war in Asia that is well known. In general, however, the exploits of Canadian flyers, and particularly fighter pilots, are unknown. What follows is just a small biographical sampling of Canadian flyers who helped defeat the Japanese.

I had the good fortune to interview seven men who had served as fighter pilots in Southeast Asia. They describe a natural environment that was considerably more hostile and an enemy more implacable than anything in Europe, which is saying a great deal. Fred Sproule served on Hurricanes, Bert Madill on Hurricanes and Thunderbolts, Harold Hope and Atholl Sutherland Brown on Beaufighters and Brick Bradford on Spitfires (see his story in Part Four). Bill Atkinson and Donald Sheppard served on Royal Navy carriers flying the F4F Hellcat and the F4U Corsair (see their stories in Part Twelve).

Canadians were serving in the China-Burma-India theatre well before Pearl Harbor and, as already noted, more than 7,500 flyers from

Canada and the RCAF had served there by 1945. Exact figures are unknown and no one considered it important back then to keep close tabs on RCAF people in uniform with the Royal Air Force. Our largest single contingent in the early days were not flyers, but RCAF radar technicians, or radio direction finding (RDF) technicians as they were then known. We had more than seven hundred of that secret trade there, in some cases responsible for setting up radio/radar networks in China as a defensive screen for the China-Burma-India theatre.

Fighter pilots such as Howard Low of Vancouver and Russell Smith of Kamsack, Saskatchewan, served with 607 Squadron RAF during the battle of Singapore in January 1942, flying outclassed Hurricanes against Japanese Zeroes. When Low and Smith reviewed their combat experiences at the Japanese prison camp in Batavia (Jakarta), they decided to attempt an escape by stealing an aircraft at a nearby airfield. They almost made it, but were captured and shortly thereafter beheaded. Hundreds of Allied prisoners of war in Asia were summarily executed in this way, but particularly flyers who had been shot down attacking Japanese installations.

Reconnaissance pilot Brick Bradford carried a disassembled Sten gun simply to ensure that he was never taken prisoner. The one Spitfire pilot from his squadron who was known to have been captured was dragged through the streets until he died. In Europe it was often considered safer to be unarmed so as to pose no threat after being shot down and apprehended by the Germans. In Southeast Asia it was essential to be armed with both a gun and a knife, and to avoid surrender if at all possible.

Atholl Sutherland Brown in his home in Victoria, 2001.

Profile – ATHOLL SUTHERLAND BROWN

Born – June 20, 1923, Ottawa; grew up in London, England, and Victoria, BC

Father – Brigadier General James Sutherland Brown, CMG, DSO, army officer, Canadian Army, 1895–1933

Mother – Clare Temple Corson

Decorations & Medals – DFC, Jubilee Medal, Ambrose Medal of Geological Survey of Canada

Degrees & Awards – BASc, PhD, PEng

Post-war occupation – Geologist, chief of the Geological Survey of BC

Marital status – Married his first wife Barbara in 1948, she died in 1996; married second wife Ruth in 2001; son Brian

Hobbies – Golf, gardening

Atholl Sutherland Brown is the youngest of three sons of a career officer, Brigadier General James Sutherland Brown of the Canadian Army. Brothers Malcolm and Ian had graduated from Royal Military College (RMC), Kingston, and had the war not intervened it is very likely Atholl also would have. Malcolm became an officer in the Royal Canadian Engineers, receiving a DSO for his wartime accomplishments. Ian became a flying instructor at No. 3 Service Flight Training School (SFTS) in Calgary with his fellow RMC graduate Dick Forbes-Roberts, but was killed in a flying accident in the spring of 1941. As soon as Atholl turned eighteen in June 1941, he signed up for pilot training, receiving his wings and being commissioned in September '42 at the same SFTS at which Ian had taught.

After his General Reconnaissance Course (GRC) training in PEI, he asked to go to Coastal Command fighters. As he admits today, he had no clear notion as to what that entailed in 1942, but it sounded good, and far more promising than bomber or reconnaissance aircraft. While waiting at Bournemouth to go to an operational training unit (OTU), Atholl chanced to see a Beaufighter for the first time, flying below the cliffs along the English Channel, silently making its way, and suddenly he realized with excitement that was to be his future.

He qualified on TFX Beaufighters in Catfoss, Yorkshire, the X standing for Mk 10, the TF for torpedo fighter. He and his English navigator, Flight Sergeant Alf Aldham, ferried a Beaufighter (manufacturer's serial number LX996) out to India via Fez, Castel Benito, Cairo and Bahrain. Instead of arriving on an operational squadron with the fresh machine they had been handed at the Bristol factory, the two men were quickly separated from LX996 and sent to the aircrew pool in Poona. After frittering away three months in Poona, they were posted to Southeast Asia Communications Flight in Delhi, where Atholl flew a variety of aircraft in VIP and utility transport duties. It was a good way to be educated about the weather and geography of India, but he wanted to fly operations on Beaufighters. After three more months he and Alf managed to escape, joining 177 Squadron RAF stationed at Feni, near the Bay of Bengal.

The three Beaufighter squadrons, 27, 177 and 211, formed 901 Wing RAF, which belonged to 224 Group of the Third Tactical Air Force. The Beaufighter squadrons operated from separate airfields and the personnel of the three squadrons knew little about each other. They rarely flew together in joint operations. No. 27 Squadron started operations earlier in 1943 and learned on the job and, because of that, suffered higher casualties.

The main job of the Beaufighters was ground attack; they flew solo or with one other aircraft to targets up to six hundred miles away, sometimes logging up to seven hours. This set them apart from short-range single-engine tactical fighters. Their targets were far from the front. They included shipping and transportation for the Japanese army; the trains on the twenty-five hundred miles of Burmese railroad; and the military vehicles on the paved and dirt roads. The Beaufighters also attacked the paddle steamers, sailing schooners, sampans and barges on the rivers and in the coastal waters of the Bay of Bengal and Gulf of Martaban. Other important targets included oil wells, pipelines and, most challenging of all, the Japanese airfields. Each Beaufighter at 177 was modified by squadron maintenance personnel to carry a Fairchild F24 camera in the nose, ensuring good photographs of anything they saw or attacked in daylight.

Aldham and Sutherland Brown commenced operations on March 8, 1944, but Aldham went down sick and, when well, was sent away for a jungle survival course. Sutherland Brown explained to the author that skin rashes, festering lesions and intestinal disorders like dysentery were the most common illnesses that hospitalized military personnel. In his case it was a complete body rash; in Aldham's case, dysentery. So for the first few weeks, Atholl flew with other navigators who were not quite up to Alf's level. Atholl was relieved to have Alf back from jungle survival and eager to hear more about what he had learned on the course. Without missing a beat his favourite navigator stated: "If we come down in the jungle, I'll shoot you to save you all that trouble."

Some six weeks later, on April 28, led by Flying Officer Joe Van Nes, of Flin Flon, Manitoba, Atholl and Alf attacked freight trains and trucks west of the Salween River (which flows out of Tibet), in the Shan plateau near Lashio, Burma. Seven more ops followed in May, in which they severely damaged five locomotives and thirteen trucks.

The learning process that resulted in a competent operational crew came at some cost. In his indoctrination period with 177, Atholl did one hard landing, knocking off the tail wheel, and while flying the commanding officer's Tiger Moth he tipped it up and broke the prop. The latter upset resulted in a red-ink endorsement stamp in his logbook, alerting future squadron commanders to his shortcomings (good deeds resulted in a similar endorsement stamp in green ink).

The main enemy of the Beaufighter in these day and night attacks was anti-aircraft guns. Only occasionally did fighter aircraft shoot down Beaufighters, because the Japanese army kept its Oscars (the Nakajima Ki-43 Hayabusa) hundreds of miles behind the front and, during the monsoon season, in Siam (now Thailand). However, this did not prevent Japanese army fighter pilots from flying the Oscar up to six hours at a time, allowing them to reach the Imphal battlefields in Assam province, India. The maximum low altitude, on-the-deck speed of 260 knots for the Beaufighter was comparable to the Oscar, so Beaufighter crews were rarely attacked. But on long, six-hour trips, the cruising speed was much lower at 180—three miles a minute. The United States Army Air Force (USAAF) P38 twin-engine fighters had a habit of attacking the Beaufighters, presuming them to be Japanese, and 901 Wing lost two Beaufighters to friendly fire from P38s.

The Beaufighter did not generate a lot of engine noise before arriving overhead. In the humid tropics, whenever the aircraft was flown in steep turns, pulling "G," it trailed conspicuous white vortices off the wingtips and also made a distinctive whistling sound. It was these unique characteristics of the Beaufighter that perhaps led the Japanese to nickname it "Whispering Death." By flying at fifty feet, popping up to identify targets and using terrain masking to conceal the aircraft, Allied pilots discovered that Japanese radar units had difficulty detecting a Beaufighter. This further reinforced its nickname, as it seemed to arrive out of nowhere. The motto of 177 Squadron inscribed on its crest was: "*Silently into the midst of things.*"

Unquestionably, the environment of Burma— its weather, high terrain and thick jungles—was as hazardous as the enemy. Of the 40-per-cent losses suffered by the squadron, many were caused by crashes into terrain or the ocean. A total of forty-eight pilots and navigators were reported missing in action and presumed killed while either with 177 or on loan to 27 Squadron; another seven were listed as missing but later were found to be prisoners of the Japanese. Frequently, a crew and aircraft did not return and were never heard from; the loss could have been due to enemy action, storms or low-level flight into obstacles. One-third of 177 Squadron's personnel were killed or died in service. Sutherland Brown recounts in his memoirs and squadron history:

> Skill and knowledge were of fundamental importance if a crew was to have a good chance of survival. There's the word—chance. Undoubtedly luck was of equal importance and most successful crews thought they were lucky. Although subject to intense fear at times and a low subliminal level of apprehension all the time, practically no one thought they would be dealt the card. We all considered ourselves immortal. If we hadn't, our behaviour would scarcely have been "press on regardless."

The squadron was a happy and operationally outstanding one with a mixture of men from all over, including one navigator of Indian background, as well as Australians, New Zealanders, Canadians and Britons. They got along well and did not feel hard done by that they were stationed in a remote corner of the Empire fighting in a little-known war. Sutherland Brown and the other pilots believed they had the best job in the air force: low-flying all the time against an enemy that was evil and deserved to be eradicated:

> Our life on the squadron was motivated by these scarcely discussed attitudes [towards the enemy], but it was driven by routine, by a love of flying, by companionship, by a sense of fun, and more personally, by hope and fear. The morale of the aircrew under the stress of severe losses always appeared to be good ... [One] must consider the excitement, especially for pilots, of limitless low flying. The aircrew were barely adults and the rewards of this excitement to most of them outweighed the risks. Friendship was a support but less than might be imagined. Amongst those at the frontline strips, friendships tended to be sincere but shallow, inhibited by a fear of possible loss. Friendship among many survivors today is much stronger and deeper. We were thrown together by chance, having no common geographic origins

and not much common background, except flying. Still, we probably had our share of pride in not wanting to let the side down.

A crew did an op every third day; before flying, they equipped themselves with survival goods—items such as a money belt of silver rupees, a *kukri* (the knife of the Ghurkha soldier), a silk escape map and a "Goulee" chit that offered a reward to any person who helped an "Allied fighter ... to the nearest Allied Military Post." Tea was served before an early-morning launch, and tea with a bit of rum when you made it back from a night sortie. Daytime attacks were frequently near sunrise, which meant a departure in darkness. Evening attacks were around sunset, which meant the cover of darkness when returning home.

Most true night operations were flown during the two-week period each month when moonlight helped light the terrain below. Although the crew had parachutes, they were unlikely to save anyone's life because all flights were just above the trees or so low over the water that the navigator could look back and see the wake from the prop wash on the surface. The survival items were important if one survived a forced landing in the jungle or on a beach, but that was by no means a certainty.

In July 1944 the Beaufighters at 177 were fitted with rocket rails, and training commenced on using the rocket projectile. This was at their new airfield at Ranchi in Bihar Province, two hundred miles west of Calcutta. The airfield was much more pleasant and there were many more amenities. But because it was monsoon season, the rocket firings on the range were done in heavy rain at low altitude. The front windscreen of the Beaufighter was thick enough to repel bullets, a comforting feature, but it was impossible to see out to the front with rain streaming down. As Atholl recalls, one could open the side windows to see, craning one's neck giraffe-like to get an idea of where one was. The excitement of learning to fire the rockets in such grim weather easily matched any operational trip.

By the first week of August the squadron had moved south to Chiringa, India, between Chittagong and Cox's Bazar. On September 10, Sutherland Brown and Aldham led four Beaufighters in an attack on eight freighters with Japanese navy escorts, south of Moulmein, Burma, near Kalegauk Island in the Gulf of Martaban. It was at the extreme radius of action of the Beaufighter (a round-trip time of six hours, forty minutes), so cannon and rocket attacks were necessarily brief. But the Allies set fire to one vessel and damaged others, and 177 and 211 Squadrons received congratulations from US General George Stratemeyer for the ground-crew work that made it possible, and for "the determined and courageous attacks" that impeded the Japanese supply line and reinforcements.

Atholl's final op, his forty-ninth, was on the night of December 28, attacking a train at Pegu, Burma. There was brilliant tracer firing back at the Beaufighter in the moonlight and something exploded under Atholl's feet, forcing him to break off his attack. It was actually an exploding cannon shell from his own aircraft that wounded him, causing his right boot to fill with blood that congealed around the cockpit floor. The injuries from the exploding cannon shell left fragments, which had to be removed from his legs.

But after two weeks of pleasant rest in hospital, his sick leave was cancelled. He was assigned to command a direct-air-support control unit with the Fourteenth Army. Not feeling well-treated by the authorities and now separated from his beloved Beaufighter, Atholl must have wondered what he had done so terribly wrong to earn a trek overland on the central plains of Burma to join the Fourteenth Army. After the comforts of squadron life, he was now obliged to set out guards at night to protect his men from stray tigers and Japanese soldiers separated from their own army.

Fortunately, his transfer to Bombay arrived as his air-support control unit made it to the army HQ, so he escaped and was sent back to Britain, where he enjoyed VE Day in London. In April 1945 his award for the Distinguished Flying Cross was gazetted, with the following citation:

This officer has completed many operations over Burma and Siam. He has attained outstanding results and has inflicted most severe damage against enemy technical transport. He has at all times shown the utmost determination and courage in low level attacks. His

unfailing keenness and devotion to duty have been most praiseworthy.

The DFC was formally presented while Atholl was completing his studies in science at the University of British Columbia.

Sutherland Brown went on to complete his doctorate in geology at Princeton University in 1954. He is retired now from his career with the BC Geological Survey, living well with his wife, Ruth, in Victoria, BC, playing golf, writing and publishing. He has written a critically acclaimed history of 177 Squadron, *Silently into the Midst of Things*; has written studies on the air war in Southeast Asia in scholarly journals; and, in October 2004 his biography of his famous father, *Buster: A Canadian Patriot and Imperialist—The Life and Times of Brigadier James Sutherland Brown*, was released.

Atholl believed his navigator, Alf Aldham, had been killed after he left the squadron; happily this was "duff gen," and the two met again in 1971 and frequently thereafter, most recently (at this writing) in 2003. In 1997, Atholl toured many of his former attack sites in Burma/Myanmar, and visited the graves of ten members of 177 buried in Rangoon. It was a squadron that existed for less than two years but received four DSOs, fourteen DFCs, two DFMs and an MBE. Its surviving personnel from the British Commonwealth have made distinguished lives in business; the professions; education; government service; as well as military and/or civil aviation.

Profile – HAROLD TAYLOR HOPE
Born – July 21, 1917, Vancouver; raised in Port Alberni and Armstrong, BC
Father – Albert Hope, baker
Mother – Margaret Ann Taylor
Post-war occupation – Jeweller, watchmaker, investment broker
Marital status – Wife Irene Morris, daughters Geraldine (killed in a VI buzz bomb attack, 1944) and Jacqueline, sons Graham and Roger
Hobbies – Aircraft owner and restorer

Harold Taylor Hope, of Armstrong, BC, had the misfortune on his arrival in Britain to be assigned Bristol Beaufort torpedo bombers, an operational

Harold Hope in his office in Vancouver, 2002.

Canadian pilots, on the Beaufighters in 901 Wing. Harold is now eighty-seven years old, but he fondly remembers Jack Pettifer as the finest navigator any pilot could wish for, "one of the great men in my life, and make sure you mark down his name." The two survived their tour together despite the odds against it at 27 Squadron.

Harold is the youngest son of the baker and owner of Hope Bakery in Armstrong. He had trained before the war as a watchmaker and gemologist with a Mr J.R. Clark because Albert Hope paid Clark $2 a week to teach his son a good trade. Harold was turned down at the recruiting centre in 1940 because the RCAF thought he was twenty-eight pounds underweight, but Mrs Rose, his landlady at the boarding house at 1326 West 13th in Vancouver, helped him gain weight by feeding him extra portions. Her son Bob was a pal of Harold's at the time and they both made it into the RCAF, but Bob was killed in 1944 flying as a navigator with 415 Squadron RCAF. Harold's brother Ken was an RCAF instrument technician with the RAF in England and survived the war, as did brother Art who served as a radio operator on tanks in Italy with the Canadian Army.

Harold's flying career got off to a rocky start in India. On one of his first operational trips at 27 Squadron they refuelled at Ramu, and one aircraft of the four in the section became unserviceable. Harold and Jack, as the inexperienced crew, were ordered to return to Parasharam with the defective Beaufighter which was consuming about 15 per cent more fuel than it ought to. Disobeying orders, Hope followed the other three aircraft to the target, which they strafed successfully. But Harold was almost shot down by anti-aircraft fire and it was dark as he approached the aerodrome. As he raised the nose of the aircraft to level off from his descent, the engines failed due to fuel starvation and Harold was forced to land his Beaufighter in the bush short of the runway.

Not long after this episode, he had an engine failure on takeoff and crashed through the operations room and out the other side directly into a Beaufighter belonging to 177 Squadron. Atholl Sutherland Brown had watched the 177 Squadron Beaufighter being refuelled from a bowser less than five minutes before the collision and recalled his sense of relief that a great explosion had been avoided, but only by a narrow margin.

assignment with a dismal survival rate that matched or sometimes exceeded anything in the Bomber Command campaign over Europe. He flew a few stressful patrols off the Norwegian coast in this heavy and ponderous machine, but then was taken off ops and retrained on the Mk X Beaufighter. In his heartfelt words, "the Beaufighter was wonderful after the Beaufort." He ferried his new Beaufighter through the Middle East to India with his navigator, Jack Pettifer. Jack was from Birmingham, England, and had crewed with Harold at the OTU.

They joined No. 27 Squadron, commanded by Wing Commander James Nicholson, VC, DFC. Nicholson was one of only two fighter pilots to be awarded the Victoria Cross in the Second World War, for his actions as a Hurricane pilot with 249 Squadron in the Battle of Britain in 1940. He left 27 Squadron in March 1944, and was killed in action in May 1945 while flying with the crew of a B24 Liberator bomber from 355 Squadron.

Hope and Pettifer, a "Canada" and a "Brit," were a typical crew on Beaufighters in Southeast Asia as there were no Canadian navigators, but many

Harold Hope, Beaufighter pilot with 27 Squadron, got married in 1943 in Britain to Irene Morris, an RAF WAAF from Dagenham, Essex. While Harold was serving in India, their new born child, Geraldine, was killed in a British hospital when a wing of the hospital was struck by a V1 buzz bomb attack.

One of the most memorable events for Hope and Pettifer involved the rescue of a Spitfire pilot who was down in a large field north of Henzada, Burma. The field had been harvested and what was left was hard-packed stubble, able to support the weight of his aircraft, so Hope circled around and landed. He taxied up to the pilot and offered him a ride, flying him to his airfield north of Cox's Bazar where Harold managed to land on the short runway.

In order for the Beaufighter to get off that runway they had to clear the brush so the twin-engine fighter could be backed up to provide just enough distance for the takeoff. Fortunately, they were able to lift off pointed towards the Bay of Bengal, with Harold skimming the surface, flaps down, gaining the critical airspeed needed to climb. Hope was reprimanded by his commanding officer for misusing the Beaufighter to rescue someone when that was not his job, and for being late getting home. He does not know, if he ever did, the name of the Spitfire pilot he rescued.

While serving at 27, Harold was commissioned and immediately made a flight lieutenant. The powers that be decided that, as a commissioned officer, Hope's tour of operations commenced from date of commissioning, and his ops flown as an NCO pilot were not to be counted. This had serious implications for Harold's survival because the loss rate at 27 Squadron was more than 50 per cent during his tour. Despite setbacks such as this, Hope retained the courage of his own convictions; this was best demonstrated in a conflict with the squadron's engineering officer when Hope refused to fly a Beaufighter that he believed had a defective engine. Twice he took it out for takeoff, but despite the normal engine instrument indications he could feel a murmur that disquieted him. The engineering officer believed that Hope was simply using a false pretext to get out of a sortie. Nevertheless, Harold did not back down. He refused that aircraft and the sortie was subsequently scrubbed:

The engineering officer went to the CO to have me put on charge ... the next day, another pilot with his navigator took off with this aircraft and the engine blew a pot. He force-landed with the gear up, and there was no access out

from below. The navigator could not get out from above, and he burned to death. The engineering officer was sent back to the UK.

But for one of the characteristic misfortunes of war, Harold and Jack might have received DFCs for sinking two heavily laden ships, setting them on fire with their 20mm cannons in the Gulf of Martaban near Moulmein. Their commanding officer in April 1945, Wing Commander T.P.A. Bradley, showed Harold and Jack the photos from their aircraft camera, the ships on fire, burning from end to end. Bradley congratulated them, saying that it was one of the best accomplishments for the unit in a long time. As he was leaving in a jeep to go on an op he further stated or strongly implied that he had started the paperwork for a decoration because of this outstanding work.

Several hours later Wing Commander Bradley and his navigator Pilot Officer Holmes returned to the aerodrome. Harold and Jack were standing around and watched the CO's Beaufighter enter the circuit. One of the most hazardous aspects of takeoffs and landings from airfields in India was the numerous vultures that soared in the vicinity of the runways. The impact from hitting one of these large scavengers threw the Beaufighter out of control.

As luck would have it on this trip, standing behind Bradley's seat in the plane was a newspaper journalist who had gone along for the ride. He intended to file a story about Beaufighter operations for his newspaper. There were no extra seats in the Beaufighter so a third person of necessity had to stand in the cavity directly behind the pilot's seat. The entry hatch into the cockpit formed the floor of that cavity. In an act of profoundly quick thinking, Bradley pulled the lever for the floor hatch on which the journalist was standing. The journalist fell from the aircraft, pulled the rip cord on his chute and landed safely. Bradley crashed and he and his navigator were killed.

After Hope's tour ended, he served in Cyprus with the RAF, while his navigator, who had finally been commissioned, ended up with a great job running the officers' mess at Gibraltar. When the war ended, Hope went back to his job at Shore's Jewellery in Vancouver, but in 1959 joined the investment firm of Pemberton Securities. Harold finally retired in 2004; his offices were within a block of the site where Shore's Jewellery once stood.

Harold travels to Britain annually, touring the many military museums there and attending reunions of the Burma Star Association. He has been a recreational pilot and an aircraft owner ever since the war. Among many aviation activities, he spent eight years restoring an Avro Anson that is now housed at the Reynolds Alberta Museum in Wetaskiwin, Alberta. When he thinks back on the war, his most vivid memory is of the ships he set on fire, packed with Japanese soldiers. Their deaths did not bother him then, because he believed in the cause for which he was fighting, but today he finds himself remembering the ships burning end to end, and the men jumping in the water to escape the flames.

Profile – BERT DENNIS MADILL
Born – January 20, 1923, Edmonton
Father – Granville Madill, grocery store owner, fox and mink farmer
Mother – Irene Sunderland
Decorations & Medals – DFC, CD and Clasp
Post-war occupation – Air force officer, RCAF/CAF, Squadron Leader; after retirement, a property manager
Marital status – Wife Florence Peterson died in 1995; sons Eric (died in 2003), Gregory and Douglas; daughter Beverley
Hobbies Music

Benjamin Madill, Bert Madill's grandfather, had owned a lot of land on the south side of Edmonton, but lost most of it in the Depression. Bert's father, Granville, ran a grocery store during these tough years. In 1938 his father sold the store and ventured into the fur-ranching business with his brother Oscar, setting up on forty acres in the north Edmonton area. Bert boarded out with friends in south Edmonton to complete his junior high schooling at King Edward School, later attending Eastwood High School in the northeast end of the city. It was tough to make ends meet, even with two paper routes—a noon and an evening edition—and he left school after Grade 11 to work for a chartered accountant. This proved to be dull and tedious work, but the office was around the corner from the RCAF recruiting centre.

Bert Madill at home in Edmonton in 2003, holding a model of the P47 that he flew with 123 Squadron, RAF, in India.

Bert had watched American pioneer flyer Wiley Post land his aircraft "Winnie Mae" on Kingsway Avenue and this, plus a love of airplanes, proved irresistible. Lack of money stopped any thoughts of his obtaining a pilot's licence, but the recruiting centre was not far away; one day, Bert left the office at lunchtime and by late afternoon was an airman, serial number R113041.

His parents were very unhappy when they found out that evening that their only child was now in the military. His father threatened to get him out of the RCAF, but that attempt never went anywhere. Bert felt his life had been transformed. He had musical ability and had played the sousaphone and the tenor and baritone horns in the Schoolboys Band in Edmonton. When this ability became evident at the Brandon Manning Depot, there was no guard duty for Madill because he was drafted into the station band.

Madill says, "I thoroughly enjoyed my pilot training, and my first instructor, on the Tiger

Moth, was a US pilot named 'Sparky' Wilcox. He was a great instructor and a real fine man. He once told me that 'anytime I thought I knew all there was to know about flying, be sure to quit—before I killed myself!'" On completion of Elementary Flying Training School (EFTS), Bert was sent to No. 2 SFTS Uplands, Ontario, where he trained on the Harvard and graduated as a sergeant pilot. He went overseas to Britain on a Polish ship, SS *Batori*:

On arrival we were sent to No. 5 AFU [Advanced Flying Unit] for about three weeks' training on the Miles Master aircraft—a glorified Harvard—and a first trip on the Hurricane. From here we were sent to No. 55 OTU at Annan, Dumfriesshire, Scotland, for a couple of months' training as a fighter pilot on the Hurricane. After graduating we were sent on "indefinite leave" pending transfer instructions, but after about one week, we received word to report to the PDC [Posting Demarcation Camp] at Blackpool for further instructions. There we were informed that we were bound for the tropics, and were duly kitted out for a tour in India. We boarded the troopship *Stirling Castle* (a converted luxury liner) and set forth for India. This proved to be quite a trip—the ship was impressive (manufactured as I recall about 1935), and accommodation typical of wartime, six to a small cabin. The food was substandard and rotten on one occasion. We travelled from October 29th to December 18th, 1943, via Bahia, Brazil, and Durban, South Africa.

For one month, December 1942, Bert lived in a tent at Bombay. While he was wondering what he had let himself in for, his commission came through, and he was now Pilot Officer Madill. Posted to 28 Squadron RAF at Ranchi, India, he learned that he was going to be a photo reconnaissance pilot on the Hurricane. The squadron was relinquishing its Lysanders as he arrived. Bert, unlike Bill Carr and Brick Bradford, received not one formal hour of photo reconnaissance training. He was expected to learn on the job. Unlike the Mk XI Spitfire, 28 Squadron Hurricanes were equipped with eight .303-calibre

machine guns in the wings and three cameras in the fuselage—one oblique, two vertical. Unlike the fortunate pilots flying Mk XI PRU Spitfires at 350 mph above thirty thousand feet, pilots at 28 Squadron simply could not avoid the enemy by flying high and fast. All of 28 Squadron's photographic reconnaissance was carried out between eight thousand and twelve thousand feet, always with two aircraft. No. 1 did the photography; the No. 2 was a lookout protecting the pilot doing the photography.

Bert was never told what a tour consisted of, and he was disappointed to be taking pictures of instead of firing his guns at the enemy. After a year of lobbying with Squadron Leader Larson, he was transferred to 123 Squadron, a fighter squadron that featured Hurricane IIC aircraft, equipped with four 20mm cannon. This was a squadron that had a reputation as lucky, with few pilots being lost, and Bert joined as the battles in the Imphal Valley were raging in the first months of 1944. He spent day after day providing airborne artillery support for General Slim's Fourteenth Army.

A big improvement came in the fall of '44 when the squadron re-equipped with the Republic P47 Thunderbolt. While Madill was talking to me about the fighter bomber, he pointed out his detailed model painted with his own squadron markings, XE, followed by his own number, "R," and the tail number, HD255. Many fighter pilots named their aircraft; Bert's was called "Birth of the Blues," and had a painting of a stork carrying a bomb on the nose of the aircraft.

Built like a tank, heavily armoured, with eight 50-calibre machine guns and the ability to fly for more than five hours, the P47 was a vast improvement over the Hurricane, and Bert fell in love with it. Among its virtues was the way it withstood crashes. There were many Hurricane and Spitfire pilots who were badly burned and injured in crash landings, but few Thunderbolt pilots because the P47 did not burn easily. At a weight of fourteen thousand pounds the P47 could run through solid obstacles, shedding many parts, but its cockpit seemed to survive just fine, protecting the pilot from harm.

Bert has one confirmed official victory on the P47. But as he explained to me, confirmed or not, it didn't happen and wasn't true. His story of how he received a confirmed victory provides a great insight into how complicated air warfare can be:

I was relaxing at the bar after a five-hour escort of twelve B24 bombers to a target well south of Rangoon, in the Moulmein area. They were attacking a prominent bridge with a specialized bomb. My squadron was close escort on this do and, while we were over the target, a few Jap fighters below us made two or three ineffective passes at us. My No. 2 and I left the formation and flew down and towards them, at which time they rolled over and headed for the deck. We pulled back up into formation—standard procedure, nothing further to report.

While at the bar the telephone rings and our commanding officer, "Mac" Macgregor, answers it. It was the commanding officer of the B24 squadron wanting to make sure I got credit for shooting down a Zero. He, and so he reported, several of his crew members, had my aircraft ID and had personally seen me shoot one of these guys out of the sky! "Mac" turned from the phone and told me this story, and asked me why I hadn't said anything about it at debriefing. "Quite simple," I said, "I had not fired my guns and did not shoot anyone down!" The American commander and his crews were adamant about the whole thing and stated that he had far too many witnesses to disregard the "facts," and that they were officially crediting me (i.e., my Thunderbolt) with one destroyed. After a bit more conversation, "Mac" hung up the phone and said: "Whether you like it or not—you have one confirmed to your credit." Well, there was no way I would paint a small rising sun flag on the nose of my TBolt for this escapade.

For his service with 28 and 123 Squadron over more than two years, Madill was recommended for the DFC. Gazetted in November 1945, the citation read:

Flight Lieutenant Madill has been engaged on operational flying over the South East Asia area of war operations for over two years. He has completed numerous tactical reconnaissance sorties over the difficult terrain of northwest Burma. He has also flown on many long range reconnaissances and taken part in bombing attacks against varied targets in Burma. Throughout this officer has maintained a high standard of skill and devotion to duty.

When the war ended, Bert found he was, like many veterans, at a loss as to what to do with his life. Following his release he worked for the weather services of the Department of Transport, but after eleven months the RCAF offered him a short-service commission and a flying job with the Communications Flight of Northwest Air Command in Edmonton. He served in the RCAF and Canadian Forces for twenty-nine years, retiring as a squadron leader (or major in the new Canadian Forces rank system). He then had a second career in property management for, among others, the University of Alberta—before retiring fully in 1986.

Profile – FREDERICK HOWARD SPROULE
Born – September 22, 1918, Vancouver; raised in Winnipeg till age 9, then moved back to Vancouver
Father – William Howard Sproule, self-employed real-estate financier
Mother – Ada Gertrude
Decorations & Medals – DFC, CD, Coronation Medal
Post-war occupation – Business executive with Chevron Canada; Wing Commander, RCAF Auxiliary; civil servant, BC government
Marital status – Wife Jean Beverley Martin; daughter Deena (deceased); sons John, Ronald, Martin and Gordie; daughter Janice
Hobbies – Military historian, avid reader, docent at an aviation museum

Many aspiring pilots were trained in the army before transferring into the RCAF, and Fred Sproule was one of the best-trained soldiers of any fighter pilot I interviewed. The military had played a strong role in his father's family: one of William's brothers had been killed in the Boer War, and a second had been killed at Ypres in the Great War. Fred enlisted in 1934 as a *Boy* (a rank not a description), at half the pay of a private, in the 72nd Seaforth Highlanders of Canada, Vancouver. The next year he graduated from a course in infantry tactics run by the Princess Patricia's Canadian Light Infantry (PPCLI) at Workpoint Barracks at the Royal School of Infantry in Victoria, being promoted to corporal. In the early months of the war the RCAF preferred university graduates, so Fred's first attempt to become a pilot failed.

While serving with an anti-tank artillery regiment he was selected to become an instructor at the No. 1 Infantry Training Centre at Currie Barracks, Calgary. After a period of instructing recruits of the Edmonton Regiment, Calgary Highlanders and Seaforth Highlanders, Fred walked into the RCAF recruiting centre and this time they signed him up. He recalls how he took his release from the army:

I had to get papers from the station adjutant, an old bow-legged captain of the Strathcona Horse. He signed the papers and said to me, "So you're going into the air force. Well, you have had good training here. See that you carry it on into the air force because they are a bunch of undisciplined bastards!" "Yes, sir," I replied.

Sproule avoided guard duty while waiting to fly because of his extensive army experience, and he was made a drill instructor at the Manning Depot in Toronto. He went through his pilot training on the same course with the American pilot-poet John Gillespie Magee. Unlike Magee, Sproule did not get overseas after graduation, being retained as an instructor at No. 2 SFTS.

After a year Sproule asked, in the RCAF vernacular, to "be paraded" before the commanding officer at Uplands. He said that he wasn't doing himself or any of his students any good as an instructor. They sent him to No. 1 Convalescent Hospital at Muskoka for a rest. There were no duties, just boating, swimming, dining and relaxing. A Dr Hudson at the hospital recommended that Sproule be taken off instructing. However, he still did not get his overseas posting; the RCAF sent him to 133 Squadron on Hurricanes, stationed at Lethbridge, Alberta, then Boundary Bay, BC, along with soon-to-be-well-known decorated RCAF fighter pilots Donald Laubman and Dick Cull.

Sproule's first overseas flying job was also on Hurricanes, a version equipped with two 40mm cannon or eight rockets for tank busting. He recalls that each gun had six rounds and the force of the rounds leaving the two barrels would drop the nose of the

Fred Sproule at home in Victoria, 2001.

Courtesy of the Wayne Ralph Collection

aircraft three degrees, so that after each firing, the nose had to be raised. The guns were calibrated for fifty feet off the deck at two hundred yards' distance. The squadron, No. 186 RAF, at Heathfield, Ayr, re-equipped with the Typhoon and was sent to Tain, Scotland, halfway between Inverness and Wick. But the bugs had not been worked out on the Typhoon and, unlike the Beaufighter, it did not have the range to reach the Norwegian coast and hang around.

Sproule then transferred at his own request to 183 Squadron at Tangmere, England, flying ops in the Typhoon against V1 facilities in France and Belgium. On one op his high-speed blower failed to cut in at twelve thousand feet; he burned more fuel because of it. He just made landfall at Beachy Head, at a peacetime location that was known as Lover's Leap, and got down safely at an emergency field, but there was not enough fuel left to taxi in, so he shut down and walked in.

In late March he was sent as a supernumerary flight lieutenant to No. 5 PDC at Blackpool,

Fred Sproule in India in 1944.

before shipping out to an unknown destination. Fred learned through a friend, whose luggage had similar tags, that the destination was India; their ship was HMT *Strathaird* and the voyage took one month, transiting the Mediterranean, the Suez Canal and the Indian Ocean. As for most air force personnel, the first stop was at Bombay, at No. 5 BR (Reception) Depot, Worli Camp.

Sproule was sent to Jungle School at Mahableshwar, a hill station for the civil servants of Bombay during the hot season. This was followed by refresher flying at No. 3 Refresher Flying Unit at Poona, then a month at Ranchi to take the so-called SLAIS course, at the Specialized Low Attack Instructional School.

Then Sproule was posted to 42 Squadron in the Imphal Valley. Between July 1944 and July 1945, he flew 224 hours in 167 sorties with this unit. The squadron flew Hurricane IVs that were fitted with long-range internal fuel tanks and, therefore, were equipped with only two .303 machine guns. These aging fighter bombers carried 250- or 500-pound bombs, as well as supply canisters for clandestine groups belonging to Force 136, part of the Special Operations Executive.

Where Fred's squadron operated, Force 136 had two operational divisions, "E" Group and "Z" Force. It was the latter that 42 Squadron supported. "Z" Force was a cadre of a few men with an army officer in command; their job was to scout out Japanese HQ ammunition dumps which the air force could then bomb. Fred described what was involved to support them:

As I recall, the container, which fitted onto the bomb rack under each wing, was about ten to twelve feet long with a special parachute fitted to the end ... They were dropped at three hundred feet above the ground. We flew in pairs, sometimes both Hurricanes carrying containers. These being intelligence patrols, they weren't going to be anywhere near a town or village or any outstanding spot the Japanese might be. We were given an eight-figure map reference to find them. They were usually out in a clearing, waving their arms, and we would descend to 300 feet and let them go. There was no circling around to look for them or

anything like that. If you missed them you had to carry on for several miles and have another go at finding them.

Stationed just south of Imphal City at Tulihal, the members of the squadron lived in buildings made of bamboo with thatched roofs, lacking any doors or windows because it was unnecessary in that climate. The runways were made from rolls of oiled bituminous material, overlapped and built up in the middle so that water ran off. Later the squadron moved north to Kangla, India, and then into Burma, some eight miles behind the front lines at a place called Tabinguang, then immediately moved again to Onbauk, Burma, near the Irrawaddy River to the north of Mandalay. They were so close to the enemy that when attacks were launched, sometimes the maintenance crews stood on the wings of the remaining Hurricanes so they could watch their pilots bomb the front lines.

We bombed and strafed within fifty yards of our own troops at times. The Japanese put up pretty severe anti-aircraft fire that often included small-arms fire from soldiers lying on their backs ... Also, they moved mainly at night. They had to cross many rivers over bridges that we targeted. The Japanese were clever because on some of the bridges they would take the boards off in the early morning before light and put the boards back at night. We attacked the bridges using time-delayed fuses, some set to explode between four and twelve hours later.

As Wing Commander Sproule was explaining his final op to me in his living room, he handed me his map of Burma—the map he had carried that day. It had a large rust-coloured spot on it. "You know what that is?" "No, but it looks like dried blood." "Yes, my blood. The map was under my hip."

As "B" Flight commander at 42, Fred was leading an operation against Japanese dug-in positions at the base of two pagodas on either side of a road leading south out of Mandalay. He was surprised at the amount of anti-aircraft fire, and while on a strafing run, he had a stoppage on one of his two .303s, and then was hit on the portside of the Hurricane.

I was hit in my left leg, but my kukri knife was on my left side, and my .38 revolver was on my right side. The shrapnel and bits of my own aircraft struck the knife and shielded me somewhat. I got back to the base, but they had hit the hydraulic lines and I had no brakes and no flaps. Fortunately there was no wind on the aerodrome ...

I was carried on a stretcher in an L5 aircraft [the Stinson L5] to No. 60 Military Field Hospital at Monywa, Burma. As my wounds were not serious, I had a white ribbon attached to my stretcher, and I waited for many hours. I can remember watching them drain blood from the lungs of badly wounded soldiers. I have never forgotten the sound that made as the blood drained, as I lay there waiting.

On returning to his squadron, he continued on ops until he contracted jaundice in May and had to go into hospital again. While there he was posted home. He was in Bournemouth in August 1945, and then travelled home to Canada on the ship *Louis Pasteur*.

Squadron Leader Bob Stout recommended Sproule for the DFC and it was gazetted in October 1945:

Flight Lieutenant Sproule has frequently led formations against Army support targets in Burma. In March 1945, whilst leading an attack on a gun position, he was wounded and his aircraft was damaged by heavy anti-aircraft shells. He returned to base where he completed a successful landing without further damage. He has at all times shown the greatest keenness on operations and his courage and determination have played a large part in the fine results which his squadron has achieved.

After the war, Fred served with the RCAF's 19 Wing Auxiliary under Group Captain Geoff Northcott and then Group Captain Ernie Alexander, rising to the rank of wing commander. Retired now from provincial government service and Chevron Oil, Fred lives with his wife, Jean, in a condominium complex adjacent to Victoria Harbour's seaplane terminal on Vancouver Island.

Courtesy of the Atholl Sutherland Brown Collection

177 Squadron Beaufighter over the Irrawaddy deltaic plain.

217

Robert Hampton Gray, VC, DSC, MiD, of Nelson BC, Fleet Air Arm, Corsair fighter pilot.

THREE PILOTS OF THE FLEET AIR ARM IN THE PACIFIC THEATRE

Canadians distinguished themselves in all branches of military aviation during the Second World War. However, in the Royal Navy Fleet Air Arm the contribution of Canadians was out of all proportion to their relatively small numbers. Only two Victoria Crosses were awarded to fighter pilots in the war; the second one was posthumously conferred on Fleet Air Arm Lieutenant Robert Hampton Gray of Nelson, British Columbia. The dramatic and sad story of how he came to receive the VC was played out in the last thirty-six hours of the Second World War.

Profile – ROBERT HAMPTON GRAY

Born – November 2, 1919, Trail, BC

Died - August 9, 1945, off the coast of Japan[1]

Father – John Balfour Gray, born in Brechin, Scotland, owner JB Gray Jewelers, Nelson, BC

Mother – Wilhelmina McAllister, accountant, born in Listowel, Ontario

Decorations & Medals – VC, DSC, MiD

Degrees & Awards – In 1938-39 was attending UBC in pre-Medicine; he was a Phi Delta Theta fraternity member, and a supporter of the Student Peace Movement

Marital Status – Unmarried; his brother John Balfour "Jack" Gray, wireless air gunner, was killed in action in February 1942 with 144 Sqn RAF; sister Phyllis Gautschi lives in West Vancouver, BC

At 10:58 a.m. local time on Thursday, August 9, 1945 a single B29 of the 509th Composite Group, US Army Air Force (USAAF), dropped an atomic bomb codenamed "Fat Man" on the city of Nagasaki, Japan. The following morning a message of surrender ordered by the Japanese Emperor Hirohito, against the wishes of his military commanders, arrived in Washington, DC, ending the war in the Pacific theatre. The message came one day too late for Hammy Gray and several other Fleet Air Arm flyers. Major Charles Sweeney and his crew had released the first plutonium nuclear weapon, with a yield of 22,000 tons of TNT, almost twice as powerful as that dropped on Hiroshima three days before. It was the only bomb Sweeney had dropped on an enemy target in his war career.

The B29 had circled for fifty minutes, from 8 a.m. to 8:50 a.m., over Yakoshima, Japan, while Sweeney waited for his two observation aircraft to arrive for his final run in to the target. During this same period Lieutenant "Hammy" Gray launched in his Corsair, No. 115, from HMS *Formidable*. He was the leader of Ramrod Two, two sections of eight fighter bombers of 1841 Squadron, each carrying two five-hundred-pound bombs.

As Hammy had walked out to his Corsair a few minutes before 8 a.m., fellow Canadian Bill Atkinson, who had already finished his dawn patrol, walked alongside him. Bill helped Hammy strap in. The two young fighter pilots were just gossiping about the events of the past week, speculating that the war might end soon. A few days earlier the entire British Pacific Fleet had been ordered off station, out to 500 miles from the Japanese coast from the fleet's usual position of 100 to 150 miles. No one knew why. Bill and Hammy and the others wondered, since they were being moved away from the action, if they had done something wrong. However, the lull gave the Corsair pilots a welcome reprieve; they had suffered many casualties over the previous weeks.

It was the habit of the ship's personnel on HMS *Formidable* to listen to the daily BBC radio broadcast. They heard that on August 6 a new so-called

[1] "Hammy" Gray was killed in action on August 9th, 1945, at Onagawa Bay, Japan. He is the only Canadian fighter pilot of the Second World War to receive the Victoria Cross, and the last Canadian recipient of Canada's highest military decoration for valour.

atomic bomb had been dropped on Hiroshima. This was the reason the British fleet had been moved away from the coast. But an atomic bomb seemed minor news given that the ship's company knew that the invasion of Japan was on for November 1. The pilots were gradually being fitted for cold-weather suits in preparation for this invasion. After Bill stepped down from the wing of the Corsair, Chief Petty Officer Dick Sweet climbed up on the wing and advised Hammy that a coastal convoy had been sighted in Onagawa Bay, Honshu. Ramrod Two's primary target was not an airfield as had been planned, said Sweet, but this group of vessels.

The Japanese ships at anchor were protected by the steep hills surrounding Onagawa Bay. Gray led his two sections in a descent from ten thousand feet down the hills, through the ravines, levelling out at fifty feet for the attack across a short stretch of open water from the shoreline. There was intense opposing anti-aircraft fire from shore-based batteries and the gun batteries aboard the ships, all of which were anticipating an attack from the direction of the shoreline.

Gray's Corsair was set on fire during his run in and one of his two bombs was shot away. He pressed on against the Japanese navy ocean escort *Amakusa*, and his remaining bomb penetrated the ship's engine room and exploded. As he pointed his aircraft out towards the open ocean, the plane became enveloped in smoke and flames and flick-rolled into the water. *Amakusa*'s ammunition magazine exploded and the vessel sank rapidly, with a loss of seventy-one men. A few of the Japanese who witnessed Gray's actions, familiar as they were with their own kamikaze attacks, were a little in awe of this unknown pilot who had pressed on against such intense fire.

Gray had been a greatly admired and well-liked flight commander and senior pilot of 1841 Squadron. His death was devastating for his buddies on Ramrod Two—T. Storheill, Alan Maitland, Leslie Reeve, Lachlan MacKinnon (the deputy leader), Albert Hughes, John Blade and Philip Abbott.

With Gray lost, MacKinnon immediately reformed the remaining aircraft and assumed the lead of the first flight of four, with Maitland taking the lead for the second flight of three. The seven Corsair

pilots came around in two more attacks in the face of intense anti-aircraft fire, sinking *Ohama* and damaging a minesweeper. Sadly, the following day Maitland was shot down and killed on his third strafing pass of an airfield, this on the last day of war operations for the Royal Navy's Pacific Fleet.

A few months earlier, Hammy had learned that his friend and course mate Bud Sutton had been killed on operations in northern Java in January. Bud had been flying a Corsair in an attack on an airfield, had been damaged and set on fire and dove his aircraft into a hangar full of aircraft. Sutton received a Mention in Despatches, his second, because his nomination for the Victoria Cross could not be validated, given that he may have been unconscious in the last moments of his flight into the hangar.

In *A Formidable Hero*, Gray's biographer, Lieutenant Commander Stuart E. Soward, quotes from a letter Hammy wrote to his mother and father, Wilhelmina and John:

> I know you will be sorry to hear that Bud Sutton, my friend from Saskatoon, has been killed in action. I have been looking forward to seeing him for a long time now, but I was too late. He died very gallantly. How I cannot tell you, but you might like to write to his family. He was an only child and I cannot think how badly they will feel about it.

Eight days after his death, and two days after the Pacific war had come to a formal end, Wilhelmina and John received a telegram about their oldest son, Hammy. They had been so looking forward to his return, especially John, a Boer War veteran who had raised a beer at the local Royal Canadian Legion branch in Nelson to mark the war's end. The Gray family had already received one telegram in the war about their younger son, John Balfour, a Royal Canadian Air Force wireless-operator air gunner, who had been killed in action in February 1942 while flying with 144 Squadron Royal Air Force.

Vice-Admiral Sir Philip Vian (later Admiral of the Fleet Vian, GCB, KBE, DSO) was the commander of all air operations of the British Pacific

Fleet. He was liked very much by his officers and men, and he had a habit of saluting them *faster* than they could salute him. He met with his flying officers after Gray's death and they decided that Hammy should be recommended for the VC. In addition to his example as a leader, Vian felt that Gray was a deserving representative from Canada, a country that had contributed much to the training of flyers during the war.

Gray had already received a Mention in Despatches in 1944 for attacks in Norwegian waters against German destroyers protecting *Tirpitz*. His Distinguished Service Cross, for which he had been recommended before his death for his previous operations in July, came through on August 31. When his Victoria Cross was gazetted in November 1945, it was historic on several counts: it was the last VC for an action by a Canadian, the only one for a fighter pilot of the Fleet Air Arm and the only one for any Canadian serving in the Pacific campaign.

On the forty-fourth anniversary of his death, a monument was erected to Hammy Gray overlooking Onagawa Bay. Through the personal efforts of Lieutenant Commander Soward, and many generous private and corporate citizens, various military personnel—including Japanese war veterans and the Canadian diplomatic staff in Tokyo—the two-ton monument on a 20-foot by 20-foot site was unveiled by Gray's sister, Phyllis Gautschi. The consecration ceremonies were broadcast on CNN Television, and three Fleet Air Arm veterans from HMS *Formidable* stood adjacent to the Japanese navy veterans who had lost their friends in Onagawa Bay, 171 of them in the attack by the eight Corsair pilots of Ramrod Two. The monument to the twenty-four-year-old fighter pilot is the only one ever erected in Japan to a foreign war hero.

Profile – DONALD JOHN SHEPPARD

Born – January 21, 1924, Toronto

Father – Ross Sheppard, lawyer

Mother – Mabel Heron, schoolteacher

Decorations & Medals – DSC, CD and Two Clasps

Post-war occupation – Naval officer, RCN, Commander

Marital status – Wife Gwendolyn Alice Falls; sons Robert and Michael; daughters Christine, Nancy and Susan

Hobbies – "Walking the dog since I turned 80"

Commander Donald Sheppard is Canada's only Corsair ace of the Second World War, and was the first Fleet Air Arm pilot of any nation to become an ace in the war against Japan. He is one of the youngest veterans I have had the privilege of meeting and one of the most self-possessed, humorous and candid. After my meeting with him, he generously offered to drive me to the Finch subway station on the north side of Toronto, many miles from his home in Aurora.

The weather was nasty, with freezing rain and ice pellets falling, and the streets icy. It was dark, and in bumper-to-bumper traffic, a northbound Toronto taxicab crossed the median and struck our car and a couple of others. Sheppard reacted quickly and with slightly more room and a dry pavement might have evaded the taxicab driver who, according to our best guess, had had a seizure. Many drivers stuck in the traffic jam behind us as we awaited the ambulance handed us telephone numbers, volunteering to provide witness testimony on our behalf.

Don's Toyota Camry was badly damaged and could not be driven, but we were both unhurt. It took several hours before Don left for home in a rental vehicle and I boarded the subway southbound. I was mortified that I had exposed this war hero to such risks for such inconsequential reasons. However, Sheppard did not seem in the least dismayed about events, allowing only: "I have had better days."

In describing his war career, Commander Sheppard applies the same kind of dry wit to his more hazardous adventures, with perfect comic timing. His first operation as a rookie twenty-year-old Corsair pilot was to provide top cover at 18,000 feet on the April 1944 attacks against *Tirpitz* and the German fleet in a Norwegian fjord. He recalls that they had no idea where they were going or what assignment they might have when they sailed from Scapa Flow in the Orkney Islands. After they sailed, the captain of HMS *Victorious* called the airmen into the admiral's dining room. They stood up as he entered, and just like in a war movie, he announced: "Gentlemen, your target is the *Tirpitz*!" Sheppard laughs today as he recalls that scene and says, "'Jesus,' we thought to ourselves, 'the *Tirpitz*. Well, that's the end of us'—one operation that would do us in before we got any experience."

Don Sheppard in the Second World War.

Sheppard in Aurora, ON., at his home, 2002.

Donald John Sheppard, born and raised in Toronto, joined the Fleet Air Arm at the age of seventeen, after reading a brochure that his brother Robert, a Sea Cadet officer, had requested. He decided that he was actually better qualified than Robert to join up. Their older brother William was already in the Royal Navy under the Raleigh Scheme; he had been in the same 1940 intake as Hammy Gray. The Raleigh Scheme enlisted university students with the rank of seaman and sent them to study at King Alfred School, Brighton, England, to become officers.

While at Royal Navy Air Station (RNAS) Lee-on-Solent in England, Don Sheppard successfully passed his interview with a panel of senior Royal Naval officers. When pressured by these officers to become an observer, Don balked. As luck would have it, the RCAF doctor doing the Fleet Air Arm medical exams had given Don a strong sales pitch to become an RCAF pilot. Sheppard advised the officers that he already had an offer elsewhere, so he would not compromise. The panel capitulated.

After the interview, he consoled a well-known athlete from Toronto who had been rejected. Apparently, the panel had a couple of trick questions to see if candidates listened carefully before answering. On this day, the question was: "Can you marry your widow's sister?" The athlete pondered carefully and said, "No sir, that's not done." Don pointed out to his despondent friend that the correct answer was: "No sir, I can't do that because I'm dead."

Sheppard says that his military training in the 48th Highlanders in Toronto stood him in good stead at the shore establishment HMS St Vincent, Gosport (near Portsmouth), but he found the course demanding and challenging for a city kid. It included many nautical skills such as boat-pulling, sailing, knot-tying and ship recognition, in addition to night guard duty watching for air raids, and of course the usual 5:30 a.m. physical education.

Offered a choice of RCAF or United States Navy (USN) training, Sheppard had no prob-

Courtesy of the Donald Sheppard Collection

Corsair on fire due to snagged drop tank, pilot survived.

lem selecting Pensacola, Florida, over Kingston, Ontario. He believes that the American training was a better preparation for carrier operations, and his class had no serious upsets in carrier qualification. The Chance Vought F4U Corsair, however, was nicknamed in some circles "The Widow Maker" because inexperienced pilots often were killed or injured checking out on the plane, also known as the "Bent Wing Bird." The USN initially refused to operate the planes on their carriers and promptly handed half of the initial aircraft production to the US Marines and the other half to the Royal Navy under a lend-lease scheme.

The Royal Navy had already suffered through the operational limitations of the Skua, and knew from experience aboard carriers the fragility of the Seafire, a navalized Spitfire, and the inadequate speed of the Martlet (the RN name for the Grumman F4F Wildcat). It was therefore thrilled to get such a high-performance fighter with an engine rated at more than 2,000 horsepower and a top speed of over 400 miles per hour. The RN equipped nineteen squadrons with the fighter. Nevertheless, there is no question that the Corsair was complex, demanding to fly and unforgiving of mistakes. Sheppard recalls

that on his initial flights with the fighter he felt as though he was sitting on the tail of a torpedo. On one trip he had a malfunctioning pitot head, which meant he had no airspeed indicator. He landed on the carrier with extra velocity:

[I] grabbed the No. 9 wire, which was referred to as the "For Christ's Sake" wire. But if the guy on the barrier was quick in getting it down, you would not strike your prop on the deck. Well, he was quick, and though I tipped up, there was no damage. My friends liked to say I was the only pilot in the history of the Royal Navy to engage the No. 9 wire and the barrier and not scratch my aircraft … that particular landing was observed by King George VI, who had been invited to watch carrier air operations aboard *Victorious*.

Commander Sheppard recollects being interviewed by the King after the incident, and that he praised the fighter pilots for their keenness and professionalism. Don says that all the pilots hoped that King George would recommend that the carrier pilots be given increased risk allowance (to no avail).

After arriving in the Far East in June 1944, Sheppard learned that his first op was an attack at Sabang in Sumatra (now Indonesia) in July. As he recalls, "My main fear was just of the unknown. I thought little about my mortality until I saw one of my friends, Cutler, go down in flames at Padang. I was not religious, though I had gone to church and Sunday school. I figured that I was too young to go." Sheppard showed me his logbook to emphasize how little flying practice pilots got in the British East Indies Fleet. He flew about ten hours in July 1944 and the same in August. Don believes that there was a tragic waste of aircraft and lives for the amount of damage inflicted, and he still remembers vividly the flaming deaths of his friends Eric Hill and John Chandler during attacks on the Nicobar Islands in the Bay of Bengal.

Sheppard received the Distinguished Service Cross for his contributions flying with 1836 Squadron on the January 4, 1945, attack against the oil refinery at Pangkalan Brandan, Sumatra. He provides a hair-raising yet hilarious account of how he became a hero flying as No. 2 to one of the most original characters of the Fleet Air Arm, an ace during the Palembang operations and also later in the Pacific campaign:

Aerial view of the oil refinery at Pangkalan Brandan under attack on January 4, 1945.

Major Ronnie Hay, Royal Marines, was the air coordinator, like a master bomber, something we had never seen before in any of our operations; he was controlling the fighters and the bombers to the target. He wore white gloves—a great showoff, but a very good one. He reached down into the two fighter squadrons and picked up three pilots from each squadron to support him on operations. Well, the first time I went up with him, he said, "Now, Sheppard, your job is to make sure nothing happens to me. I am the most important guy up there and I don't care what happens to you, but you are to make sure nothing happens to me. Never take your eyes off me." Jesus, what a job that was!

I stuck to him like glue. Every time we ran into fighters he would take them on instead of sticking to his job of air coordinator—he would rush right in. We came in high over the target, and Hay had a camera in his aircraft, and we stayed behind to take pictures. Of course, the Japanese pilots would come up after us, and here we were the only four Fleet Air Arm pilots left over the target! It was a great opportunity to shoot aircraft down, but very dangerous. I shot down one on the first attack against Palembang on January 24th, '45, and Major Hay got two. Five days later, during the second attack on the 29th, Hay and I shared two more victories.

I had got two Oscars [Nakajima Ki-43 Hayabusa] on the previous attack on Pangkalan Brandan on the 4th ... that was another one where I was high cover. I saw a guy sneaking in between us and low cover ... and just before I was going to shoot, he rolled over and bailed out, and he fell from his parachute harness. I climbed back up, I looked down and saw another, and fired at about two hundred yards, and he blew up.

After the second attack on Palembang, Ronnie Hay was promoted to lieutenant colonel and received a DSO. It is interesting that he transferred to the Royal Navy after the war and we both retired from our naval careers as commanders. We were good friends after the war and last met in Portsmouth, UK, for the fiftieth anniversary of the "Forgotten Fleet,"

the British East Indies and British Pacific Fleets of the Royal Navy.

Don's brother, Robert, followed him into the Fleet Air Arm and also qualified on the Corsair. He was a member of 1841 Squadron on HMS *Formidable*. During a routine training takeoff on March 21, 1945, the left wheel of his Corsair struck the eighteen-inch ramp projection on the forward flight deck. He climbed steeply, stalled and crashed into the sea. Don flew over to *Formidable* from *Victorious* to learn what had happened, but there was little that could be done, with the battle for Okinawa getting underway. He continued flying with his squadron and tells of how he became the first FAA ace in the Pacific:

My last victory was in Okinawa on May 4th, I was up at 20,000 feet over the fleet, a combat air patrol ... As we were climbing out the fighter direction officer said, "I have a very high target." I said I could see him, but I lied, I couldn't, because I knew the fighter direction officer did not want me getting too far away. Then I did spot a tiny speck much higher than our patrol. The Japanese pilot was obviously reporting on the fleet for the kamikaze pilots. We called such aircraft the "Gestapo Aircraft," as they directed the attacking aircraft. It was a Judy [Yokosuka D4Y3 Suisei bomber], and as he started to turn, I put up the throttle and left my three other guys and dumped my drop tank. I gave him a short burst from 250 yards at a high closing speed. When I gave him the second burst he blew up. I was going so fast I had to pull back the throttle, but still the debris hit my aircraft and set my fabric elevators on fire. I said to my guys, "We are going home" ... My rudder and tail plane were all wrinkled.

After the battles for Okinawa, Sheppard, who had been on duty for two years, was sent on a home leave to Canada. He decided to stay in the military and had a distinguished career with the Royal Canadian Navy. Among his many duties, he was the RCN assistant to the commandant of the Joint Air Training School at Rivers, Manitoba. At the prodding of his Canadian Army counterparts, he qualified as a paratrooper at Rivers and received his paratrooper's badge.

Courtesy of the William Atkinson Collection

Bill Atkinson in the Second World War.

Courtesy of the Wayne Ralph Collection

Bill Atkinson at home in Surrey, BC, 2002.

Profile – WILLIAM HENRY ISAAC ATKINSON

Born – April 22, 1923, Minnedosa, MB

Father – John Lawrence Atkinson, train engineer with the CPR, farmer

Mother – Selena Black

Decorations & Medals – DSC, MiD, CD and Clasp

Post-war occupation – Naval officer, RCN, Commander

Marital status – Wife Valgerdur Sigurdson, sons Larry and Tom, daughters Pamela and Lynne

One of the Fleet Air Arm veterans at the 1989 Onagawa Bay memorial service for Hammy Gray was Canada's only ace on the Grumman F6F Hellcat in the Pacific campaign—Commander William Henry Isaac "Bill" Atkinson, of Minnedosa, Manitoba. When Bill was six years old, his father had entertained a distinguished visitor at their home: the famous Great War VC recipient

Billy Bishop, who at the time was en route by train to Edmonton. John Atkinson, a CPR train engineer, farmed 160 acres two miles northwest of Minnedosa, but he had been with the Lord Strathcona's Horse (Royal Canadians) in the First World War, and he had served on horseback with Bishop before Bishop went on to fame with the Royal Flying Corps.

Bill Atkinson's mother, Selena, gave her son $5 for a short flight at age eleven with bush pilot legend Connie Johanneson and, five years later in Winnipeg, another $100 to take flying lessons from Jim Syme in a Taylorcraft. On graduation in 1942 from Daniel McIntyre High School in Winnipeg, Bill decided that ships and aircraft were more exciting than just aircraft. He wrote to the senior Royal Navy officer at Kingston, Ontario; he then applied through HMCS *Chippewa*.

His initial administrative processing was done in Winnipeg by an RCAF Women's Division flight lieutenant. After months had passed, and pleading letters had been sent to no avail, Bill visited the RCAF offices and while the administrative officer was out, he looked through her desk drawers. There on top in a folder were his application documents. He presumed that the RCAF did not like Canadian boys going off to the Fleet Air Arm, and the woman had deliberately stuffed his application in her desk drawer.

Like many other Canadians wanting to fly with the RN, Atkinson went through an interview with senior officers at RCAF Station Kingston before proceeding to HMS *Saker*, at Dartmouth, Nova Scotia. He recalls with a chuckle how fond he was of his green overcoat and green bowler hat, purchased in high school, and the only dressy clothing he had for his important trip down east. He was enlisted as a naval airman, second class, at a pay scale of three shillings a day. As Bill recalls, "There was no third-class rank." If you failed the interview, you paid your own way back home; if you were successful, you were outfitted and sent immediately to Dartmouth. When Atkinson exchanged his civvies for a sailor's uniform, his overcoat and bowler were taken from him, never to be seen again.

The training of a Fleet Air Arm pilot or observer was more extensive than that of his counterpart in the RAF or RCAF, and for a Canadian it involved two crossings of the Atlantic. On Atkinson's first crossing he sailed on the same ship his father had with the Canadian Overseas Expeditionary Force in 1915—SS *Aquitania*. For three months he trained as a recruit at HMS St Vincent, and was then promoted to leading naval airman; this promotion brought a large increase in pay and status. Flight training was conducted by either the USN in Florida or the RCAF in Ontario. Of Bill's class of just over 260, one-third went to Pensacola and two-thirds to Aylmer and Kingston.

Bill graduated with his wings from Aylmer in February 1944 and was promoted to the enlisted rank of petty officer. The USN provided more hours of flying training on more types of aircraft than the RCAF, and foreign students met all the requirements to receive the coveted gold aviator's wings of a USN flyer. As a result of the more thorough training, few of the USN-trained Fleet Air Arm pilots of Atkinson's HMS St Vincent course actually flew on operations before the war ended.

All the RCAF graduates were then sent overseas to Scotland to learn how to fly from carriers. It was here that Bill's friend, Jack Taylor, asked to trade positions with him on the deck qualification course. Like so many things in the military, be it training, punishment or pay parade, the alphabet decides who goes first or ends up last. Jack Taylor wanted to visit his family in London before shipping out to an unknown destination. The only way he would have time to do so was if someone near the front of the course, someone like Atkinson, swapped places. Bill agreed and Taylor qualified and went on leave. The weather turned sour and Atkinson never qualified. It was a simple decision by Bill but it had an unintended benefit. As he recalls those days, Bill gets tears in his eyes about Jack because he drowned in June 1945 after ditching his Seafire off Sydney, Australia, not long after completing a tour of operations at Okinawa. He knows that had he not switched, Taylor's parents would not have had that last week with their son before he shipped out.

Atkinson arrived with his fellow pilots in Ceylon (now Sri Lanka) at an aerodrome carved out of the jungle called RNAS Puttalam. There was every type of fighter that the RN used in the Pacific: the Seafire, the F4F Wildcat, the F6F Hellcat and the F4U Corsair. Bill points out that "the RN, once you had your wings, was most informal about aircraft check outs. If you wanted to fly a new aircraft you simply read the pilot's notes and then signed it out."

Atkinson found the F4U Corsair too massive, with a starting checklist that ran, so he recalls, to about one hundred items. It was the Grumman F6F Hellcat he fell in love with ("everything about it just felt right—it had bags of power") and, as luck would have it, he was assigned to a Hellcat squadron, No. 1844, on the carrier HMS *Indomitable*. When he commented that he was not qualified to land on carriers, the ops officer instructed him to sign out a Hellcat and complete a couple of landings. Bill did those two landings on January 27, 1945; two days later he participated in his first operation.

Bill's baptism in combat was on one of the largest, most dangerous air operations of the Pacific war, the attacks against the Japanese oil refineries at Palembang, Sumatra. Essential to the Japanese war effort, the refineries had many anti-aircraft batteries and also were vigorously defended by Japanese army pilots. In just two days, January 24 and 29, the Royal Navy lost forty-one aircraft and fifty flyers.

While Bill was waiting to take off in his Hellcat on his first do, as No. 4 in the formation, seven twin-engine Sally bombers, on their final kamikaze attack, aimed for the British Pacific Fleet. It was the largest fleet of Royal Navy vessels on a war assignment since the days of Lord Nelson in the nineteenth century, and the Japanese pilots had plenty of targets: four carriers (the flagship *Indomitable*, along with *Illustrious*, *Indefatigable* and *Victorious*), two battleships, four cruisers and eight destroyers. One Sally was shot down by a Seafire some thirty-five miles out, and then No. 1 and No. 2 Hellcats launched from the deck and destroyed two more. Anti-aircraft fire from the ships and other Seafires took care of the remaining four. No. 3's Hellcat became unserviceable and was sitting on the down elevator, blocking Bill's position:

I was back behind the after-lift, stuck behind the down elevator, unable to take off until the elevator returns to deck level ... meanwhile all guns are firing at these kamikaze attackers, including the 4.5-inch guns near me. The entire fleet starts to turn hard to starboard, so a "clear the deck" call is announced. I am the only human being on that deck, one green pilot on his first op in one lonely Hellcat. Well, a carrier bounces about two or three feet when turning hard, so my aircraft is skidding sideways along the deck to port. By this time, *Indomitable* is doing thirty-five knots and is ninety degrees out of the wind. Above me I can see six bombers in flames in the air simultaneously. I said to myself, "To hell with this," and took off without permission. The lead and No. 2 have formed up and I join them. My leader later asks me where the hell I had gotten to during all the excitement.

After the operation on Palembang, the British Pacific Fleet proceeded to its main base in Sydney. Admiral King, commander of the United States

Navy, had no time for the Royal Navy. If it had been his decision, the British would have played no role in the defeat of Japan. Roosevelt and Churchill decided otherwise. To protect the USN's resources, Admiral King said that no support services, not even replenishables, would be provided to the British Pacific Fleet. This meant the Royal Navy had to set up an 11,000-mile-long supply line for all the provisions of war. That they did so was a remarkable achievement, but in the official histories of the Pacific campaign little credit is given to the Royal Navy or its Fleet Air Arm, or to its contributions in the taking of Okinawa and the battles over Japan.

Atkinson and his fellow pilots on Hellcats with 1844 and 1839 supported the US landings at Okinawa between March and May 1945, in Operation Iceberg. Approximately ten thousand Japanese aircraft, including four thousand kamikazes, defended Okinawa, flying out of airfields in Formosa, southern China and Indonesia. Hellcats did a bit of everything: escort Grumman Avengers during the dive-bombing on the Sakishima group of islands and on Formosa; dive-bomb and strafe anti-aircraft positions and other targets; and fly Combat Air Patrol over the fleet shooting down kamikaze and "snooper" aircraft.

An independent thinker with a disobedient streak, Atkinson had great gunnery skills, learned quickly and was involved in aerial combats where he frequently damaged or destroyed more than one aircraft. He damaged a twin-engine bomber on March 26 and got his second damaged enemy aircraft on April 12 against a Tony (a Japanese equivalent to the Me109) and his first confirmed victory against a Zeke (Mitsubishi A6M Reisen Zero-sen). He got his first victory by disobeying his flight leader and pursuing an enemy target that his leader could not see:

I was blessed with great eyesight (all Prairie boys have great eyesight) and I would not return to the formation and go home because I just knew the target was straight ahead. I hit him with the first bloody burst in line astern, 800 to 900 yards away, and he blew up. [*Bill shows me the tiny speck on the gun film print that looks like a flaw on the negative, not an aircraft.*]

I was somewhat reticent to go to the Wardroom to have a drink after we debriefed, and as I entered the commanding officer said, "Bill, that was pretty damn wild!"... He wasn't amused because my judgment had proven better than his. But he did not have long to live. From then on I was known on the squadron as "Wild Bill."

The commanding officer was killed on May 3 while leading a special op against anti-aircraft sites. Just before launch, Bill's Hellcat became unserviceable. He jumped out of it, ran forward, leaped up on the wing of his commanding officer's machine and told him he was taking the spare Hellcat. As he jumped down to the steel deck, the CO advanced power and blew Atkinson across the deck almost into the turning propeller of the next Hellcat. He rolled under the huge prop ("the closest that I came to dying in the war") and leaped in the spare, which was armed and running, and took off.

The pilot flying as No. 3, a rookie pilot, did not jink to starboard, as was customary after takeoff, and Bill, now No. 4, struck his wake turbulence. Flying along nose-up, at low speed, his Hellcat could not climb through the turbulence. After about one mile, Bill's starboard wing struck the sea; the impact straightened him out and off he went, joining his formation. While Bill was wondering if his Hellcat would crash into the sea or climb away, the fleet had stopped launching aircraft; the "plane guard" destroyer went to full power to rescue Bill because it looked as though he would ditch. It was a very close run thing.

The commanding officer had briefed for an attack in combat formation, line abreast with three hundred feet between Hellcats. It was hoped that the Japanese would believe them to be merely passing by and not fire, but the anti-aircraft batteries opened up anyway, wreaking havoc:

The target was on our portside, and as I rolled in to a fifty-degree dive, the batteries started firing. I was hit in the engine, and I looked over my shoulder to see my CO entirely in flames. We called him on the radio, but he never responded. I think he had been killed by the flak, and he crashed in the vicinity of the target. We carried on with our bombing and strafing attacks and formed up to fly back, a distance of one hundred miles. My wingman checked my belly and it was covered in oil, but the engine instruments were normal. After I landed on *Indomitable*, still with normal engine power, and my aircraft was taken below, the engineering officer spoke to me. He said the engine had no oil, not a drop in the oil tank, and the two bottom pots [cylinders] on the Pratt & Whitney engine were gone.

After Okinawa fell, the fleet returned to Sydney, and *Indomitable* went into dry dock for repairs. In July, Bill was selected along with five other pilots to detach from 1844 with six Hellcats and go aboard HMS *Formidable*, now Admiral Sir Philip Vian's flagship. Four of the Hellcats provided night-fighter capability and two were for photo reconnaissance. Atkinson claims that he was selected partly because he was a good deck hockey player and would help defeat the deck hockey team on *Formidable*, hockey being a pastime that occupied much of the pilots' down time.

Admiral Vian, the air commander of the British Pacific Fleet, was now aboard the *Formidable* and had specifically requested the Hellcats to defend his flagship because, in his opinion, they were so capable. This rather upset the captain of *Formidable*, who liked his Corsairs and thought he needed no help from Hellcat pilots. Nevertheless, at Vian's request two Hellcats were kept "hot" and at five minutes' readiness. There was little action at night, though, and the pilots lobbied the admiral to let them strafe trains and other shore targets, the main job of the Corsair.

This boring standby duty for the Hellcat detachment came to an end on the evening of July 25, with Atkinson, call sign "Lucky 37," flying an op as No. 2 to Dick Mackie, along with No. 3, Bill Foster, and No. 4, Harry Taylor. Bill recalls how he became an ace that night:

Taylor had to return to the carrier with failing electrics, being led there by Foster. Shortly afterwards Mackie and I were given an interception heading by the radar controller towards a target. I could see these planes in the dusk [they were the new high-performance Aichi B7A Grace], but Mackie could not, so he said: "You have the lead. Go for them." He followed me up in the climb, and I fired from ten degrees below with about ten degrees angle off, getting the leader first and his No. 2 right afterwards with two short bursts. They both exploded. The third guy on the right turned away towards Mackie and he shot him down after a long chase. In the meantime I pulled up to get the advantage of altitude.

I then felt a whack in my fuselage not far behind my head and I knew that I had been hit. I turned tightly towards this fourth aircraft and managed to set fire to his starboard side. This Grace pilot knew what he was doing, he was experienced. I claimed him as a probable, but the next day they found the two crew members alive in the water, so the probable was upgraded to a confirmed. I heard that the two Japanese flyers attempted to commit suicide by ritual hara-kiri but were apprehended by our sailors, and thereby survived the war.

Atkinson received the Distinguished Service Cross for his actions in his last weeks of operational service. He was the only Fleet Air Arm pilot to achieve a triple victory in a single op. The Royal Navy citation, characteristically brief and colourless, consisted of eleven words: "For determination and address in air attacks on targets in Japan." Bill had earlier received a Mention in Despatches.

On the afternoon of August 9, Bill watched a close friend, Lieutenant Gerald A. "Andy" Anderson, of Trenton, Ontario, strike the roundown[2] on the carrier deck. Damaged by flak on an op led by Lieutenant Richard Bigg-Wither and by Canadian Charles Butterworth, his Corsair ran out of fuel and its engine failed just as he approached the deck. The severe impact caused the fuselage to break in two behind the cockpit. With the wheels of the Corsair physically on the deck, Bill thought Andy might make it. As he recalls today, "just a cupful of fuel would have made all the difference." But the aircraft tumbled backwards into the ocean. Andy may have been wounded, as he seemed to be unconscious after

his aircraft hit the roundown. Lieutenant Anderson was the last Canadian flyer in the Fleet Air Arm to die in the war against Japan, and was the final fatality among Canadian fighting men in the war.

Of the seven Canadian pilots with *Formidable*, five died. Only Charles Butterworth and Bill Atkinson survived to lay a wreath in August 1989 at the grave markers of their friends in the British Commonwealth War Graves Cemetery near Yokohama, Japan. Butterworth flew on the afternoon of the 9th and returned with a flak-damaged aircraft and an eye wound caused by windshield fragments; Atkinson flew two sorties on August 10 and made it back unharmed. Bill felt relieved not so much that he no longer had to fight but rather that he no longer had to attend requiem church services on the carrier every Sunday for the men lost the previous week.

I have had the good fortune to have many meetings with Commander Atkinson, and to get to know him better. Feeling rather bold one day, I asked Bill if he had ever done anything in combat that he might

[2] Navy term for the rounded edge of the stern of the carrier where the steel surface of the flight deck curves downwards towards the sea, like a lip.

feel uncomfortable about or ashamed of. He recalled a low-level op during the Battle of Okinawa where he passed over the jungles of an island of the Sakishima Gunto group early one morning:

I came to a clearing in the jungle and Japanese troops were formed up in a parade-square formation while they raised the Japanese flag. Instinctively, I just squeezed the trigger and I could see them falling ... It was over in a few seconds and I flew onward toward my carrier. That memory is tough on the conscience, and I dreamed about it sometimes.

When Bill arrived home in Manitoba in December 1945, he had another dream that reoccurred for days and days. In the dream, he stands in his mother's house and the doorbell rings; a man is at the door holding a telegram. He wakes up. When I asked Bill to speculate on what the dream could mean, he observed, "Perhaps I was just experiencing

the fear that my mother had lived through [during] my time overseas."

Atkinson carried on with the Royal Canadian Navy permanent force and had a distinguished career as a naval aviator and ship's captain. One of his great regrets, shared with most other RCN pilots, was that the Canadian government in 1946 rejected a no-conditions donation by the United States of fifty new Hellcats and an Essex-class aircraft carrier to fly them from. Instead the RCN went "British," operating Seafires and Fireflys—and then Sea Furies—on British carriers, in exchange for Canadian products sent to Britain.

Commander Atkinson, like his friend Don Sheppard, qualified for his paratrooper's badge while serving at Rivers, Manitoba. His last ship command, just before he retired, was HMCS *Haida*, the famous Second World War destroyer that he took on its final cruise through the Great Lakes to its berth-side home in Toronto as a museum exhibit (it has since been relocated to Hamilton).

Courtesy of the William Atkinson Collection

Left to right: Sub Lt Harry Taylor, British; Sub Lt Bill Foster, British; Lt Dick Mackie, New Zealander, RNZNVR; Lt Bill Atkinson, Canadian, RCNVR—all recipients of the Distinguished Service Cross.

Fighter ace Geoffrey Northcott, of Minnedosa, MB, dances with unidentified WAAF at RAF station Digby, Britain, circa 1943.

PART THIRTEEN

REHABILITATION, READJUSTMENT AND RE-ENTRY

Canadian fighter pilots, like virtually all veterans, came home to Canada by ship. Unlike soldiers, however, who often came home with their regiment, fighter pilots did not return to Canada with the squadron they had served on, but rather as individuals. There was no assembly parade at Halifax or Montreal or New York City for fighter pilots prior to marching away from the dock. Sometimes the process of being discharged back into civilian life was solitary and quick. The men you had joined up with were never those you took your discharge alongside. Well, almost never.

Ivan Mouat, Typhoon pilot, and Jack Moul, Spitfire pilot, both prisoners of war at Stalag Luft III, took their discharge at the same time and place and in the same lineup. It was a particularly rare coincidence, since they had joined up at the same time and place, in the same lineup. They had even been given adjacent serial numbers; the third serial number in the sequence was given to Roy Burden, Typhoon pilot. The three learned about this synchronicity of serial numbers well after the war, when comparing notes with each other at fighter-pilot reunions.

Burden had married right after getting his pilot's wings in 1941. When he returned to Vancouver, a local newspaper featured a story about his first meeting with his daughter in two years. Lynne, of course, did not remember him, but her mother, Virginia, had saved every letter Roy had written to her during the war, and he had saved all her letters. There are many hundreds of them, tied with string or ribbons and stored in a big cardboard box. For the past three years, they have taken to rereading the letters aloud to each other, then burning them, especially the risqué and mushy ones. A few deemed acceptable for outsiders have been passed along to the author.

When James Edwards was sent home on leave he was assigned to the Royal Canadian Air Force's No. 2 Training Command Headquarters in Winnipeg. There he encountered an old friend and ace, Geoffrey Northcott, DSO, DFC and Bar. The two were among the most decorated and highest-scoring young RCAF aces alive, and there were senior officers at the HQ who had heard no guns fired in action. They resented cocky young wartime temporary squadron leaders.

The two had the misfortune to ride up in an elevator with a pre-war RCAF group captain who tore a strip off them for their scruffy appearance and flat hats without interior reinforcing bands. As luck would have it, the rank of the two combat veterans was hidden by their wrinkled raincoats. Northcott fixed a beady eye on the group captain and said: "Do you always speak to senior officers in that tone of voice?"

Edwards was aghast at his friend's comment and moved sideways towards the corner of the elevator, not wanting to be associated with the outcome. Northcott's bluff worked, and within moments the group captain apologized to the two and backed out of the elevator in confusion. Edwards had always admired and liked Northcott and never more so than after this bit of reckless fighter pilot's intimidation.

Air Vice-Marshal Broadhurst, commander of the Second Tactical Air Force, and well known for his antipathy to Canadians, specifically requested that the RCAF send Northcott back to Britain. Geoffrey, aged twenty-four, the son of a farmer in Minnedosa, Manitoba, was promoted to wing commander and given command of 126 Wing in late January 1945. He had the nerve to walk into Air Vice-Marshal Kenneth Guthrie's office at Winnipeg and thumb his nose at him. He declared: "I told you I would be out

Roy Burden poses on one of the two 1,000-pound bombs carried by his Typhoon.

of here soon. After I get over there, I am going to have Edwards transferred as well."

True to his word, he spoke to Broadhurst, and Edwards, aged twenty-three, went back to Europe in March 1945 to replace the famous Johnnie Johnson, now a group captain, as wing commander (flying) of 127 Wing. When Edwards went into Ken Guthrie's office to say goodbye, he was more diplomatic than Northcott, but still expected a frosty reception. Instead, Guthrie, who in 1917 had lied about his age to join the Royal Flying Corps (he was only sixteen at the time), stuck out his hand and said to Edwards, "You take care of yourself over there, young fellow."

Jimmie Edwards did take care of himself and when the war ended he felt, by his own admission, rather confused. Now Jimmie would wake up in the morning not knowing what his day would be. He knew only that there were no more sorties to be flown against the enemy. War's end became a traumatic letdown for some pilots, and one individual whom Edwards had known for some period, a happy-go-lucky figure seemingly without a care in the world, climbed his Spitfire up to thirty thousand feet and

dove it straight into the ground. Most did not feel that alienated, but quite a few did feel something akin to it: the knowledge that nothing the future had to offer could possibly match what they had experienced either in intensity or comradeship. Most warriors moved past this feeling, shaping successful careers, but a few never did. Their minds were forever reliving experiences that had no parallel in the mundane world of peace.

When Doug Booth came home for his first leave after his tour at 416, he failed to telegram his mother and father that he was on his way. Doug was the newly commissioned pilot who had sent a telegram to his mother asking for money, not realizing the impact such a telegram could have on her nerves. When Doug walked into his family home on Trinity Street in Vancouver, he heard his mother washing clothes in the basement and went downstairs to say hello.

It was a great shock to her to see her only child walk in unannounced, but when she got over it, she was furious ("God, I don't think I have ever seen her so angry!"). She yelled at him about how disap-

Courtesy of the Roy Burden Collection

Two days home in Canada, Roy Burden reconnects with his daughter Carol Lynne.

pointed she was that he had not provided her the opportunity to dress up and go to the train station to meet him. It had never entered Doug's mind that his mother cared about such ceremonies.

After thirty days' leave, Doug was sent to Halifax to catch a ship back to Britain. Someone in authority asked if he was willing to do a second tour. Doug replied, "No, not really. Hell, you have plenty of pilots clamouring to go overseas. If you can do without me, I prefer to stay in Canada." Without further ado, they sent him back to Vancouver by train and placed him on the Class E Reserve List, subject to call-up if required.

He started his university education in commerce at the University of British Columbia in January 1945. At university he was pleased to run across George "Pat" Patterson, DFC, who had served with him at 416. Pat had stayed on through D-Day, flying with Al McFadden, Dick Forbes-Roberts, Derrick England and Bill Mason, and he had ultimately shot down four enemy aircraft and destroyed about one hundred vehicles in strafing attacks.

Doug was shocked to see that Pat's left arm was missing. Pat filled Doug in. He had been shot down on September 26, '44, bailing out of his burning Spitfire. He was then strafed by a German pilot as he descended in his chute. The cannon fire shattered his arm, and German surgeons amputated it above the elbow. Pat was repatriated in February 1945 from Germany and received back pay and a disability pension.

With the back pay Patterson bought a new blue Dodge, and asked Doug to drive with him to California. Under wartime federal laws, the two were not allowed to take more than $150 out of the country. They ran out of money in San Diego and slept on the beach at La Jolla, then headed to Reno to make money at craps. They didn't, of course. They spent their last dollars on an overnight bender. On the morning after, with the help of a few coins and folded one-dollar bills plus a gasoline company credit card, they drove through Oregon and Washington, arriving home flat broke. Like every DFC or DFM recipient, Patterson got $4.17 every month for his Distinguished Flying Cross; the stipend has never been adjusted for inflation, and at the end of the century it was still $4.17.

Patterson graduated as an engineer and became president of Armco Canada, a construction product company. He never wore a prosthesis, and his life was in no way impaired by the loss of his arm. He golfed well, driving the ball over two hundred yards, and even had a rare hole in one. He made inventions for himself, one-off tools that helped him to fish and to fire a hunting rifle. It was never a good idea to hold open the door for Patterson: he did not appreciate the gesture. A few months before he died in 2001 of congestive heart failure, he was mowing his lawn. His neighbour asked the former fighter pilot why he did not get Veterans Affairs Canada to mow the lawn, since he was, after all, a veteran. He replied, "That help is for handicapped people."

Booth had named his Spitfire "Lorraine" for a girl he knew in high school. They dated after the war, but the relationship did not bloom, and they went on to marry others. Similarly, Doug's wingman of 1943, Al McFadden, named his Spitfire "Margie" after his girlfriend, Marjorie Lenore "Lennie" Wilson. Lennie and Al did reconnect, marrying in the fall of 1944. Al, now Class

E Reserve, commenced his agricultural education at the University of Alberta, then went on to agricultural engineering at the University of Saskatchewan.

Al and Lennie lived in converted army barracks on the north side of Saskatoon and ate their meals in a common dining room with other veterans. The cost for Al, Lennie and their baby, Murray, was about $90 a month, and they took home about $120. As a stenographer for the Provincial Mediation Board, Lennie had made $70 a month during the war. But as Mrs McFadden she was forbidden to earn more than $30 per month, as it would jeopardize the financial assistance that Al as a veteran could receive for education. She still resents the government for it.

Derrick England was badly wounded on September 25, 1944—the day before Pat Patterson—while breaking up a bomber attack against a bridge near Arnhem. As he admits, it is the enemy you don't see that gets you, and in the intense dogfight that took place, England's focus was in front of him:

I was hit by somebody I did not see. My aircraft virtually exploded. I was really badly hit and I flopped over at twenty thousand feet, and went straight down. I took a cannon shell right in the starboard wing—blew a hole through it the size of a forty-five-gallon drum. I had taken a cannon shell through the side and it almost blew this leg off ... I was trying to decide whether to get out, but the explosion of the cannon shell jammed the canopy. I fought the controls, finally the nose of the aircraft slowly started to come up ... they had not hit a vital part of the engine, so I still had power. I had to run the engine at full power, or my aircraft would want to roll over ...

I decided to try to reach the airfield just outside Brussels. I could not slow down and had to fly the aircraft right onto the ground. I pulled back on the throttle slightly, the nose dropped, and I remember coming over the fence and cutting the switches ... Then I woke up in the hospital. Luckily there was a field hospital right on the aerodrome, or I wouldn't be here.

Next I woke up on an operating table. They were cutting away my clothes. Blood was gushing out of my leg. Into the operating tent came Group Captain Bill MacBrien: "I just looked at your aircraft, and you're dead; you can't be alive." I don't recall any more and then I woke up in a hospital in Brussels, don't know when. I stayed there six or eight weeks. Then they flew me to London in a Dakota.

I arrived back in Canada in March 1945, and got back to flying again. I was sent to Saskatoon, my old original stamping ground. I was told there were fire balloons being sent over from Japan. I was to be in control of a three-aircraft Hurricane unit to shoot down these balloons. We chased this one balloon over Moose Jaw, at our maximum altitude of thirty-two thousand feet. We zoomed up and fired at this balloon way above us at forty thousand. This was the only balloon we ever saw... Then I went to Yorkton, and I ended the war there...

I got married. My father-in-law was keen that I get out of the RCAF, though I was in the permanent RCAF. So I accepted his offer to go into the plumbing, heating and air-conditioning business. But later I flew in the RCAF Auxiliary on Mitchells with 406 Squadron.

Frank Hubbard, a fighter pilot at 401 Squadron in 1943–44, had had several serious crashes in his war career, the last one on May 28, '44. The auxiliary slipper tank was not feeding properly and the engine cut out at fifteen hundred feet. Frank remembers seeing the airfield at Hawkinge ahead of him, and then amnesia caused by the crash and subsequent fire blanked out the rest. His next memory is of coming to in the Medical Officer's office at Hawkinge, his hands and knees burned, his face, eye sockets and eyelids burned.

Eventually he was sent to Queen Victoria Hospital at East Grinstead, but his condition was considered marginal. Leading Air Woman Shirley "Red" Chambers, a stenographer at RCAF Headquarters at Lincoln's Inn Fields during the week, was up for the weekend at the hospital to help the Canadians on the ward. She had been visiting since 1943 and found the work was gratifying, even though as she recalls, "the smell took getting used to." She had heard the nurse indicate that Hubbard might not last, and she walked over to look at him. Frank, his eye socket burned and his eyelids gone, looked up at Shirley, reached out for her hand and declared: "I am going to marry you." The attending nurse watching this said, "Well, there is life in the old dog yet."

The following weekend when she looked in on Flying Officer Hubbard, Shirley knew immediately that his declaration was the truth. Frank's face was reconstructed using hair from his temple for eyebrow, and skin grafts from other body parts to build up the eye socket and eyelids. Shirley and Frank were married in September 1944; they went on a one-week honeymoon, and then Shirley returned to work at RCAF HQ and Frank went back into hospital. Dr Ross Tilley at Queen Victoria Hospital paraded Frank and his bride around the ward, complimenting Frank on how much more mobility he had in his burned arm since the honeymoon. Shirley had wanted very much to go to France with the RCAF, but when she got pregnant she was released from the service ("Boy, I was so mad."). The wing commander decided that Frank should be sent back to Canada rather than continue on operations, so his war was over.

The couple's first child, simply named Frank after his father and grandfather, was born in Toronto in July 1946 while Hubbard was attending the University of Toronto. Six more children followed: Michael, Kathleen, Ross, Kristen, Lauren and Moira. Frank graduated in aeronautical engineering, worked at Orenda Engines on the Iroquois program and was a scientific officer with the Defence Research Board and later with Transport Canada. He retired in 2001. He and Shirley live in Chilliwack, BC, and fly recreationally. They attend annual gatherings of the Guinea Pig Club and the Canadian Fighter Pilots Association.

Bill Roddie was a tour-expired 416 Squadron pilot waiting at Bournemouth to go home. He was contacted by the Eighth Army Air Force Headquarters at High Wickham, Buckinghamshire. The Americans wanted him to come north to fill out a deposition for use in the court martial of a P51 pilot. The request related to an op on March 31, '45, when two pilots in Bill Roddie's section had been shot down by a P51. Both pilots, Mullen and Round, survived the attack, ending up as prisoners of war.

At first it was assumed that a captured P51 flown by a German pilot was involved. When the American

major's gun film was developed and the roundels on the Spitfire wings were quite visible, a court martial proceeding was initiated. As Bill recollects:

I wasn't very popular [as they knew why I was there], but they had good accommodation and food. They already had depositions from Squadron Leader Mitchner [later Wing Commander John D. Mitchner, DFC and Bar, CD], and the two other pilots, but, when those statements had been taken I had left because I was tour-expired. It was not our first loss in this way. [Alexander George] "Sandy" Borland had been killed on Christmas Day over the Ardennes by a P47 Thunderbolt pilot. So, after this last incident, we were told that if any American aircraft made an attempt on us, we were to kill them.

Flying Officer John Philip Wiseman "Red" Francis had joined the RCAF in 1940. Just before the war he had finished his training for his limited commercial pilot's licence and had planned a career in bush flying. He was older than the average fighter pilot, having been born in Battleford, Saskatchewan, in 1913. He and Bill Barker joined 442 Squadron at the same time. Red shot down a Focke-Wulf 190 on his first day of operations, November 2, 1944, in a formation where he flew as No. 2 to Squadron Leader Bill Olmsted. He is philosophical about the achievement: "A lot depended on luck. We saw plenty of enemy aircraft, and yet you could go up ten minutes later and see nobody ... you could go a whole tour and see nobody."

Red Francis went on to destroy three other enemy fighters and two Ju52s on the ground, receiving the DFC. His last aerial fight while serving at 401 Squadron was memorable; on April 20, '45, he was in a line-astern chase. "There were four of us going in a circle, Robert W. 'Andy' Anderson was leading with a German on his tail, and I was on that German's tail, and another German was on my tail ... so Anderson went down, then my target went down in flames."

Red's father, John, had died in 1939, so when Red came home from the war he thought he should help his brother Tom on the farm eight miles west of Battleford; their youngest brother, Lloyd, had been killed in action in Normandy while serving as a signaller in the artillery. A fourth brother, Manley Francis, survived his war with the RCAF, having served as Wing Commander Buck McNair's fitter in England; he farmed as well in the Battleford region. Red had a brief civilian flying career with Saskatchewan Government Airways in the 1950s, but decided, partly due to his age, to return to farming. He does not look back on the war with nostalgia: "Sometimes I think it was a waste of time. Things have not improved all that much. It was something that had to be done at that time, but the end result has not been that great."

In 2001, Francis received a telephone call asking him to provide more information to an Elizabeth Anderson Gray in Britain about the death of her father, Robert Anderson. Red wrote to Mrs Gray, and her heartfelt reply is in the box at the bottom of this page.

Squadron Leader Rod Smith, DFC and Bar, returned from the war and attended engineering school at McGill University. He also flew Vampires with 401 Squadron, an RCAF Auxiliary squadron in Montreal. Like many Montreal-based fighter pilots he occasionally crossed paths with George Beurling, who was considering whom to fight for in the war in the Middle East. Later, George encouraged Rod to come with him to Israel, but Rod turned him down, wanting to finish his education. Some of Rod's contemporaries from Malta and northwest Europe did go to fight for Israel.

After receiving his engineering degree, Rod decided he wanted to become a lawyer. While attending Osgoode Hall Law School in Toronto, he was promoted to wing commander and took command of 411, the RCAF Auxiliary unit in Toronto. I had written a short draft biography of Rod Smith, which Rod reviewed before he died in April 2002. In the section where I listed him as a bachelor, he crossed it out and wrote in red ink: "never married." To Rod, a craftsman with words, there was a significant difference, and there were many red corrections on my draft. In discussing the women in his life, he admitted that his longest relationship had terminated because "I failed to ask the right question."

In 1990, Rod Smith received a telephone call from Frankenberg, Germany. The man on the other end of the line, struggling with his few words of English, explained that he was the navigator who had bailed out of the burning Ju88 over Malta on July 25, 1942. He was the only survivor from the bomber and his name was Heinz Heuser. He had paid a researcher to investigate who the Spitfire pilot was that day.

Heuser invited Rod to visit him in Germany. Before they could meet, within a few months of the telephone call, Heuser died. His widow extended the same invitation, and Rod went to Germany the following year for a visit. In one of life's peculiar little twists, it just so happened that Rod's long-time friend at his

ELIZABETH ANDERSON GRAY, BODRIGAN COTTAGE, TRESARRETT, NEAR BODMIN, CORNWALL

Dear Mr Francis, thank you so much for your letter about my father, Robert Anderson. With Al Gamble's help [at 401 Squadron] I have been able to piece together a complete record of my father's RCAF career, but you are the first person I have found who actually knew him. It has made him become so real. My natural mother is so touched to hear about him because sadly no-one thought to tell her that he had been killed, so she believed until I met her for the first time 18 months ago that he had gone back to Canada after the war. Thank you very very much for taking the time to write to me with your memories. They are so appreciated.

With best wishes, Mrs E. Anderson Gray.

PS – Al sent me a college photograph of my father. We have often wondered who our son David took after in looks, and now we know. He is 23 years old so he is not so much older than my father when he was killed.

law office, Margarete, had been born in Germany, had grown up in the same town as Mrs Heuser—though Margarete was some years younger—and had even attended the same high school in Frankenberg.

The year before Rod died, Air Vice-Marshal Johnnie Johnson died. There was a memorial service in the spring of 2001 for Britain's highest-scoring Second World War fighter pilot at the Church of the Royal Air Force, St Clement Danes, Strand, London. Johnson's family allocated pews directly behind the family for Canadians; Johnson had been especially proud of being an honorary Canadian. While Johnson was commanding the Kenley (Canadian) Wing, south of London in Surrey, the Canadian fighter pilots had invited him to wear Canada flashes on his RAF uniform. They asked him to speak like a Canadian, but the results were so painful that they told him to stop. Johnson came to Canada many times after the war, and had many friends, including legions of young people interested in his story.

I spoke with Rod when he returned from the memorial service. He declared that Johnnie's death was the passing of an era. He lamented that long-distance flying was too onerous for him; his flight to Johnnie's memorial, he said, was his last. He mentioned that Ian Maclennan and he had shared a room at the Royal Air Force Club on Piccadilly. He marvelled that General Gunther Rall, 275-victory Luftwaffe ace, had sat next to him in the pew at Johnnie's memorial. Throughout his post-war life, Johnson frequently socialized with surviving aces of the Luftwaffe.

* * *

In November 2000, Flight Lieutenant Don Walz travelled to France with one of his sons, Mike. Don wanted to visit the country and particularly the location he had parachuted into on June 16, '44. He reconnected with the French family that had hidden him from the Germans at the risk of summary execution should they be caught. After giving him his peasant clothing and his cover story as a deaf mute, they had taken away all of Walz's military clothing. The old farmer wore Don's flying boots for years after the war, and as he was throwing them out, he happened to come across a man's gold bracelet in the hollow heel. The bracelet was inscribed "F/L Don-

Burdette Gillis at home in Rouleau, SK, 2001.

ald Walz, C12586, 443 Sqn." The farmer handed the bracelet to his daughter, Loissette Delarue and instructed her to give it back to the Canadian pilot should he ever return to France.

The bracelet had been given to Don as a gift for good luck by his New Brunswick girlfriend, Genesta Tower, later his wife. He never flew without it, and so that it did not snag on aircraft parts, he put it in the heel of his flying boot whenever he was flying on operations. The bracelet was with him when he alone, of four RCAF pilots, survived an attack by an overwhelming force of German fighters. He came home from the war and returned to farming, but also founded West-Air Ltd, a flight training and charter operation out of Swift Current and later Moose Jaw. He forgot about the bracelet until Loissette, now over eighty, handed it to him in 2000. Don's wife, Genesta, who had given him the bracelet to keep him safe, had died of cancer in December 1980.

I had called Don Walz from Rouleau, Saskatchewan. It is a village of 435 people best known in 2005 as the film set for a CTV comedy program, *Corner*

Gas. The call was made from the home of Burdette Gillis, a fighter pilot who had served two years in the Western Desert with 145 and 238 Squadrons and finished the war with 403 at Hamburg, Germany. I had spent the afternoon with him and his caregiver, Byrnece Henderson.

Gillis, born in 1919 just a few miles away at Pence, had been a successful businessman at Rouleau after the war, establishing a locker plant, a grocery store, a liquor store and a car dealership. After his retirement in the 1970s, Rouleau went into decline and the businesses did not last. Burdette's wife, Freda, died in 1999 and a lifelong friend of the family, Byrnece, moved in to take care of him following several strokes. Though late in the day, Gillis said I should telephone Walz, as he would want to meet me, he said, and then he handed me the telephone.

Walz said that 7 p.m. was just fine. He described how to get there by driving south on Highway 2. He told me that if I missed his place, I would be headed for the Montana border. I did miss it and when I retraced my route, my breath was taken away by the golden colour of the crops in the August sun. When I arrived at the farm, I rang the doorbell of the house closest to the highway. A young woman answered the door, and when I explained who I was, she said: "He's in the house behind this one. But he won't remember anything about asking you to drop by."

This didn't sound promising, but Walz *did* remember, having written my name on a piece of paper that he placed next to the sink. He had coffee made, and he had bottles of liquor on the counter. He was a man without an ounce of fat on him, with muscular forearms and strong rough hands. He looked like an old rodeo cowboy. I knew very little about what he had done in the war, and was looking forward to learning more. His name had come to me from other fighter pilots who admired and liked him: "You got to go see Don, he's a great guy." It was the American Phil Vickers who first mentioned Don to me as a must-do interview.

Unfortunately, Walz's memory was substantially gone. It was more than an hour later while sipping his own drink that he realized he had not offered me one, and told me to help myself from the bottles on the kitchen counter. Don could re-

Burdette Gillis and caregiver, Byrnece Henderson, at home in Rouleau, SK, 2001.

member people if I asked about them by name, but randomly and unpredictably. If he could not remember, he simply told me that was a tough question I was asking and stopped talking. I spent one of the most entrancing and frustrating evenings I have ever experienced.

Knowing that I wanted him to talk about the war, he would, after long periods of silence, tell a story ... a great story, but fragmented. One that made him laugh was of how he protected Flying Officer Gordon Ockenden, DFC, aged twenty [the late Air Vice-Marshal Ockenden, RCAF, retired], from an affectionate French prostitute. After a period of silence, he smiled and said: "Well, I shot down four, and I was shot down twice. So I'm still two ahead!"

He did not know where his logbook was; he thought he had the Croix de Guerre, but couldn't be quite sure as his medals were also missing. We looked through a cigar box of old photos and war memorabilia, curled-up military prints of targets, cancelled ticket stubs. He then showed me some family photo albums, including photos of women in the war, showgirls in Montreal nightclubs, and his special girl, Genesta. Then he and I ran out of conversation, and silence descended on the living room, decorated in shades of peach by his late wife.

Somewhat later he turned the television on, the volume quite loud, but there seemed to be only one channel, CNN. They were reporting on floods somewhere. After we had both stared at the screen for a long period, he turned to me and asked: "Do you want to see my airplane?" It was 10 p.m. on a moonlit night on a farm in southern Saskatchewan. He put his hat and coat on, took a key off the hook by the kitchen door and walked me out into the yard. It was easy to see where he was headed by the light of the full moon. I could hear the hum of semi-trailers on Highway 2, heading to Montana or north into Moose Jaw. I did not know what to expect, but half thought that Walz was hallucinating. He unlocked the door to a large building, turned on the fluorescent lights, and sure enough, there sat a 1950s Beechcraft Debonair, in original colours of brown and yellow. After all, he was an old fighter pilot, why wouldn't he have an airplane on his farm?

We went back inside and he asked me where I was staying. I had made no reservations because I could not know at the end of a day where I would be. The interviews determined my location. I said I wanted to visit Eastend, the childhood home of American novelist and teacher Wallace Stegner, and thought I might find a motel at Assiniboia. Don said, "That is a long way to go. Why not stay here?" I murmured that I did not want to inconvenience him. He said: "Well, my wife is gone and I am here alone. We have several bedrooms to choose from."

Before going to sleep he insisted that I wake him in the morning so we could have breakfast together. He showed me his bedroom, got into bed in his underwear. I noticed the gun rack above his bed. When I went to turn off the hall light, he asked me to leave it on. Don liked to get a glass of milk from the fridge in the kitchen when he woke up in the middle of the night. I realized he would have to pass my bedroom on his way to the kitchen. He might not remember who I was at 3 a.m. I took the precaution of closing the bedroom door, placing my suitcase against it.

At about 7 a.m. I woke him up. Don sat on the side of the bed and lit a cigarette. I don't know if he knew at all who I was, but he spoke assertively: "Put on some coffee." I went to his kitchen, found what I needed, and made coffee. He came out in his denim shirt and pants, lit another cigarette and sat opposite me. I had made us toast, and I was having cereal. We did not talk. We drank our coffee, and the sun lit up the front yard, the same yard I had seen in moonlight on the way to view an aircraft. He had not heard from Phil Vickers, his wartime wingman, for a long time. He could not recall how long, so I dialled Vickers's number in Sedona, waking him up at 7:30 Arizona time so he could talk to his buddy.

I got ready to leave, loaded my suitcase in the car and went back to say thank you. He had the most intense blue eyes, and his smile as he wished me well transformed his face. As I pulled out of the yard, I was thinking of the three hours to Eastend and the decades behind me since last I had driven Highway 13 westbound from Assiniboia. I looked back to see Don Walz, former fighter pilot, waving goodbye to me from his kitchen window.

Don Walz seated at the kitchen table in the house on his farm, owned by his family since 1910. He was born at Moose Jaw on Christmas Day 1917 and died there May 13, 2004 (this photo taken on August 2, 2001).

APPENDICES

APPENDIX 1:
"OVERHEARD AT THE BAR"

Recollections by Various Anonymous Fighter Pilots about Friendly Fire and General Stupidity, Fleeting Affairs and Tragic Outcomes

"We had a great commanding officer, and he was replaced by one who was only interested in getting a gong. Well, he was getting into all kinds of mischief and eventually he does not come back ... he is reported missing. I can recall vividly R.A. _____ coming out of the dispersal hut kicking his hat gleefully in front of him with the news that B _____ has bought it."

"P _____ was on his last operation for his tour and had a new guy as his No. 2. They are being vectored towards two bogies at low altitude heading towards the south coast. As they get them in sight, No. 2 opens fire spontaneously. P _____ calls out, 'Stop firing, they're ours, they're Mustangs.' No. 2 keeps firing and one Mustang goes down. The other Mustang pilot turns into the attack, opens fire, and kills P _____. No. 2 comes home alone."

"I am travelling on a train at night and meet a young WAAF. She and I are sitting alone in the train compartment, and we are on the way to our home stations. In the dim light of the compartment, as she undresses for me, I see that her pubic area is shaved. I went to Europe a virgin Canadian kid and had seen nothing like this. I worried later that she might have had crabs, and that was why she was bare." Question by the author: "Was she pretty?" Answer: "My, aren't we fussy now!"

"I am in the bar following an op and am enjoying the company of my buddies. A WAAF sidles up to me and invites me to her room, where she says she has a bottle ... I am not that interested in going, but eventually I do. The following morning I wake up with a headache. The WAAF is not there, the bottle is not there. When I put on my tunic, I look down and see that she has neatly cut off the wings above my left breast pocket."
"There are no rooms to be had in London and I am stumbling around the park in the blackout looking for a place to lie down. A man approaches me and says I can bunk in with him. I follow him to his flat, at which point he says he would like to reveal his soul to me, would like to get to know me better. I say, thanks, but no thanks, and make my way back to the park bench."

"My flight commander and I were rendezvousing for the bombers right off Beachy Head, low over the water, and suddenly, without any warning, his drop tank comes off right in my face. He aborted the mission, and I was lucky as hell as his No. 2 not to have to ditch—that drop tank came very close ... I was not impressed."

"Lead and No. 2 get into a scrap over the French coast, in the course of which No. 1 has to bail out, but not until he has damaged one Me109 and sent another down in flames. Ultimately, No. 1 is taken prisoner, while No. 2 comes home and puts in a personal claim for one destroyed and one damaged. The IO [intelligence officer] credits him with No. 1's achievements."

"One of the pilots on our Mosquito squadron contracted venereal disease, and in those days they sent you down to the hospital at Alton for treatment. When he came back from the hospital, he related to me that he was embarrassed to have to report in to the nurse at the desk, giving his name. She produced his file, laying it on the counter, and to his horror the front of the file had large red letters, 'VD,' across it. He flipped over the file to hide the letters, only to find that the back of the file had similar large red letters, 'VD.'"

"One of my buddies in the maintenance section of our wing, Frank M_____, a non-smoker, had made $18,000 Canadian in Belgian francs by selling cartons of cigarettes for one British pound apiece. On leave in Paris he exchanged the money for French francs, and went into a bar to have a drink. There he met a lovely woman—a veritable vision named Teddy A_____. She was with a US Army major. At least she was until Frank showed her his bankroll. She agreed to spend the week with him on condition that she looked after the money.

At the end of a blissful week the money was gone, the leave was over, and Frank returned to the wing. Noting the smile on his face, I asked where he had been. He told me of his week in Paris and when I said, "Frank, don't you think that was a lot of dough to lose so fast?" Frank replied, "It was worth every bloody nickel!" When I saw the photo of Teddy A_____, I had to agree."

"At the front there was no social life after the retreat to Alamein. We did not have a radio or a piano. On one occasion we travelled into Alexandria, had a fight in a bar and stole their piano (there were some good strong airmen from the squadron with a truck out front). We were not allowed into Alexandria or Cairo without a sidearm. The Egyptians were pro-German. The British were not liked, and it was not hard to understand why they were not liked. They would kick Egyptians off the sidewalk. As a Canadian, it was shocking to see that kind of treatment. We had no idea such things existed, and we got into arguments with the British about their treatment of the locals."

"I landed my Spitfire in a stiff crosswind, striking and damaging the left hand flap on the metal matting of the runway. I had had a successful op and destroyed an enemy aircraft. My commanding officer was congratulating me when my fitter opened his big mouth and announced the damage. The CO's face clouded over and he said, "Bill, consider yourself confined to base for the next seven days." Within two days the CO is shot down and M.J. takes over the squadron. Being a more laid-back personality, far more of a gentleman than his predecessor, he countermanded my punishment, so I could go into town."

"It was the last day of hostilities in Germany, and we knew that as of 0800 hours the shooting stopped. Foolishly, I think, we launched several sorties at dawn as though this was a day like any other day. One eager beaver spotted a Luftwaffe float plane stooging along at slow speed, a helpless target. He hosed it down; it crashed and burned. Aboard the plane were several Luftwaffe officers who were simply looking for a place to land so they could surrender to us. What a callous, meaningless act that was to kill a bunch of Germans who only wanted to give up and go home."

APPENDIX 2:
PROFILE OF THE MEN INTERVIEWED FOR THE BOOK

By January 2005 I had completed tape-recorded interviews with 106 veterans. Some 15 to 20 individuals declined to be interviewed personally, but provided information and advice on how to reach other men (favourite rejection line: "All I did was drink and chase women, so you won't learn anything useful from me"). In many other cases, surviving family informed me that the individual had died or was now too ill to be interviewed. Nineteen of the tape-recorded interviewees are known to have died. During 2005, the year that this book was going to press, the oldest two men still living would be turning ninety-two (Francis and Fumerton); the youngest eighty (West); with the majority falling between eighty-two and eighty-five years of age.

Fifty per cent of those interviewed received at least one award for gallantry and/or a mention in despatches for their performance on operations. About 90 per cent of the flyers completed at least one tour of operations. Ten pilots became prisoners of war, including two individuals shot down in the first twelve months of the war and three in the last twelve months of the war. In addition, several pilots were shot down in enemy territory but evaded capture (e.g., Barker, Goldberg, Jowsey, Kennedy, Locke and Walz). At least nine had serious wounds as the result of combat, and five were burned and/or crushed and required reconstructive surgery at the Queen Victoria Hospital in East Grinstead, West Sussex.

Remarkably, more than 15 per cent of those interviewed had brothers who also served in an aircrew or technical capacity with the Royal Canadian Air Force. At least ten lost their brothers in action during the war, and one other in a military flying accident following the war. One lost a brother who had been serving with the Canadian Army in Holland. Two of those interviewed served on operations with their brothers in the same squadron (R.I.A. Smith and D. Warren).

At least 25 per cent of those interviewed had one or two victories, with one or more probables or damaged, or some variation thereof. One pilot had more than fifteen aerial victories to his credit, and six achieved ten to fifteen victories, seven achieved between five and nine, while three had four victories. In addition, those working in the fighter-bomber and anti-shipping roles destroyed hundreds of vehicles, trains and ships.

Fighter pilots on the whole make good entrepreneurs: quite a few of these men established successful businesses and could fairly be described as wealthy. One of the wealthiest entrepreneurs interviewed had been a radio detection finding (RDF) technician; another was a former Beaufighter pilot. Of the men who left the family farm to join the RCAF, a few returned to farming after the war (Evans, Ferguson, Francis, Martyn, G.N. Smith and Walz), but most did not.

About 25 per cent were invited to stay on in the permanent RCAF or Royal Canadian Navy, frequently with a reduction in rank. A few came back into the RCAF after further education and civilian work experience. Many others served in the RCAF Auxiliary. Several pilots and two of the six mechanics had successful RCAF careers in non-flying specialties such as engineering, air traffic control and administration. Of those who served in the post-war military, there are two retired lieutenant generals; three major generals; five colonels; four group captains, two wing commanders and a flying officer with the RCAF Auxiliary; four lieutenant colonels; two squadron leaders; two captains and one flight lieutenant; and two commanders and one lieutenant commander with the RCN.

However, the majority of the fighter pilots interviewed had no interest in flying professionally or recreationally and have not flown since the war. Due to the post-war airline demand for multi-engine flying experience, few fighter pilots obtained positions with Trans-Canada Airlines (TCA). Of the 240 veterans hired during the war and up to July 1947 by TCA, only six came from a fighter background—two of those six have been interviewed (March and Marr). Indeed, of all the pilots interviewed, only four made their careers entirely in airline flying (Bradford, March, Marr and Moul). But a significant number of others went into bush flying; founded general aviation firms; or had careers as charter, corporate, provincial or federal government pilots (Bradford from age sixty to seventy-seven, Hanton, Heacock, Phillip, Porter and Walz). Those who had a career in civil aviation typically logged in excess of twenty-five thousand flying hours, the highest being thirty-three thousand. A few became executives in aerospace manufacturing and/or test pilots (e.g., Bannock, J. Phillips).

Almost without exception, these men had what can be considered successful post-war careers. Quite a few have degrees in medicine or law, and many of the others have undergraduate or advanced degrees in aeronautical engineering, architecture, geology, mining engineering, commerce and the arts. Their degrees and other awards are shown after their names.

Many pilots, having been witness to and participants in massive destruction and death, wanted to build. They were drawn to education, medicine, dentistry, law or engineering. One ace became a Church of England minister (Noonan). The post-war civilian occupations of this group also include a United Nations executive, a stage actor and later a sculptor, an artist, a newspaper publisher, an office-supplies salesman, a car salesman, a tax revenuer, a postal clerk, a bus driver, a stockbroker and a realtor. One hundred and six people is not a large sampling from the thousands who flew, yet from this small group one former fighter pilot has received the Order of Canada, the Saskatchewan Order of Merit and an honorary doctorate; a second recently received the Order of Canada; a third is a member of the Agricultural Hall of Fame; and three others have been inducted into Canada's Aviation Hall of Fame (CAHF).

APPENDIX 3:
THE INTERVIEWEES

Alphabetical listing of interviewees, showing post-war rank and accreditation, province (if in Canada) and date of birth, date of death where applicable, and wartime squadrons served in.

1. George D. **Aitken**, AFC: b. Alberta on June 21, 1920—416, 403
2. Commander William H.I. "Bill" **Atkinson**, DSC, MiD, CD: b. Manitoba on April 22, 1923—1844 Fleet Air Arm
3. Russell W. "Russ" **Bannock (Bahnuk)**, DSO, DFC and Bar, CAHF: b. Alberta on November 1, 1919—418, 406
4. Group Captain Robert B. "Bill" **Barker**, DFC, CD: b. British Columbia on December 4, 1918—130, 442, 412
5. C. Keith **Barlow**, BEd: b. Ontario on March 7, 1923—72
6. Lt Commander Richard E. **Bartlett**, CD: b. Saskatchewan on April 21, 1919—803 Fleet Air Arm
7. Group Captain Roy F. **Begg**, Croix-de-Guerre, ED: b. British Columbia on August 5, 1915; died April 17, 2003—414, 83 Group
8. Frederick S. "Fred" **Berg**: b. British Columbia on December 2, 1922—438 (armourer)
9. Squadron Leader L.P.S. "Pat" **Bing**, DFC and Bar, CD: b. Saskatchewan on July 28, 1920—406, 89 (navigator)
10. Colonel Donald J. M. **Blakeslee**, USAF (retired): b. Ohio on September 11, 1917—411, 401, 133, 4th Fighter Group USAAF
11. R. Douglas **Booth**, BComm, CGA: b. British Columbia on July 4, 1920—416
12. John W. "Brick" **Bradford**, DFC: b. Ontario on July 18, 1920—681
13. H. Roy **Burden**, MiD: b. British Columbia on November 15, 1919; died January 28, 2005—118, 438
14. D. Fraser **Campbell**, BComm: b. Nova Scotia on December 23, 1919—253, 14, 411
15. Lt General William K. "Bill" **Carr**, CMM, DFC, CD, CAHF: b. Newfoundland on March 17, 1923—542, 683
16. Squadron Leader William **Cartwright**, MiD, CD: b. British Columbia on September 15, 1919—Halton course No. 33, 1936-38; 73, 3, 242, 260 (Fitter)
17. William C. "Bill" **Clifford**: b. Ontario on February 23, 1923—440
18. Roy **Cuthbert**, BASc, PEng: b. Saskatchewan on November 20, 1921—radio direction finding (RDF) technician (i.e. radar)
19. Arthur H. **Deacon**: b. Saskatchewan on July 22, 1916—242
20. William A. "Bill" **Doyle**: b. Manitoba on July 18, 1920—403, 132
21. Squadron Leader Harold G. "Curly" **Edwards**, CD: b. Nova Scotia on February 2, 1917—487
22. Wing Commander James F. "Stocky" **Edwards**, DFC and Bar, DFM, MiD, CD, OC: b. Saskatchewan

on June 5, 1921—94, 260, 417, 274, 127 Wing

23. Derrick J. "Dyke" **England**: b. Quebec on February 10, 1921—416

24. Robert J. **Evans**: b. Ontario on January 25, 1921—145, 601

25. Gordon H. T. **Farquharson**, DFC, LLB, QC, LSM: b. Ontario on May 10, 1921; died June 13, 2004—54, 126, 416

26. Robert R. "Bob" **Ferguson**, MiD, BA, BSc, LLD, OC: b. Manitoba on May 13, 1917—96, 410

27. J. Terrance "Terry" **Field**: b. British Columbia on September 24, 1921—601, 213, 417

28. Ross H. **Finlayson**, DDS: b. Ontario on February 22, 1921—409

29. Reginald L. **Follett**, LLB: b. Manitoba on July 15, 1924—567, 414, 411

30. Wing Commander Richard D. "Dick" **Forbes-Roberts**, CD: b. Saskatchewan on July 18, 1918—416

31. John P.W. "Red" **Francis**, DFC: b. Saskatchewan on August 1, 1913—130, 401, 442

32. R. Carl "Moose" **Fumerton**, DFC and Bar, AFC: b. Quebec on March 20, 1913—32, 1, 406, 89, 406

33. Colonel John W. **Garland**, DFC, BSc, CD: b. Ontario on June 15, 1922—80, 3

34. Flight Lieutenant Zella **Gibson**, CD: b. Ontario on January 23, 1912, widow of Flight Lieutenant John "Gibby" Gibson, CD—14, 417

35. F. Burdette **Gillis**: b. Saskatchewan on January 11, 1919—145, 238, 403

36. Group Captain David **Goldberg**, DFC, BBA, LLB, QC, LSM, CD: b. Ontario on March 20, 1917—416, 417

37. Francis E.W. "Frank" **Hanton**, DFC: b. Ontario on August 18, 1920; died December 2001—243, 400, 402, 443, 416

38. Harry J. **Hardy**, DFC, CD: b. Manitoba on May 30, 1922—440

39. Alan J. **Harris**, MASc, PEng: b. Ontario on February 10, 1920—radio direction finding (RDF) technician (i.e. radar), 96, 243, 450

40. Harold A. **Heacock**: b. Alberta on June 21, 1920—167, 412

41. Harold T. **Hope**: b. British Columbia on July 21, 1917—27

42. Frank T. **Hubbard**, BASc, PEng, AFCASI: b. Ontario on December 12, 1919—123, 403, 401

43. John C. "Hughie" **Hughes**: b. Manitoba on April 13, 1919—402, 249, 401

44. Dr Norris E. "Joe" **Hunt**, MD: b. Ontario on September 13, 1920; died October 19, 2004—65, 403

45. Robert S. "Bob" **Hyndman**: b. Alberta on June 28, 1915—411 (also Official War Artist)

46. Michell **Johnston**: b. Manitoba on February 29, 1920; died March 8, 2004—72, 402, 442, 443

47. Milton E. **Jowsey**, DFC, BSc, PEng: b. Ontario on May 21, 1922; died August 14, 2004—33, 92, 442

48. Dr Irving F. "Hap" **Kennedy**, DFC and Bar, MD: b. Ontario on February 4, 1922—263, 421, 249, 111, 93, 401

49. Edgar A. **Ker**, DFC, BSc, BEd: b. Ontario on January 5, 1922—145, 401

50. Stanley J. "Stan" **Kernaghan**, AFC, DFM: b. Manitoba on May 30, 1921; died April 16, 2001; and his widow Agnes Kernaghan—252

51. Clarence J "Kirk" **Kirkpatrick**, DFC, BAcct, CA: b. Saskatchewan on August 7, 1918; died October 7, 2004—406 (navigator)

52. Lt General Donald C. **Laubman**, CMM, DFC and Bar, CD: b. Alberta on October 16, 1921—133, 412, 402

53. Major General Kenneth C. **Lett**, BSc, CD: b. Ontario on July 13, 1923—402

54. Colonel James D. **Lindsay**, DFC, DFC (US), Air Medal, CD: b. Ontario on September 16, 1922—403, 416, and 39th FIS (Korean War)

55. J. E. Roland "Junior" **Locke**, MiD: b. Ontario on May 27, 1923—417, 416

56. Ian R. **Maclennan**, DFM, BArch, FRAIC, RCA: b. Saskatchewan on April 9, 1919—610, 401, 1435, 443

57. Squadron Leader Bert D. **Madill**, DFC, CD: b. Alberta on January 20, 1923—28, 123

58. Ian A. **March**, DFC—b. Scotland on July 11, 1921; died January 24, 2005—410

59. William L. "Bill" **Marr**, AFC: b. England on July 4, 1917—409

60. D. E. George **Martyn**: b. Ontario on November 20, 1923; died September 26, 2004—132, 137

61. William F. J. "Bill" **Mason**, BComm: b. Ontario on February 5, 1918—416
62. Allan R. **McFadden**, BSc: b. Alberta on December 11, 1918—416
63. H. Douglas **McNabb**: b. Manitoba on August 9, 1920—406
64. William R. "Bill" **McRae**: b. Scotland on September 9, 1919—132, 128, 401, 1490 Flight
65. Wing Commander Robert G. "Bob" **Middlemiss**, DFC, CD: b. Quebec on July 30, 1920—41, 403, 249, 130, 442, 130
66. Wing Commander Warren M. "Mid" **Middleton**, DFC, CD: b. Ontario on October 1, 1918; died December 1, 2002—430
67. Dr Hugh F. **Morse**, DFC, DDS: b. British Columbia on March 1, 1919—132, 14, 442
68. W. Ivan **Mouat**, BA, BEd: b. British Columbia on July 16, 1920—412, 56, 198
69. Arthur John "Jack" **Moul**: b. British Columbia on November 20, 1920—416
70. Flight Lieutenant Donald G. **Murchie**, BEd, CD: b. Alberta on February 14, 1923—412
71. Group Captain G. Bremner "Scotty" **Murray,** DFC: b. Manitoba on December 2, 1920—401, 412
72. W. Barry **Needham**: b. Saskatchewan on August 8, 1920—412, 401
73. Rev Daniel E. **Noonan**, DFC, BA, BD: b. Ontario on September 2, 1921—416
74. George R. "Pat" **Patterson**, DFC, BSc, PEng: b. British Columbia on July 4, 1921; died December 16, 2001—416
75. Martin J. "Pat" **Peterson**: b. Ontario on December 27, 1911; died December 23, 2003—118, 438, 143 Wing (Fitter)
76. Robert D. "Dagwood" **Phillip**, DFC: b. Ontario on April 5, 1921—416, 421
77. Howard L. "Tex" **Phillips**: b. Texas on October 12, 1914—112, 412
78. Wing Commander John H. "Jack" **Phillips**, DFC, CD: b. Ontario on April 23, 1923—418
79. John W. **Porter**: b. British Columbia on November 12, 1921—247
80. Rex H. **Probert**, DFC: b. Saskatchewan on March 19, 1921—33, 92
81. Lt Colonel Clive L. **Rippon**, DFC, LLB, CD: b. England on April 7, 1921—23 (navigator), 116 (pilot)
82. David "Lofty" **Roberts**: b. Alberta on April 30, 1922—Halton 1938–40, fitter in Malta, 298
83. William G.D. "Bill" **Roddie**: b. Quebec on November 5, 1923; died circa April 2002—416
84. Philip G. **Rogers**: b. Quebec on July 25, 1917—403, 33, 99
85. Arthur H. **Sager**, DFC, BA: b. British Columbia on October 22, 1916—421, 416, 443
86. Group Captain Rayne D. **Schultz**, DFC and Bar, OMM, CD, CAHF: b. Alberta on December 17, 1922—410
87. Commander Donald J. **Sheppard**, DSC, CD: b. Ontario on January 21, 1924—1835, 1836 Fleet Air Arm
88. Squadron Leader Sidney **Shulemson**, DSO, DFC, CEM and Clasp: b. Quebec on October 22, 1915—404
89. C. Ivan **Smith**: b. Ontario on September 24, 1921—268
90. George N. **Smith**: b. Ontario on December 11, 1920—411
91. Wing Commander Roderick I.A. **Smith**, DFC and Bar, BSc, LLB: b. Saskatchewan on March 11, 1922; died April 16, 2002—412, 126, 401
92. Robert E. **Spooner**, DFC: b. British Columbia on September 12, 1920—438
93. Wing Commander Frederick H. **Sproule**, DFC, CD: b. British Columbia on September 22, 1918—133, 186, 183, 42
94. Atholl **Sutherland Brown**, DFC, PhD, PEng: b. Ontario on June 20, 1923—177
95. Group Captain George "Red" **Sutherland**, CD: b. Alberta on July 2, 1918—406
96. Edgar L. **Taylor**: b. Manitoba on August 30, 1918—416, 238
97. Thomas E. "Tommy" **Vance**: b. Ontario on July 26, 1922—595, 411
98. Philip G. **Vickers** (Bockman): b. Oklahoma in September 1919; died circa June 2003—127, 443
99. Air Vice and Marshal William H. **Vincent**, his wife Margaret Vincent, CMM, CD: b. Manitoba on January 31, 1922—410, 409
100. Donald M. **Walz**, Croix de Guerre: b. Saskatchewan on December 25, 1917; died May 13, 2004—127, 443
101. Wing Commander Douglas "Duke" **Warren**, DFC, Air Medal, CD: b. Alberta on May 28, 1922—165, 66, 39th FIS (Korean War)

102. Squadron Leader Donald **West**, BSc, MBA, CD: b. Ontario on May 9, 1925—166, 401 (fitter / aero engine mechanic)
103. Group Captain David J. "Blackie" **Williams**, DSO, DFC, CD: b. British Columbia on January 6, 1919; died August 21, 2004—408, 406
104. Flight Lieutenant Leonard H. "Len" **Wilson**, CD: b. Ontario on August 4, 1923—442
105. R. Roy **Wozniak**, BScPharm: b. Saskatchewan on June 29, 1919—416, 403
106. James **Wright**, DFC, BSc, PEng: b. Saskatchewan on August 28, 1921—418 (navigator)

APPENDIX 4:
GLOSSARY OF MOST COMMON BRITISH EMPIRE AWARDS TO FIGHTER PILOTS

(Listed in descending order)
VC—Victoria Cross: Awarded to all ranks; of 1,354 awarded in 150 years, less than 60 have been to flyers, and only 2 to fighter pilots in the Second World War.
CGM—Conspicuous Gallantry Medal: Awarded to non-commissioned ranks.
DSO—Distinguished Service Order: Awarded to officers of all branches of the armed forces. For aircrew it was typically given to officers of the rank of flight lieutenant and higher. According to Surgeon Commander John Blatherwick, OC (as noted in his book *Canadian Orders, Decorations and Medals*, The Unitrade Press, 1983), a total of 1,291 DSOs and Bars have been awarded to Canadians in all our wars.
DFC—Distinguished Flying Cross: Awarded to air force officers; the most common decoration for flyers. According to Blatherwick, 4,237 DFCs and Bars were awarded to Canadian flyers during the Second World War.
DFM—Distinguished Flying Medal: Awarded to non-commissioned ranks, less common, and for that reason more coveted. 516 DFMs and one Bar were awarded to Canadian flyers during the Second World War.
DSC—Distinguished Service Cross: Awarded to officers of the Royal Navy. 143 DSCs and Bars were awarded to Canadians during the Second World War.
DSM—Distinguished Service Medal: Awarded to non-commissioned ranks.
AFC—Air Force Cross: Awarded to officers, for actions not directly involving enemy engagements. George VI awarded 427 AFCs and one Bar to Canadians.
AFM—Air Force Medal: Awarded to non-commissioned ranks, for actions not directly involving enemy engagements. George VI awarded 42 AFMs and one Bar to Canadians.
MiD—Mention in Despatches: Awarded to all ranks.
Note: A Bar worn on the ribbon of the award is indicative of a second award for that decoration, hence a DFC and Two Bars is equal to three Distinguished Flying Crosses. A clasp is provided on the Canadian Decoration (CD) to indicate additional awards, similar to a Bar. Total Numbers shown as awarded are from Blatherwick, "Canadian Orders," op.cit.

S O M E   O B S E R V A T I O N S   O N   T H E
D I S T I N G U I S H E D   S E R V I C E   O R D E R

Rarely conferred upon pilot officers and flying officers (George Beurling in Malta being an example), the DSO was notable in the Second World War as an award more for leadership than just bravery. At the same time, because the DSO is an order, rather than a medal or cross, its cachet owes something to unarticulated notions of social class. The order was created in 1885 to recognize junior officers of the British Army who were until then eligible only for a VC or CB (Commander of the Bath). But the DSO was most frequently conferred for air operations on higher ranks such as squadron leader, wing commander and group captain.

      The award of the DSO to Canadian flyers usually followed after the award of a DFC. Approximately one hundred Canadian flyers received a DSO. However, it is notable that only two Canadians received it after a DFM (the equivalent medal for an NCO flyer) even though they had subsequently been commissioned. According to author Hugh Halliday, the two Canadians were Beurling, serving in the RAF, and RCAF Flight Lieutenant Russell E. Curtis, of 428 Squadron, 6 Bomber Group. Halliday notes that only four RCAF pilots received the DSO twice (i.e., DSO with a Bar), two of those four being Wing Commanders Lloyd Chadburn and George Keefer, the latter ace born in 1921 in New York City of a Canadian mother and American father, who spent his childhood summers on Prince Edward Island. Group Captain John Faquier, a Pathfinder with 405, was unique in the RCAF in receiving the DSO three times, having two Bars to his DSO.

Most common foreign awards that have been conferred on Canadian fighter pilots include:

LdeH—Legion of Honour, France
CdeG—Croix de Guerre, France or Belgium
DFC—Distinguished Flying Cross, United States
Silver Star, United States
Air Medal, United States
DFC—Distinguished Flying Cross, Netherlands
Order of Orange-Nassau, Netherlands
VM—Virtuti Militare, Poland
War Cross, 1939, Czechoslovakia

Air Force Ranks—RCAF and RAF—Second World War
(Listed in ascending order from lowest to highest rank)

Aircraftman 2nd Class (AC2): rank when joining up
Aircraftman 1st Class (AC1)
Leading Aircraftman (LAC): rank for flyer in *ab initio* training
Corporal (Cpl)
Sergeant (Sgt)
Sergeant Pilot: usual rank for newly graduated non-commissioned flyer
Flight Sergeant (F/Sgt)
Warrant Officer 2nd Class (WO2)
Warrant Officer 1st Class (WO1)
Pilot Officer (P/O): usual rank for newly graduated flyer if commissioned immediately
Flying Officer (F/O)

Flight Lieutenant (F/L)
Squadron Leader (S/L)
Wing Commander (W/C)
Wing Commander (Flying): the highest rank of flyer that might regularly be engaged in combat flying
Group Captain (G/C)
Air Commodore (A/C)
Air Vice-Marshal (AVM)
Air Marshal (AM)
Air Chief Marshal (ACM)
Marshal of the Royal Air Force: (no equivalent in the RCAF)

Primer on RCAF and RAF fighting structures
Author's note: the following is a general guideline only and, as many veterans can attest, the reality may not have accorded with what is described below.

Single-engine day-fighter squadrons were normally commanded by a squadron leader, with the two flights within the squadron commanded by flight lieutenants. A typical flight consisted of six to nine aircraft; a typical squadron twelve to eighteen aircraft, but sometimes more. Nominal strength of eighteen aircraft could well be reduced to half that number in heavy combat, for example, in Malta.

Roughly eighteen to twenty-five pilots served in a **fighter squadron**, but there were also a large number of support personnel, including fitters, riggers, armourers, as well as an intelligence officer, an administration officer and a flight surgeon. Experienced and senior-ranking pilots were most likely to have their own assigned aircraft and designated fitter and rigger. Rookies were assigned whatever aircraft might be available, sometimes a machine that had a troublesome maintenance history. Frequently in air combat, squadrons and even wings were led by the most capable or experienced leaders, regardless of rank. This practice varied from air force to air force, theatre to theatre, and no generalizations can be made.

In the air, two aircraft were, in American parlance, "an element," but in the RCAF or RAF just "a **section** of two" or simply "No. 1 and No. 2." Four aircraft in formation were a "section." The first two of the section were numbered No. 1 and No. 2, and the second two No. 3 and No. 4. In the Fleet Air Arm, however, "a section" was two aircraft; "a **flight**" was four. The characteristic battle formation in the latter stages of the war for four aircraft was called "finger four," positioned like the tips of the fingers when extended, with several hundred feet of horizontal distance between each aircraft.

Twin-engine night-fighter, intruder, anti-shipping and Coastal Command fighter squadrons were normally commanded by a wing commander, with the two flights commanded by squadron leaders. This was parallel to the arrangement for Bomber Command squadrons. Night-fighter and most intruder operations were flown solo, i.e. with only one fighter aircraft manned by a pilot and a navigator. This was also the norm for unarmed photographic reconnaissance. Armed photographic reconnaissance was often flown in a section of two fighters—one to photograph, one to protect the photographic aircraft against enemy attack.

A **wing** consisted of two or more squadrons, led by a wing commander (flying) and commanded by a group captain. A group that constituted two or more wings was typically commanded by a group captain or an air vice-marshal. An **air force**, such as the Second Tactical Air Force, RAF, consisted of two or more groups and was usually commanded by an air vice-marshal.

REFERENCES

Books, memoirs, articles and papers cited, quoted or used for background.

INTRODUCTION

Hartley, Lesley Poles. 1953. *The Go-Between*. London: Penguin Modern Classics.

Funk & Wagnalls. 1980. *Standard College Dictionary*, Canadian ed. Toronto: Fitzhenry and Whiteside, p. 466.

Herrigel, Eugen. 1989. *Zen in the Art of Archery*. New York: Vintage Books, p. 31.

Shores, Christopher, and Hans Ring. 1969. *Fighters over the Desert: The Air Battles in the Western Desert June 1940 to December 1942*. New York: Arco, p. 220.

Halliday, Hugh. 1978. *The Tumbling Sky*. Stittsville, ON: Canada's Wings, p. 279.

Shores, Christopher, and Clive Williams. 1966. *Aces High: The Fighter Aces of the British and Commonwealth Air Forces in World War II*. London: Neville Spearman, pp. 72–81.

Ralph, Wayne. 1999. *Barker VC: The Classic Story of a Legendary First World War Hero*. London: Grub Street, p. 274.

Jack E.G. Dixon. July 25, 2000. "Wing Commander Vernon Woodward: Fighter Pilot Was One of Canada's Leading Aces. Won Rare Honour for 20 Kills in Second World War." *National Post*, p. AB.

PART ONE:
KITTYHAWK ACE OF THE
WESTERN DESERT CAMPAIGN

Edwards, J.F. (Stocky), Wing Commander, with J.P.A. Michel Lavigne. 1983. *Kittyhawk Pilot*. Battleford, SK: Turner-Warwick Publications.

Lavigne, J.P.A. Michel, with James F. Edwards, Wing Commander, and artwork by Alain Gagné. 2002. *Kittyhawks over the Sands: The Canadians & the RCAF Americans*. Victoriaville, QC: Lavigne Aviation Publications.

McCallum, Neil. 1959. *Journey with a Pistol: A Diary of War*. London: Victor Gollancz.

Hess, William N. 1966. *Famous Airmen Series: The Allied Aces of World War II*. New York: Arco, copyright by A.G. Leonard Morgan.

Sheppard, Lionel J., DFC. 1994. *Some of Our Victories: Life with a Desert Air Force Fighter/Bomber Squadron*. Unpublished memoir of British P40 pilot of 260 Squadron. East Rising, Humberside, UK.

Gilboe, Nelson. Circa 1998. *The Flying Adventures of Nelson Gilboe, Flight Lieutenant, RCAF: A True Story Written by Nelson Gilboe—1940 to 1945*. Unpublished memoir of Canadian P40 pilot of 260 Squadron, Windsor, ON.

Ireland, Bernard. 1993. *The War in the Mediterranean, 1940–1943*. London: Arms and Armour Press.

Clayton, Tim, and Phil Craig. 2003. *The End of the Beginning: From the Siege of Malta to the Allied Victory at El Alamein*. New York: The Free Press.

PART TWO:
CANADIANS IN THE SIEGE OF MALTA

Granfield, Linda. 1999. *High Flight: A Story of World War II.* Toronto: Tundra Books, p. 26.

Beurling, George, with Leslie Roberts. 2002. *Malta Spitfire: The Buzz Beurling Story.* Toronto: Penguin Books Canada, p. 234.

Nolan, Brian. 1981. *Hero: The Buzz Beurling Story.* Toronto: Lester & Orpen Dennys, pp. 74–79.

Shores, Christopher, Brian Cull, and Nicola Malizia. 1991. *Malta: The Spitfire Year, 1942.* London: Grub Street Publishing.

———. 1987. *Malta: The Hurricane Years 1940–41.* London: Grub Street Publishing.

Smith, Peter. 1970. *Pedestal: The Convoy that Saved Malta.* London: William Kimber.

Lucas, Laddie. 1994. *Malta: The Thorn in Rommel's Side: Six Months That Turned the War.* Anstey, Leicestershire: F.A. Thorpe (large print), p. 414.

Jones, Frank A., Group Captain. Circa 1985. *A Journal of a Return to the Postings during WWII of Group Captain Frank Jones Accompanied by His wife Joyce.* Unpublished memoir. Pender Island, BC.

Personal letters of Rod and Jerry Smith; newspaper clippings, condolence letters of the Smith family, courtesy of Wendy Noble; and the letters of Henry Wallace McLeod, courtesy of Library and National Archives Canada.

Pete McMartin. November 12, 1997. "Dawn Patrol Gathers to Remember Comrades Who Didn't Make It Back." *The Vancouver Sun.*

PART THREE:
THE WESTERN DESERT, 1942–43,
AND ITALY, 1943–44

Cundy, W.R. (Ron), DFC, DFM, MiD. 2001. *A Gremlin on My Shoulder: The Story of an Australian Fighter Pilot.* Loftus, Australia: Australian Military History Publications, pp. 60–61.

Olmsted, Bill, DSO, DFC and Bar. 1987. *Blue Skies: The Autobiography of a Canadian Spitfire Pilot in World War II.* Toronto: Stoddart, pp. 53–54 ("Advice to Rookie") and p. 259 ("Bill Olmsted Recalls …").

Houle, Albert U., with J.P.A. Michel Lavigne, and artwork by Alain Gagné. 2000. *G/C A.U. "Bert" Houle, DFC & Bar: The Man & the Aircraft.* Victoriaville, QC: Lavigne Aviation Publications, p. 72.

Lavigne, J.P.A. Michel, with Wing Commander James F. Edwards. 2003. *Hurricanes over the Sands (Part One): The Canadians & the RCAF Americans.* Victoriaville, QC: Lavigne Aviation Publications.

Duke, Neville. 1953. *Test Pilot.* London: Allan Wingate, p. 93.

Nesbit, Roy C. 1995. *The Armed Rovers: Beauforts & Beaufighters over the Mediterranean.* Shrewsbury, UK: Airlife Publishing, pp. 59–70, 98, 159.

Waugh, Evelyn. 1986. *Officers and Gentlemen.* London: Methuen.

Jowsey, Milton E., DFC. Circa 1990s. *The Story of Milton Jowsey,* an unpublished memoir. Copper Cliff, ON.

Kernaghan, Stanley J., AFC, DFM. Circa 1990s. *My Life,* an unpublished memoir. Vancouver.

Kennedy, I.F., Squadron Leader, DFC & Bar. 1994. *Black Crosses off My Wingtip.* Burnstown, ON: General Store Publishing House, pp. 164–65.

No author. 1983. *417 Squadron History.* Published under the authority of L/Col J.H. Newlove, commanding officer, 417 Squadron. Belleville, ON: The Hangar Bookshelf.

PART FOUR:
THE WORLD OF THE UNARMED
PHOTOGRAPHIC RECONNAISSANCE PILOT

Schiff, Stacy. 1996. *Saint-Exupéry: A Biography*. Toronto: Vintage Canada, p. 434.

Telegraph Group Limited. <http://www.telegraph.co.uk/news/main.jhtml?xml=/news/2004/04/08/wstex08.xml&sSheet=/portal/2004/04/08/ixportal.html>. "Wreckage of Little Prince Author's Plane Found in Sea" (accessed December 15, 2004).

Carr, William K., Lieutenant General, CMM, DFC, CD (ret). 2001. "Getting the Picture: Memories of a PRU Spitfire Pilot," in *The Canadian Aviation Historical Society Journal*, vol. 39, no. 4.

———. 2000. "Unarmed Against the Enemy: Memories of a Photo Recce Pilot," in *Airforce Magazine*, vol. 24, no. 3.

Bradford, John W. 2004. *The Life and Times of John William "Brick" Bradford*. Self-published memoir. Richmond, BC.

PART FIVE:
CANADIANS IN THE RAF
AND FLEET AIR ARM, 1939–40

Halliday, Hugh A. 1981. *No. 242 Squadron: The Canadian Years—The Story of the RAF's "All-Canadian" Fighter Squadron*. Belleville, ON: Canada's Wings.

———. 2000. *The First of the Many: Canadians in the Royal Air Force, 1920–1945*. Paper presented at the 6th Annual Air Force Historical Conference, sponsored by the Office of Air Force Heritage & History, Department of National Defence, Winnipeg.

Allison, Les. 1978. *Canadians in the Royal Air Force*. Roland, MB: self-published.

Library and Archives Canada. Manuscript Group 30, Series E527, Volume 1, File of McKnight, William Lidstone, Letters: 23 July and 16 Sept 1939; 25 Feb; 24 April; 18 July; 22 Sept 1940.

Interview by the author with Mike Pegler about his childhood friend Willie McKnight, 2004.

Brickhill, Paul. 2001. *Reach for the Sky: The Story of Douglas Bader, Legless Ace of the Battle of Britain*. Annapolis, MD: Naval Institute Press.

Bartkiewicz, Jeff. August 29, 2004. "Calgary Flying Ace Lived Hard, Died Young." *Calgary Herald*.

Heathcote, Blake. 2002. *Testaments of Honour: Personal Histories of Canada's War Veterans*. Toronto: Doubleday Canada.

Soward, Stuart E., Lieutenant Commander RCN (ret). 1993. *Hands to Flying Stations: A Recollective History of Canadian Naval Aviation*, vol. 1. Victoria, BC: Neptune Developments.

James, B.A. "Jimmy". 2002. *Moonless Night: The Second World War Escape Epic*. UK: Pen & Sword Books/Leo Cooper.

PART SIX:
THE DEADLY YEARS: RHUBARBS, CIRCUSES AND MANY, MANY WULFIES

Dunmore, Spencer. 1996. *Above and Beyond: The Canadians' War in the Air, 1939–45*. Toronto: McClelland & Stewart.

———. 1994. *Wings for Victory: The Remarkable Story of the British Commonwealth Air Training Plan in Canada*. Toronto: McClelland and Stewart.

Barris, Ted. 1992. *Behind The Glory*. Toronto: Macmillan Canada.

Hatch, F.J. 1983. *Aerodrome of Democracy: Canada and the British Commonwealth Air Training Plan 1939–1945*. Ottawa: Monograph Series No. 1, Directorate of History, Department of National Defence.

Forbes, Robert W. 1997. *Gone is the Angel: The Biography of Another Unsung Canadian Hero: Wing Commander Lloyd Chadburn, DSO and Bar, DFC*. Oshawa, ON: 151 Chadburn Squadron, Royal Canadian Air Cadets, pp. 149–50 (for quoted material from Chadburn's May 1944 letter, written just before he died).

No author. 1984. *416 Squadron History*. Published under the authority of L/Col W.A. Kalbfleisch, commanding officer, 416 Squadron. Belleville, ON: The Hangar Bookshelf, p. 35 ("Travelling Circus" extract) and p. 50 (May 22, 1944, Etrepagny air battle).

Chadburn, Wing Cmdr L.V. "We Bagged a '109' a Minute." *The Star Weekly*. Magazine Section, Number Two. Toronto, Friday, December 31, 1943.

Rees, Ken, Wing Commander, with Karen Arrandale. 2004. *Lie in the Dark and Listen: The Remarkable Exploits of a WWII Bomber Pilot and Great Escaper*. London: Grub Street, p. 179.

Caygill, Peter. 2001. *Spitfire Mark V in Action: RAF Operations in Northern Europe*. Shrewsbury, England: Airlife Publishing, pp. 45–46 ("The Focke-Wulf 190 and Mounting Losses").

Greenhous, Brereton, Stephen J. Harris, William C. Johnston, and William G.P. Rawling. 1994. *The Crucible of War, 1939–1945: The Official History of the Royal Canadian Air Force*, vol. 3. Toronto: University of Toronto Press in cooperation with DND and CGPC, Supply and Services Canada, pp. 217–18 ("Account in the Official History of the RCAF" extract) and p. 220 (Leigh-Mallory quotation).

Deere, Alan, C., Air Commodore, DSO, DFC and Bar. 1999. *Nine Lives*. London: Goodall.

Smith, Richard C. 2004. *Al Deere: Wartime Fighter Pilot, Peacetime Commander*. London: Grub Street Publishing.

Hunt, Dr Norris E. "Joe." 1995. *Are You Ready, Hunt?* Unpublished memoir of Dr Norris Hunt, Huntsville, ON.

———. 2003. *Muskoka: Change of Seasons*. Hunstville, ON: Fox Meadow Creations.

Johnson, Johnnie. 2000. *Wing Leader: Top Scoring Fighter Pilot of World War Two*. Toronto: Stoddart Publishing.

Sarkar, Dilip. 2002. *Johnnie Johnson: Spitfire Top Gun—Part One*. St Peter's, Worchester, UK: Ramrod Publications.

Sager, Arthur, DFC. 2002. *Line Shoot: Diary of a Fighter Pilot*. St Catharines, ON: Vanwell Publishing, p. 20 (quoted material about Sager's flying test).

Linton, Karl, DFC. 2003. *Lucky Linton: A Second World War Spitfire Pilot's Memoir*, self-published by Karl Raymond Linton. Halifax.

Warren, D., DFC. 2001. *Gemini Flight, a Self-Published Memoir by Wing Commander Douglas Warren, DFC*. Comox, BC.

Franks, Norman. 2001. *Buck McNair—Canadian Spitfire Ace: The Story of Group Captain R W McNair DSO, DFC & 2 Bars, Ld'H, CdG, RCAF*. London: Grub Street Publishing.

Bracken, Robert. 1995. *Spitfire: The Canadians*. Erin, ON: The Boston Mills Press.

———. 1999. *Spitfire II: The Canadians*. Erin, ON: The Boston Mills Press.

PART SEVEN:
THE WORLD OF THE BEAUFIGHTER AND MOSQUITO IN BRITAIN

Nijboer, Donald, with photos by Dan Patterson. 1998. *Cockpit: An Illustrated History of World War II Aircraft Interiors*. Erin, ON: The Boston Mills Press, pp. 38 and 42.

Houston, Stuart C. 1991. *R.G. Ferguson: Crusader Against Tuberculosis—Canadian Medical Lives Series, No 17*. Toronto and Oxford: Hannah Institute and Dundurn Press.

McIntosh, Dave. 1981. *Terror in the Starboard Seat*. Markham, ON: Paperjacks, p. 34 (quotation about Sid Seid) and pp. 92–96 (extract on the women of London).

The Weather Doctor website. "Weather Phenomenon and Elements: The Fire of St Elmo." <http://www.islandnet.com/~see/weather/elements/stelmo.htm>

Cooper, Royal. 1999. *Tales from a Pilot's Logbook: A Love Affair with Airplanes*. St. John's: Flanker Press.

RCAF Air Historian. Circa 1945. *A History of 410 Squadron*. Photocopy in the possession of Squadron Leader Ian March, DFC.

Halliday, Hugh. 1978. *The Tumbling Sky*. Stittsville, ON: Canada's Wings, p. 179 (quote about Donald MacFadyen).

Kostenuk, Samuel, and John Griffin. 1977. *RCAF Squadron Histories and Aircraft 1924–1968*. Toronto, Sarasota: Samuel Stevens, Hakkert and Company, pp. 92 and 111 (casualties at 406 and 418).

Deadly Duo: No 404 Squadron (Buffalo), RCAF and the Rocket Projectile, 1943–45. 2002. Paper presented by Guevremont, Stéphane, at the 8th Annual Air Force Historical Conference, conference sponsored by the Office of Air Force Heritage and History, Department of National Defence, Winnipeg.

Nesbit, Roy Conyers. 1995. *The Strike Wings: Special Anti-shipping Squadrons, 1942–45*. United Kingdom: The Stationery Office Books.

Humphries, Colonel Terry, air attaché. April 1995. *Airforce* feature story about the grave of George Beurling and others in Israel, p. 43.

PART EIGHT:
TWO AMERICANS IN THE RCAF

Dunmore, Spencer. 1994. *Wings for Victory: The Remarkable Story of the British Commonwealth Air Training Plan in Canada*. Toronto: McClelland and Stewart, p. 243.

Internet Movie Database (IMDb) website. Filmography of Philip Vickers, actor. <http://us.imdb.com/name/nm0896019/>

Johnson, Johnnie. 2000. *Wing Leader: Top Scoring Fighter Pilot of World War Two*. Toronto: Stoddart Publishing, pp. 273–74.

PART NINE:
RCAF SPITFIRE OPERATIONS FROM BRITAIN AND EUROPE

Bashow, David L. 1994. *All the Fine Young Eagles: In the Cockpit with Canada's Second World War Fighter Pilots.* Toronto, New York: Stoddart Publishing.

Johnson, Johnnie. 2000. *Wing Leader: Top Scoring Fighter Pilot of World War Two.* Toronto: Stoddart Publishing, p. 236 (discussion of Wally McLeod's shooting).

Berger, Monty, and Brian Jeffrey Street. 1994. *Invasions Without Tears: The Story of Canada's Top-Scoring Spitfire Wing in Europe During the Second World War.* Toronto: Vintage Books.

PART TEN:
CANADA'S TYPHOON PILOTS

Halliday, Hugh A. 1992. T*yphoon and Tempest: The Canadian Story.* Toronto: CANAV Books.

Hardy, Harry James, DFC, CD. 2004. *Autobiography of Harry James Hardy DFC CD—From Canoeist to Typhoon Fighter-Pilot.* Self-published memoir. Burnaby, BC.

Johnson, Johnnie. 2000. *Wing Leader: Top Scoring Fighter Pilot of World War Two.* Toronto: Stoddart Publishing, p. 130.

Madsen, Chris (University of Victoria). "Victims of Circumstance: The Execution of German Deserters by Surrendered German Troops under Canadian Control in Amsterdam, May 1945." <http://info.wlu.ca/~wwwmsds/vol2n1circumstancemasden.htm> (accessed January 5, 2005).

Burrill, William. 1994. *Hemingway: The Toronto Years.* Toronto: Doubleday Canada, p.51.

Clark, Gregory. Circa summer 1944. "Diving 6000 Feet Straight Down: Pilot's Body Weighs Two Tons at End of Descent." *Star Weekly.*

Clifford, Bill. No date. *Reflections on November 11th.* Self-published memoir by 440 Squadron Typhoon pilot. St Catharines, ON.

Le Gear, Victor H.J., DFC. No date. Unpublished memoir by 440 Squadron Typhoon pilot. Cobble Hill, BC.

PART ELEVEN:
THE FIGHTER PILOTS' WAR IN INDIA AND BURMA

Axis History Forum. September 18, 2004, reprint of *Daily Telegraph,* obituary of Air Commodore Leonard Birchill.< http://forum.axishistory.com/viewtopic.php?t=60023> (accessed January 5, 2005).

Hamilton, Angus, 1998. *Canadians on Radar in South East Asia, 1941-1945: The Saga of Seven Hundred and Twenty Three RCAF Radar Mechanics who served with the RAF in South East Asia in World War II.* Fredericton, ACH Publsihing.

Innes, David J. 1985. *Beaufighters over Burma: No. 27 Squadron, RAF, 1942–45.* Poole, Dorset, UK: Blandford Press.

Sutherland Brown, Atholl, DFC, PhD, Peng. 2001. *Silently into the Midst of Things: 177 Squadron Royal Air Force in Burma, 1943–45: History and Personal Narratives.* Victoria, BC: Trafford Publishing (originally printed by The Book Guild Ltd., Sussex, England), pp. 39 and 75.

———, 1995. *Indian Days—Burmese Nights: Personal Reminiscences of Wartime Service with the RAF.* Self-published memoir. Victoria, BC.

———. 2004. *Buster: A Canadian Patriot and Imperialist—The Life and Times of Brigadier James Sutherland*

Brown. Waterloo, ON, and Victoria, BC: Laurier Centre for Military Strategic and Disarmament Studies at Wilfrid Laurier University, and Trafford Publishing.

PART TWELVE:
THREE PILOTS OF THE FLEET AIR ARM IN THE PACIFIC THEATRE

Rhodes, Richard. 1986. *The Making of the Atomic Bomb*. New York: Simon and Schuster, A Touchstone Book, pp.739–42

Daily Telegraph. July 21, 2004. "Obituary: Major-General Charles Sweeney."

Vian, Admiral of the Fleet Sir Philip, GCB, KBE, DSO. 1960. *Action This Day: A War Memoir*. London: Frederick Muller.

Soward, Stuart E., Lieutenant Commander, RCN (ret.). 2003. *A Formidable Hero: Lt R.H. Gray, VC, DSC, RCNVR*, 2nd ed. Victoria, BC: Neptune Developments.

Eadon, Stuart, ex-Lieutenant RNVR. 1988. *Sakishima and Back: "Where Men with Splendid Hearts May Go"*. Upton-upon-Severn, Worcestershire, UK: Charity Books in association with The Self Publishing Association.

Reid, Wallace. 1996. *Japan and Aspects of Naval Operations Pacific World War II*. A lecture delivered to Eton College History Society. Illustrated pamphlet, Rustington, West Sussex: Beauclerk.

Brown, David, ed. 1995. *The British Pacific and East Indies Fleets: "The Forgotten Fleets," 50th Anniversary* (illustrated commemorative paperback for fiftieth anniversary of war's end). Liverpool: Brodie Publishing.

Poolman, Kenneth. 1955. *Illustrious*. London: William Kimber.

PART THIRTEEN:
REHABILITATION, READJUSTMENT AND RE-ENTRY

Personal letter written to Red Francis, DFC, by Elizabeth Anderson Gray, Cornwall, England.

681 Squadron ground crew standing in front of Spitfire Mk XI

Courtesy of the John "Brick" Bradford Collection

INDEX
PEOPLE AND PLACES

A

Abbott, Phillip, HMS Formidable, on Ramrod Two with Gray, 220

Aberdeen, Scotland, 61, 122

Abu Sueir, Egypt, 30, 165

Acklington, Northumberland, 30, 124, 138

Aiken, ACM Sir John, RAF course mate of Ferguson, 60 OTU, 116

Aitken, George, pilot with 416, 403 RCAF, 82(family profile), 82-84, 86, 90, 91-92, 93(photo), 246

Aitken, G/C Sir Max, CO Banff Strike Wing RAF, son of Lord Beaverbrook, 157

Aldham, "Alf," navigator with Sutherland Brown at 177 RAF, 204-207

Alexander, Sgt, maintenance chief 118 RCAF, Annette Island, AK, 197

Alexandria, Egypt, 3, 15, 31, 38, 244

Anderson, Gerald "Andy," HMS Formidable, Canadian Fleet Air Arm pilot, 230(KIA)

Anderson, J.W., with Moul on first enemy action for 416 RCAF, 86

Anderson, Robert "Andy," pilot with 401 RCAF, 237, 238(KIA)

Andrews, Bernard, RAF navigator with Kernaghan at 252 RAF, 45, 47

Angus, Allen, first Canadian ace in WWII, with 85 RAF, 14, 16(KIA)

Annette Island, Alaska, 190, 197

Anzio, Italy, 53, 54, 62

Arbuthnott, Bill, 96

Archer, pilot with 416 RCAF, first 416 victory, 96

Argue, pilot with 403 RCAF, 88

Armstrong, Tom, RAF navigator with Kernaghan at 252 RAF, 47

Aston Down, England, 22, 101

Atkinson, Cmdr William H. I. "Bill," Canadian ace with Fleet Air Arm, 1844, HMS Indomitable and Formidable, xi, 203, 219, 220, 226(family profile; photos today; in WWII), 226-231, 231 (photo), 244

Atkinson, Val, wife of Bill Atkinson, xi

Audet, Richard J. "Dick," Canadian ace in the RCAF, 411 Sqn, 172(recalled by Lett and Campbell)

Aurora, ON, 83, 222

Aylmer, ON, 142, 153, 227

Ayr, Scotland, 94, 192, 194, 214

B

Bader, G/C Sir Douglas, legendary RAF amputee ace, 16, 68, 72

Bagotville, Quebec, 23, 176, 177, 190

Ballantyne, James, pilot in Malta, 17

Bannock, W/C Russell "Russ," Canadian ace with 418, CO 406 RCAF, 128, 135, 143, 147(family profile), 148-151(photo), 152, 245

Barker, W/C Anthony, RAF CO of 418 RCAF, 147, 149(photo with Bannock, Gray)

Barker, G/C Robert "Bill," pilot with 442, 412 RCAF, xi, 176(family profile, photo), 176-178, 245, 246

Barlow, Keith, Canadian pilot with 72 RAF, 244

Bartlett, W/C Christopher, Dick Bartlett's brother, CO 434 RCAF, 73, 77 (KIA)

Bartlett, Lt Cmdr Richard "Dick," HMS Ark Royal, Fleet Air Arm, 72(family profile), 73(photo), 74-77, 246

Bassett, Peter, RAF navigator with Shulemson at 404 RCAF, 154

Battleford, SK, 4, 6, 237, 238

Beachy Head, England, 107, 214, 243

Begg, G/C Roy, CO 414 RCAF, 83 Group RAF, 246

Beresford, W/C, 233 Wing RAF, 6

Berg, LAC Fred, 438 RCAF armourer, xi, 194(describes 20mm gun accident), 244

Bergen Belsen concentration camp, 190, 195(recalled by Vic le Gear), 199

Berlin, Germany, 21, 150, 177, 185

Beurling, George Frederick, Canadian top ace of WWII, 249 RAF; 403, 412 RCAF, 1, 16(arrival in Malta), 18, 25(photo), 25-27(recalled by Maclennan), 31-33(crash at Gibraltar), 37, 41, 49, 90, 118(recalled by Ferguson), 159(death, final interment in Israel), 167(recalled by Tex Phillips), 174(recalled by Lindsay), 238, 250

Biernes, S/L Jake, CO 438 RCAF, killed in flying accident, 195

Bigg-Wither, Richard, Pilot with Fleet Air Arm, HMS Formidable, 230

Billing, G.D. "Jerry," pilot in Malta, 17

Bing, S/L L.P.S. "Pat," navigator ace with Fumerton at 89 RAF, 17, 29(family profile, photo), 30-31, 246

Birchall, AC Leonard, pilot with 413 RCAF, "Saviour of Ceylon," 203

Birks, Lt Gerald A., WWI ace with 66 RAF, 1

Bishop VC, AM William Avery "Billy," RCAF Director of

Recruiting in WWII, 30, 49, 60(photo presenting wings), 226

Blade, John, HMS *Formidable*, on Ramrod Two with Gray, 220

Blakeslee, Colonel Donald, American pilot in the RCAF, CO 4th FG, USAAF, 22(photo), 22, 244

Blatchford, W/C Howard Peter "Cowboy," pilot from Edmonton in RAF, 82(KIA)

Boal, Earl W., Canadian ace navigator with Johnny Caine at 418 RCAF, 144

Bockman, Philip G, *see* Vickers, Philip "Phil"

Bombay, India, 207, 212, 216

Bond, Brendan, xi

Booth, Joy Rathie, wife of Doug Booth, 103

Booth, Richard Douglas "Doug," pilot with 416 RCAF, xi, 101(family profile), 102(photos), 103-110, 234-235, 246

Boothman, AVM Sir John, RAF commander, 61

Borland, Alexander George "Sandy," pilot with 416 RCAF, 78(in group photo), 110, 237(KIA, friendly fire)

Bournemouth, England, 61, 83, 116, 130, 165, 193, 204, 170, 204, 217, 237

Bradford, John "Brick," Canadian pilot with 681 RAF, xi, 59(family profile), 62, 63(photo), 64(citation), 65(photo), 203, 212, 245

Brandon, MB, 5, 48, 83, 87, 109, 169, 211

Bradley, W/C T.P.A., CO 27 RAF, 210(KIA)

Bradwell Bay, Essex, England, 120,185

Breadner, AM Lloyd, RCAF commander, 43, 52, 175

Broadhurst, ACM Sir Harry, RAF commander, 51, 199, 233, 234

Brown CGM, S/L Kenneth, Canadian pilot with 617 RAF, The Dambusters, 88

Brown, W/C Mark "Hilly," Canadian ace in RAF, 13, 14, 16, 23

Brown, Marvin, pilot with McKnight on last op, 242 RAF, 70

Bruce, Robert Roy, navigator ace with Bannock at 418 RCAF, 148-150, 152

Buckham, W/C Robert "Bob," CO 416 RCAF, 41, 86, 96(at Dieppe)

Burbidge, Maurice "Moss," bush pilot, Edmonton, 148

Burden, George, pilot with 143 Wing RCAF, 195(KIA)

Burden, H. Roy, pilot with 118, 438 RCAF, 189(family profile, childhood photo), 190, 191(photo), 194, 195-196, 233, 234-235(photos), 246

Burden, Virginia Hampson, wife of Roy Burden, 189, 190

Butler, Mickey, pilot in Malta, 17

Butterworth, Charles E., Canadian pilot with Fleet Air Arm, HMS *Formidable*, 1842, 230

C

Caen, France, 167, 187

Caine, John Todd "Johnny," Canadian ace with 418 RCAF, 143, 144(description), 146(citation)

Cairo, Egypt, 12, 39, 43, 45, 98, 204, 244

Calgary, AB, xi, 41, 67, 68, 70, 94, 99, 129, 130, 169, 172, 204, 214

Calcutta, India, 12, 58(aerial photo), 62, 206

Campbell, Don, pilot at 403 RCAF, POW, 91

Campbell, S/L Kenneth, CO 403 RCAF, POW, 88

Campbell, Fraser, pilot with 411 RCAF, with Audet on five-victory op, 172, 246

Campbell, Moore, friend of Lindsay, 173

Carpenter, J.L. "Joe," navigator with Marr at 409 RCAF, 138-139,

Carr, Lt General William K. "Bill," Newfoundland pilot with 683 RAF, 17, 59, 60(family profile, photo), 61-62(citation), 64, 212, 246

Cartwright, MB, 45, 49

Cartwright, S/L William "Bill," Halton graduate in RAF, Edward's fitter at 260 RAF, 67, 246

Casson, Lt Cmdr John, CO 803 FAA, HMS *Ark Royal*, 74

Caterpillar Club, badge and ID card, qualifications for, 104, 105(photo)

Catfoss, Yorkshire, England, 45, 48, 204

Caygill, Peter, author, 96, 109

Chadburn, W/C Lloyd, Canadian ace in the RCAF, 39, 83, 84(family profile, photo), 85(recalled by pilots), 96, 101, 102, 103, 109-110, 111(photo with 416), 111(KIA)

Chambers, Lorne, pilot in 242 RAF, POW, 72

Chandler, John, Fleet Air Arm pilot, friend of Sheppard, 224(KIA)

Charles, W/C E.F.J. "Jack," Canadian ace in RAF, 79, 107

Chennault, Major General Claire, head of the AVG "Flying Tigers," 5

Charlottetown, PEI, 52, 153

Chez Moi Club, London, 33, 82

Chilliwack, BC, 130, 237

Crichton, J.M.S. "Joe," Canadian pilot with Tex Phillips at 112 RAF, 166

Church, Jack, pilot with Hap Kennedy in Italy, 51

Churchill, Sir Winston, WWII Prime Minister of Britain, 11, 47, 89, 131, 228

Clark, Frank J., pilot with 421 RCAF, KIA in collision with Chadburn, 110-111

Clark, Gregory, journalist for *The Star Weekly*, reporting from Normandy, 192

Cliff, F. Lindy, Canadian pilot with 94 RAF, xvi(photo)

Clifford, William "Bill," pilot with 440 RCAF, 188, 246

Clubley, George, pilot with 137 RAF, 186

Cluderay, "Al," Canadian pilot with 56 RAF, 184

Cohen, Cheryl, line editor, xii

Colquhoun, pilot with 165 RAF, 96

Connell, Bud, pilot in Malta, 17

Conrad, W/C Walter A.G. "Wally," Canadian ace with 274 RAF, 35-36(shot down)

Contonu, Dahomey, Africa, 99

Coombes, Wally, Canadian pilot with 56, 199 RAF, 184

Cooper, Royal, Newfoundland pilot with 125 RAF, 121(memories from autobiography)

Copacabana Club, London, 171

Cotterill, Stanley H.R., pilot with 418 RCAF, 145(KIA)

Crackers Club, London, 33, 59

Crawford, D.H., WAG with W/C Bartlett, sole survivor, 77(POW)

Creed, Donald, RCAF navigator with Ferguson at 410, 116-117, 135

Crespi, Countess Vivian, friend of Beurling, 25

Crosby, Gordon, pilot with Goldberg to Spain, 56

Crosby on Eden, England, 83, 85

Crowley-Milling, AM Sir Denis, at 610 RAF, 23

Cull, Dick, pilot with 133, 401, 412 RCAF, friend of Laubman, 173, 175, 214

Cundy, Ron, RAAF pilot, with Edwards at 260 RAF, 37-38

Cunningham, Admiral Andrew Browne, Royal Navy commander, 15

Cuthbert, Roy, RCAF RDF technician, 246

D

Daddo-Langlois, Edward, pilot with 249 RAF, Malta, 18

Darling, E.V. "Mitzi," British pilot with 403 RCAF, 89, 90(KIA)

Dartmouth, NS, 108, 122, 163, 227

Dauphin, MB, 22, 50, 83, 87, 98, 116

De Courcy, Tom, CO 443 RCAF, 163(recalled by Vickers)

de Havilland, Geoffrey, manufacturer-pilot, 152

De la Haye, "Al," pilot with 404 RCAF, 154

de Nancrede, Gerry, pilot in Malta, 17, 18

Deacon, Arthur "Art," Canadian pilot with 242 RAF, 70(photo, family profile), 71(first victory), 72(POW), 246

Deere, AC Alan, New Zealand ace in RAF, CO 403 RCAF in 1942, 88-92, 95

Dickins, Punch, bush pilot, Edmonton, 148

Dieppe, France, 91, 96(19 Aug 42 air battles)

Digby, Lincolnshire, 13, 82, 93, 100, 101, 103, 109, 163, 170, 232

Dixon, Jack, journalist, *National Post*, 41

Dodd, Wilbert, pilot in Malta, 17

Doleman, Australian navigator with Ferguson, 96 RAAF, 116

Donaldson, W/C Arthur, RAF, B24 crash, Gibraltar, 31, 33

Douglas, ACM Sir Sholto, RAF head of Coastal Command, 157

Dover, S/L Dean H., CO 412 RCAF, 175

Doyle, William "Bill," Canadian pilot with 132 RAF, xi, 246

D'Oyly-Hughes, Capt Guy, HMS Glorious, 76

Drake, G/C Billy, RAF ace, CO 112 RAF, 165

Drem, Scotland, 116

Driver, Gordon, pilot with 421 RCAF, friend of Tex Phillips, 166

Dubé, Tim, archivist, NAC Ottawa, xi

Duego, Bob, Canadian pilot with 198 RAF, 184(KIA)

Duke, S/L Neville, ace in the RAF, 40(desert life), 43

Dunmore, Spencer, author, 161

Duval, H.P., pilot with 403 RCAF, 88(KIA)

E

Eardley, Cpl Albert, 143 Wing RCAF, 196(KIA)

East Grinstead, West Sussex, England, 104, 166, 236-237

Easton, Admiral Ian, Royal Navy commander, commenting on FAA crews, 230

Edmonton, AB, 5, 67, 82, 83, 87, 144, 146, 147, 148, 197, 211, 213, 214, 226

Edwards, S/L Harold "Curly," Canadian pilot with 487 RNZAF, xi, 246

Edwards, W/C James F. "Stocky," Canadian ace with 94, 260, 92, CO 274 RAF; CO 127 Wing RCAF, xi, 2(photo), 3(family profile), 6(first victory), 7(leadership), 35-38, 50, 53-54(Anzio, six victories), 149, 176-177, 233-234, 246

Edwards, Toni Antonio, wife of James Edwards, xi

Eindhoven, Holland, 186, 192, 196

El Alamein, Egypt, 39, 165

Elwood, AVM, CO 18 Group, Coastal Command, 154, 157

England, Derrick "Dyke," pilot with 416 RCAF, 98(recalls bravery of Beaufighter crews), 108, 111, 236(wounded in combat; repatriated), 247

Entrepagny, France, 110

Espelid, Hal, Norwegian in the Great Escape, 77

Evans, Robert, Canadian pilot with 145, 601 RAF, 245, 247

Executions, Bruno Dorfer and Rainer Beck, 189-190

Eyolfson, Kristjan, RCAF navigator with March at 410, 122-123

F

Falaise, France, 182

Fairbanks, S/L David Charles, American ace in the RCAF, 161

Fairbanks, Jr, Douglas, movie star, USN officer, USS Wasp, 10

Fano, Italy, 56

Farquharson, Gordon, pilot with 126 RAF; 416 RCAF, 17, 31(family profile), 31-33(B24 crash, Gibraltar), 108, 166, 247

Ferguson, Norma, wife of Bob Ferguson, xi, 115

Ferguson, S/L Robert "Bob," pilot with 410 RCAF, xi, 114, 115(family profile, photo), 116-119, 121, 135, 245, 247

Field, Terrance "Terry," pilot with 213 RAF; 417 RCAF, 38(family profile), 38-39, POW, 247

Finlayson, Dr Ross, pilot with 409 RCAF, 135, 136(family profile), 136-138, 137(combat report), 138, 247

Fischer, Harold, USAF ace, Korean War, 174

Floody, Walter "Wally," pilot with 401 RCAF, of the Great Escape, Stalag Luft III, 86, 184

Focke-Wulf 190, Luftwaffe fighter, 80

Follett, Reginald L., Canadian pilot with 567 RAF; 414, 411 RCAF, 247

Forbes-Roberts, W/C Richard "Dick," RMC graduate, 78(group photo), 85(recalls Chadburn), 99, 100(family profile), 110, 111, 204, 247

Fort McLeod, AB, 130

Fort Qu'Appelle, SK, xi, 73, 114, 115

Fort William, ON, 101, 116

Foster, William "Bill," FAA British pilot, 229-230, 231(photo)

Fox, Charles, pilot with 412 RCAF, 111

Francis, John P.W. "Red," pilot with 442, 401 RCAF, 177, 178, 237-238, 245, 247

Francis, Lloyd, Red Francis's brother, artillery signaller, 238(KIA)

Francis, Manley, Red Francis's brother, RCAF fitter for Buck McNair in England, 238

Freetown, Sierra Leone, Africa, 98

Frizelle, Jack, pilot with Jack Phillips, 1 SFTS, 142

Fumerton, Madeleine Reay, WAAF, wife of Carl Fumerton, 31, 97

Fumerton, W/C Robert Carl "Moose," Canadian ace in 89 RAF, CO 406 RCAF, 17, 29(family profile, photo), 30-31, 97, 128, 130, 131, 245, 247

G

Gardiner, Ed, 403 RCAF, buried near Dieppe, 91

Garland, Col John W., Canadian ace with 80 RAF, 247

Garratt, Phillip, de Havilland Canada CEO, 152

Gasson, Johnny, SAAF pilot with Edwards, 92 RAF, 54

Gates, pilot with 165 RAF, 96

Gatward, S/L Ken, RAF pilot with 404 RCAF, 156-157

Gautschi, Phyllis Gray, sister of Hammy Gray, 221

Gazala, Libya, 5, 38,

Gibraltar, 10, 15, 26, 29, 31, 32, 33, 50, 56, 59, 210

Gibson VC, W/C Guy, CO 617 RAF, The Dambusters, 88

Gibson, F/L John "Gibby," pilot with 417 RCAF, xi

Gibson, F/L Zella, wife of John "Gibby" Gibson, xi, 247

Gillis, Burdette, Canadian pilot with 145, 238 RAF; 403 RCAF, 192, 240, 247

Glasgow, Al, navigator with Shulemson on first op, 404 RCAF, 153-154

Glass, Floyd, BCATP instructor, 22

Gobeil, S/L Fowler, RCAF CO of 242 RAF, 71

Godefroy, W/C Hugh C., Canadian ace with 401, 403 RCAF, 49

Godwin, Harley, BCATP flying instructor, 119, 169(taught Schultz inverted falling leaf)

Goldfish Club, badge and ID card, qualification for, 104, 105(photo)

Goldberg, G/C David, pilot with 416; CO 417 RCAF, 54(family profile), 55(photos), 55-57(citation), 245, 247

Goldberg, Irwin, 6 Bomber Group RCAF, brother of David Goldberg, 56

Graafstra, John, pilot in 242 RAF, KIA, 71

Grand Bank, Newfoundland, 60

Grandview, MB, 81, 114

Grandy, G/C Roy, Newfoundland WWI pilot with RCAF in WWII, 122

Granfield, Linda, Magee biographer, 14

Grangemouth, Scotland, 13

Grant, S/L "Bitsy," CO 416 RCAF, 100, 101(KIA with 403 RCAF)

Grant, W/C Frank, CO 143 Wing RCAF, 195

Gravesend, England, 73, 95

Gray, Colin, RNZAF ace, about Bill Olmsted, RCAF, 36

Gray, Elizabeth Anderson, daughter of Robert Anderson, 401 RCAF, 238(KIA)

Gray, John Balfour, Hammy's brother, WAG 144 RAF, 220(KIA)

Gray VC, Robert Hampton "Hammy," FAA, HMS Formidable, 1841, only WWII Canadian fighter pilot awarded Victoria Cross, 100, 218(photo), 219(family profile), 219-221

Gray, Ross, Canadian ace with 418 RCAF, 145, 149(photo with Bannock and Barker)

Green, Bud, pilot with 410 RCAF, conflict at West Malling, 118

Green, Frederick E. "Freddie," pilot 411. 412, 421, CO 416 RCAF, American in the RCAF, 101, 108, 160(photo)

Green, Joe, navigator with 406 RCAF, post-war Liberal cabinet minister, 151

Greenwood, NS, 48, 49, 142, 148

Guevremont, Stéphane, historian, U of C, xi, 156,

Guinea Pig Club, badge, qualifications for, 104

Guthrie, AVM Kenneth M., WWI pilot and WWII RCAF commander, 233-234

H

Halifax, NS, 122, 176, 185, 233, 235

Hall, S/L James, pilot with 443 RCAF, 102(KIA)

Hall, John, RAF navigator with McNabb at 406 RCAF, 127-128(photo, first victory)

Halliday, Hugh, author, xi, 1, 70, 153, 250

Hamburg, Germany, 21, 199, 240

Hamilton, ON, 54, 57

Hamilton, Lord Douglas, RAF commander, 61

Hanbury, O. V. "Pedro," CO of 260 RAF, Western Desert, 35, 36

Hanks, W/C Peter Prosser, ace in the RAF, in Malta with Smith, 27, 28

Hanton, Francis E.W. "Frank," pilot with 400 RCAF, 245, 247

Hardy, Harry, xi, pilot with 440 RCAF, 180(photo), 181(family profile), 181-184, 187-188, 190, 247

Harris, Sgt Alan, Canadian RDF tech with 243 RAF; 96, 450 RAAF, 42, 116, 247

Harris, ACM Sir Arthur, RAF, head of Bomber Command, 21

Hawkins, Lise, xii

Hay, Lt Col "Ronnie," Royal Marine air coordinator, Operation Lentil, 224-225(recalled by Sheppard)

Hayward, S/L Robert "Bob," Newfoundland ace in RCAF, CO 411 RCAF, 122(with March in training)

Heacock, Harold, Canadian pilot with 412 RCAF, post-war RCMP pilot, 245, 247

Heinbuck, "Red," RCAF navigator with Vincent at 410 RCAF, 125

Heinemann, Stephen, historian, xi

Hemingway, Ernest, author, 192

Henderson, Byrnece, of Rouleau, SK, friend of Burdette and Freda Gillis, 240

Heuser, Hans, Luftwaffe navigator, shot down in Ju88 by Rod Smith, Malta, 238

Hill, Eric, Fleet Air Arm pilot, friend of Sheppard, 224(KIA)

Hiroshima, Japan, 220

Hogg, S/L Jimmie, CO 438 RCAF, killed at gunnery camp, 192-193

Holmes, navigator with W/C Bradley at 27 RAF, 210(KIA)

Holmes, LAC John, with 438 RCAF, 198(KIA)

Hope, Harold, Canadian pilot with 27 RAF, 203, 207-208(family profile, photo), 209(photo), 210-211, 247

Hope, Irene Morris, Harold Hope's wife, 209(photo)

Hope, Kenneth, Harold Hope's brother, instrument tech RCAF, 208

Houle, G/C Bert, Canadian ace, CO 417 RCAF, 40(describes desert life)

Hubbard, Frank, pilot with 403, 401 RCAF, 97, 236-237(Guinea Pig), 247

Hubbard, LAW Shirley Chambers, RCAF Overseas HQ, wife of Frank Hubbard, 97, 236-237

Hughes, Albert, HMS *Formidable*, on Ramrod Two with Gray, 220

Hughes, John "Hughie," pilot with 402, 401 RCAF; 249 RAF, 247

Hunt, Norris "Joe," pilot with 403 RCAF, 90(family profile), 90-92, 93(photo), 247

Hurst, Doug, pilot at 403 RCAF, POW, 91

Hyndman, Robert "Bob," pilot with 411 RCAF, also Official War Artist, 49, 161, 175, 247

I

Ireland, G/C E.G. "Irish," RCAF fighter pilot, 170

Irrawaddy River, Burma, 216, 217(photo)

J

Jacobs, William, pilot with 416 RCAF, 108, 110(KIA)

Jenvey, Donald "Buck," pilot with 440 RCAF, 188(KIA)

Job, Bernard, RAF navigator with Phillips at 418 RCAF, 143, 144(photo with pilot)

Johanneson, Connie, pre-war pilot, 226

Johnson, AM George, RCAF commander, 152

Johnson, AVM John F. "Johnnie," British top ace of RAF, 11, 100, 103, 111, 163(memories by Vickers), 164(about McLeod's death), 166, 174, 192, 234, 239(funeral in 2001)

Johnson, Vic, *Airforce Magazine*, xi

Johnston, S/L Michell "Mich," pilot with 403 RCAF; CO 442 RCAF, 87(family profile, photo), 88, 92, 177, 247

Jones, Dale, pilot in 242 RAF, KIA, 72

Jones, G/C Frank, pilot in Malta, 17, 26(recalls Beurling)

Jones, Geoffrey, RAF navigator with Sutherland at 406 RCAF, 132, 133(wedding), 135

Jones, Rick, pilot in 126 RAF, 28(KIA)

Jowsey, S/L Milton "Milt," Canadian pilot in 33, 92 RAF; CO 442 RCAF, 43(family profile), 45(citation), 245, 247

K

Kallio, S/L Oliver "Sandy," American in the RCAF, CO 417 RCAF, 41, 42, 56

Kassel, Germany, 130

Keefer, W/C George, American ace in the RCAF, 166(recalled by Tex Phillips)

Keller, Ross, pilot with 143 Wing RCAF, 196(KIA)

Kennedy, Carleton, brother of Hap Kennedy, 434 RCAF, KIA, 52

Kennedy, Dr Irving F. "Hap," Canadian ace in 249, 111, 93 RAF; CO 401 RCAF, 17, 49(family profile), 50(photo), 50-53, 245, 247

Kennedy, Robert, brother of Hap Kennedy, 6 Bomber Group RCAF, 52

Kent, W/C John, Canadian ace in RAF, 79

Ker, Edgar, 247

Kernaghan, Agnes Borody, wife of Stan Kernaghan, 49

Kernaghan, Stanley "Stan," Canadian pilot with 252 RAF, 45(family profile), 47-49, 247

Kiel, Germany, 167

Kimmel Club, London, 171

King George the VI, British reigning monarch in WWII, 95, 223

King, W. L. Mackenzie, WWII Canadian Prime Minister, 32

Kirkpatrick, Barbara Copper, WAAF, wife of Kirk Kirkpatrick, 97, 135

Kirkpatrick, Clarence "Kirk," navigator ace at 406 RCAF, 97, 132, 134(photo), 135(family profile), 151, 247

Koch, R., Luftwaffe night fighter ace, shot down by Finlayson and Webster, 136

L

Lacombe, AB, 99

Larson, S/L, CO 28 RAF, 212

Lambros, Andy, pilot with 438 RCAF, 193

Laubman, Lt General Donald Currie, Canadian ace with the RCAF, CO 412 RCAF, 167(recalled by Tex Phillips), 168(portrait by Hyndman), 172, 173(family profile), 173-175, 214, 247

Laubman, Margaret Gibson, wife of Don Laubman, 173, 175 (Creil, France) 59

Le Gear, Victor, pilot with 439 RCAF, 195(recalls Bergen-Belsen)

Le Touquet, France, 89

Lethbridge, AB, 83, 173, 214,

Leech, Sgt, 408 RCAF, crew of D. Williams, 130

Leigh-Mallory, AVM Sir Trafford, RAF commander, 92

Levigne, Michel, author, 40

Lett, Major General Kenneth Charles, pilot with 402 RCAF, 169(family profile, photo), 170-172, 247

Letter, 1945, Harry Hardy, 440 RCAF, to Mrs Passmore, 188

Letter, 1945, Robert Hammy Gray, 1841 FAA, to parents about Bud Sutton, 220

Letter, 2001, Elizabeth Anderson Gray to Red Francis, 401 RCAF, 238

Letters, 1939-40, William McKnight, 242 RAF, to H.F. "Mike" Pegler, 68-70

Lindbergh, Charles, flies over St John's, Edmonton, 122, 148

Lindsay, Col James Douglas "Doug," Canadian ace with 403 Sqn RCAF, 173(family profile), 173-175, 247

Linton, Carl "Ozzie," pilot in Malta, 17

Linton, Karl "Lucky," pilot with 416, 421 RCAF, 106, 255

Lipton, W/C Maurice, CO 410 RCAF, 117

Lisbon, Portugal, 33

Lloyd, ACM Sir Hugh, RAF commander, Malta, 9

Locke, Roland "Junior," pilot with 417 RCAF, 245, 247

Loney, Don, editor, xii

Lovell, W/C Tony, CO 1435 RAF in Malta, 13, 23

Low, Howard, Canadian pilot with 607 RAF, 203 (POW executed by Japanese)

Luqa, Malta, 9, 20, 26, 30

Lynton, Tex, American in the RCAF, 10 SFTS, 22

M

MacFadyen, S/L Donald, Canadian ace at 418 RCAF, 136, 150(V1 attacks),

Macgregor, S/L "Mac," CO 123 RAF, 213

Mackie, Richard "Dick," FAA New Zealand pilot, 229-230, 231(photo)

MacKinnon, Lachlan, HMS Formidable, on Ramrod Two with Gray, 220

Maclean, Chuck, pilot in Malta, 17

Maclennan, Bruce, Ian Maclennan's brother, WAG in 419 RCAF, 21(KIA), 22

Maclennan, Ian, Canadian ace with 1435 RAF in Malta; 443 RCAF, xi, 7, 9, 17, 21(photo), 21-24(Malta decoder wheel), 26(recalls Beurling), 27, 239, 247, POW

Madill, Bert, Canadian pilot with 28, 123 RAF, 211(family profile, photo), 211-213(citation), 247

Madore, Garfield, pilot in 242 RAF, 71(KIA)

Magee, Jr, John Gillespie, pilot-poet, poem *High Flight* (13), 14(death), 82, 214

Mahar, RAAF pilot, B24 crash, Gibraltar, 32

Maitland, Alan, HMS *Formidable*, on Ramrod Two with Gray, 220(KIA)

Malta, description of the Malta Siege and Malta convoys, 14-15

March, S/L Ian A., pilot with 410 RCAF, 122(family profile), 123, 247

Marples, W/C Roy, RAF CO 143 Wing RCAF, 192

Marr, Henrietta McAteer, wife of Bill Marr, 138

Marr, William "Bill," 409 RCAF, xi, 138(family profile), 139-140(photos, citation), 141, 247

Martlesham Heath, Suffolk, England, 92, 102

Martuba, Libya, 6

Martyn, George, Canadian pilot with 137 RAF, 185-187, 186(family profile), 243, 247

Martyn, Olive Mason, wife of George Martyn, 185, 187

Mason, William "Bill," pilot with 416 RCAF, 78(in group photo), 85, 108(family profile), 109(photo), 110, 111, 248

Maximow, Hans-Werner, Luftwaffe pilot, shot down by Kennedy, 51

McBrien, G/C William "Bill," RCAF commander, RMC graduate, 236

McConachie, Grant, CP Airways founder, 148

McConnell, Joseph, USAF ace, Korean War, 174

McConvey, Carl, pilot with 438 RCAF, 198(KIA)

McDonald, Ralph, pilot with 440 RCAF, 187(KIA)

McDougall, CO of 94 RAF, 6

McElroy, John, pilot in Malta, 17

McFadden, Allan "Al," pilot with 416 RCAF, 78(group photo), 96(family profile), 97(photos), 98-99, 101, 104, 106, 110, 235-236, 248

McFadden, Marjorie Lenore "Lennie" Wilson, wife of Al McFadden, xi, 96, 97(photo), 235-236

McFadden, Dr Murray, son of Al and Lennie McFadden, 96, 236

McGregor, G/C Gordon Roy, 2 RCAF, Battle of Britain, 79

McGuire, Wally, BCATP flying instructor, 169-170(taught Lett inverted falling leaf)

McIndoe, Dr Archibald, surgeon, Queen Victoria Hospital, East Grinstead, 166

McIntosh, David, navigator 418 RCAF, author, 117, 133, 150

McKendy, pilot with 165 RAF, 96

McKnight, William Lidstone "Willie," Canadian ace with 242 RAF, 67(family profile), 68-70 (letters home to Mike Pegler), 70(MIA), 79

McLaughlin, S/L William "Bill," xi

McLeod, S/L Henry Wallace "Wally," RCAF top ace of WWII, 1, 17, 23, 25(photo of bust), 163, 164(death in combat), 174, 177

McLeod, J.C. "Wulfer Bait," 416 RCAF, 108, 110

McMartin, Pete, journalist, *Vancouver Sun*, 22

McNab, G/C Ernest A. "Ernie," CO 1 RCAF, Battle of Britain, 79

McNabb, Donald, RCAF transport pilot in Southeast Asia, brother of Doug McNabb, 126

McNabb, Harold Douglas "Doug," pilot with 406 RCAF, 126(family profile, photo), 127(photo), 128 (recalls Fumerton and Williams), 135, 248

McNair, G/C Robert W. "Buck," Canadian ace in the RCAF, CO 126 Wing RCAF, 12-14, 17, 23, 166

McNaughton, Andrew, pilot in Malta, 17

McRae, William "Bill," Canadian pilot with 132, 128 RAF, 1490 Flt Takoradi; 401 RCAF, 248

Medicine Hat, AB, 94

Melville, SK, 114

Middlemiss, W/C Robert "Bob," Canadian pilot with 249 RAF, Malta, 17(photo), 18-19(family profile), 248

Middleton, W/C Warren "Mid," pilot with 430 RCAF, 248

Minnedosa, MB, 110, 226

Mitchell, General William "Billy," US air power advocate, 15

Mitchner, W/C John Davidson, Canadian ace with 416 RCAF, 109-110, 237

Monchier, Norm, 403 RCAF, buried near Dieppe, 91

Moncton, NB, 122, 138

Montreal, Quebec, 18, 35, 49, 122, 125, 147, 148, 152, 155, 158, 159, 233, 238, 240

Moon, Chris, pilot in Edmonton, 83

Moore, LAC Peter, armourer with 143 Wing RCAF, 194

Moose Jaw, SK, xi, 26, 31, 39, 163, 236, 239, 240, 242

Morse, Hugh, pilot with 442 RCAF, 248

Mouat, Ivan, Canadian pilot with 56, 199 RAF, 184(family profile), POW, 233, 248

Moul, Jack, 416 RCAF, 85, 86(family profile), 86(first probable for 416), POW, 233, 248

Moulmein, Burma, 62, 207, 210, 213

Mullen, pilot with 416 RCAF, POW (friendly fire), 237

Munich, Germany, 21, 61, 145

Munn, pilot with 403 RCAF, 88

Murchie, Donald, pilot with 412 RCAF, 246

Murray, Bremner "Scotty," pilot with 401, 412 RCAF, 248

Mussolini, Benito, WWII Italian leader, 3

N

Nagasaki, Japan, 219

Nanton, AB, 93, 94

Neal, S/L Eugene "Jeep," pilot at 401 RCAF, 23

Needham, Barry, pilot with 412 RCAF, 81(family profile, photo), 82, 166, 167(recalled by H. Phillips), 175, 248

Needham, Martha Kerluke, wife of Barry Needham, 81

Nesbitt, G/C A. Dean, 143 Wing RCAF, 199

Nesbitt, Roy, author, 48

Newsome, Albert "Buck," pilot with 438 RCAF, 193(KIA)

Nicholson VC, W/C James, CO 27 RAF, British fighter pilot awarded Victoria Cross, 208(KIA)

Niger River, Africa, 99

Nijmegen, Holland, 164, 167, 175

Noble, Wendy, sister of Rod Smith, xi, 11, 23

Nolan, Brian, Beurling biographer, 32

Noonan, Rev Daniel "Danny," Canadian ace with 416 RCAF, 103, 108-109, 110, 246, 248

North Weald, England, 86, 88

Northcott, G/C Geoffrey W., Canadian ace, CO 402; 126 Wing RCAF, 17, 110, 170, 172, 177, 217, 232(photo), 233-234

North-Lewis, W/C Kit, 124 Wing RAF, 186

Nuremburg, Germany, 21

O

Ockenden, AVM Gordon, Canadian ace with 443 RCAF, 241(recalled by Don Walz)

Okinawa, Ryukyu Islands, Operation Iceberg, 225, 227, 228

Olmsted, William "Bill," CO 442 RCAF, 36, 51, 237

Onagawa Bay, Japan, 220, 221, 226

Operation Bodenplatz, 1 January 1945, Luftwaffe attack, 196

Operational Wings, qualifications for, 103

Oshawa, ON, 83, 108, 186

Ostend, Belgium, 72

Ottawa, ON, xi, 25, 42, 43, 49, 56, 67, 90, 108, 111, 120, 148, 161, 169, 178, 204

Ough, Robert "Bob," pilot-historian, xi, 25

Oxford, England, 61

P

Padua, Italy, 57

Palembang, Sumatra, 224, 225, 228

Palmer, William "Bill," 416 RCAF, 78(group photo)

Paris, France, 21, 52, 56, 69, 122, 131, 149, 199, 244

Park, ACM Sir Keith, RAF commander, Malta, New Zealander, 9, 11

Parr, Jack, pilot with 403 RCAF, 91(POW)

Passmore, Deke, pilot with 440 RCAF, 188(KIA)

Patterson, George "Pat," pilot in 416 RCAF, 78(in group photo), 235, 236, 248 (wounded) (POW)

Pattle, Marmaduke "Pat," SAAF ace, 41

Pearsons, Don, xi

Pederson, pilot with 165 RAF, 96

Pedley, Flt Sgt Leon, maintenance chief 143 Wing RCAF, 198, 199

Pegler, H.F. "Mike," McKnight's friend in Calgary, 68, 69, 70

Pensacola, Florida, 223, 227

Perez-Gomez, Luis, Mexican pilot in the RCAF with 443, 102(KIA)

Perugia, Italy, 61

Pétain, Philippe, Marshal, WWII leader, Vichy French State, 9, 98

Peterborough, ON, xi, 32

Peterhead, Scotland, 39, 83, 84, 85, 86, 97

Peterson, LAC Martin John "Pat," fitter with 438 RCAF, xi, 196(family profile), 196-198, 200(photo), 201, 248

Pettifer, Jack, navigator with Harold Hope at 27 RAF, 208, 210

Phillip, Margaret Vincent, wife of Dagwood Phillips, 85(photo)

Phillip, Robert "Dagwood," Canadian pilot with 416, 421 RCAF, 85(family profile, photo), 86, 100-101(citation), 245, 248

Phillips, Chester, brother of Tex Phillips, B24 pilot, 44th Bombardment Group, 167(KIA)

Phillips, S/L George H.R., RCAF and OPAS pilot, father of Jack Phillips, 142, 147

Phillips, Howard Lynn "Tex," American in the RCAF, 112 RAF, 412 RCAF, 164(family profile), 165, 166(photo), 167, 248

Phillips, W/C John "Jack," pilot with 418 RCAF, xi, 142(family profile), 143-144(photo), 145-147(citation), 245, 248

Phillips, Olga "Sunny," wife of Jack Phillips, xi, 145 (photo)

Phillips, pilot in 94 RAF, 6

Pieri, Donald Mathew "Tex," American ace in the RCAF, 442, 412 RCAF, 176, 177, 178(MIA)

Poona, India, 204, 216

Port Alberni, BC, 85

Port Arthur, ON, 77

Porter, Charles, brother of John Porter, pilot with 419 RCAF, 185(KIA)

Porter, John W., Canadian pilot with 247 RAF, 185(family profile, photo), 245, 248

Post, Wiley, American pilot, Edmonton, 148, 211

Pow, L.G.D. "Les," pilot with 411, 416 RCAF, 106

Powell, Archie, RAF navigator with Kernaghan, 252 RAF, 47, 48(photo with pilot)

Powell, L.W. "Ping," B24 crash, Gibraltar, 32

Probert, Rex, Canadian with 33 and 92 RAF, 39(family profile), 43, 45(citation), 248

Proctor, W/C Fred, CO of 681 RAF, India, 63(photo)

R

Ralph, Dan, xii

Ralph, Elaine, xii

Ramsay, Chuck, pilot in Malta, 17

Ranchi, India, 206, 212, 216

Rangoon, Burma, 207, 213

Raynor, LAC "Alf," fitter 438 RCAF, 196

Reid, Donald, pilot in Malta, 17

Red Deer, AB, 83

Reeve, Leslie, HMS *Formidable*, on Ramrod Two with Gray, 220

Regina, SK, 8, 9, 12, 19, 23, 81, 87, 99, 114, 115, 163, 164, 189

Richards, Lloyd, British gunner with Bartlett on Skuas, HMS *Ark Royal*, 74-77

Rippon, Clive, British pilot with 23, 116 RAF, 248

Robb, Ken, pilot with 412 RCAF, 166

Roberts, David "Lofty," Halton graduate in RAF, 67, 248

Roberts, Leslie, Beurling biographer, 32, 33

Robinson, Doug, 488 RNZAF pilot, with Schultz at OTU, 120

Roddie, William "Bill," pilot with 416 RCAF, 237(friendly fire), 248

Rogers, Philip, Canadian pilot with 403 RCAF, remustered to Blenheims, 248

Rommel, Field Marshal Erwin, Africa Korps commander, 5, 15, 36, 111(wounded)

Roosevelt, Col Elliott, USAAF pilot, 132

Roosevelt, Franklin D., United States president in WWII, 10, 132, 228

Roscoe, Art, pilot, B24 crash, Gibraltar, 32

Rose, Robert, navigator with 415 RCAF, friend of Harold Hope, 208(KIA)

Ross, Gary, author, editor, *Saturday Night*, xi

Rouleau, SK, 192, 239-240

Round, pilot with 416 RCAF, POW (friendly fire), 237

Royal Military College of Canada, Kingston, ON, 99, 108, 204

Russel, W/C Blair Dalzell "Dal," 1 RCAF, Battle of Britain, CO 126, 127 Wing RCAF, 79, 102, 175

Russel, Hugh, brother of Dal Russel, pilot in 416, 443 RCAF, 96(at Dieppe), 102(KIA)

S

Sager, S/L Arthur H., pilot with 421, 416, CO 443 RCAF, 100(family profile), 101(photo), 108, 110, 111, 163

Saint-Exupery, Antoine de, French author-pilot, 31 July 44, 59(MIA)

Salween River, out of China and Burma, 62

Sang, Fugel, Norwegian in the Great Escape, 77

Saskatoon, SK, 4, 5, 88

Sault Ste Marie, ON, 142

Saunders, B24 pilot, 511 RAF, Gibraltar, 32

Savage, Doc, pilot with 92 RAF, 45

Scapa Flow, Orkneys, Scotland, 84, 221

Schaller, Wolf, Luftwaffe pilot, Western Desert, shot down by Edwards, 36

Schulz, Otto, Luftwaffe ace, Western Desert, KIA by Edwards, 35-36

Schultz, G/C Rayne "Joe," Canadian ace with 410 RCAF, 112(photo), 113, 119(family profile), 120-121, 123

Scoles, S/L Joe, xi

Seid, Sidney P., pilot with 418 RCAF, 117, 133, 150

Selkirk, MB, 87

Sherlock, Eric and Allan, bomber pilots, twins, 95

Sherlock, John, pilot in Malta, 17

Sheppard, Cmdr Donald John, Canadian ace in the Fleet Air Arm, 1836, HMS *Victorious*, 203, 221(family profile), 222(photos today, in WWII), 221-225, 231, 248

Sheppard, Robert, brother of Donald Sheppard, pilot on HMS *Formidable*, 225(KIA)

Sheppard, William, brother of Donald Sheppard, Raleigh Scheme, Royal Navy, 222

Shore, Patrice, author's wife, dedication on page v, xii

Shores, Christopher, author, 51

Shulemson, Sydney, pilot with 404 RCAF, 147, 152(family profile), 155(photos), 153-156(citations), 157-159

Smiley, Joseph "Bev," Canadian in 242 RAF, 71(POW)

Smith, A.P.L. "Apple," pilot with 412 RCAF, 82

Smith, Blanche Robertshaw, mother of Rod and Jerry Smith, 19(photo), 23

Smith, George "Smitty," pilot with 411 RCAF, 172, 245, 248

Smith, Ivan, Canadian pilot with 268 RAF, xi, 248

Smith, Jerry, Canadian pilot with 126 RAF, brother of Rod Smith, 10(photo, USS Wasp), 11, 17, 19-20 (KIA), 23, 27, 95

Smith, W/C Rod, Canadian ace in 126 RAF; 412, CO 401 RCAF, xi, 1, 7, 8(photo), 9, 11-14, 17, 19(childhood photo), 23, 29, 31, 34(log book photo), 53, 248, 19-20(first victory), 27-28(shot down), 33(in London after Malta), 81, 95, 111(dislike of strafing), 149, 164, 238(contacted by Luftwaffe victim), 245, 248

Smith, Russell, Canadian pilot with 607 RAF, 203 (POW executed by Japanese)

Somers, Larry, 403 RCAF, 88, 91(POW)

Soward, Lt Cmdr Stuart E., author-pilot, 75, 220

Spooner, Richard, Bob Spooner's brother, bomb aimer RCAF, 193

Spooner, S/L Robert "Bob," CO 438 RCAF, 192, 193(family profile), 194(photo), 194-195, 196, 248

Sproule, W/C Frederick H., Canadian pilot with 133 RCAF; 186, 183, 42 RAF, 213(family profile), 214(photo), 215(photo), 216-217, 248

St Catharines, ON, xi, 86

St Hubert, Quebec, 101, 152

St John's, Newfoundland, 122

St Petersburg, Florida, 108

Stalag Luft I, Barth, Germany, 77

Stalag Luft III, Sagan, Poland, 21, 72, 86, 184, 233

Stegner, Wallace, author, childhood home at Eastend, SK, 241

Stewart, William "Bill," American in the RCAF; with Edwards at 260 RAF, 35

Storheill, T., HMS *Formidable*, on Ramrod Two with Gray, 220

Sugden, Derric, pilot with 440 RCAF, 187(KIA)

Sully, AVM J.A., RCAF commander, meets with Bannock, Ottawa, 148

Sutherland Brown, Atholl, Canadian pilot with 177 RAF, 202(photo), 204(family profile, photo), 204-207(citation), 208, 248

Sutherland Brown, Ian, Atholl's brother, RMC graduate, BCATP instructor killed in flying accident, 204

Sutherland Brown, Malcolm, Atholl's brother, RMC graduate, Royal Canadian Engineers, 204

Sutherland, G/C George "Red," pilot with 406 RCAF, 129(family profile, photo), 130-132, 133, 248

Sutton, Bud, Canadian pilot in Fleet Air Arm, 1830, HMS *Illustrious*, 220(KIA)

Sweeney, Major General Charles, USAF, commander of B29 that dropped atomic bomb on Nagasaki, 219

Sweet, CPO Dick, HMS *Formidable*, speaks with Gray about Ramrod Two, 220

Sydney, Australia, 227, 228, 229

Syme, James "Jim," bush pilot, 226

T

Takali, Malta, 20, 26

Takoradi, Gold Coast, Africa, 39, 45, 98

Taylor, Charles, xii

Taylor, Edgar L., Canadian pilot with 54, 238 RAF, 248

Taylor, Fletcher, RCAF navigator, 23

Taylor, Harry, FAA British pilot, 229-230, 231(photo)

Taylor, Jack, FAA pilot, course mate with Atkinson, 227(KIA)

Terrine, Georgette and Henri, citizens of Brussels, 199

Thompson, Walter R "Punch," Canadian Pathfinder pilot, 124-125

Thorpe, David, navigator with Vincent at 409 RCAF, 124

Tilley, Dr Ross, Canadian surgeon, Queen Victoria Hospital, East Grinstead, 166, 237

Timbuktu, French West Africa, 99

Tindall, Brian, RAF navigator with McNabb at 406 RCAF, 126, 127, 128, 135

Tobruk, Libya, 5, 36, 47(Operation Agreement),

Toronto, ON, 5, 16, 29, 31, 54(Manning Pool, CNE Grounds), 57, 85(Barker Field), 86, 95, 102, 108, 111, 125, 142, 143, 151, 153, 165(Manning Pool, CNE Grounds), 186, 214, 221, 222, 231, 237, 238

Townsend, G/C Peter, CO at Drem, trained Ferguson on Beaufighter, 116

Trainor, S/L Charles, Canadian ace in RCAF, CO 401 RCAF, 52, 53

Trenchard, Marshal of the RAF Hugh "Boom," Halton School founder, 67

Turner, G/C Percival Stanley "Stan," Canadian ace in RAF and RCAF, 16, 17, 30, 47(aboard HMS *Coventry*), 68, 69

Turner, Flt Sgt, 408 RCAF, crew of D. Williams, 130

Turp, Robert J. "Bob," pilot with 416 RCAF, 102(KIA)

Typhoon Memorial, Noyers Bocage, Caen, France, description of, 187

U

Union Jack Club, London, 33

V

Valetta, Malta, 15, 27

Vance, Thomas "Tommy," 248

Vancouver, BC, xi, 9, 11, 21, 38, 41, 45, 48, 49, 86, 91, 101, 106, 123, 129, 148, 176, 178, 185, 196, 197, 203, 207, 208, 210, 213, 219, 233, 234

Van Nes, "Joe," Canadian pilot with 177 RAF, 205

Vernon, S/L Jerrold "Jerry," historian-engineer, xi

Vian, Admiral Sir Philip, Royal Navy commander, 220-221, 229

Vickers, Philip "Phil," 25(McLeod bust), 161(family profile), 162(photo), 163-164, 240, 241, 248

Victoria, BC, 1, 41, 49, 73, 193, 196, 204, 207, 213, 214, 217

Vincent, Carl, AVM Vincent's brother, 123

Vincent, Margaret Harrison, WAAF, wife of AVM Vincent, 123, 125

Vincent, Peter, AG with 192 RAF, 123(KIA)

Vincent, AVM William H. "Bill," pilot with 409, 410 RCAF, 123(family profile), 124-126, 248

W

Wade, W/C Lance, American ace in RAF, 39, 41, 42

Walker, R.H. "Kelly," CO 416 RCAF, 101

Walton, B24 pilot, 511 RAF, Gibraltar, 32

Walz, Donald, pilot with 127, 443 RCAF, xi, 102, 163, 164(with McLeod and Johnson), 165(photo), 239-241, 242(photo), 245, 248

Walz, Genesta Tower, wife of Don Walz, 239, 240

Walz, Mike, one of Don Walz's sons, accompanied father to France in 2000, 239

Warburton, W/C Adrian, RAF, Malta, 59(MIA), 60

Warren, Bruce "Duke I," Douglas Warren's twin, Canadian pilot in 165, 66 RAF, 93, 94(childhood photo), 95(photo), 94-96, 147

Warren, W/C Douglas "Duke II," Canadian pilot in 165, 66 RAF, xi, 93(family profile), 94(childhood photo), 95(photo), 94-96(about Dieppe losses), 245, 248

Warren, Melba Bennett, wife of Duke Warren, 96

Washington, DC, 14, 161, 162, 164, 219

Waterton, William "Bill," pilot in 242 RAF, 72

Waugh, Evelyn, author, 47

Weaver, Claude, American ace in the RCAF, 161

Webster, Alan, RCAF navigator with Finlayson at 410 RCAF, 135, 136-138

Weeks, William "Bill," pilot with 442 RCAF, 111

West, S/L Donald, engineer, 245, 249

West Malling, Kent, England, 118(rivalry)

White Rock, BC, xi, xv, 103, 201

Whitney, Alexandra, sculptor of Beurling bust, Ottawa, 25

Wick, Scotland, 153, 214

Wilcox, Sparky, American BCATP flying instructor, 212(recalled by Madill)

Williams, G/C David "Blackie," pilot with 408, CO 406 RCAF, 128, 129(family profile, photo), 130-131, 132(citation), 134(photo), 135, 249

Williams, David, son of Blackie Williams, 135

Williams, John "Willie the Kid," Canadian in 249 RAF, Malta, 17, 31(killed, B24 crash, Gibraltar)

Williams, Vern, navigator with Schultz at 410 RCAF, 112(photo), 114, 119-120

Wilman, LAC Richard, with 438 RCAF, 198(KIA)

Wilson, Gordon, Canadian with 213 RAF, 38(photo)

Wilson, Leonard H. "Len," pilot with 443, 442 RCAF, 249

Wilson, S/L Pete, CO 438 RCAF, 193(KIA), 196

Windsor, the Duke of, in Alberta in 1941, 87

Winfield, Phil, CO 126 RAF, Malta, 20(wounded)

Winnipeg, MB, xi, 49, 79, 87, 108(402 Sqn), 115, 123, 126, 135, 148(112 Sqn), 213, 226, 233

Wise, G/C Bill, CO RAF Element Reconnaissance Force, India, 64

Wood, pilot with 403 RCAF, 88

Woodward, W/C Vernon Crompton, Canadian ace in 33 RAF, CO 213 RAF, 1, 41(family profile)

Wozniak, Margot Martin, WAAF, wife of Roy Wozniak, 97

Wozniak, Roy, 403 RCAF, 91(family profile), 91-92(photo), 97, 249

Wright, James, navigator ace with MacFadyen at 418 RCAF, 136(family profile), 150(V1 ops), 249

X, Y and Z

Yorkton, SK, 81, 114, 165, 176, 190, 192, 236

Zoochkan, pilot with 403 RCAF, 88

INDEX – RCAF, RAF, RAAF, RNZAF, and RN FAA units and ships in each chapter

PART ONE—KITTYHAWK ACE
94 Squadron RAF, xvi (photo), 5-6
112 Squadron RAF, 5
233 Wing RAF, 6

PART TWO—CANADIANS IN MALTA
2 SFTS, Uplands, 12
6 EFTS, Prince Albert, 22
10 SFTS, Dauphin, 22
32 SFTS, Moose Jaw, 31
41 Squadron RAF, 18
52 OTU, Aston Down, 22
58 OTU, Grangemouth, 12-13
89 Squadron RAF, 30
126 Squadron RAF, 11, 20
133 Squadron RAF, 22
242 Squadron RAF, 16
249 Squadron RAF, 16, 18, 26
401 Squadron RCAF, 14, 22, 23
406 Squadron RCAF, 30
411 Squadron RCAF, 13, 22
412 Squadron RCAF, 13-14
419 Squadron RCAF, 21
443 Squadron RCAF, 23
511 Squadron RAF, 31
610 Squadron RAF, 22, 23
1435 Squadron RAF, 23, 26

PART THREE—WESTERN DESERT AND ITALY
2 (C) OTU, Catfoss, 45, 48, 204
4 SFTS, Saskatoon, 55
6 SFTS, Dunnville, 55
8 OTU, Greenwood, 48
10 SFTS, Dauphin, 50
12 SFTS, Brandon, 48
15 Squadron RAF, 45
33 Squadron RAF, 39, 41, 43, 45
80 Squadron RAF, 54
92 Squadron RAF, 43, 45, 53-54
94 Squadron RAF, 35
134 Squadron RAF, 47
145 Squadron, 41
213 Squadron RAF, 38
229 Squadron RAF, 54
243 Squadron RAF, 42
244 Wing RAF, 57
249 Squadron RAF, 50
252 Squadron, 45, 47-48

260 Squadron RAF, 35, 37, 44(photo)
263 Squadron RAF, 50
274 Squadron RAF, 35, 54
401 Squadron RCAF, 52, 53
416 Squadron RCAF, 39, 41, 56
417 Squadron RCAF, 41, 47, 53, 56-57
421 Squadron RCAF, 50
434 Squadron RCAF, 52
442 Squadron, 45
450 Squadron RAAF, 42
601 Squadron RAF, 38

PART FOUR—PHOTO RECONNAISSANCE
9 OTU, Dyce, 61
542 Squadron RAF, 61
681 Squadron RAF, 62, 63 (photo), 64
683 Squadron RAF, 62, 61

PART FIVE—RAF AND FAA, 1939-40
School of Technical Training, Halton, 67
6 FTS, RAF, Little Rissington, 67
85 Squadron RAF, 71
242 Squadron RAF, 68-72
434 Squadron RCAF, 77
607 Squadron RAF, 71
615 Squadron RAF, 71
803 Squadron FAA, 74

PART SIX—THE DEADLY YEARS
1 Squadron RCAF, 79
2 ITS, Regina, 83, 87
2 EFTS, Fort William, 101
3 SFTS, Calgary, 99
4 SFTS, Saskatoon, 100, 108
5 EFTS, Lethbridge & High River, 83, 93
10 SFTS, Dauphin, 83, 98
11 SFTS, Yorkton, 81
12 SFTS, Brandon, 109
13 SFTS, St Hubert, 101
15 EFTS, Regina, 81
15 SFTS, Claresholm, 87
18 EFTS, Boundary Bay, 87
34 SFTS, Medicine Hat, 94
52 OTU, Aston Down, 101, 103
55 OTU, Usworth, 98
58 OTU, Grangemouth, 95
66 Squadron RAF, 95
126 Squadron RCAF, Dartmouth, NS, 108
127 Wing RCAF, 110
165 Squadron RAF, 94-95, 96(at Dieppe)
222 Squadron RAF, 89

242 Squadron RAF, 79

303 Squadron RAF, 79

331 Squadron RAF, 89

400-numbered RCAF squadrons, outline, 80

401 Squadron RCAF, 86, 111

402 Squadron RCAF, 108, 109-110

403 Squadron RCAF, 86, 88-93, 95, 101

412 Squadron RCAF, 82

416 Squadron RCAF, 78(photo), 83, 85, 86, 96 (at Dieppe), 98, 100, 101, 102, 103, 106-108, 109-111

421 Squadron RCAF, 85, 100, 101, 111

442 Squadron RCAF, 111

443 Squadron RCAF, 102

PART SEVEN—BEAUFIGHTER AND MOSQUITO IN BRITAIN

Second Tactical Air Force, RAF, 142

Technical Training School, RCAF, St Thomas, 130

Central Flying School, Trenton, 138, 147

Central Flying School, Arnprior, 148

1 SFTS, Camp Borden, 142, 148

2 EFTS, Fort William, 116

2 SFTS, Uplands, 122

7 SFTS, Fort Macleod, 119, 130

7 OTU, Debert, NS, 123, 131

8 EFTS, Vancouver (1941), 119

8 SFTS, Moncton, 122, 138

10 SFTS, Dauphin, 116

14 SFTS, Aylmer, 142, 153

54 OTU, Charter Hall, 123, 126

60 OTU, East Fortune, 116

96 Squadron RAAF, Wales, 116

112 Squadron RCAF, Rockcliffe, 148

125 (Newfoundland) Squadron RAF, 121

192 Squadron RAF, 123

401 Squadron RCAF, 142

404 Squadron RCAF, 153-157, 158(photo), 159(photo)

406 Squadron RCAF, 126-128, 130, 131-132, 134(photo), 142, 151

408 Squadron RCAF, 130

409 Squadron RCAF, 123-125, 136, 137(combat report), 138-141

410 Squadron RCAF, 112 (photo), 116, 117-120, 122, 125

411 Squadron RCAF, 122

418 Squadron RCAF, 136, 141-42, 143-147, 149-152

PART EIGHT—AMERICANS IN THE RCAF

11 SFTS, Yorkton, 165

44th Bombardment Group, USAAF, 167

61 OTU, Sudan, Africa, 165

112 Squadron RAF, 165

126 Squadron RCAF, Dartmouth, NS, 163

127 Squadron RCAF, Gander, NF, 163

412 Squadron RCAF, 166, 167

416 Squadron RCAF, 166

421 Squadron RCAF, 166

443 Squadron RCAF, 163, 164

PART NINE—RCAF SPITFIRES OPS, BRITAIN AND EUROPE

Central Flying School, RAF, 176

Second Tactical Air Force, RAF, 170, 171

2 SFTS, Uplands, 170

5 ITS, Belleville, 169

11 SFTS, Yorkton, 176

13 EFTS, St Eugene, 169

39th Fighter Interceptor Squadron USAF, Korea-1952, 173

125 Wing RAF, 171

126 Wing RCAF, 171, 177

130 Squadron RCAF, Bagotville, Goose Bay, 176

133 Squadron RCAF, Lethbridge, Boundary Bay, 173

401 Squadron RCAF, 177

402 Squadron RCAF, 170, 171

403 Squadron RCAF, 173, 175, 177

411 Squadron RCAF, 168 (photo), 172

412 Squadron RCAF, 173, 175, 177-178

442 Squadron RCAF, 177, 178 (photo)

PART TEN—CANADA'S TYPHOON PILOTS

1 ITS, Toronto, 186

3 Repair Depot, RCAF, Vancouver, 197

6 Bomber Group RCAF, 185

11 SFTS, Yorkton, 190

20 EFTS, Oshawa, 186

56 Squadron RAF, 184

59 OTU, Millfield, 185

83 Group RAF, 183

111 Squadron RCAF, 192

118 Squadron RCAF, Annette Island, AK, 190, 197

123 Squadron RCAF, 190-191

124 Wing RAF, 186

137 Squadron RAF, 186, 187

143 Wing RCAF, 182, 183, 184, 186, 187, 189, 192, 197, 198(photo), 199-200

198 Squadron RAF, 184

199 Squadron RAF, 184

238 Squadron RAF, 192

247 Squadron RAF, 185

401 Squadron RCAF, 184

419 Squadron RCAF, 185

438 Squadron RCAF, 182, 183, 190, 192-196, 197, 198

439 Squadron RCAF, 182, 192, 195

440 Squadron RCAF, 182, 187-188, 190
616 Squadron RAF, 192

607 Squadron RAF, 203
901 Wing RAF, 204

PART ELEVEN—INDIA AND BURMA—BEAUFIGHTER, HURRICANE, THUNDERBOLT
Force 136, India-Burma, 216
Third Tactical Air Force, RAF, 204
2 (C) OTU, Catfoss, 204
2 SFTS, Uplands, 212, 214
3 SFTS, Calgary, 204
3 RFU, Poona, 216
19 Wing RCAF Auxiliary, 217
27 Squadron RAF, 204, 208, 209 (photo), 210
28 Squadron RAF, 212, 213
42 Squadron RAF, 216-217
123 Squadron RAF, 211, 212, 213
133 Squadron RCAF, Lethbridge, Boundary Bay, 214
177 Squadron RAF, 204-207, 208
183 Squadron RAF, 214
186 Squadron RAF, 214
211 Squadron RAF, 204, 207
224 Group RAF, 204
249 Squadron RAF, 208
355 Squadron RAF, 208
415 Squadron RCAF, 208

PART TWELVE—FLEET AIR ARM IN THE PACIFIC
1836 Squadron FAA, HMS *Victorious*, 221, 224
1841 Squadron FAA, HMS *Formidable*, 219-220
1839 Squadron FAA, HMS *Indomitable*, 228
1844 Squadron FAA, HMS *Indomitable*; HMS *Formidable*, 227-231
509th Composite Group, USAAF, 219

PART THIRTEEN—REHABILITATION, READJUSTMENT AND RE-ENTRY
126 Wing RCAF, 233
127 Wing RCAF, 234
145 Squadron RAF, 240
238 Squadron RAF, 240
401 Squadron RCAF, 236, 237
403 Squadron RCAF, 240
416 Squadron RCAF, 234, 235, 236, 237
442 Squadron RCAF, 237
443 Squadron RCAF, 239

A scene of the celebrating crowds in Piccadilly Circus, London on VE-Day, May 8, 1945.

Courtesy of the Airforce Magazine Collection